Civil war London

Manchester University Press

Politics, culture and society in early modern Britain

General Editors
Professor Alastair Bellany
Dr Alexandra Gajda
Professor Peter Lake
Professor Anthony Milton
Professor Jason Peacey

This important series publishes monographs that take a fresh and challenging look at the interactions between politics, culture and society in Britain between 1500 and the mid-eighteenth century. It counteracts the fragmentation of current historiography through encouraging a variety of approaches which attempt to redefine the political, social and cultural worlds, and to explore their interconnection in a flexible and creative fashion. All the volumes in the series question and transcend traditional interdisciplinary boundaries, such as those between political history and literary studies, social history and divinity, urban history and anthropology. They thus contribute to a broader understanding of crucial developments in early modern Britain.

Recently published in the series

Chaplains in early modern England: Patronage, literature and religion
HUGH ADLINGTON, TOM LOCKWOOD and GILLIAN WRIGHT (*eds*)

The Cooke sisters: Education, piety and patronage in early modern England   GEMMA ALLEN

Black Bartholomew's Day   DAVID J. APPLEBY

Insular Christianity   ROBERT ARMSTRONG and TADHG Ó HANNRACHAIN (*eds*)

Reading and politics in early modern England   GEOFF BAKER

'No historie so meete'   JAN BROADWAY

Writing the history of parliament in Tudor and early Stuart England
PAUL CAVILL and ALEXANDRA GAJDA (*eds*)

Republican learning   JUSTIN CHAMPION

News and rumour in Jacobean England: Information, court politics and diplomacy, 1618–25   DAVID COAST

This England   PATRICK COLLINSON

Gentry culture and the politics of religion: Cheshire on the eve of civil war   RICHARD CUST and PETER LAKE

Sir Robert Filmer (1588–1653) and the patriotic monarch   CESARE CUTTICA

Doubtful and dangerous: The question of succession in late Elizabethan England   SUSAN DORAN *and* PAULINA KEWES (*eds*)

Brave community   JOHN GURNEY

'Black Tom'   ANDREW HOPPER

Reformation without end: Religion, politics and the past in post-revolutionary England   ROBERT G. INGRAM

Freedom of speech, 1500–1850   ROBERT G. INGRAM, JASON PEACEY *and* ALEX W. BARBER (*eds*)

Connecting centre and locality: Political communication in early modern England   CHRIS R. KYLE *and* JASON PEACEY (*eds*)

Revolution remembered: Seditious memories after the British Civil Wars   EDWARD JAMES LEGON

Royalists and Royalism during the Interregnum   JASON MCELLIGOTT *and* DAVID L. SMITH

Laudian and Royalist polemic in Stuart England   ANTHONY MILTON

The crisis of British Protestantism: Church power in the Puritan Revolution, 1638–44   HUNTER POWELL

Lollards in the English Reformation: History, radicalism, and John Foxe   SUSAN ROYAL

The gentlewoman's remembrance: Patriarchy, piety, and singlehood in early Stuart England   ISAAC STEPHENS

Exploring Russia in the Elizabethan Commonwealth: The Muscovy Company and Giles Fletcher, the elder (1546–1611)   FELICITY JANE STOUT

Loyalty, memory and public opinion in England, 1658–1727   EDWARD VALLANCE

Church polity and politics in the British Atlantic world, c. 1635–66   ELLIOT VERNON *and* HUNTER POWELL (*eds*)

Full details of the series are available at www.manchesteruniversitypress.co.uk.

Civil war London

Mobilizing for parliament, 1641–5

Jordan S. Downs

MANCHESTER UNIVERSITY PRESS

Copyright © Jordan S. Downs 2021

The right of Jordan S. Downs to be identified as the author of this work has been asserted by him in accordance with the Copyright, Designs and Patents Act 1988.

Published by Manchester University Press
Oxford Road, Manchester M13 9PL

www.manchesteruniversitypress.co.uk

British Library Cataloguing-in- Publication Data
A catalogue record for this book is available from the British Library

ISBN 978 1 5261 4881 0 hardback
ISBN 978 1 5261 7444 4 paperback

First published 2021
Paperback published 2023

The publisher has no responsibility for the persistence or accuracy of URLs for any external or third-party internet websites referred to in this book, and does not guarantee that any content on such websites is, or will remain, accurate or appropriate.

Typeset by Newgen Publishing UK

Contents

List of figures	*page* viii
Acknowledgments	ix
List of abbreviations	xi
Introduction	1
1 London, Ireland, and the Protestant cause	27
2 Mobilizing the metropolis	60
3 A third house of parliament	119
4 London's *levée en masse*	180
5 A "rebellious city"?	224
Archival materials	301
Index	315

Figures

1 Frontispiece from Captain John Williams, *Londons Love to her neighbours in generall* (London, 1643). Worcester College, Oxford, LR. 4.12 (10) — *page* xii
2 The London assessment of November 1642 and payments by ward — 99
3 Claes Visscher, *The Visscher Panorama of London*, etching from 1616 — 146
4 Wenceslaus Hollar, *Long View of London from Bankside*, etching from 1647 — 146

Acknowledgments

Gratitude is due to the many librarians and archivists who directed me to sources, disabused me of illusions, and offered patience in general. Chris Scales and Patricia Dark at the John Harvard Library offered friendly accommodation as I rushed in from a summer rainstorm. Archivists from the Goldsmiths' Company, the Drapers' Company, the Clothworkers' Company, and the Mercers' Company all took time out to open their doors and records. Particular thanks are reserved for Katie George of the Salters' Company as she kindly allowed me to access company records on more than one occasion. Late thanks are due to Renée Prud'Homme of Worcester College Library.

Financial support for this project came by way of short-term research grants from The Huntington Library, the Andrew W. Mellon Foundation, the Institute of Historical Research, the William Andrews Clark Memorial Library, and UC Riverside's History Department. The single greatest help came by way of the freedom to research and write during a two year postdoctoral appointment at Vanderbilt University. The time afforded by this opportunity was of course valuable; truly invaluable, however, was the advice, friendship, and conversation offered by Peter Lake, Sandy Solomon, and Michael Questier.

The Skinners Arms sits at a marvelous intersection. It is a mere stone's throw from Thanet Street, a block from the British Library, a short one-mile walk from the London Metropolitan Archives, just down the road from UCL, and very near to the Institute of Historical Research. This Bermuda Triangle of early modern scholarship kept me read, fed, housed, quenched of thirst, engaged in conversation, and generally lost to the surrounding world. Natives and denizens of the triangle include a group of scholars who have offered endless advice and encouragement. The rotating cast has included Tim Reinke-Williams, Chris Kyle, David Como, Ed Legon, Peter Lake, Richard Bell, Robert Ingram, Leanna McLaughlin, Ariel Hessayon, Bill Bulman, Noah Millstone, Laura Stewart, Joel Halcomb, Simon Healy,

Steven Teske, Elliot Vernon, and Tim Wales. Missing only was Stefania Tutino, who was likely off in the Vatican archives anyway. Five veterans of the triangle have since become close friends: John Collins, Sam Fullerton, Matt Growhowski, Dave Magliocco, and Isaac Stephens made research trips a genuine pleasure and they never hesitated to share research material and manuscript sources. My greatest debt in this area is to Jason Peacey; Jason's knowledge of archives and their contents is matched only by his persistent generosity. This book would also be in far worse shape were it not for the tireless advice of Ann Hughes. Ann knows 1640s London inside out and she has proven unfailingly kind with her knowledge.

Three scholars have guided this project from well before its inception. Sears McGee first conjured the dead when I entered his Tudor history class many years ago at UC Santa Barbara. Since then, he has never failed to offer up sage advice and his scalpel of an editorial pen. I owe him a great deal. Thanks is also due to Richard Cust, who gave up his own valuable research time to show me the ropes at the British Library and the National Archives. Last but not least is, of course, Tom Cogswell. If there is a British archive you've heard of, it is likely that Tom has been to it. Check the call slips – no, really, check them. Tom has proven an unflinching and tireless supporter of his students and their projects, and the present case is no different. His is the voice I still hear saying "yes, yes, good, but did you go *here*? What about Kingston? What news from Kew?" Tom's guidance, feedback, and keen sense of what was missing – and as importantly, what was needed – made this book possible. All errors in this work remain my own.

Beyond the realms of scholarship are a phalanx of supportive friends and family. Blake Beaudette, Aron and Geneva Ives, Jessica Lohr, Jessie Sprague and Bruce Davis, Sean Scott, and Mark Vedder often remind me that some of the best historians I know are the ones who never received formal training. Katie Macias has never balked when I asked for help, day or night. Doug and Kate Downs, my parents, have provided unflagging support since well before history was a thing. Their love and encouragement has meant more than I can say. For Joey and Annette, my newer parents, and for Nancy Smith, whose conversation and views often kept the sky from falling down, profuse thanks are due.

Oliver and Jack give renewed meaning to all things past and present. Above all others and all else is Meghan. Meghan explored London tirelessly while I burned the days away in the archives. She continues to offer unreasonable kindness, patience and forbearance while I chase Laplace's demon and shout out avian names. This book is for Meghan and the youth we shared together in London.

Abbreviations

AHR	*The American Historical Review*
A&O	*Acts and Ordinances of the Interregnum*
BL	British Library
CJ	*Journal of the House of Commons*
CSPI	*Calendar of State Papers Relating to Ireland*
CSPV	*Calendar of State Papers Relating to English Affairs in the Archives of Venice*
EHR	*English Historical Review*
GL	Guildhall Library
HJ	*Historical Journal*
HL	Huntington Library, San Marino
HLQ	*Huntington Library Quarterly*
JBS	*Journal of British Studies*
LJ	*Journal of the House of Lords*
LMA	London Metropolitan Library
PA	Parliamentary Archives
PH	*Publishing History*
TLJ	*The London Journal*
TNA	The National Archives, Kew
TRHS	*Transactions of the Royal Historical Society*

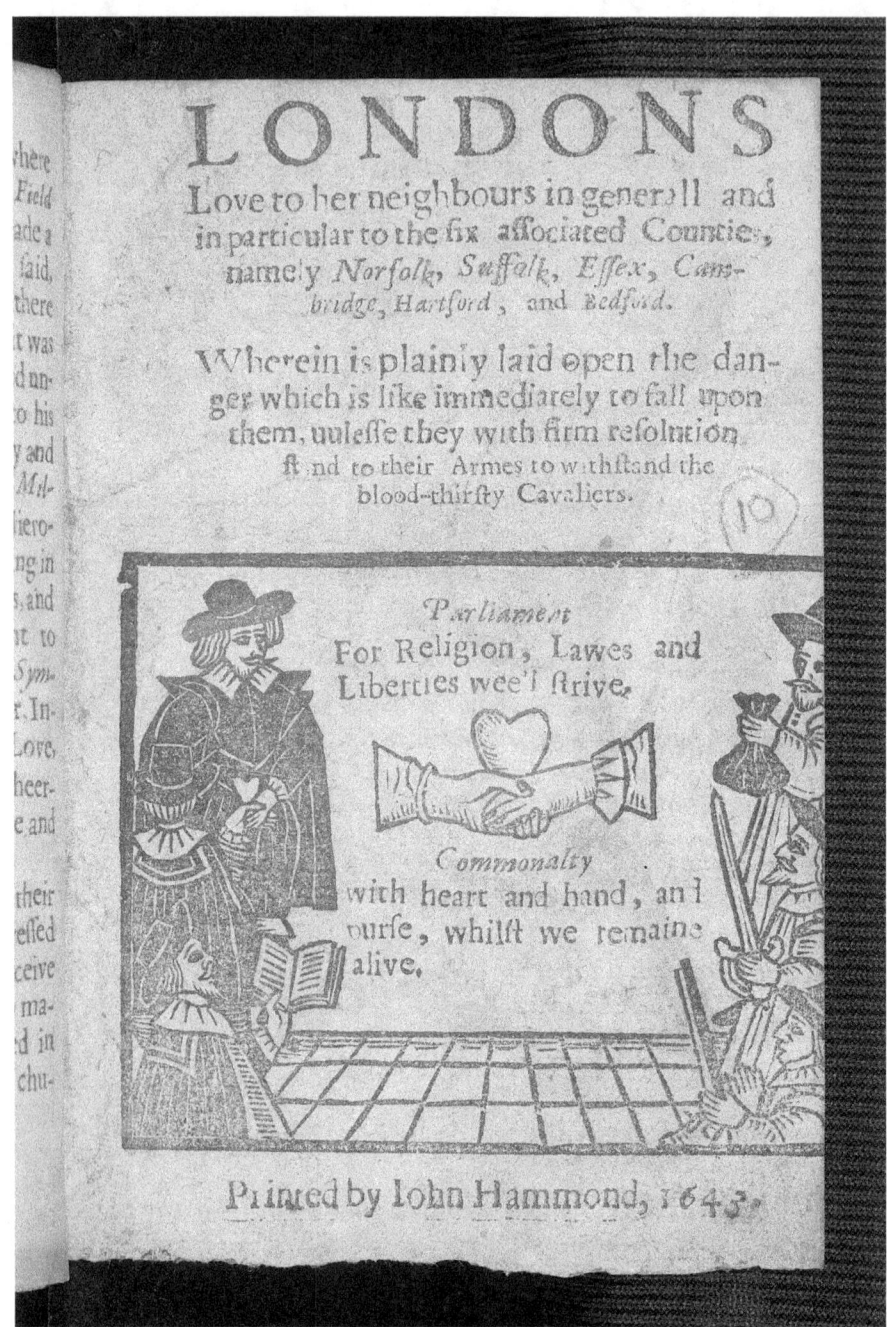

Figure 1 Frontispiece from Captain John Williams, *Londons Love to her neighbours in generall* (London, 1643). Worcester College, Oxford, LR. 4.12 (10).

Introduction

"The proud, unthankful, schismatical, rebellious, bloody City of London"

In early January 1642, Londoners committed themselves to a twenty-four-hour double watch. Guards stood "well weaponed" between the curfew hours of eight o'clock in the evening and five in the morning and took care to patrol and see that "gates and portcullices" and other "leading places" were "shutt and thoughly [sic] guarded." By ten the streets were "chained up" and barricaded. On the evening of 6 January, shops were closed and windows shuttered in preparation for another uncertain evening. Shortly after dark, rumors began to circulate. Reports of pistol fire and the "clashing" of swords came from Covent Garden, accompanied by the allegation that the king, along with "fifteen hundred horse," was preparing to ride on the City in order to seize five parliamentary opponents of the Crown who had recently been charged with treason. By midnight a "great cry was up and down" the streets, followed by banging on doors and "the thundring of Drums." Rumor seemingly became reality; members of the London trained bands equipped themselves and took to the streets in anticipation of "ware horse and foote coming against the City." At home, wives hung lanterns so "that each man might know the way to his house again" and boiled water to fend off the approaching "*Cavaleeres*."

The morning light revealed streets littered with "joynt-stooles, foormes, and empty tubbes" which had been "throwne" into piles in order to hinder the rumored horses and their riders. Although the enemy had ultimately failed to materialize, contemporaries were left with an appreciation for the reactivity of Londoners. Nehemiah Wallington, a godly woodturner, diarist, and parishioner from St. Leonard Eastcheap, recalled that "feare and trem[b]ling entered on all," and that even if the City's inhabitants had succumbed to more "fright than hurt," their collective ability to "bestirr ourselves" had prevented a situation that "would have gon hard enough with us." The royalist Samuel Butler concluded that "no lesse" than fifty or sixty thousand inhabitants had prepared that night "to incounter they knew not what." If prone to exaggeration, one thing had become crystal clear: Londoners could – and indeed would – assemble in self-defense.[1]

When looking back and attempting to account for the many years of bloody civil war that had laid waste to England during the 1640s, Edward Hyde, earl of Clarendon, remarked that it was the nation's capital – its "rebellious city" – that was chiefly to blame. It was London, and more specifically its people, who drove Charles I from peace and security to open hostility; Londoners, he lamented, were "always an enemy to the crown," and their city had long served as "a bit in his [majesty's] mouth and a bridle upon his neck."[2] If hyperbolic, Clarendon's was an assessment more often echoed than denied by contemporaries. Thomas Hobbes offered a similar view in his *Behemoth*, a controversial account of the war that was initially kept from public eyes by request of Charles II. Once printed in 1682, this revealed a characteristically Hobbesian, and thus causal, reading of the war: if it were not "for the City," claimed Hobbes, "the Parliament could never have made the War." Without such a war, there could of course be no "Rump" Parliament; and without the Rump Parliament there would never be the trial that "murdered the King."[3] So went two lasting assessments of London's place in the English Revolution.[4]

Indeed, both accounts resonate to this day. If not necessarily the "rebellious city" of Clarendon's mind, London remains for many the parliamentarian stronghold that made for the defeat of the king. If not synonymous with "parliamentarianism," most scholars readily acknowledge that the nation's capital made parliament's war efforts possible. It was the City that sheltered the notorious "Five Members" in January 1642; it was the City that marched out to stop the king at Turnham Green in November of that same year; and it was the City, again, that supplied the men-at-arms and money needed to launch parliament's war in the first place. If, as Butler claimed, "beggarly Confederates" such as Viscount Saye and Sele, John Pym, and Lord Brooke conceived the rebellion, it was most certainly the City that also provided them with "money to Levie an Army against their Leige Lord." Shortly after the descent into open conflict, royalists like Butler could lament that "in all of *England* there is but one *Rebell*, & that is *London*." With the rebellion "conceived (some *Say*) neere *Banbury*, & shaped in *Grays-Inne-Lane*," it was most certainly "put out to Nurce in *London*" and subsequently allowed to "creepe into the world."[5] Money was most certainly at the heart of such assessments, and although Clarendon and a handful of other outspoken loyalists might call the metropolis the "sink of the ill humors of the kingdom," most contemporaries of all political views would readily agree "that the rebellion was continued, as it had been raised, by the wealth and submission only of the city of London."[6] So adamant were contemporaries about London's centrality to parliament's war, both ideologically and financially, that questioning their claims would scarcely seem reasonable.

If largely true, revisionist historians nevertheless took up the challenge to counter such notions about a monolithic "parliamentarian city" as overly rudimentary, Whiggish, or "*simpliste.*" Valerie Pearl first opposed the idea of a uniform metropolitan parliamentarianism over half a century ago with *London and the Outbreak of the Puritan Revolution, 1625–1643*, a book of lasting importance.[7] Recognizing the scope of her undertaking, Pearl set about to provide "a many-sided approach" that would both explain London's constitution and show how a revolutionary "parliamentarian puritan party" came to dominate the City's government between 1641 and 1642. As the first of its kind, her book proved to be an almost unqualified success, leaving scholarship with a clear picture of an elite City revolution in the early 1640s that more or less mirrored a revolution of county elites in parliament.[8] Pearl's impression of London's revolutionary "upper sorts" became yet more entrenched with her later claim that wartime London persisted "without a popular uprising."[9] Scholarship has more or less followed in Pearl's wake by seeking to qualify, rather than challenge outright, her picture of a revolution waged by London merchants. Robert Ashton's pathway for explaining "why" the City became "parliamentarian rather than royalist," for instance, led him to focus on the economic interests of leading Londoners starting with James I's reign in 1603 and ending with the "events of 1640–2."[10] Robert Brenner took this line of inquiry several steps further by evoking the ghost of Stone to provide an expansive – and at times remarkably detailed – reconstruction of London's merchant revolutionaries that spanned from 1550 to 1653.[11] We have thus inherited three books that explain civil war London in increasingly social and economic terms, which boast progressively ambitious chronological purviews (and in the case of Brenner, page counts), and which all take as their primary focus London's revolutionary mercantile leaders. If by intention or not, London's historiography has thus remained on Pearl's revisionist trajectory.

Two important challenges to this view arrived in the 1990s. The first of these was *London and the Civil War*, an invaluable collection of thematic essays about the City's military and political cultures edited by Stephen Porter; next was Keith Lindley's *Popular Politics and Religion in Civil War London*.[12] Porter's volume contributed significantly to our understanding of the citizenry and their dynamic relationships to the war and indeed of some of the important divisions that were present throughout the civil wars. Lindley's book, meanwhile, which covers the years 1640–6, offered a remarkably different view of the period – one that accounts for popular wartime factionalism in terms of numerous shifting binary categories that blurred the lines between religion and politics, between royalists and parliamentarians, and between the admittedly tricky categories of presbyterians and independents. Lindley's account, which provides numerous valuable insights, and succeeds in moving us past a limited analysis of elite interests, unfortunately suffers from something akin to organizational paralysis. Rather than set his numerous participants – including artisans, apprentices, and plenty of London's "ordinary" and "middling" sorts – within a comprehensive narrative arch, he has produced a series of episodic and thematic vignettes; these provide valuable, if also somewhat disjointed, windows into wartime London, but we are in the end left to sort through a rotating cast of free radicals who appear and disappear, only to return chapters later. While this may in a sense be faithful to London's voluminous and sprawling sources, it ultimately leaves even the most dedicated of London's revolutionaries stripped of motivations, and, perhaps worse, context.[13] With Lindley's challenge hitting slightly wide of the mark, Pearl's original thesis has remained mostly intact: ergo, post-Pearl and post-Lindley London remains a landscape dominated by an often "puritan," self-promoting, and distinctly parliamentarian Common Council and Militia Committee – a landscape, then, of the City elites. This is, on the one hand, all fine and well; City authorities have an indispensable place in the story of London's mobilization. Yet it remains the case that we have no more than half of the picture of London's mobilization.

Indeed, with Pearl's side of the equation firmly in place, historians – and their historiographies – have moved on. Recent endeavors have seen the metropolis carved up into increasingly specialized, and in some cases quite compelling, studies. Ben Coates's exploration of the impact of the civil war on the economy of London stands out, both for its originality and its extensive archival breadth. Despite numerous valuable insights into London's wartime economy, Coates's research does little to impact our sense of the City's role in parliament's war. Admittedly, this is foremost due to perspective; rather than ask how the economy of London impacted the civil war, and thus challenge and qualify revisionist scholarship vis-à-vis Pearl and her followers, Coates seeks to explain how the civil war impacted the economy of London. When keyed into the historiographical trajectory below, Coates's research provides a new array of insights. Aside from Coates, and recent work by Gavin Robinson on horse conscription, most historians have focused on London within the scope of urban history, and thus treat the capital's wartime years in passing.[14] A sustained interest in the metropolis means that we now have a veritable range of what might be labeled "early modern metropolitan studies." These now cover, in edited volumes and monographs, London's cultural and social history, its dead, its diversity, its "ordinary women," its memory, and the roots of metropolitan environmental pollution.[15] Each of these histories contend with their own issues, and each makes its own, unique set of historiographical interventions and contributions. Long-standing and contentious debates about London's stability have, for instance, been sufficiently put to rest by Paul Griffiths, whose exhaustively researched study of metropolitan crime and policing paints a picture of a dynamic, ever-changing, and rapidly modernizing City.[16]

Other scholars, meanwhile, have aided our understanding of the wartime metropolis by focusing on boroughs. Jeremy Boulton generated an invaluable survey of the "neighborhood" borough of Southwark, while Julia Merritt has crafted compelling accounts of Westminster, both in terms of its respective development as an early modern city and in terms of its relationship to the civil war.[17] Importantly, Merritt captured the experience of war in the metropolis, illustrating in particular how the "streets of Westminster" saw a "heavy military presence," and how inhabitants engaged with both "low-level military interference in civilian life" and at times the "significant impact" of being in close proximity to parliament's mobilizing efforts.[18] She has also observed the extent to which wartime "London was exercising more control than ever before over its suburbs" as a matter of "revenue raising." However, where Merritt places emphasis on the ways that Westminster "vigorously" resisted the encroaching interests of the City (both in terms of bids for incorporation that lasted from the outset of the war until 1654, and due to the "scarcely more than four years" when Westminster and London were encompassed by the same defensive fortifications known as the Lines of Communication), the present study regularly discusses the urban area as a component of the larger metropolis. This is possible for a number of reasons. Foremost is the fact that over the course of 1641–5 Westminster fell increasingly under the authority of London's Common Council and the City Militia Committee. By 1643, the boroughs of Southwark, Tower Hamlets, and Westminster were ordered to raise "auxiliary" forces to supplement London's trained bands. More than this, by the time the City fortifications were built, ordinances issued by Common Council began regularly addressing Westminster and other outlying areas. Indeed, contemporaries navigated (often seamlessly) the wider metropolitan area, traversing the City's parishes and wards as they gathered in tumults, or regularly delivered petitions from London to parliament. For all practical purposes, then, Westminster, like Southwark or Tower Hamlets, will be treated here as an important constituent component of metropolitan London. Westminster's parishes, including St. Giles in the Fields, are here used to supply information about the ways in which the metropolis mobilized for parliament's war.[19] If circuitously, then, research on Westminster and London's boroughs has added indispensably to our picture of the wartime metropolis.

Like the capital, the civil war and revolution have continued to attract scholarly attention. Having fallen decidedly out of fashion since the 1980s, the topic of revolution has seen something of a minor recent resurgence. Within the past decade and a half, a handful of historians have reconceptualized the ways in which people participated in the conflict, and indeed, by extension, the nature and scope of the conflict itself.[20] Rather than see the war in terms of fixed ideologies of allegiance – as a matter of subscribing to reified notions of "parliamentarianism" or "royalism" – they have favored the more fluid categories of situation and action (of context, in short). This line of inquiry, which stems from pioneering work by David Underdown, has since been developed upon and adapted by scholars such as David Scott, whose research continues to investigate how to better understand wartime politics and party alignments.[21] Among the most compelling early efforts to do away with overly static categories, however, are John Walter's research on crowd tactics and mobilization in Colchester and Ann Hughes's study of Thomas Edwards's *Gangraena*, an exploration of the ways in which print – considered through multiple contextualizations – helped to shape a landscape of "rival parliamentarian mobilizations."[22] In the wake of these seminal studies, questions about the dynamics of mobilization – of moving men, money, and, importantly, ideas – have crept into other scholarly accounts of the war.[23] Michael Braddick, for instance, has proposed that we "might be better to think in terms of people's responses to particular mobilizations rather than a fixed allegiance of two sides."[24] This shift in attention has had important – if perhaps at times seemingly obvious – implications. For one, it has redirected scholarly attention away from questions about the long-term "causes" of the war, and in doing so has made space for other matters such as the reconsideration of short-term agents, participatory contextualization, and of the dynamics of wartime activism.[25] We have thus been able to set aside overly rigid, problematic, and crudely imposed explanations in favor of an effort to understand participation, which has in itself helped to reduce our reliance on, and indeed the explanatory power of, monolithic party identities which leaves us with fewer capital "R" Royalists and capital "P" Parliamentarians. Tom Leng, for instance, has proposed a more subtle exploration of the discursive practices of mobilization by looking at the parliamentary cause as a moving target, as a thing that remained inchoate as opposed to fully-fledged.[26] Ergo, we might take the cue and happily avoid unnecessary taxonomic parsing. Second, and on a somewhat more abstract level, this has allowed for an important reevaluation and reappraisal of lasting chronological and historiographical conventions surrounding the civil war. Rather than cling too tightly to periodizations of the war – to the 1642–6 paradigm, for instance – we might now seek more subtle chronologies of mobilization, of momentary, if also situational and finite, developments that help to explain participation.[27] This approach allows for a novel consideration of London's wartime mobilization that spans between the outbreak of the Irish "rebellion" in late 1641 to the establishment of the New Model Army in early 1645. If valuable as a window into a period of unprecedented popular participation, this periodization does also omit important mobilizing efforts, like, for instance, the Root and Branch petition of December 1640.[28] It is my humble hope that things lost here might make way for other things gained.

Shared notions of self-preservation often guided Londoners, as did of course their deeply held religious and political convictions. The City could thus be as much a place for "neuters" as it was for activists. This explains in part why Philip Skippon's November 1642 speech at Turnham Green registered the cause as one "for God, and for the defence of yourselves, your wives and children." And likewise it helps to explain why we find analogous terms of mobilization deployed eight months later when Londoners were asked to participate in a "general rising" to defend both "Religion, Lawes, Liberties" and the wellbeing of their "Wives, Children, [and] Estates."[29] Less pleas to join up and fight for a reified or ideologically clear "parliamentarianism," these entreaties to action were made in light of tangible – and in contemporary minds, very real – threats. Both cases, for instance, saw Londoners endangered by loyalist armies. Yet Skippon's motivating speech and the later urgent call for Londoners to partake in a "general rising" had drastically different outcomes. We might thus acknowledge from the outset that popular mobilization did not depend entirely upon immediate circumstances. To make such a claim would be conveniently and problematically Hobbesian. Rather, it is here suggested that the success of mobilizing efforts owed to complex intersections between preexisting assumptions and propensities *and* immediate catalysts. Agitators, propagandists, and wartime participants in general were the ones left with the unenviable burden of rendering, crafting, and deploying arguments and accounts that might sway popular opinion – or better yet, spur action. A wide and at times by definition inclusive cross-section of players worked to win over the hearts and minds of Londoners.

This dynamic, and indeed the extent to which Londoners were both politically engaged and willing to entertain mobilizing efforts, is revealed in striking detail by John Walter's exploration of the politics surrounding the 1641 Protestation oath. Walter uncovered a remarkable moment of metropolitan mobilization that was "the result of an independent initiative undertaken by an alliance of City radicals, parish activists, and Puritan ministers." City preaching (especially, in this case, by Richard Culverwell, Thomas Case, and the later presbyterian George Lawrence) and petitioning saw the capital's inhabitants at the forefront of national politics surrounding questions that centered around loyalty to Charles I. As Walter reveals, parochial mobilizing efforts in some instances saw Londoners taking the oath "the day before the mayor gave his agreement," a matter that clearly broke with precedent. Mobilizations of this nature, as I hope to show, were by no means limited to the Protestation oath. Indeed, from Walter's painstaking reconstruction we might readily assume aspects of the dynamic structure of mobilization to be part of a process; and thus we might think in terms of processes when considering wartime mobilizations. With the descent into war mobilizing processes became both more robust and, with time, they permutated. London hosted numerous dynamic efforts to mobilize military and financial resources for what began as a largely defensive effort against the king and his supporters. Likewise, counter-mobilizing efforts were in place from day one. As with the Protestation, the success of these rival mobilizing efforts depended upon an intersection of efforts, matters that tied parochial politics to London's corporate authorities and indeed on to parliamentary procedure itself. While we might ultimately acknowledge that activists and oath takers helped define the early "character of the English Revolution," as Walter suggests, we might also see that Londoners would spend the coming years contending with and redefining both the character and tenor of the war.[30]

Our modern pursuit of these defining characteristics has been aided considerably by David Como's *Radical Parliamentarians and the English Civil War*. Through an ambitious and compelling account of the most radical components of the parliamentarian coalition, Como's research uncovers the emergence of "new or newly adapted ideas and programs" of parliamentarianism and concomitant moments of ideological escalation that saw parliament's war effort develop from nascence to revolution.[31] This proves a remarkable trajectory. Whereas Como's focus rests on the permutations of radical (and often, then, sectarian) ideas within parliament's wartime coalition, and by extension a limited coterie of players who were engaged in intra-parliamentarian debates, the present study accounts for radical mobilization in a far broader sense. Explored here are the extreme and progressive views and tactics of a broad sweep of Londoners (including, notably, those who were opposed to the sectarian visions presented in the early 1640s such as Stephen Marshall, Edmund Calamy, Thomas Case, and other future presbyterian leaders) who sought to extract military and financial resources from the City. Efforts to agitate Londoners, or indeed to assess and obtain weapons, warriors and wealth often broke with long-standing precendents and assumptions and by definition were thus novel or "radical."

Mobilizing efforts encompassed metropolitan communities that ranged from unreceptive to widely recalcitrant, or at times even outspokenly opposed to war. In exploring the full dynamics of metropolitan wartime mobilization, we might as often engage with the efforts and opinions of individuals who were deemed "radicals" within a wider parliamentarian coalition, just as we might also engage with counter-mobilizations in terms of peace protests, peace petitioners, and loyalist preachers who were "radical" or "radicalized" in their own respects. In so far as efforts to move money and men broke with precedent – or indeed, for that matter, with prevailing, and at times fundamental opinions – both parliamentarians *and* loyalists might at any point be deemed "radicals." Ergo, we find here both radicals who remained committed to the moving ideological target that was the parliament's effort, just as we find a rotating cast of Londoners who were equally committed to testing and challenging parochial, City, and parliamentary actions as a means to stymie war or promote peace. London's loyalists were at times no less driven by seemingly extreme means than were their ideologically opposed counterparts.

With this broad definition of radicalism in place, and with an eye to mobilization as process, we might finally seek to ask how and why so many Londoners moved their vast resources and why the lion's share went not to the king but to parliament. How, it should now be asked, does this serve to qualify Pearl's original claims? We might, on the one hand, accept the lasting importance of London's leading revolutionaries and activists; but meanwhile, on the other hand, we might challenge the notion that London's war effort commenced "without a popular uprising." The latter disagreement returns to the fold the inclusory and participatory nature of London's wartime politics, from the actions of the many who signed petitions, to the nameless crowds of agitators and protesters, down to the very parishioners who sat steadfast through countless sermons.

Focus on the "popular" component of wartime mobilization stands to sharpen – or at the very least shed valuable light – on the efforts of the political leaders, propagandists, preachers, petitioners, agitators, and others who sought to move money and people. But it also allows us to hone in on various actors and groups that were at the fore of any given mobilizing effort. Within a year of the war's start, Butler felt confident that he might identify fomenters of "rebellion." Like Clarendon's later assessment, these included the "*Puritans*" who had preached in the "*Military-yard or Artillery-Garden*" such as Obadiah Sedgwick and Calybute Downing, and lecturers who preached "fire from the pulpit" to "foment disloyalty," including Stephen Marshall, Edmund Calamy, Cornelius Burgess, and Hugh Peter. Butler added to their ranks a handful of civic leaders who proved overwhelmingly "disaffected to the Government." These men were aldermen, such as Thomas Atkins, John Towse, and John "*Fowke the Traytor*." And with them now were the "beggarly Captaines" John Venn and Randall Mainwaring, along with the war petitioners Sir David Watkins and "*Satten [Richard] Shute*." None figured more prominently in Butler's "*bloody City*" than Isaac Pennington, "the pretended Lord Mayor" and burgess for London who helped to oust and replace his predecessor, the loyalist mayor

Richard Gurney, in August 1642. Pennington was nearer than most to the beating heart of parliament's wartime mobilization.[32] Indeed, both the Lord Mayor and his equally zealous wife, Mary, made parliament's success their primary purpose.[33] When not clearly manifested in terms of popular agitation, petitioning, or casting votes in parliament, Pennington wielded the mayoralty to implement controversial financial expedients and bring loyalists to heel. These efforts helped in the short term to finance parliament's war; in the long term, they served to develop and hone the apparatuses of the City and the state.[34]

In his published Ford Lectures, Peter Lake proposed engagement with "the full range of contemporary media" as a means to get to the heart of "public politicking" in late Elizabethan England.[35] The present work must humbly aspire to do the same for the early 1640s, a period that affords parallel, if decidedly unique, methodological challenges to those of a half century earlier. Indeed, the "full range" of material that must be accounted for with regards to London's wartime mobilization is, by any reasonable account, staggering. Whereas the Elizabethan and early Stuart periods contended with their own polarizations, the early 1640s created arenas for contention on a scale that would previously seem unfathomable.[36] The resulting landscape is one of political interests that often aspire to – but normally defy – neat categorization. Our best efforts, for lack of more precise and accepted taxonomies and classifications, see us working with a dialogue of polarities (between, again, on a crude level, Parliamentarians and Royalists, and for those working within the parliamentarian coalition itself, between shifting "war" and "peace" parties). As the civil war progressed, these interests became both more and less pronounced and, indeed, increasingly fragmentary, with groups clinging, on the one hand, ever more tightly to their sentiments regarding either the exigency or termination of war, and groups, on the other hand, diverging in opinion about how to best manage and even expand the fight. It was not long after the outset of war that segments of parliamentarian coalition, and indeed many Londoners, began to make known their opposition to the ideological and logistical demands of war. Fatigue, financial losses, physical deterioration, and widespread disillusionment eventually led many in the metropolis to avoid, or even protest outright against, a continuation of the conflict. Added to this already fitful scene must eventually be an awareness of how contemporaries grappled with the prospect of peace, and further what to do in the case of an actual peace settlement. The resulting narrative – or, perhaps more accurately, narratives – are cacophonous. Well aware of the fluctuating state of politics, the present account explores how mobilizing efforts shifted over time and how, in turn, London's vast resources and manpower were mobilized. If, and when, successful, methods of mobilization were maintained, adapted, and repeated. Here, then, is an attempt to explore the dynamics of mobilization across social and political categories, as they change – in some cases minutely or subtly – over time.

These demands necessitate engagement with numerous sources and fragmentary chronologies. Naturally, this means that the present work must rely upon sources as a representative cross-section of the material available – alas a mere sampling of "the full range of contemporary media" – that can and should be used to shed light on London's mobilization. Fortunately for modern scholarship, and indeed for this author, London does not suffer from a dearth of accessible sources. Indeed, quite the opposite is true: the City boasts a wealth of archives and archival materials relating to the civil war period. Much of this owes to clerical and lay diligence, and in particular that of contemporary churchwardens. Much later, this survival owed (and to this day owes) to the care and attention of thoughtful archivists. It is perhaps telling that the bulk of accounts from livery companies and parishes survived fire on the ground in 1666 and lightning from the sky in 1940–1. Modern scholars might consult with thirty-nine accounts and numerous minute books that were deposited by livery companies into the London Guildhall Library. The Clothworkers, the Drapers, the Goldsmiths, the Leathersellers, the Mercers, and the Salters all, meanwhile, retain accessible court books and minute books in their own archives. Parochial records are much the same with regard to record retention; more than a hundred unique vestry minutes and churchwardens' accounts from dozens of City parishes have been deposited in the London Metropolitan Archives. Westminster and the Boroughs of Southwark and Tower Hamlets likewise retain records from the period.

To these valuable resources must be added a wealth of other manuscript materials that shed light on wartime narratives and, where possible, corroborate, or detail, mobilizing efforts. Considered here are numerous scribal receipts, manuscript libels, lampooning songs, petitions, private correspondences, and marginalia notes that detail mobilizations. Increasingly, the wartime years see examples of manuscript and print working interdependently. Vestry and livery company records, for instance, show directly (and at times quantifiably) how contemporaries responded to printed loan requests and charitable collections, or indeed how liverymen reacted to mayoral precepts, ordinances, and requests issued by parliamentary committees. Receipts provide a classic example of the interdependence between printed and scribal components; petitions, likewise, might readily be found printed and written out, and indeed often copied yet again by hand, each a link in a chain of production. Not least here are parish minutes, churchwardens' accounts, and official scribal records of the Corporation – the journals, cash accounts, letter books, repertories and other materials that recall proceedings in Common Council, Court of Aldermen, and Common Hall. Here are found orders, requests, and replies, with printed materials pasted into books, or sometimes with print copied out verbatim. Revealed in the interaction between print and manuscript at this time – in unavoidably structurated relationships – are processes of mobilization as much as examples of novel processes of communication and the expanding apparatuses of state.

Printed sources provide their own unique challenges. Not least of these is the breakdown in censorship laws in 1640 and 1641, a matter that has attracted its fair share of scholarly attention.[37] Indeed, the voluminous print of the era has led historians, attempting to grapple with their sources, and eager to capture prevailing conditions, to employ a range of metaphors; we thus deal with a period, and specifically a capital, that experienced print as a "deluge," an "avalanche," or even, at times, a "flood."[38] Presented with such meteorological challenges, the present study must nevertheless swim and persist. Charting London's mobilizations requires, where possible, engagement with the participatory dynamics that surrounded print and the sophisticated ways in which contemporaries produced and used printed newsbooks, ordinances, proclamations, tracts, sermons, pamphlets, polemics and ephemera.

Aiding our efforts here are methods of analysis uncovered by Jason Peacey and Ann Hughes, scholars who have teased out sophisticated ways to situate print in relation to political engagement. Peacey, in particular, has revealed how print operated situationally and organizationally in processes of mobilization, and how we might estimate the role that "printed texts played in mass politics," or how print might serve "as a tactical device."[39] Print as propaganda, ergo, has an important place here. In his original study of London's Restoration crowds, Tim Harris suggested some of the ways in which propaganda could be used to "throw much light on the political assumptions of the populace."[40] Where possible, the present study hopes to do the same; propaganda is employed here as a means to investigate the opinions of leading activists and the groups of Londoners that they sought to influence. Print, as we will see, was deployed on numerous occasions and with an equally numerous range of intentions. Often, it was used to promote or censure – to legitimize or delegitimize – the perceptions of readers and listeners. But most notably, it was used as a means to mobilize directly, to organize and move people and resources. Throughout the first civil war, print was deployed tactically to agitate crowds, to direct popular protests, and at times to intimidate or incite violence. As the war progressed, printed propaganda took on different and sometimes more subtle roles. It became an important means to promote and legitimize preferred political narratives, to stymie peace propositions, and to evoke and amplify direct threats or allay lingering concerns.[41] Moments arose when demotic libelous printed tickets were "scattered about the Streets in the night" or distributed "up and downe in the Citty of London" to spur popular mobilization, shape opinion, and influence debate.⁴² Popular opinion and debate might then, in turn, influence proceedings in parliament, eroding convenient demarcations between politics of the street and high politics. Herein lies the danger that we might simply assume that print mobilized, that readership implied belief, or indeed that surviving materials might constitute roadmaps to action. Such assumptions are, in short, untenable. Rather than be taken as conclusive and concrete, it should be noted that what follows is at times suggestive or speculative.

When taken together – and indeed when understood as interdependent – the period's extensive manuscript and print sources offer views of the many struggles to win over the hearts and minds of Londoners. Under scrutiny, this disparate range of sources can link the ideological concerns of leading activists and institutions to piecemeal processes of mobilization. Emerging from these weblike connections are, for want of a better phrase, what might be termed "topographies of mobilization," rough sketches of London's wide participatory political landscape. Here we might trace the production of an ordinance from its introduction in parliamentary committee, to debate and vote in Commons, to delivery to Common Council, and on to print as an ordinance or precept approved by Common Council and signed by the lord mayor. Onwards, we might espy the letter pasted in, or copied out scribally in livery and parish account books, discussed or debated in minutes, and then reported back to a parliamentary committee or the council. At this point we might find out responses were sufficient or considered for further action. Likewise, we might trace sermons from venue to print, and in terms of notes and marginalia. London's many churchwardens at times note the merits or shortcomings of a preacher or sermon, of approbation or criticism, or of the quantity and quality of the money or goods collected in the wake of a sermon or on a day of thanksgiving. By triangulating efforts – by identifying individuals within recorded processes – we can at times trace and gauge the effectiveness of mobilizing efforts that were both robust in intention and granular in response. From this vantage point, we can, as one royalist contemporary suggested, locate "a kind of discipline in disorder." Sweeping demands for money might thus break down into their constituent parts, down even to the level of group or individual payments. "Tumults," likewise, might become less unruly, disorganized affairs, and instead take on the characteristics of orchestrated events in which individual participants stand "ready at command, upon a watch-word given."⁴³ Sermons, likewise, become less clearly anodyne matters of tending to spirituality than they do specifically timed pleas to action. What emerges collectively is a landscape of mobilization, and with it a topography that does not simply account for intent and action, but rather exposes processes that moved from closed committees to companies, from pulpits and pews, and from London's streets to parliament.

Source-driven analysis on this scale is not without its fair share of pitfalls and shortcomings. Naturally, the matter of record survival has shaped the scope of the present work, and while it can only be guessed at how additional sources – surviving petitions, printed sermons, and others – may have influenced the story of mobilization that unfolds here, it seems likely that, given the relative resilience of the communities that are here considered, and indeed the resulting patterns of mobilization that emerge, and the corroboration and verification afforded by multiple sources, the majority of the present findings might hopefully stand to be qualified rather than corrected. It is nevertheless still worth reiterating that the present findings are, once again, putative.

Finally, we might also take into account how rumors and events were intentionally manipulated to serve specific purposes. The "propagandized event" has a distinct place in any account of 1640s London. Here is no different. Seemingly frenzied and unorganized moments of iconoclasm could unfold as "exercise[s] in propaganda" – episodes when, as the historian Julie Spraggon has shown, "parliamentarian authorities" sought "to stir up anti-Catholicism and to promote the godly cause."[44] Wartime London played host to numerous incidents that could afford similar – if not necessarily always anti-Catholic – opportunities. Scores gathered to spectacles, to see and be seen. Military companies mustered in fields and processed through the streets, waving flags and rattling drums; church bells pealed to announce the return of brigades of soldiers and their celebrated commanders; jeering crowds amassed to witness executions at Tyburn Tree, Royal Exchange, and Tower Hill. Agitators and petitioners, meanwhile, participated in their own public performances as they affixed colored ribbons to their hats and clothes and marched petitions from London to Westminster, and indeed as they waylaid officials, cried out in chorus, lit bonfires and toppled monuments. With assembly and dispersal, Londoners relayed – intentionally or unintentionally – their own social cues to fellow inhabitants; these could as soon legitimize or delegitimize their purposes, inspiring allies and critics alike. Similar to moments of popular iconoclasm, these various "organic events" generated secondary and tertiary opportunities to promote, publicize, and propagandize, and to churn out new rumors, responses, and indeed counter-mobilizations. Behind this all, which contemporaries frequently labeled simply as "tumults," or which they might simply dismiss as the rearing head of the *mobile vulgus*, were numerous subtle processes.

A trip up the Thames during the early 1640s would provide sweeping views of this teeming city, of a city that had clearly outgrown its medieval footprint. Following the river's silt-rich waters inland would reveal wooden embankments and moored merchant vessels, pulled east or west by the prevailing tide. Bisecting the Thames was London Bridge, the sole river crossing that served as both a southern gateway to the bustling metropolis and a barrier to the large seaward vessels since the early thirteenth century. Upriver would be numerous smaller sailing barges, eel ships and wherries, slender riverboats that docked in clusters as watermen waited to ferry passengers who wished to avoid the City's crowded alleyways and dirty streets. Dominating the river's north side was St. Paul's, an imposing medieval cathedral around which huddled countless half-timbered buildings and brick chimneys. Rising from the City's centre were scores of parish towers and steeples, including those of St. Mary-le-Bow, All Hallowes the Great, St. Martin Thames Street, St. Laurence Pountney, and St. Michael Cornhill. Tucked amidst London's parishes and northeast of St. Paul's was Guildhall, the center of City government that remained invisible from the river. Southeast of the medieval hall and also obscured from view was Royal Exchange, a commercial center that sat between Cornhill and Threadneedle Street. The contrasting "south bank," or Bankside, was underdeveloped by comparison. Bankside had decidedly fewer spires, although the largest by far belonged to St. Mary Overie, Southwark's own cathedral that was dedicated in the twelfth century and had since gained its title for being "over the river." A glance past Overie would reveal rows of half-timbered structures and "stews," brothels near to the famous theaters that parliament would order shuttered in September 1642. Further up Bankside was the Bear Garden and open spaces that followed the curve of the river on toward Lambeth Palace, the metropolitan residence of the Archbishop of Canterbury. Looking north again, the river bent gradually to reveal Essex House, Arundel House, and Somerset House, imposing walled and gated estates with walkways and piers that dominated the Thames foreshore and spanned from the western edge of London's crowded square mile all the way to the meeting point of St. Martin's Lane and Charing Cross, an area where the river narrowed slightly and where the Palace of Westminster stood. Here the view was defined less by towers, steeples, and half-timber gables than by an architectural hodgepodge; Inigo Jones's neoclassical Banqueting House stood downriver from the Norman Great Hall and the Abbey turned Royal Peculiar. Near to these imposing landmarks and perpendicular to the river stood St. Stephen's Chapel, the meeting place for the House of Commons.

London had grown rapidly over the course of the sixteenth and seventeenth centuries. Steady immigration and regular growth had coupled with relatively few recent outbreaks of the plague so that the City's population quadrupled between 1500 and 1600; and it doubled yet again over the course of the early Stuart period.[45] If once seen as something of a backwater by European standards, London had by the 1640s become a bustling international center. Estimates suggest that the City was home to between 350,000 and 400,000 people during the 1640s. Indeed, growth in the capital steadily outpaced that of other English cities. The substantial market town of Norwich, which was by most accounts the nation's "second city," was estimated to have upwards of 32,000 inhabitants by 1622, a mere fraction of London's total.[46] Smaller yet – but still relatively large – were Coventry, York, and Bristol, important regional hubs of activity that served thousands, respectively, but paled in size when compared to London.

London's size and population were impressive by wider archipelagic and Continental standards. Edinburgh was home to between 25,000 and 36,000 people by the middle of the century, while Dublin remained smaller yet with its approximately 20,000 inhabitants.[47] Looking further afield revealed that London's population was on par with – and even in some cases exceeded – some of Europe's largest civic centers. Paris had steadily grown over the course of the fifteenth and sixteenth centuries to provide for nearly half a million people in 1645.[48] Some 350,000 inhabitants called Naples home in 1647, while Amsterdam boasted a population of 140,000.[49] Only one European city was considerably larger than London by the middle of the seventeenth century and it sat at the meeting point between continents and cultures on the Bosporus; estimates suggest that Constantinople's diverse population had grown well past 600,000.[50] More staggering than London's rapid growth was the fact that it contained some "7 per cent of England's population in 1650," an impressive figure at a time when compared to the approximately "2.5 per cent of Frenchmen [who] lived in Paris" contemporaneously.[51]

Paralleling London's demographic ascendancy was its path to economic preeminence. As Coates suggests, the capital had by this time settled into a "dominant position" over "England's internal and external trade," acting as the nation's "main port" and the "centre of the transport network."[52] Beyond its apparent geographical advantage, London had long been home to livery companies, "ancient" City guild trade associations that controlled manufacturing and trade beyond the boundaries of the metropolis. Over the centuries, liveries had become inextricably connected to the political operations of the City. They were, to borrow Lindley's apt phrasing, "London's most important social organisations." Liveries at once provided "aid, discipline and a sense of community and fellowship for their members," while liverymen often found themselves elected to fill seats in City government.[53] A major part of London's social world revolved around its liveries, which included wardens and assistants, apprentices, householders, journeymen, and, at the top, liverymen, who were named for their company gowns. In 1515 it was decided that there would be "twelve great worshipful companies": The Mercers, Grocers, Drapers, Fishmongers, Goldsmiths, Skinners, Merchant Taylors, Haberdashers, Salters, Ironmongers, Vintners, and Clothworkers. Of nearly 100 City liveries, London's twelve great were preeminent in terms of the status of their members, wealth, and their historic accounts of themselves. Liverymen from the twelve were disproportionately nominated and selected to fill the upper ranks of City government. For instance, just four liverymen from outside the "twelve great" found their way to the mayoralty over the course of the entire seventeenth century, and each of these came to the position after 1650.

As some of the City's wealthiest and oldest institutions, livery companies were regularly called upon to make loans to the Crown. However, in the wake of escalating tensions and the king's abrupt departure from London in early 1642, this function was readily subsumed by parliament. Over the course of the war parliament repeatedly turned to London's Corporation for loans, which were issued as direct requests for loans in cash, arms, and armor by the Lord Mayor and Common Council. More than supplying the sinews of war, liveries helped to facilitate parliament's day-to-day proceedings by offering up their "great halls" and chambers for the use of parliamentary committees.[54] As the demands of war shifted and intensified, companies were called upon to mobilize in other ways; apprentices soon marched under company colors to help construct London's fortifications while others were conscripted directly into parliament's armies.

The vast majority of Londoners were engaged in sundry occupations and fell well below the priviledged staus of liverymen or citizen. Most were shopkeepers, artisans, apprentices, and day laborers, just as they were denizens, vagrants, refugees, and beggars. Regardless of status, nearly all Londoners experienced the quotidian aspects of war from within their respective parochial communities; as was the case throughout the nation, parishes made up the foundations of metropolitan life. As volunteer lay officials who oversaw the daily operations of their parishes, churchwardens and vestrymen engaged with the majority of the population and thus could play a conspicuous part in mobilization. Church officials regularly oversaw numerous wartime responsibilities. Not least, they read out and implemented parliamentary acts and City ordinances – actions that brought Londoners into direct contact with parliamentary and metropolitan interests. When the prior and latter aligned, parochial administrators served as a highly effective ground level means for mobilizing resources. Indeed, church officials oversaw numerous seemingly quotidian matters that related directly to mobilization and the experience of war. Churchwardens, for instance, managed accounts and receipts, including the crucial roles of charitable collections and payments to the poor. But they also oversaw church maintenance, inventories, rents, scavenging, and matters such as the ringing of bells. Such day-to-day tasks, ostensibly devoid of political meaning, could in fact reveal clear partisanship; extra payments for continued ringing on days of thanksgiving for military victories, for example, might be taken to reveal a dynamic "wartime soundscape," a space where the pealing of bells might literally sound for support, or indeed in some instances, for dissent. Moreover, as the war pressed on, church officials helped to keep track of parishioners who loaned – or who refused to loan – money toward parliament's effort; they paid for and oversaw the removal of idolatrous and "popish" images; they purchased books to record and return the names of oath takers and breakers; and, increasingly as the war pressed on, they managed the distribution of money for sick and injured soldiers. Lastly, and in many regards most importantly, lay parochial administrators were often responsible for the appointment and maintenance of clergymen (by advowsons or other means) and preachers. They might thus stock the very pulpits that "administered fuel, and blowed the coals" of what Clarendon called the "strange wildfire among the people," rebellion against the king.[55] Or they might just as soon snuff out sparks that could turn to conflagrations.

Londoners found themselves living under overlapping and often confusing jurisdictions that spanned between the parish, ward, City, and in some cases the county. London's Corporation consisted of three main courts: that of Lord Mayor and Aldermen, Common Council, and Common Hall. The greatest authority resided with the Lord Mayor and Aldermen, a governing body made up of twenty-six aldermen who served for life and a Lord Mayor who was appointed annually. Aldermen were nominated by annual wardmotes of the City's freemen, and ultimately selected by existing members of the aldermanic bench. Once chosen, aldermen could only be removed by vote of their peers. As Pearl observed, this meant that the aldermanic bench became an increasingly "oligarchic and almost self-perpetuating" body. Over time, the court became dominated by some of the capital's "wealthiest citizens."[56] Common Council, which drafted and issued legislation, precepts, and petitions, was comprised of four to eight citizens from each of the City's twenty-six wards. Like the Court of Aldermen, freemen and householders chose councilmen during annual wardmotes. Although this meant that there could be upwards of 200 members of Common Council at any given time, proceedings were overseen by the Lord Mayor and aldermen, who both selected matters for the Court's consideration and "exercised a veto over its proceedings."[57] Common Council was for all outward purposes, then, a legislative extension of the Court of Aldermen. Common Halls operated in an altogether different manner. These assemblies, at times referred to by contemporaries as "congregations," were open to all of the City's liverymen and were called and dissolved at the discretion of the Lord Mayor. Attendance at Common Halls regularly numbered in the thousands during the 1640s. Aside from regular annual September meetings for the election of the Lord Mayor, Common Halls became increasingly political and partisan affairs, called upon strategically as a means to disseminate favorable political news, or in some cases to celebrate providential delivery from dangerous plots.

As chief magistrates of the City, Lord Mayors were appointed annually by vote of Common Hall. Common Halls nominated two aldermen who were sent on for final consideration by the Court of the Mayor and Aldermen. An important break in procedure occurred in August 1642, when Isaac Pennington was appointed as a replacement for the expelled royalist Lord Mayor, Sir Richard Gurney. More than simply elevating an outspoken critic of the Crown to the position of chief magistrate of the City, Pennington was also permitted to retain his seat in the Commons. Contemporary critics were quick to point out that this gave him undue influence over political affairs. Indeed, by August 1643, *Mercurius Aulicus* complained that parliament's war effort was being directed by "my Lord Say, or Pym, or Isaac Pennington" who could each be found in "any of the three Houses wherein they are leaders."[58] The extent to which Pennington utilized his position for parliament's cause – the ways in which he presided over Common Council as a "third house," the extent to which he exploited the mayoralty, and his limited actions as a Member of Parliament, are central considerations of the present work.

If noteworthy as an unrivaled and closely governed economic center, London was also an unparalleled source of manpower. The City had long enjoyed traditions of martial display, especially in terms of the fashionable public and private companies that met to drill in the capital's open spaces and adjacent areas. Both the public Artillery Garden and the Military Garden held regular meetings in Bishopsgate and St. Martin's Fields. Muster books from London's Honorable Artillery Company reveal a robust membership that extended back to the reign of Henry VIII. Many of the leading officers who would go on to serve either the king or parliament had enjoyed membership in the company. Sir Philip Skippon, for instance, served as Captain-General of the Honorable Artillery Company long before parliament appointed him as commander of the trained bands in 1642.[59] If not participants themselves, Londoners frequently encountered scenes of drilling that included formational marching to the beating of drums, the waving of banners, and occasionally the discharge of cannons and muskets.

Regular practice and drilling was sometimes supplemented by private performance. One such meeting took place in October 1638 at the Merchant Taylors' Hall when "fourscore" of the Honourable Artillery Company staged a mock battle between Saracens and Christians. The occasion was as much a performance as it was a chance to exercise and display military precision and discipline. Twenty-two Saracens marched into the hall under the command of Captain Thomas Whitley, decked in turbans and to the beat of a "Turkey Drumme" along with "a hideous noise making pipe" fashioned from buffalo horn. Next came thirty-two men in "Moderne Armes" – pikes and muskets – led in formation by Captain John Venn. Once in the hall, the men took to striking their drums to coordinate "a lofty English march." The introduction of the two sides was followed by speeches, music, a display of drilling formations, and a mock battle that saw the Christian Englishmen defeat the Saracens "in a triumphant manner."[60] Barbara Donagan points out that the "exotic presentation" resembled a masque for its "combined music, drill, and drama," but it was also a display that reinforced the "theme of the soldier-citizen."[61] When the carefully choreographed performance ended, participants marched out of the hall to resume their regular lives as "either Merchants or Shopkeepers." Such well-rehearsed performances raise important questions about the place of military theater in daily metropolitan life.[62] But they also reflected the growing sense among contemporaries that Londoners were collectively "no younglings in the Art Millitary."[63] Londoners, argues David Lawrence, were among the nation's most capable soldiers; indeed, some of the very men who reveled in their parts as soldier-citizens, or who drilled with the Honourable Artillery Company and other fashionable military companies, went on "to lead the regiments of the London trained bands."[64] The same Captain Thomas Whitley who fought a mock battle against Saracens in 1638, served also as a lieutenant of the City's Green regiment in 1642; and while John Venn may have paraded in formation indoors in 1638, he later served in the field as a colonel in Essex's army.

As London's only official armed force and its first line of defense, the trained bands were expected to muster and drill regularly. When war broke out, the vast majority of the nation's standing forces were organized in local militia regiments comprised of householders and freeholders. If unprepared or unwilling to defend their families and livelihoods, able-bodied men were expected to find and pay for replacements. London's trained bands were by far the largest and best organized in the nation, and these included some 6,000 men who were organized into four regiments. In February 1642, amidst tensions surrounding rebellion in Ireland, Common Council issued orders for the expansion and reorganization, making way for 8,000 infantry divided into six regiments. Each regiment fell under the command of colonels and was named according to the color of their ensigns, including Blue, White, Orange, Red, Green, and Yellow. Nine additional "auxiliary" regiments were added in the following year, including those from Southwark, Tower Hamlets, and Westminster, along with six others raised within London's environs and thus once again designated by color. By late 1643, the City militia could call upon upwards of 20,000, a force unrivaled until the creation of the New Model Army in 1645. Active throughout the first two years of war, London's trained bands supplied desperately needed men-at-arms in a series of brigades that marched from the City to supplement strained parliamentarian armies and relieve sieges.

"The City" is accounted for here in the broadest sense. As the war progressed, the boundaries between London and its neighboring cities, boroughs, and environs blurred, just as, in many cases, jurisdictional boundaries were tested and transformed. London is here taken to include its traditional twenty-six wards and 111 parishes, along with a handful of "out-parishes" that were traditionally beyond the reach of the Lord Mayor and Common Council, but which were eventually subsumed by parliament. Londoners regularly moved throughout the wider metropolitan area for any number of reasons – to join in popular protest, for instance, or to deliver petitions from the heart of the City to the doors of the Commons. As the war progressed, parliamentary ordinances, Common Council orders, and mayoral precepts increasingly targeted areas that fell "within the Lines of Communication." Upon completion in 1643, eleven miles of fotifications encircled London, Southwark, and Westminster. As a means to account for this new administrative scope, both parliament and Common Council began using the designate of the "Bills of Mortality," an area that produced annual records of burials for victims of the plague who lived within the Liberty of Westminster, the Tower and its Liberty, parts of the Borough of Southwark, and parts of Middlesex and Surrey. These areas were, as Tim Harris has suggested, "increasingly becoming part of the urban metropolis" at the time of the Restoration.[65] Indeed, the establishment of the Lines helped to precipitate this urbanizing process. While it will at times be useful to distinguish between London and its environs – and especially in terms of the parishes and livery companies that operated within central London and those in neighboring Westminster, Southwark, and Tower Hamlets – the present study will most often concern itself with the urban metropolis, with "the City," and the spaces that fell within the defensible Lines of Communication.

Notes

1 TNA, SP 16/488/28; *The Rebellion in Covent Garden* (London, 1642), pp. 2–3; BL Add MS 21935, fol. 163r; Samuel Butler, *A Letter from Mercurius Civicus to Mercurius Rusticus: Or, Londons Confession but not Repentance* (London, 1643), p. 13.
2 Edward Hyde, *The Life of Edward Earl of Clarendon*, vol. 2 (Oxford, 1857), p. 295.
3 Thomas Hobbes, *Behemoth* (London, 1682), p. 334.

4 Indeed, the epithet of "the rebellious city" extended well into the nineteenth century. See, for instance, William Wray, *The Rebellious City Destroyed: Being an Anniversary Sermon in Memory of the Dreadful Fire of London* (London, 1682); Daniel Neal, *The History of the Puritans* (London, 1736), p. 105; S. R. Gardiner, *History of the Great Civil War 1642–1649*, vol. II (London, 1894), p. 208; Charles Knight, *The Popular History of England* (New York, 1880), p. 574.
5 Butler, *A Letter*, p. 3.
6 Edward Hyde, earl of Clarendon, *The History of the Rebellion*, vol. III (Oxford, 1888), pp. 291, 381.
7 Valerie Pearl, *London and the Outbreak of the Puritan Revolution, 1625–1643* (Oxford, 1961), pp. 1–3. Pearl here challenges the "simpliste" views set out by John Forster in *Arrest of the Five Members by Charles the First* (London, 1860); Reginald R. Sharpe's *London and the Kingdom* (London, 1894); and S. R. Gardiner's *The History of England, 1603–1642* (London, 1883).
8 Pearl, *London*, p. 5.
9 Valerie Pearl, "Change and Stability in Seventeenth-Century London," *TLJ*, 5 (1978), p. 5.
10 Robert Ashton, *The City and the Court, 1603–1643* (Cambridge, 1979), pp. 2–3.
11 Robert Brenner, *Merchants and Revolution: Commercial Change, Political Conflict, and London's Overseas Traders* (Princeton, 2003).
12 Stephen Porter (ed.), *London and the Civil War* (London, 1996); Keith Lindley, *Popular Politics and Religion in Civil War London* (Michigan, 1997).
13 These contexts are best revealed in Keith Lindley's articles on London and in particular with his valuable interventions over the question of "stability." The present work avoids engagement with this matter. See Keith Lindley, "Riot Prevention and Control in Early Stuart England," *TRHS*, 33 (1983), pp. 109–126; Keith Lindley, "Whitechapel Independents and the English Revolution," *HJ*, 41 (1998), pp. 283–291.
14 Ben Coates, *The Impact of the English Civil War on the Economy of London, 1642–50* (Aldershot, 2004); Gavin Robinson, *Horses, People and Parliament in the English Civil War: Extracting Resources and Constructing Allegiance* (Farnham, 2012).
15 Paul Griffiths and Mark Jenner (eds), *Londinopolis: Essays in the Cultural and Social History of Early Modern London* (Manchester, 2000); Julia F. Merritt (ed.), *Imagining Early Modern London: Perceptions & Portrayals of the City from Stow to Strype 1598–1720* (Cambridge, 2001); Vanessa Harding, *The Dead and the Living in Paris and London, 1500–1670* (Cambridge, 2002); Jacob Selwood, *Diversity and Difference in Early Modern London* (Farnham, 2010); Eleanor Hubbard, *City Women: Money, Sex, & the Social Order in Early Modern London* (Oxford, 2012); Andrew Gordon, *Writing Early Modern London: Memory, Text, and Community* (Basingstoke, 2013); William Cavert, *The Smoke of London: Energy and Environment in the Early Modern City* (Cambridge, 2016). For a valuable summary of the earlier historiography

of London, see Vanessa Harding, "Recent Perspectives on Early Modern London," *HJ*, 47 (2004), pp. 435–450.

16 See F. F. Foster, *The Politics of Stability: A Portrait of the Rulers of Elizabethan London* (1977); Ian Archer, *The Pursuit of Stability: Social Relations in Elizabethan London* (Cambridge, 1991); Paul Griffiths, *Lost Londons: Change, Crime, and Control in the Capital City, 1550–1660* (Cambridge, 2008), pp. 28–35.

17 Jeremy Boulton, *Neighborhood and Society: A London Suburb in the Seventeenth Century* (Cambridge, 1987); Julia F. Merritt, *The Social World of Early Modern Westminster: Abbey, Court and Community, 1525–1640* (Manchester, 2005); Julia F. Merritt, *Westminster 1640–60: A Royal City in a Time of Revolution* (Manchester, 2013).

18 Merrit, *Westminster*, pp. 53–63.

19 Ibid., pp. 171–177.

20 See in particular, Laura Stewart, *Rethinking the Scottish Revolution: Covenanted Scotland, 1637–1651* (Oxford, 2016).

21 See David Underdown, "The Problem of Popular Allegiance in the English Civil War: The Prothero Lecture," *TRHS*, 31 (1981), pp. 69–94; David Underdown, *Revel, Riot and Rebellion: Popular Politics and Culture in England, 1603–1660* (Oxford, 1985); John Adamson, "The Baronial Context of the English Civil War," *TRHS*, 40 (1990), pp. 93–120; Conrad Russell, "Issues in the House of Commons 1621–1629: Predictors of Civil War Allegiance," *Albion*, 23 (1991), pp. 23–39; Wilfrid Prest, "Predicting Civil War Allegiance," *Albion*, 24 (1992), pp. 225–236; Ian Gentles, "Why Men Fought in the British Civil Wars," *The History Teacher*, 26 (1993), pp. 409–411; Barbara Donagan, "Casuistry and Allegiance in the English Civil War," in Derek Hirst and Richard Strier (eds), *Writing and Political Engagement in Seventeenth-Century England* (Cambridge, 1999), pp. 89–111; See most recently, John Adamson, *The Noble Revolt: The Overthrow of Charles I* (London, 2007); David Scott, "Politics in the Long Parliament," in George Southcombe and Grant Tapsell (eds), *Revolutionary England, c. 1630–c.1660: Essays for Clive Holmes* (London, 2016), pp. 32–55; for an earlier instance, see David Scott, "The Barwis Affair: Political Allegiance and the Scots during the British Civil Wars," *EHR*, 115 (2000), pp. 843–863. Andrew Hopper presents another important challenge to allegiance in *Turncoats and Renegadoes: Changing Sides during the English Civil Wars* (Oxford, 2012), a monograph in which he has suggested that some participants may have "had no deep or lasting attachment to either side in the first place" (p. 14).

22 John Walter, *Understanding Popular Violence in the English Revolution: The Colchester Plunderers* (Cambridge, 1999); Ann Hughes, *Gangraena and the Struggle for the English Revolution* (Oxford, 2004), p. 8.

23 See David Cressey, "The Protestation Protested, 1641 and 1642," *HJ*, 45 (2002), pp. 251–252. For a historical sociologist's consideration of the formation of mobilizing networks in London, see Henning Hillmann, "Mediation in Multiple Networks: Elite Mobilization before the English Civil War," *American Sociological Review*, 73 (2008), pp. 426–454.

24 Michael Braddick, *God's Fury, England's Fire: A New History of the English Civil Wars* (London, 2008), p. 236. See also Michael Braddick, "Mobilisation, Anxiety and Creativity in England during the 1640s," in John Morrow and Jonathan Scott (eds), *Liberty, Authority, Formality: Political Ideas and Culture, 1600–1900* (Exeter, 2008), pp. 175–193; Michael Braddick, "History, Liberty, Reformation and the Cause: Parliamentarian Military and Ideological Escalation in 1643," in Michael Braddick and David Smith (eds), *The Experience of Revolution in Stuart Britain* (Cambridge, 2011), pp. 117–134.

25 See in particular Michael Braddick and Phil Withington (eds), *Popular Culture and Political Agency in Early Modern England and Ireland: Essays in Honour of John Walter* (Woodbridge, 2017).

26 Tom Leng, "'Citizens at the door': Mobilizing against the Enemy in Civil War London," *Journal of Historical Sociology*, 28 (2015), pp. 26–48.

27 The benefit of unorthodox periodization can be seen in David Cressey, *England on Edge: Crisis and Revolution, 1640–1642* (Oxford, 2006).

28 Mobilizations surrounding Root and Branch were indeed massive; upwards of 15,000–20,000 Londoners purportedly signed the petition to abolish episcopacy. The petition, however, does not survive.

29 *A Memento to the Londoners: To put them in minde how neere their destruction is, and what means is left to prevent it* (London, 1643).

30 John Walter, *Covenanting Citizens: The Protestation Oath and Popular Political Culture in the English Revolution* (Oxford, 2017), pp. 1, 86–92, 113–120.

31 David Como, *Radical Parliamentarians and the English Civil War* (Oxford, 2018), p. 16.

32 Butler, *A Letter*, pp. 3–4, 8–9, 13, 15, 29, 31. For the Military Company sermons, see Obadiah Sedgwick, *Military discipline for the Christian souldier* (London, 1639); Calybute Downing, *A sermon preached to the renowned Company of the Artillery* (London, 1641).

33 Robert Chestlin, *Persecutio Undecima* (London, 1648), p. 57. Mary Pennington, as Pearl recounts, kept their house open as a "randevouz" point for visiting "scandalous and schismaticall Lecturers." See Pearl, *London*, p. 179.

34 See most notably Michael Braddick, *State Formation in Early Modern England c. 1550–1700* (Cambridge, 2000), p. 1. Braddick here distinguishes, importantly, between "state formation" and "state building"; D'Maris Coffman, *Excise Taxation and the Origins of Public Debt* (Basingstoke, 2013).

35 Peter Lake, *Bad Queen Bess? Libels, Secret Histories, and the Politics of Publicity in the Reign of Queen Elizabeth I* (Oxford, 2016), p. 468.

36 Apart from Lake, see, for instance, Paul Hammer, *The Polarization of Elizabethan Politics: The Political Career of Robert Devereux, 2nd Earl of Essex, 1585–1597* (Cambridge, 1999); Thomas Cogswell, *The Blessed Revolution: English Politics and the Coming of War, 1621–1624* (Cambridge, 1989).

37 See especially Christopher Hill, "Censorship and English Literature," in *The Collected Essays of Christopher Hill*, vol. 1 (Brighton, 1984), pp. 32–71; Anthony Milton, "Licensing, Censorship, and Religious Orthodoxy in Early Stuart England," *HJ*, 41 (1998), pp. 625–651; Cyndia Susan Clegg, "Censorship and the Courts of Star Chamber and High Commission in England to 1640,"

Journal of Modern European History, 3 (2005), pp. 50–80; Cyndia Susan Clegg, *Press Censorship in Caroline England* (Cambridge, 2008).

38 Andrew Pettegree, *The Invention of News: How the World Came to Know About Itself* (2014), p. 226; Cressey, *England on Edge*, p. 282; Hughes, *Gangraena*, p. 295.
39 Jason Peacey, *Print and Public Politics in the English Revolution* (Cambridge, 2013), *passim*, but especially pp. 331–363; Hughes, *Gangraena*, introduction; Jason Peacey, *Politicians and Pamphleteers: Propaganda During the English Civil Wars and Interregnum* (Aldershot, 2004).
40 Tim Harris, *London Crowds in the Reign of Charles II: Propaganda and Politics from the Restoration until the Exclusion Crisis* (Cambridge, 1987), pp. 96–129.
41 See in particular, Ethan Shagan, "Constructing Discord: Ideology, Propaganda, and English Responses to the Irish Rebellion of 1641," *JBS*, 36 (1997), pp. 4–34.
42 *Alas pore Parliament* (London, 1644); BL, Harley MS 165, fol. 145v. For the significance of the tickets, see Peacey, *Print and Public Politics*, p. 354.
43 Dudey Diggs, *An Answer to a Printed Book* (Oxford, 1642), p. 55.
44 Julie Spraggon, *Puritan Iconoclasm during the English Civil War* (Woodbridge, 2003), p. 119.
45 Derek Keene, "Material London in Time and Space," in Lena Cowen Orlin (ed.), *Material London, ca. 1600* (Philadelphia, 2000), p. 57.
46 A. Hassell Smith, *County and Court: Government and Politics in Norfolk, 1558–1603* (Oxford, 1974), p. 10.
47 Keith Wrightson notes the lower estimate in *Earthly Necessities: Economic Lives in Early Modern Britain, 1470–1750* (London, 2002), p. 164. The second, higher estimate is based on James McGrath, "The Medieval and Early Modern Burgh," in Thomas Martin Devine and Gordon Jackson (eds), *Glasgow: Beginnings to 1830* (Manchester, 1995), p. 45; M. Perceval-Maxwell, *The Outbreak of the Irish Rebellion of 1641* (Montreal, 1994), p. 31.
48 Karen Newman, *Cultural Capitals: Early Modern London and Paris* (Princeton, 2007), p. 2.
49 Jack Goldstone, *Revolution and Rebellion in the Early Modern World* (Berkeley, 1991), p. 167; For the population of Amsterdam in 1647, see Friso Wilenga, *A History of the Netherlands from the Sixteenth Century to the Present Day* (London, 2015), p. 66; See E. Anthony Wrigley, "Urban Growth and Agricultural Change: England and the Continent in the Early Modern Period," *The Journal of Interdisciplinary History*, 15 (1985), pp. 683–728; see Boulton, *Neighborhood and Society*, p. 1.
50 Charles Issawi, "Economic Change and Urbanization in the Middle East," in Ira Marvin Lapidus (ed.), *Middle Eastern Cities* (Berkeley, 1969), p. 103.
51 Roy Porter, *London: A Social History* (Cambridge, MA, 1998), p. 131.
52 Coates, *The Impact*, pp. 6, 15.
53 Lindley, *Popular Politics*, p. 158; see also Ian W. Archer, "The Livery Companies and Charity in the Sixteenth and Seventeenth Centuries," in Ian Anders Gadd and Patrick Wallis (eds), *Guilds, Society and Economy in London 1450–1800* (London, 2002), pp. 15–28.

54 For a valuable discussion of the extent to which committees acted as an interface between parliamentary proceedings and the people, see Chris Kyle and Jason Peacey (eds), *Parliament at Word: Parliamentary Committees, Political Power and Public Access in Early Modern England* (Woodbridge, 2002).
55 Edward Hyde, *The History of the Rebellion*, vol. 3 (Oxford, 1834), p. 216. See in particular Stephen Baskerville, *Not Peace but a Sword: The Political Theology of the English Revolution* (London, 1993).
56 Pearl, *London*, pp. 59–60.
57 Ibid., pp. 54–55, 57.
58 Peter Heylyn, *Mercurius Aulicus* (Oxford, 1643, TT E. 67[7]), p. 475.
59 Barbara Donagan, *War in England, 1642–1649* (Oxford, 2008), pp. 55, 59; G. A. Raikes, *The Ancient Vellum Book of the Honourable Artillery Company, Being the Roll of Members from 1611–1682* (London, 1890).
60 William Barriffe, *Mars his Triumph* (London, 1638), pp. 1–2, 6, 40.
61 Donagan, *War in England*, pp. 58–59; see also G. A. Raikes, *History of the Honourable Artillery Company*, 2 vols (London, 1878); G. Goold Walker, *The Honourable Artillery Company* (London, 1926).
62 For a recent valuable investigation of the place of pageantry, see Tracey Hill, *Pageantry and Power: A Cultural History of the Early Modern Lord Mayor's Show, 1585–1639* (Manchester, 2010); for the classic treatment, see Clifford Geertz, *Negara: The Theatre State in Nineteenth-Century Bali* (Princeton, 1980).
63 Barriffe, *Mars his Triumph*, p. 39.
64 David Lawrence, *The Complete Soldier: Military Books and Military Culture in Early Stuart England, 1603–1645* (Leiden, 2009), pp. 157–167.
65 Harris, *London Crowds*, p. 13.

1

London, Ireland, and the Protestant cause

The 5th of January 1642 must be recounted as one of the more unsettling days in Charles I's twenty-four-year reign. The king spent the morning at London's Guildhall where he pled with common councilors for the delivery of the five MPs whom he had accused of high treason and attempted to arrest in the Commons the previous day. Like most who were present, the king suspected that the men were "shrowded" somewhere nearby, protected by a sympathetic citizen – or perhaps citizens.[1] Charles's request, which he believed to be imminently reasonable, fell upon a crowd with decidedly mixed sympathies; some responded to his plea by calling out to bless the royal person, while others shouted instead for parliamentary privileges. The king's frustrations escalated when John Fowke, a newly elected common councilor, offered "a Saucy, Insolent Speech" in which he expressed his hope that the accused members should be "tried but in a *Parliamentary* way."[2] Being thus rebuffed, Charles departed from the Guildhall to take his midday supper at the house of Sir George Garrett, a city sheriff and well-respected draper who lived nearby.[3] Rumors suggested that the five men were in fact hiding in Coleman Street at the house of Alderman Isaac Pennington, the future Lord Mayor of London. No matter their location the king would remember both his failed plea and Fowke's insolent response.

Charles departed from Garrett's residence around three o'clock, but his return to Whitehall was halted when a crowd of Londoners surrounded his cavalcade. Some may have come to capture glimpses of their sovereign, but others in "the rude multitude," as Thomas Wiseman later suggested, had come specifically to cry out for the "priveledges of parlament."[4] Within the clamorous crowd was Henry Walker, an ironmonger who had spent the day distributing copies of a newly printed pamphlet. Aware of the unusual opportunity, Walker decided to deliver a copy directly to the king. John Taylor's contemporary account suggests that Walker stood at the ready amidst a group of drapers, watching as the king's coach rolled slowly through St. Paul's churchyard. "Having one of his Pamphlets in his hand," but being some distance back, Walker then decided in a "most impudently sawcy" way to throw it so that it would fly "over the folks heads and into his Majesties Coach." Notwithstanding the details of his delivery, Walker was clearly determined that his writings should reach "the very face of the King."[5] That afternoon, Charles held before him a pamphlet bearing an Old Testament verse that might distress any dread sovereign – I Kings 12:16, "*To your Tents, O Israel*" – a verse so explicit and inflammatory that its production later saw Walker pilloried and orders issued for the confiscation and destruction of his pamphlet.

Having survived, a copy of the pamphlet reveals both the reason for Walker's urgency and the cause of the king's post-supper perturbation. Walker's brief but disconcerting request was "that your most Excellent *Majestie*, would be, Gratiously pleased to meditate on" I Kings 12:15–12:16, "*Wherefore the King* hearkened not unto his people, for the cause was from the Lord." Failure to do so, the verses went on, would see the people sound for war, "to your tents, O *Israel*."[6] Like Charles I, Londoners who acquired copies of Walker's pamphlet were expected to "meditate on" the similarities between the world of the Israelites of I Kings 12:15–12:16 and their own world in the early 1640s. Even a cursory knowledge of scripture would remind readers of the time when the Israelites had been called to their tents of war to rebel against Rehoboam, the fourth king of Israel who sought to expand his father's burdensome and unpopular taxation upon the people. Indeed, most contemporaries were acutely aware of the recent collapse of a decade of "personal rule" by the king, a controversial time when Charles maintained his court through unpopular and legally dubious forms of taxation such as distraint of knighthood and ship money. After the calling of the Long Parliament, and in light of the recent jeopardizing attempt on the five members, Walker had devised a poignant way to urge the king to "listen to the people." That Walker had done so in a deeply provocative and problematic manner was beyond dispute. Contemporaries would also readily note the parallels between the tyranny of Rehoboam and Charles's own personal rule. Taylor, who was admittedly no friend to Walker, concluded that the pamphlet had made it appear "as if the King were a Tyrant, bidding as it were every man to take his Sword and Armor; and oppose all authority whatsoever."[7] Indeed, when later asked to return to London, the king refused on grounds that dangerous pamphlets such as Walker's were still being allowed to circulate throughout the City unchecked.[8]

A bold comparison to the first king of Judah was just one of a number of pressing issues faced by the king at the outset of 1642. The refusal to turn out the five members of course added another stinging dimension to what was by some estimates "the most disastrous week" of Charles's "reign."[9]

But Londoners remained as anxious as they were defiant. "Wee are not free from the fears of an insurrection," wrote Thomas Wiseman on 6 January 1642.[10] "Everything," wrote Captain Carterett shortly thereafter, seemed "inclinable to ruin."[11] Tensions escalated and open conflict seemed plausible. The king's guards stood at the ready in Whitehall, while the trained bands were posted outside of the Grocers' Hall, with each force ready to move against the other. "The City and people in adjacent parts" were preparing themselves, "fearing some suddaine execution may be done upon the Parliament."[12] As we have seen, these events culminated on the night of 6 January, when rumors suggested that the king was assembling "a force to fetch" the five members out of their hiding place; Londoners thus sounded their night alarms, blockaded the streets, and saw "all men woeman & children to geet up."[13]

Again, little had changed by the time that the streets were cleared of furniture and chains. Efforts moved forward to help assure that "the enemy" should not breach the City. That day, Commons ordered the Committee for Irish Affairs to meet at the London Guildhall to confer with Common Council about London's continued safety. Two days later, both the Committee and the Council agreed "that Captaine [Philip] Skippon shalbee Serjeant Major general of the Forces of the City."[14] The nation's single largest force, which was traditionally under the command of the king, thus passed seamlessly into the hands of the Captain of London's Artillery Company and a known parliamentary sympathizer. Held up in his palace in Whitehall as news of these events unfolded, Charles may indeed have found some fleeting moments to heed Walker's advice and "meditate" upon the wider implications of Kings 12; not least, he may have considered how fear of a popular uprising drove Rehoboam to mount "his chariot in haste and flee to Jerusalem." Rehoboam's departure marked the beginning of a seventeen-year civil war and the Israelites' perpetual rebellion against the house of David. Charles's own hasty escape, as we of course know, would have its own dire consequences. On the night of 10 January, in the wake of news that the London trained bands were no longer his own, and fearing for the safety of his family, the king boarded a barge for Hampton Court. His departure marked the end of a calamitous week in the capital and the beginning of the slide toward civil war.

On the day after Charles's departure, London revealed Viscount Mandeville and the five "shrowded" MPs. The viscount was escorted from the City to Westminster by Skippon and eight companies of the trained bands. The five members of the Commons – John Hampden, Sir Arthur Haselrig, Denzil Holles, John Pym, and William Strode – left from Coleman Street for the Guildhall, and were then escorted by the trained bands to a barge that took them upriver to the House of Commons. Alighting in Westminster, the five were met with triumphant cheers and salute by cannon fire. Wallington, who remained tense and had "taried at home that day," heard the cannons firing from two miles downriver and mistook the blasts for an attack on the City. He was soon relieved to discover the source of the noise.[15] Emerging from the House of Commons later that same afternoon, Sir Simonds D'Ewes, a member of the Long Parliament well-known to historians for his detailed journal-keeping, decided "to walk awhile in Westminster hall" and observe the "many of the citizens of the trained bands of London" who had come to protect the five accused men.[16] D'Ewes counted a full "8 companies which guarded us" and were "in all 2400 Men." Accompanying the City's forces were additional "companies of the Cittie of Westminster." Soldiers were prominently displaying copies of "the Protestation" that was "formerlie framed & taken by the members of the howse Commons, & afterwards by most of the citizens." "Divers of the Londoners" had attached copies "upon the topp of the pikes," while others, D'Ewes was informed, had fixed copies of the Protestation "like a little square banner" to their "muskets." Beyond simply showing up to cheer the return of leading Members of Parliament, inhabitants had come out to display their solidarity with the cause at hand – to fulfill pledges to defend their representative body.[17] In their presence – and indeed their performance – could be found what Lawson Nagel called "the germ of an army."[18] Affixed to weapons and bodies was the same document that had been framed the previous May as a means to defuse tensions between the king and parliament. Yet on this occasion the Protestation served an altogether different purpose; it was not displayed as a means to deescalate a conflict, or mollify the monarch, but instead stood out as a show of support for parliamentary privilege. It was on this occasion, as Conrad Russell has suggested, an intentional and apparent statement of support for parliament's "established authority against its lawful king."[19] It was, to borrow words from John Walter, by this point serving as a "justification for taking up arms in a defensive war."[20] The militiamen who hoisted up and proudly wore the Protestation on 11 January 1642 were indeed advertising their support for "the Power and Privileges of Parliament" and "the Lawfull Rights and Liberties of the Subject."[21] With the successful return of the five members, Londoners found, if only momentarily, an alignment of purpose and reason to celebrate.

New challenges would of course emerge over the coming weeks and months. Not least of these was the daily arrival of Protestant refugees fleeing from Catholic uprisings in Ireland. Ireland's woes soon provided Londoners with an almost constant reminder of England's long-standing and providentially sanctioned commitment to the health of international Protestantism. But more than this, as we shall see, Ireland's situation helped to prime London logistically and ideologically for the coming war at home. The need to aid refugees and the neighboring nation saw the City increase its charitable giving and begin large-scale programs for lending and raising men and goods for relief expeditions. Presaged in the reaction to the Irish Rebellion were the dynamics of London's coming civil war mobilizations.

Metropolitan machinations

Like the many other Londoners who lost sleep during January's long nights, Wallington had developed a strong impression of who the common "enemy" was. It was the same foe who had urged the king to unlawfully enter the Commons, and it was the same foe who had threatened to execute the king's demand to forcibly extract the five members from hiding; and it was, as importantly, the same enemy who repeatedly threatened "a Popish plot against" the City.[22] Londoners had spent the end of 1641 half in the grip of terror. The City was rife with rumors of terrible plots and suspected uprisings. The "plot and machinations" of some "cruell and mercilesse Papists" were overheard near Moorefields "late at night" in the middle of November.[23] A month later, a "French-man" warned authorities that Christmas "would be a bloudy day for *London*." "Seven Papists" were subsequently apprehended by London's watch under suspicion of "treachery against the City."[24] The imaginations of Londoners were thereby sparked; all the while, neighboring Ireland provided daily views of the damage that could be done by lurking rogues and plotting "papists." Fears, like those expressed by Wallington, had recently taken on the hallmark characteristics of what Peter Lake has called a "cloud of unknowing," a thing "which descended on contemporaries at times of crisis and led them to misconstrue the real nature of events."[25] Indeed, the widespread anti-popery of late 1641 and early 1642 had distilled into a general, hazy paranoia; Londoners might just as soon identify the "enemy" in the nighttime clatter of swords, assume treachery by the king's armed guards, or believe whispers about plotters in Moorefields and the warnings of itinerant Frenchmen. Concerns over an amorphous "papist" threat had intensified throughout November and December, manifesting most notably in response to the Grand Remonstrance in the shape of mass petitions and crowd violence. One petition decried the king's appointment of Thomas Lunsford as Lieutenant of the Tower of London on grounds of his suspected shared sympathies with plotting Catholics; another put thousands of hands to paper in outright opposition to episcopacy.[26] "Religion," as Anthony Fletcher proclaimed years ago, "was at the heart of it."[27] And in no place was this connection more clearly established than the uprisings in Ireland. Spurring popular protests and mass petitions were growing concerns that Middlesex might, as some contemporaries claimed, become a second Ulster.

Reports of Ireland's uprisings first reached London at the start of November, and from that point forward booksellers were awash with depictions of the grueling deaths of Protestant planters by the barbarous native Irish; crude and hastily etched scenes revealed a crisis in which men were purportedly flayed alive, "children" were hoisted "upon pikes," and women fled from their "deflowering."[28] These terrors – read, reported, and discussed daily in London's crowded streets, alehouses, and alleys – offered the sensational headline of late 1641 and early 1642. From the moment that news of the Irish "Rebellion" reached the capital, and refugees began "broadcasting their terrible tales," Londoners sought what means they could to alleviate their brethren.[29]

Historians have gone to great lengths to establish the ideological and causal relationships between the Irish Rebellion and the civil war that soon shook England. Indeed, it is worth heeding the sage advice that such "well-worn historical paths" need not be "retread."[30] But in recent years, the Irish Rebellion has taken something of an explanatory back seat in accounts of the outbreak of the English civil war. This is due in no small part to John Adamson's claim that concerns over Ireland provide an insufficient explanation for the "major conflict" that was at its heart "about the nature of sovereignty and political institutions." Adamson maintains that we have suffered from a general lack of explanation, and thus have prematurely concluded that the Irish Rebellion was a "*diabolus ex machina*," an unexpected agent that explains why "a tense but otherwise peaceable England" came to "an internal contest for the control of military power."[31] Doubtless this argument, which is at best rhetorically driven or simply overstated, deserves some reconsideration. The Irish Rebellion need not be given primary, secondary, or even tertiary status with regards to its impact on England's own wars, and nor does the topic require compartmentalization. As with most cases, there is a valuable middle ground to be found. If clearly not a "bolt from the blue," the issue of the uprising, and the subsequent and concerted attempts by the English to intervene militarily on behalf of Protestants in Ireland, deserve lasting consideration with regards to both the outbreak and continuation of war in England. This is particularly true of London, where significant military and financial efforts were undertaken to help relieve brethren abroad, and, increasingly, refugees at home.

Although the responsibility for caring for refugees and displaced ministers was by no means unique to the capital, London, the most populous city in the archipelago, seemed an obvious place to seek out help.[32] The City boasted opportunities for employment, charity, and a close proximity to the seat of national government. Moreover, Londoners had themselves revealed a seemingly bottomless, if also distinctly macabre, appetite for accounts of the suffering of their neighboring Protestants. Rather than supplant local fears over episcopacy, the degradation of parliamentary privilege, or even the king's ill-advised attempt on the five members, news of Ireland's woes seemed only to compound and reinforce local concerns by heaping on yet more evidence of Catholic corruption. Reports of the death of good Protestants at the hands of "barbarous" Catholics, for instance, confirmed anxieties that were long-term and international in scope, and which traced their roots back more than a generation to the inception of the Protestant cause.[33] Pamphlets and letters stood to confirm well-established fears. "Popery," claimed one London pamphlet, was "the nurse of rebellion and the mother of disastrous discords."[34] "The business of Ireland," wrote Robert Reade, Sir Francis Windebank's nephew, in January, "makes great noyse here." "I pray," he went on, "some tymely course may be taken for quenching that fire otherwise it may chance not only to consume that Kingdome, but to endanger others."[35] "All plots eyther against Prince or State," claimed another author, "were contrived and determined to be executed by Papists." Such "Romish Incendiaries" had devised both "the powder Treason" of James I's reign and the decision "to kill King *Henry the third*" of France. It stood to reason for some that the same culprits who had butchered Protestants in Ireland might soon carry out their designs in England. Alarmed Londoners suspected that a fifth column grew daily; "the *Strand*, *Convent*-garden, *Drury*-lane, St. *Giles*, and *Holborne*" were all "replenished with Priests and their people."[36] Hemmed in and fearful, many turned to the streets to join likeminded metropolitans in displays of "anti-popery."

Liverymen and freemen took their own precautions. In response to the "troubles and rumors of the tymes," wardens from the Fishmongers' Company ordered on 17 December that "a barrell of Gunpowder to be kept att the hall" and that a guard wait "in the greate chamber to be ready" so that they might "prevent any sudden dangers." By early January the company arranged to have "armes" prepared "for the defence of this Cyttie and hall" and further ordered that "armes enough" should be stockpiled so that the "whole company" could defend themselves "under one Capteyne."[37] Concerns led the Clothworkers to make similar preparations in January. Rather than keep their hall and armory stocked, they decided that "the armes of this Company" should be strategically placed in "severall housis belonging to this Company where it shall seeme needfull unto them in and about the city of London."[38] If violence broke out, companies would be ready to defend both their members and their respective halls.

John Venn made note of the many apprentices who gathered in Westminster's Palace Yard for three days at the end of December to "cry downe Bishops and Popish Lords." Their clamorous but otherwise peaceful assembly was interrupted when "divers Caviliers" came down and "misused most with base Language" and "did cut many." Some arrests followed and the crowd of mostly apprentices scattered until the next day when they did "swell in blood" to nearly 2,000. This time they came armed with "clubs, Swords, [and] Halberts" and threatened to storm royalist Lord Mayor Gurney's residence in order to release a handful of protesters who had recently been arrested. Further violence was narrowly avoided when Venn delivered an impromptu speech in which he pleaded that "everie man" should return to "his owne home in peace" and promised that he would go on personally to request that the mayor might release the prisoners.[39] Henry Hastings encountered the same tumult while down from the Midlands. Writing to his son just days after Venn had mollified the crowd, he recalled that nearly a "thousand prentices" had met "betwixt yorke house and Charinge Crosse with halburds Staffes and some swords." Their intention, he revealed, was to apprehend the two bishops who were recently impeached by the Commons – Durham and Coventry and Lichfield – and who they expected might pass through the street by coaches on their way to Westminster. On the night of 31 December, the apprentices "stood soe thicke that wee had much a do to passe." Although it was "thoughe it were a darke night ther inumerable number of links made it as light as day." From inside his own carriage, Hastings could see the faces of the crowd illuminated and hear their calls of "now Bishops now Papist Lords."[40] The crowds who sought to "sweep" up and deliver bishops "into the Red sea of their own blood," were as eager to alleviate the "miserable estate" of England as they were to avoid the fate of Ireland.[41] Both matters were inextricably linked.

For the king and his supporters, the tumults of December and early January were attributable to a handful of leading City agitators and they signaled that something needed to be done. An anonymous complaint from 5 January suggested that the "rabble of ignorant people sent to both Houses, but specially to the House of Peers" had been directed "by Captaine Ven[n] and his wife, and [Alderman] Isaac Pennington." Once there they set to the familiar "cry" of "Justice, Justice, and, No Bishops, No Bishops." The collective impact of their orchestration and the resulting mob was to "terrifie some Lords from the House, and awe others." At the time, it seemed as if "there were never higher breashes [sic] of Parliament priviledge then these."[42] The king's assessment, as echoed by Clarendon, was similar: it was "Alderman Pennington and captain Venn" who had "brought down their myrmidons to assault and terrify the members of both houses, whose faces or whose opinions they liked not."[43] For Edward Walker, the king's secretary at war, the "instruments" were "Doctor *Burgess, Pennington, Venne,* [Randall] *Manwaring,* [John] *Fowke* and others … who went from

House to House and brought this Hidras Head to Westminster."[44] In the anti-episcopal riots of December 1641 could be found the coming patterns of London's "rebellion," of a zealous leadership that would repeatedly agitate London's sympathetic, "calamarous, and unwarrantable multitude" to take action against the king and, increasingly, the vestiges of his authority in the metropolis, the Lords.[45] The template for war was thus in place more than eight months before its outbreak; so too, it would seem, was a model for crowd obstruction of parliamentary proceedings. In the coming days, Londoners needed only to fulfill the expectations of the king and loyalists.

Refugees and parochial charity

Ireland's uprising lasted just over half a year, from October 1641 until May 1642, but the affair had both an immediate and lasting impact on Londoners.[46] Print remains one of the simplest and best means to gauge Londoners' collective interest in the matter. Keith Lindley's valuable survey of the materials amassed by the avid London collector George Thomason in the early 1640s reveals the staggering extent to which news of Ireland came to dominate popular print. Rather than dissipating after the initial revelation of the uprising, concerns over the state of Ireland increased over the early months of 1642.[47] Much less a result of an unqualified solution to the problem, the decrease in coverage owed to a marked increase in concern over domestic matters; the preoccupation with Protestants abroad was, in short, eventually subsumed by the pressing matter of civil war at home. Londoners' persistent interest owed in no small part to proximity; London, after all, was the closest sizable metropolitan center to Dublin.[48] Grueling stories were often accompanied by their tellers. Many who fled from Ulster and neighboring areas were English by birth or descent – the same English who had in previous years left their homes and professions to pursue some of the many opportunities afforded by plantation that dated back to the end of Mary I's reign. London seemed a natural gathering place for the uprooted and "beggarly poor" who fled the conflict. Once there, refugees might seek gainful employment or benefit from the charity administered by parishes.

Shortly after news of the uprising reached the metropolis, parliament resolved to request that the City might raise a loan of £50,000 to be used for "the reliefe of his Majesties distressed Subjects in the Kingdome of Ireland." Common Council agreed with the added stipulation that remaining bishops should be arrested – an important example of their priorities and the political leanings of a Council that grew markedly more outspoken and radical in light of their 21 December elections. Orders for collections were made official in early November. Parochial responses varied according to capacity and ability. St. Stephen Coleman Street recorded the names of fifty-two inhabitants who were quick to act and brought in an impressive total of £1,171 to the Guildhall on 15 November.[49] Large sums of money were delivered from other parishes where ministers had successfully convinced their auditors to contribute. Unlike the radical enclave of Coleman Street, most parishes needed time to collect their payments in full. On 22 April, John Downham, the godly rector of All Hallows the Great, accompanied two churchwardens to transport £66 18s 2½ pence to the Guildhall. Along with their payments was a list of 185 parishioners who gave various amounts and a note about the £4 18s and 9½ pence that was "collected at the Church dore."[50] Similarly, the churchwardens at St. John Zachary in Aldersgate collected £65 12s around the time of Easter for the "reliefe of Ireland."[51] But parishioners were not always eager to part with their hard-earned money. Collectors from St. Pancras Soper Lane noted some impure "light gold that was received in the Collection for Ireland."[52] If slow to arrive, or at times debased, Londoners had paid enough coin so that preparations for a mission to Ireland could begin in earnest in January. War contracts were issued and fulfilled. On 3 March, £4,032 was released for a payment to Gilbert Moorewood, a merchant who supplied "fortie two tunn[s] of lead," which was presumably used for making musket and cannon balls. Three days later, John Hotham received funds to pay "officers and Souldiers in Hull" who were planning to go abroad into Ireland.[53]

While preparations for expeditions were under way, other schemes were being considered. One of these came from the heart of the City, which returned a petition on 11 February calling for the "speedy relief" of Ireland in exchange for profits raised from captured estates. On 25 February, parliament printed orders for their *Propositions* that would raise upwards of a million pounds "for the speedie and effectuall reducing of the Kingdom of *Ireland*." Rather than simply put forward plans for a military expedition, they intended the program as a means to capture and build upon 2.5 million acres of useful land that they valued at 1.55 million pounds. The program, known as the Additional Sea Adventure for Ireland, would require significant investment, which they hoped to raise in four phases between 20 March and 1 May.[54] While the present project cannot account for the success of the program, it is clear that considerable sums came into London's Guildhall as part of an "Adventurers fund." Three of the four collectors for the scheme, John Towse, John Kendricke, and Thomas Andrews, were among the City's leading opponents of the Crown.[55] The other collector, John Warner, remained closely involved with parliamentarian efforts. Heading the program was a mixed group of what would be parliamentary radicals and later wartime loyalists including Lord Brooke, Saye and Sele, and the earl of Warwick, and by late June efforts had generated an army of six thousand soldiers who would soon disembark on fifteen crewed ships.

As Brenner suggested, the effort foreshadowed later civil war organization; the Additional Sea Adventure provides an example of the type of mobilizing nexus that could form when City militants aligned their interests with like-minded parliamentarians and preachers.[56]

While private efforts to fund an army were underway, London's churchwardens were preoccupied with the growing number of "beggarly" refugees who sought attention and required charity. Such demands could become deeply burdensome. Wardens from All Hallows the Less kept meticulous records of the sixty days between 7 February and 24 April 1642 when they gave "amongst divers and severall Protestants of Ireland being driven away from all they had by the rebellious Irish and being in great want and misery." Each day they offered charity ranging from 2s to 8s 6d.[57] £2 was given around the same time at St. Lawrence Jewry "towards the releife of poore ministers and poore ministers wives, and maimed Souldiers and other poore distressed people" from Ireland.[58] Meanwhile, "divers poore Irish" were counted among those who received 7s 8d at St. Olave Old Jewry.[59] Small payments made in succession quickly added up. The churchwardens at St. Mary Magdalen Milk Street offered up £3 to "poore Ministers Lame Souldiers widdowes and other poore Irishe" and an additional £9 specifically "for poor ministers in Ireland."[60] £5 9s was given to "poore ministers and ministers widdowes Souldiers and other poore people that cam out of Ireland severall times" at St. John Zachary on Gresham Street.[61] £2 and four pence went "to poore ministers maimed souldiers and other distressed Irish people" in the parish of St. Peter Westcheap. Another £2 was given after Easter 1642 to "poore people English and Irish," while yet another £2 was given the next year to "poore ministers, and other poore English & Irish." So overwhelming were the number of needy that the matter of differentiating the poor had become unnecessary.[62] Sixpence was "given to a woman stripte in Ireland" and another sixpence to "two Irish women" by the wardens at St. Michael Wood Street.[63] If not recorded specifically in reference to Ireland, other parishes nevertheless provided charity in a similar capacity. £2 8s 4d, for instance, was distributed to "poore Ministers Soldiers & others" at St. James Garlickhithe.[64] The various accounts of charity given in London's churchwardens' accounts doubtless cover only a fraction of what was actually given; figures would have expanded well beyond what was recorded by churchwardens.

Although heavily burdened, London's central parishes were not the only metropolitan places to dole out extra money to care for new arrivals. Neighboring Westminster and Southwark were burdened in a similar capacity. The churchwardens at St. Giles in the Fields, for instance, were so overwhelmed with the outpouring of support for a solution that they spent six shillings "for writinge 3 bookes to gather the Contribucion money for Ireland." Individual payments included the £1 given "to Samuell Dall a poore butcher that lost all hee had in Ireland," but still needed to care for "his wife and fowre poore Children." The same amount was provided for "fower poore women and sixe Children that came out of Ireland passing to their owne Country."[65] Churchwardens from St. Margaret Westminster gave generously; 6s went to "six poore men and women which came from Ireland," while another 2d went to "the wife of John Davis" after she "was driven out of Ireland by the Rebells." One Eleanor Harte received 1s after fleeing from Ireland to London. A further 2s was given to "John Wiles and six more," while "John Strong and five more children" received the same amount after "being driven out of Ireland." A "petition and certificate" provided adequate information to procure the large sum of 20s for Mary Barnes, a widow who was also "driven out." Numerous accounts often reveal little more than sums given and the destitute nature of the recipients. One "poore woman ... who came from Ireland," for example, was given 6d after she was found nearby at "the Abbey church porch," while "a poore ministers wife and three children which came out of Ireland" were given 12d. Many other names are revealed in churchwardens' accounts without notes of origin; doubtless some owed their presence to the uprising.[66]

South of the river, at St. Mary Newington, churchwardens gave money on several occasions. The amount of 4s was "given to a poore Minister that came out of Ireland," while another 2s was given "to a poore Ministers wife that came out of Ireland." More was needed the following year when 1s was given to an "Irish gentlewoman," another 1s to "an Irish gentleman," and 6d was granted "to a poore Irishman." Faced with their own mounting problems in late 1643, churchwardens at one point dedicating 4s to see that "an Irishman with 4 children" would be sent "out of the parish."[67]

Outside of officially ordered collections, single charitable payments were the main form of aid given to Ireland's refugees in London. Although impossible to assess in totality, and obviously very different from the loan of £50,000 and the staggering £1 million proposed to support military intervention in Ireland, *ad hoc* and small-scale charitable giving added up quickly. Besides fulfilling basic parochial and civic responsibilities, frequent acts of charity connected Londoners to the greater challenge of helping their Protestant brethren in the face of a unified international – if also decidedly amorphous – Catholic threat. It is, by this light, worth noting that many of the main leading lenders for a military intervention in Ireland – including some proponents for the Additional Sea Adventure – went on to champion parliament's war effort against the king. The radical parliamentarian Henry Marten, for instance, loaned £2,000; Robert Harley, Arthur Haselrige, John Evelyn, and Philip Stapleton each gave £250. Aldermen John Towse and Samuel Warner each gave £1,000.[68] For many, the need to help their neighbors and fellow English Protestants abroad foreshadowed an escalating situation at home. As 1642 wore on, the number of refugees from Ireland would be steadily overtaken by arrival of displaced, sick, and wounded Englishmen.

Displaced refugees added unwelcome pressure in the already overcrowded metropolis, but debilitated soldiers were a different matter altogether. Replete with examples of the many other obligations that depleted local coffers, churchwardens' accounts from 1642 also make note of a steady increase in the number of maimed soldiers who required care. Caring for the sick and wounded was nothing new in 1642. Parishes paid annually toward the care of maimed soliders "by Act of Parliament" that was put in place during "the 13th year of Queen Elizabeth."[69] Collectors regularly received sums that ranged between 17s 4d and £2 3s 4d for disbursement.[70] The most common amount collected in London's parishes was £1 14s 8d.[71] Added to these sums were regular *ad hoc* payments, with some records dating back to "Count Mansfields voyage" in the middle of the 1620s.[72] The uprising in Ireland marked the beginning of a steady increase in the arrival of newly wounded men; a second more notable increase came in the wake of the first skirmishes and battles of the civil war.

Collectively burdened as they were, Londoners nevertheless raised considerable sums for the relief of their beleaguered brethren abroad. According to the contemporary accounts of Nicholas Loftus, George Henley, and John Hawkenridge, some £358,222 was paid by Londoners to "relieve" Ireland between November 1641 and October 1642.[73] Clearly, some felt it their duty to answer the call to war directly. Others, meanwhile, believed that it was their God-given responsibility to do what they could to help their fellow Protestants to escape the "barbarism" of their oppressors. In early March, Charles Travers, the orphan son of a citizen and vintner, requested leave of the Court of Aldermen to be allowed to "goe over into Ireland." The court readily agreed and allowed that his legal guardian, the haberdasher Humphrey Wrightman, should supply Travers with £30 needed for his "necessarye" outfitting and passage.[74] While it remains impossible to know precisely why Wrightman decided to outfit and send his charge off to war, or indeed why Travers and others like him wished to fight in the first place, it can be assumed that numerous motivations were present, if ultimately not evident. Explaining the extent to which Londoners enlisted to fight in Ireland, or indeed why they persistently gave money to the cause, requires at least a cursory investigation of some of the leading ideologies behind the conflict, and not least the providential and other religio-political motivations that were sometimes mentioned explicitly by participants. As we have seen, the months between November 1641 and early 1642 generated a heady climate in which fears over "papist" plots in London were conflated with episcopacy and unsettling reports out of Ireland. Accompanying the arrival of refugees were sensationalized and relentlessly propagandized accounts of the war, of affairs that were sometimes "too terrible to tell." Out of these accounts grew a pressing urgency in the minds of Londoners – a shared sense that failure to act on behalf of their beleaguered brethren might goad the Almighty to seek vengeance for complacency. Stoking these fears and bolstering a shared sense of England's responsibility were some of the nation's most capable preachers.

Providential obligation and the slide toward war

From early on, London's ministry proved indispensable to efforts to raise money and outfit soldiers for the relief of Ireland. Through preaching, ministers elucidated contemporary responsibilities, but they also revealed, in no uncertain terms, some of the alarming scriptural examples of what might befall the nation – and especially the inhabitants of its most populous city – for failing to heed divine interests. On 2 December 1641, Stephen Marshall, a minister renowned for godly preaching, delivered a sermon in the large parish church of St. Sepulchre-without-Newgate. His sermon that day harped on the almost ubiquitous themes of providential obligation and sin, but in particular he drove home the dangers that might come to subjects who stood "neuter" when it came time to "help the Lord against the mighty." Neuters and the like, Marshall proclaimed, should expect to face divine wrath and certain "ruine" if they refused to aid and "pray for *Ireland*," just as the ancient Merozites did for failing to heed God's call to join their brethren Israelites in war against Sisera and the Canaanites, as told in Judges 5:23, the curse of Meroz.[75] Joined by his godly associate, Edmund Calamy, on 22 December to preach a monthly fast-day sermon before the Commons, Marshall returned to the theme of Ireland and Judges. If toned down when compared to his previous *Meroz Curse* sermon, Marshall's *Reformation and Desolation* was nevertheless explicit about the pressing need for intervention, and indeed of the dangers of neutrality. The "turning away of Gods wrath," Marshall warned, was of the utmost importance for "*England, Scotland* and *Ireland*."[76] Calamy offered a similar view in a sermon in which he called for "a Looking-glasse for *England* and *Ireland*" and expressed his hope that England might seek out "a nationall reformation" that would help to answer the calls of "distressed *Ireland*."[77] Marshall and Calamy beseeched their auditors to consider that Ireland's fate was inextricably linked to England's, and that the looming conflict, which might seem a distant problem to some, was in fact a very real reflection of divine frustration with *both* nations. As the fate of Meroz suggested – or indeed even as the revolt against Rehoboam might indicate – failure to heed God's warnings could have dire consequences.

Historians have commented widely on the place of political providentialism in the English civil wars. Yet studies of the subject have, until somewhat recently, drawn almost exclusively from examples made by "godly" and well-known ministers whose interests aligned clearly with parliament's cause. Scholarship now readily asserts that providentialism played an important role in the day-to-day lives of most contemporaries, no matter their religious and political affiliations and beliefs – regardless, for lack of a better terminology, of what might later be called their "parliamentarianism" or "royalism."[78] Both Hugh Trevor-Roper and John F. Wilson did much to chart the political backdrops to the monthly fast-day sermons that were given to members of the Long Parliament.[79] Shared between Trevor-Roper's brief but seminal exploration of the subject, and Wilson's more systematic political contextualization of fast-day sermons, was the recognition that scriptural interpretation and providence played an important role motivating combatants during the 1640s. Religion – and more specifically providence – has retained a central explanatory place in civil war politics, with historians such as Stephen Baskerville and Glen Burgess further delineating the relationships between scripture, military mobilization, and violence.[80] More recently, these accounts have come under scrutiny by Ann Hughes, whose important research sets fast-day sermons within their "broader context" of "routine preaching" in the metropolis.[81]

Still missing, however, is a systematic consideration of the ways in which providential exhortations bridged the ideological gap between the outbreak of the Irish Rebellion and the start of the English civil war. Clearly, we do not suffer for a lack of evidence of the sensationalized print and imagery that helped to trigger England's own crisis, but absent is a thorough investigation of the ways in which the ideologies that formed in the wake of Ireland's Protestant crisis of late 1641 and early 1642 grafted onto England's own coming Protestant crisis. The eagerness with which Londoners enlisted to serve in Ireland, and later again in the summer against the king, owed in no small part to congruous – and at times consistent – fears over specific scriptural examples of divine retribution as much as they did to general anxieties over a "cavalier" or "papist" uprising. A lack of explanation regarding the precise fate of the Merozites was, thus, not a problem for contemporaries. More clearly troublesome, however, was the displeasure of an omnipotent and vengeful God, a God who was more than willing to set in motion the punishments of His choosing. Thus we find a remarkable and consistent recycling of providential warnings – of similar scriptural examples and exegetical interpretations – from one cause to the next throughout the seventeenth century in general; the relatively short period between the outbreak of the Irish Rebellion in late 1641 and the English civil war in late summer 1642 provides one of the more apparent examples of the way in which a providential warning – in this case "curse ye Meroz" – could carry over; Judges 5:23, which in one iteration was meant to mobilize Londoners for Ireland, soon transposed seamlessly to mobilize Londoners for the civil war.

Ministers could of course pick and choose from any number of cautionary tales found in scripture. With this in mind, most of the fast-day preachers who gave sermons to parliament in 1642 were careful to deploy devices that helped to explain issues that plagued both England and Ireland. Often, preachers proposed contrition as a first step toward helping aid Protestant allies abroad. But on many occasions, they also offered thinly veiled, or indeed blatantly explicit, calls to action. Edmund Calamy, for instance, carefully selected textual examples of the ways in which England could be likened to ancient Israel, a conceptual framework that allowed his listeners to both confirm their unique relationship with God and comprehend what might be done to alleviate their present troubles.[82] During his 22 December 1641 fast-day sermon, Calamy pressed his auditors to reflect on God's dealing with nations "as a Physitian with his Patient." England was suffering, no doubt, but the "lesser potion[s]" of "small-pox, unseasonable weather, [and] the Plague" were merely warnings of "greater" punishments that might soon afflict the nation unwilling to heed its prescription.[83] Two months later, on 23 February, Calamy joined Marshall again to preach a fast-day sermon to the Commons. Calamy marked the occasion by expressing his continued grief for "the warres of *Ireland*" and "the unsetled condition of *England*," and his hope that there might be "an England-and-Ireland-healing Fast." The "*Protestation against all Popery and Popish Innovations*," Calamy asserted, might prove a "good" way for England to achieve its needed "*reformation of the Church and State*." Such a reformation, Calamy went on, would serve as England's first step toward caring for neighboring Ireland. "Pitty Ireland" and "pray for Ireland," he concluded, but also maintain the "worke of *great piety*" as "a means to *roote out Popery*" in Ireland "forever."[84]

It was during the same fast-day, two months after he preached at St. Sepulchre's, and at a time when concern over Ireland had reached a fever pitch, that Marshall returned to his theme of Judges 5:23. Marshall's new *Meroz Cursed* sermon ended up being among the most celebrated and condemned of his career, later earning him derision as "Augustine ... the truly polemicall Divine of our times."[85] Indeed, Marshall's hand-picked chapter and verse – his explicit warning that England might be destroyed for failing "to help the Lord against the mighty" – ended up gaining equal, if not indeed better, purchase with disenchanted elements of the nation, with those who were losing faith in the idea that there might be a reconciliation with the king, or that some sort of armed conflict might be on the horizon. What was thus intended as a clarion call to oppose "the mighty" in neighboring Ireland soon grafted to national politics, becoming an equally alarming exhortation for the need to oppose "the mighty" advisers to the king. In the convoluted slip toward civil war, the very ambiguity of the curse became its most important feature; the unidentified enemy, the king's advisers, and, with time, the king himself became the obvious targets.

Marshall's indefatigable preaching helped precipitate the permutation of the curse. More than simply repeat the text of an ancient curse against an obscure people who had failed "to help the Lord against the mighty," and thus summon a readily understandable explanation of the divine wrath that would meet inaction, Marshall purportedly went on to preach on Judges 5:23 frequently – perhaps, as some accounts claim, "no less than sixty times."[86] Indeed, his *Meroz Cursed* sermon went into three editions that were printed in London over the course of 1642.[87] The oft-repeated theme thus readily found audiences, and subsequently a place in popular spiritual discourse. Other preachers were quick to add Meroz to their repertoires. William Laud recalled a "strangely Evil" sermon given in London on 15 May 1642 by one "Mr Joclin." The theme was apparently "*Curse ye Meroz*," and the application contained some "personal Abuse" against Laud "that was so foul and so palpable, that Women and Boys stood up in the Church, to see how I could bear it."[88] If not the central theme of a sermon, auditors were nevertheless reflecting on the place of Meroz in their own lives. After hearing "Mr Dyke" preach on Romans 8:10 at St. Martin Ludgate in late 1642, Walter Yonge was compelled to make a special note of "5 Judges Curs you Merosh." "If," he reflected, "a man be on his death-bedd & it [Meroz] comes in his mind," would "not it grieve him" and cause him to "promise better obedience" toward God?[89]

More than simply enter into the lexicon of popular preaching, Meroz grabbed the attention of authorities and helped to energize new recruits as they prepared to ship off to Ireland. On 17 June, the Committee for Irish Adventurers, which met at Grocers' Hall, ordered that all new enlistees who planned to travel across the Irish Sea to fight were to meet at the London Guildhall to "heare a sermon to bee preached by Mr Stephen Marshall, and take the protestation att St Lawrence Church."[90] Although we lack decisive evidence that Marshall's sermon was a version of Meroz, it is certainly within the realm of reason to entertain that Marshall may have touched upon his oft-repeated theme, or that even if he did not, the new recruits were being subjected to a sermon to prepare them for an international relief effort that was sanctioned by divine providence – a conflict that was, no less, well under way just two months before the outbreak of war in England.

Around this same time, copies of "the humble Petition of many thousands of Inhabitants of Norwich" began circulating in London. Dated 16 July, the petition claimed to address the many "desperate diseases which have overspread this whole body of this Kingdome, both in Church and State." Fearful that England's own "Jesuited Papists the Bishops" were preparing acts of "bloudy cruelty" like those "of the Papists in Ireland," the petitioners revealed that they might "justly fear the curse of *Merous* to befall us." One reasonable means to avert such a fate, they claimed, was to place "the Castles, Forts, and Magazines of this Kingdome into such hands as the King and Parliament may confide in." To specify further, they added that England's defensible places and munitions should only be entrusted to persons who were "bound by the Protestation by us lately taken."[91] Like Meroz, the Protestation – the same document that was affixed to the weapons and clothes of members of London's trained bands as they guarded the triumphant return of parliament's members, and the same document that London's new recruits for Ireland were expected to take – had become the marker of trust for securing the nation's arms and munitions on the eve of the civil war. Increasingly, then, as John Walter notes, "performing the Protestation" had become a matter of "raising forces and finance."[92] Ideological escalation was one thing; what had not changed, however, was the persistent threat to the nation posed by the curse of Judges 5:23. Like other providential exhortations, the curse supplied a specific but expanding ideological function, a familiar explanation for the divine retribution that would meet inaction.

On the eve of civil war, the curse provided an important example of what would happen if the nation refused the Protestation – a set of terms for what was subtly shifting from being less often a matter of "Ireland's cause" and was instead increasingly a matter of "the cause" at hand. By the time that Charles raised his royal standard at Nottingham, on 22 August, Ireland's cause had in some instances and for some participants become synonymous with parliament's struggle to overthrow the king's evil advisers. Little ideological refashioning was needed to see how the curse applied to the new dynamics of the conflict. Meroz thus made its way into fast-day sermons in Westminster for three consecutive months after the outbreak of the civil war. On 28 September, Thomas Wilson warned the Commons to beware "neuters" and the "luke-warme" as "most loathed persons" who were "cursed [like] Meroz." The following month, Thomas Case preached *God's Rising, His Enemies Scattering*, a highly charged sermon dedicated to the parliamentarian commander Sir William Brereton and urged listeners to prepare "artillery, and weapons of death" and warned that those who withheld money from parliament would suffer "the *curse* with *Meroz*." In November, Charles Herle shared his belief that Meroz, "one of the fearfullest curses in all Scripture," should be avoided at all costs.[93]

In the end, the numerous accounts of Judges 5:23 allows for a view of the many ways in which a single providential verse could be invoked to motivate, and indeed in some instances directly mobilize, Londoners. Gauging popular reactions to Meroz and other scriptural examples is in the end, of course, notoriously difficult.[94] Sermon notes from the period are relatively scarce, and short of printed sermons and a handful of letter accounts, there are few documents that shed light on how listeners reacted. Hearers and recorders, as Ann Hughes reminds us, were perhaps more eager to collect notes for personal edification and later reflection than they were to make known their personal political reactions and affiliations.[95] In the end, Marshall's sermon stands out as an important example of at least one type of inflammatory preaching that was under way in London on the eve of the civil war. It is, in this sense, a valuable indicator – or perhaps better yet, a specific marker – of the role of sermons and preaching in 1642, of what Clarendon later described as a "strange wildfire among the people."

London was at the epicenter of the ideological shifts that were taking place in late 1641 and 1642. Indeed, when looking back to explain involvement in the war, some survivors called to mind the unique and important role played by London's preaching ministry. Convicted alongside the regicides in 1661 and preparing to be hanged at Tyburn Tree, Colonel Daniell Axtell, for instance, recalled "that [when] he went out to the Warrs, at the beginning thereof," it was "by the Instigation and Encouragement of a Minister in *Ironmonger-lane*, who stirred him with many motives, to shew him it was the Cause of God."[96] As with Marshall's preaching to military recruits preparing to leave for Ireland, the sermon that Axtell heard may well not have been a version of Judges 5:23. Indeed, it would be unwise to assume that the curse held a monopoly on popular perceptions and fears, or further that preachers were limited in their exegetical interpretations of the means by which a displeased God might shape His retribution, or of the many ways in which contemporaries likened their modern nation to ancient Israel and, by extension, London to Jerusalem. After taking Isaiah 66:10 "*Rejoyce yee with Jerusalem*" as his focus during the September 1641 fast-day in the Commons, Jeremiah Burroughs turned to questions of obligation, action, and punishment, asking his audience to ruminate on Joel 3:10, "*of turning plow shares into swords*, and *pruning hookes into speares*," and Job 31:3 and the "*strange punishment for the workers of iniquity.*" Indeed, even Marshall's own *Meroz Cursed* sermon was not limited in its scope; after mentioning Judges 5:23, Marshall turned to yet another example of providential duty and reprisal, citing Jeremiah 48:10, "*Cursed is he that doth the worke of the Lord negligently*" and "*cursed be he that keepeth back his sword from Bloud.*" Years later, parliament's *The Soldiers Catechisme*, a short booklet "written for the Incouragement and Instruction of all that have taken up Armes in this Cause of God and his People," included Jeremiah 48:10 but not Judges 5:23.[97] Clearly, divine vengeance took many forms; Meroz furnished just one – albeit one highly persuasive and memorable – example of retribution for inaction, a piece of contemporary imagination that helped bridge the ideological gap between relief for Ireland and civil war at home. As Hugh Peter tellingly recalled prior to his execution during the Restoration, "preaching was Curse ye Meroz, from Scotland to England."[98]

While Londoners increasingly reflected upon the curse and other providential elucidations of their god-given responsibilities, tangible evidence of war encroached ever closer to their own lives. As 1642 wore on, metropolitan inhabitants had to look no further than their own streets and churchyards to find destitute and needy refugees from Ireland, examples – both real and prophetic – of their own fates should they rest in neutrality or remain idle. Surely, as Edmund Calamy recalled in his own fast-day preaching, the push to *"roote out"* Irish popery *"forever"* was in England's best interests. Such a preventative measure might help shield the nation from the long-standing threat of a Catholic invasion and uprising.

Murmurings of the "ill-affected"

Not all Londoners were convinced that Ireland's miseries portended their own fate, or that England's capital would suffer in the likes of the fabled city of Meroz. Nevertheless, when confronted by the spread of providential exhortations for Ireland, and made aware of the disconcerting way in which such appeals could escalate rhetoric between the king and parliament, some preachers decided to take action, to use their time in the pulpit to uphold royal authority and stave off the looming threat of war at home. William Hall was one of these men. Preaching at St. Bartholomew the Less on 27 March 1642, "the day of inaguration of our Soveraigne Lord King Charles," he chose Exodus 22:28: *"Thou shalt not revile the Gods, nor curse the Ruler of thy people."* Hall's message was unmistakably direct and his sermon apparently "found such approbation" among local auditors that Nathaniel, his father, moved that it should be printed, "so as not to be confined within those narrow limits of a small parish." Printed, his sermon bore a dedication to Sir John Banks, Attorney General and Chief Justice to the king. Clearly, Hall's view that all "must honor the King" and "consequently all who derive power from him," resonated with segments of the City, and stands out as an important early counter to escalating rhetoric and mounting criticisms of the Crown.[99]

Like Hall, others sought to use the pulpit as a means to defuse tensions and silence the king's critics. Mayor Richard Gurney, for instance, retained an important means for dissuading belligerent opponents in his ability to appoint preachers to London's cathedral. On 19 June, nearly a month before his arrest for refusing to read parliament's Militia Ordinance, legislation that placed control of the appointment of Lord Lieutenants and county militias in the hands of parliament and circumvented royal assent, Gurney selected Thomas Morton, the former bishop of Durham, to deliver a sermon at St. Paul's. The aged Morton used his time in the pulpit to identify the greatest danger to the body politic, which he took to be the very preachers who "*delightfully loveth Contentions.*" Morton lamented that London – indeed, all of England – had recently seen a wave of seditious "printed books" and sermons that hurled "invective against Church Government and Service." The "auditors," Morton opined, were guided by preachers who employed "such Texts of Scripture as speake directly of massacring," singling out Jeremiah 48:10, "*Cursed is he that doth the worke of the Lord negligently*" and "*cursed be he that keepeth back his sword from Bloud.*" Doubtless other chapters and verses came to mind when he considered the ways in which London's godly ministers had pursued their contemptible purposes. Much less than the vengeful God of war, Morton emphasized "the God of Peace" who might be found in Romans 15:13, II Corinthians 13:11, and II Thessalonians 3:16, all of which, he believed, showed in unassailable terms that "peace is a Jewell" above all others.[100] Morton's plea certainly did not fall on deaf ears – Mayor Gurney was in the audience, after all – but there is in the end no direct or conclusive evidence to suggest that his denunciation of "schismatic" preachers stifled promotion of the war. Morton would be Gurney's last appointment to the pulpit at St. Paul's, a departing mayor's swan song for peace.

If anything, sermons like those of Hall and Morton reminded London's godly and their allies in parliament of the need to further "tune" City pulpits. That same month, the Court of Aldermen ordered that a letter be drawn up to inform William Juxon, the bishop of London, about "how of late the pulpit in St Paules on Sundays hath byn furnished with meane Preachers" and how it was hoped that they might be replaced with "true orthodoxall Teachers."[101] Outside of the City's cathedral, ministers were targeted and arrested with the intention that their removal might, as Case and Goodwin suggested in their sermons, provide further reformation of the Church. But loyalists were also quick to point out that parliament might clearly benefit from having "an Orator in every Pulpit to quicken the people, to poure out their wealth Liberally, [and] to further the Rebellion intended." Butler thus opined that fomentors sought to "cause the very dregs, and scum of every Parish, to petition against the Orthodox Clergy."[102] By the early summer of 1642, concerted efforts to root out preachers were well under way. Individuals who were previously targeted as "scandalous" began to be tarred with more aggressive charges of "malignancy" for refusing to support a cause that had become as much about the king and his evil advisers as it was about relieving Protestants in Ireland. Historians have offered a range of explanations for the clerical ejections that took place in London over the course of 1641 and 1642, with some emphasizing how the upheavals of the period provided opportunities for addressing decidedly local issues, such as those delineated by Ian Green, to more general surveys of more widespread anti-episcopal sentiment, like those outlined by Tai Liu.[103] Keith Lindley, meanwhile, has described a process that "began slowly in 1640, gathered momentum in 1641 and 1642, and then accelerated very rapidly in 1643" and left London's pulpits "systematically purged." The escalating process, Lindley explains, was "largely the work of zealous minorities" who were at times "encouraged and supported by central figures like Isaac Penington."[104] Indeed, even a cursory investigation reveals that the momentum behind London's ejections often began with local concerns and accusations, but that the earnest pursuit of the "ill-affected" coincided with concerted efforts to ramp up pressure and harassment by the new Lord Mayor and his associates. Most official ejections, as we shall see, took place in early 1643, a time when Pennington was at the height of his authority and when parliament had devised more thorough means for processing those accused. Prior to this, numerous ministers had already fled London under charges of sedition for matters such as reading illegal declarations on behalf of the king, or for refusing to contribute toward the "public safety."

Pennington, who had held a seat on the Committee for Scandalous Ministers since shortly after the start of the Long Parliament, earned a deserved reputation for zeal. When the parishioners of St. Leonard Shoreditch petitioned for the removal of their vicar, John Squire, in 1641, it was then Alderman Pennington who first heard their complaints. Squire faced numerous accusations for his "corrupt and dangerous" conduct, ranging from the claim that he promoted "pictures of Christ and his Twelve Apostles" and believed that "Baptisme doth waste away Originall Sinn," to his personal engagement in "Ale house drinking" and "Bed sleeping." Squire sought to "denie" outright the complaints that were given "unto Alderman Pennington" and used against him, and further answered his charges with a petition containing 200 signatures and testimonies from "the best of my Parish."[105] Like many of his fellow embattled ministers, his official ejection did not come until 1643 following the establishment of the Committee for Plundered Ministers, months after his imprisonment in Gresham College and well after his dramatic efforts to retain his vicarage were made accessible in print.[106]

Pennington seemed at times to genuinely relish the task at hand. Robert Chestlin of St. Matthew Friday Street, for instance, came up against Pennington on several occasions. Chestlin at first faced harassment by organized and zealous parishioners.[107] Henry Burton had served as rector in the parish between 1621 and 1636, until his arrest for preaching a sermon in which he attacked episcopacy and compared English bishops to their Roman counterparts.[108] Chestlin took Burton's place at Friday Street in 1640, and held the rectorship until March 1642, when Leonard Tilley delivered the complaints of parishioners who believed that Burton "had been unjustly deprived" and hoped that he might therefore "be restored to his said living with the mesne profits taken from him since his said deprivation."[109] Pennington led the effort to acquire evidence for Chestlin's removal and subsequently obtained the warrant that led to his arrest. Among the charges against him was the claim that he had used "divers scandalous Words" in "several Sermons against the Proceedings of Parliament" and which were qualified by Chestlin's "own Interpretations."[110] Pennington had long had it out for Chestlin. When Chestlin attempted to regain the payment of his tithes in 1640, Pennington apparently turned up at his hearing to traduce him, at one point calling him a *"Saucy Jacke"* and *"brazen faced fellow."*[111] Chestlin later recalled his embarrassing treatment at the hands of then Mayor Pennington and his "Puritan Faction" in *Persecutio Undecima*. Like others, he was *"barbarously used and depived"* for maintaining *"loyalty to their Soveraigne,"* and was subsequently "sequestered, and plundered." Yet Chestlin's removal seems to have been particularly harsh. After preaching a controversial sermon in October 1642, a warrant was secured for his arrest. Subsequently, a mob of parishioners, led by John Venn, "violently assaulted" him and dragged him out of "his house." After being presented to the Lord Mayor as a "seditious preacher and delinquent," he was moved between prisons before finally landing in Colchester jail.[112]

Another opportunity arose when Thomas Swadlin, the curate of St. Botolph Aldgate, preached a loyalist sermon that upset his parishioners. After being accused by the tallow chandler John Levet of preaching "obedience to higher powers," Swadlin was arrested and brought in for examination by the Lord Mayor. During his subsequent stay in jail, which began on 29 October, Swadlin decided to print both his sermon and the nature of his examination. Available the following February, *The Soveraignes Desire Peace: the Subjects Dutie Obedience* revealed that the Lord Mayor had assured Swadlin that his continued support of episcopacy was the main reason for his incarceration. "So long as you pray for Bishops ... you shall be a prisoner," Pennington apparently professed. Further, the Lord Mayor revealed to Swadlin his profound displeasure with the Book of Common Prayer, suggesting that the only acceptable version had been approved by an "Act of Parliament" and was in fact "King Edwards Common Prayer Booke." The version "which is now extant," he continued, had since become corrupted. "Many prayers by the meanes of the wicked Hierarchie are crept into this which never were in that."[113] The cases of both Chestlin and Swadlin reveal the zealotry and hands-on approach to reform that would come to define Pennington's mayoralty.

Chestlin later estimated that there were 115 clergymen within the Bills of Mortality who would end up "sequestered, plundered, and turned out" by order of parliament. The ejected had stories that ranged from being "abused in the street" to being "forced to fly." Among those in "adjacent towns" was William Stampe, vicar at St. Dunstan's, Stepney. Stampe had been identified with the malignant party for failing to contribute toward the safety of the City in June.[114] By the following month, Stampe was considerably more active in his support of the king. He joined with his brother, Timothy, and together they sought to prevent apprentices from enlisting as volunteers under the earl of Essex. William's efforts ultimately landed him in prison for nine months. Upon release, he fled to Oxford where he was honored with the opportunity to preach before the king.[115] Where Stampe stood out for his active opposition to parliament's efforts, other City ministers found less hazardous ways to promote loyalism as the nation slid toward war. An important opportunity arrived in the middle of June, when the king issued a royal declaration in which he complained that he had been "driven by Force from Our City of *London*," that rumors of his preparation for war were false, and that blame for the state of affairs should be placed on "the Trayterous Attempts of" some "wicked and Malignant persons."[116] Several ministers chose to read the king's declaration from their pulpits and were subsequently summoned by parliament to explain their actions under charges of delinquency. On 4 July, parliament sent for five church officials from Westminster, including Mr. White, the minister at the Abbey, Richard Dukeson, rector of St. Clement Danes and Mr. Smith, his curate, along with William Fuller, vicar of St. Giles Cripplegate, and Mr. Hutton, his curate. On the following day, Francis Hall, the curate of St. Paul in Covent Garden, was called in for "for publishing in that Church his Majesty's Declaration." Upon questioning on 13 July, Dukeson and Smith were committed as prisoners to the Gatehouse. Fuller was released after it was determined that he did not read the king's declaration, but that his curate, Mr. Hutton, had done as much. Hutton was subsequently sent to the King's Bench Prison in Southwark. Further questioning revealed that Hall did indeed "publish" the king's declaration, but that he had done so under duress and threat from an unknown loyalist messenger named "Woodruff." Rather than being jailed, Hall was reprehended. Dukeson successfully petitioned and was released along with Smith eight days after being arrested.[117] Rather than keep a low profile, Dukeson shifted his efforts into peace petitioning, seeking out "royall wisdom" as a means for finding "some speedy course for an Accomodation."[118]

In the months that followed, both Pennington and parliament continued their efforts to remove London's "ill-affected" ministers. Printed at the start of November, *A Catalogue of sundrie Knights, aldermen, Doctors: Ministers and Citizens* featured the names of fifty-six individuals who had been arrested for refusing to "assist the Parliament with summes of money proportionable to their estates." Included on the list were three London doctors of divinity and a handful of church officials whose financial "inclinations" led to their immediate arrest and removal from parishes. The jailed men included Richard Holdsworth, rector of St. Peter the Poor; John Hackett, the rector of St. Andrew Holborn; Josias Shute, rector of St. Mary Woolnoth; John Squire, vicar of St. Leonard Shoreditch; Ephraim Udall, rector of St. Augustine; Benjamin Stone, rector of St. Mary Abchurch and St. Clement Eastcheap; and Matthew Griffith, rector of St. Mary Magdalen Old Fish Street. Swadlin was among the listed.[119] Each "ill-affected" individual came from a prominent City parish, or parishes; their precipitous arrests left plenty of time for later ejection proceedings. Meanwhile, their financial recalcitrance served as a demonstrable form of criticism for parliament's war.

Several of the accused had, moreover, organized their efforts in a clear response to pro-war preaching in parliament and the City. Rather than seek opportunities in St. Margaret or the Abbey, they followed Morton's lead and preached pacificity under Lord Mayor Gurney's jurisdiction in the City's cathedral. Udall had made his opinions clear in a sermon given at St. Paul's at the end of July. In this he echoed Morton's words from the previous month, calling "peace" the reasonable "desire of all men" who had "been well schooled" by "the calamities of War." Udall asked his listeners to "thinke often on the miseries that do waite on War," and in particular of Ireland, which had suffered unimaginably, its people "tossed on pikes" or "their braines dashed out against the pavement?"[120] Peace, likewise, was the subject when Griffith preached at St. Paul's in October. "Can we ever hope to prosper," he pleaded, "whilst we are thus divided?"[121] Far less a matter of failing to support the cause, Griffith had championed open opposition to war in the first place. Udall and Griffith – like Morton before them – were willing to martyr their ministerial careers in the very heart of the City if it might help to stymie belligerence. Their subsequent arrests, like those of Chestlin and Swadlin, nevertheless marked a significant step in efforts to purge London's pulpits of loyalist views.

With the line thus drawn between preaching for war and peace, it became clear that additional efforts would be needed to tip the scales. At Pennington's behest, Common Council began its own efforts to assist in the collection of evidence against London's ministers. In December, the Council appointed a group of thirteen men with the power to meet "and inform themselves of all malignant scandalous and seditious Ministers in and about this Cittye aswell [sic] those absent." Any names discovered were to be passed to "the Lord Maior."[122] Several of the appointed committee members were known for their early and vigorous support of the parliamentarian cause. Indeed, counted among their ranks was Edward Hooker, a captain in the trained bands, and William Greenhill, "the Arch-incendiary of Christ Church Parish."[123] Also present were Thomas Brightwell and John Gearing of Bread Street, both of whom were notable activists and "radicals."[124] Brightwell, for his part, brought a total of £700 for the relief of Ireland between March 1642 and January 1643.[125] The Committee's efforts proved indispensable to Pennington and parliament over the course of the following year, as official cases were built against ministers who were initially tarred by the brush of "malignancy" and would soon be ejected by official sequestration orders.

Vigorous efforts to remove oppositional views from London's pulpits did not go unnoticed. London's "heads of this Rebellion," complained *Mercurius Rusticus*, dealt with its "ill-affected" ministers in the same manner "as unjust Stepmothers do with their poor Children." They went out to "*Whip them till they cry, and then whip them again for crying.*"[126] No matter the consequences, loyalists pressed on with their efforts. Throughout the summer and autumn of 1642, a coterie of dedicants sought ways to deescalate the growing tensions between the king and parliament. Few, it would seem, ultimately chose to walk the path of open opposition to parliament. If loosely organized at first, the collective "murmurings" of London's peace activists nevertheless defined an important component of popular metropolitan mobilization; London's loyalist preachers had cut an alternative trail to one that could be heard in parliamentarian exhortations to war, and by this measure they offered an important stepping stone to the popular peace agitations that were looming on the horizon. Chestlin, Swadlin, Morton, Udall, and Griffith suffered the consequences for openly waging efforts against parliament's incipient war effort. But not all was thereby lost. By June of the following year, Griffith had become a royal chaplain, having fled London for Oxford. Some, like Dukeson, turned to promises of organized petitioning. Chestlin and Swadlin, meanwhile, answered accusations with accounts of their lives in print, hoping to persuade readers by way of the details of their own respective persecutions. In August, on the eve of the civil war, Morton, for his part, produced a short anti-war tract in which he warned of "the Nature, Danger, and ill Effects of Civill-Warre" and compared England's "blessed condition" to the "grievous calamities" of Ireland and the war-torn Continent where Germany was in a "lamentable estate," and Spain, where "whole Countries revolt against their King." To "happily avoid" the terrors of a "much feared Civill dissention," he suggested that England's "true subjects" should seek out "concord." Morton, like many others who would in time be labeled royalists, feared that England stood on the edge of a cliff. A far cry from the prophetic fate of the ancient Merozites, Morton urged his readers to simply look to neighboring lands that stood ravaged by the Thirty Years' War. Londoners might heed Morton's printed warnings about their own "imminent danger" for less than a fortnight, as this was all the time that stood between his words and 22 August, the day when the royal standard was raised at Nottingham.[127]

Notes

1 John Rushworth, *Historical Collections* (London, 1721), pp. 479–480.
2 Butler, *A Letter*, p. 16.
3 See John Forester, *The Arrest of the Five Members by Charles I* (London, 1860), p. 262.
4 TNA, SP 16/488/45.
5 John Taylor, *The whole life and progresse of Henry Walker the ironmonger* (London, 1642), sigs. A2v, A4r.
6 *VII Articles Drawn up Against Lord Kimelton M John Pinne [...] And a Petiiton to the Kings MAJESTY* (London, 1642), p. 6. Prior to David Como's discovery of the original petition (see *Radical Parliamentarians*, pp. 114–116), we were reliant on a reprinted version from *Perfect Occurrences of Parliament*, 30 August – 6 September (London, 1644) found by Nick Poyntz. My thanks are due to Dr. Poyntz for sharing his knowledge about Walker's petition.
7 Taylor, *The whole life and progresse of Henry Walker*, sig. A4r.
8 See also Ernest Sirluck, "'To Your Tents, O Israel': A Lost Pamphlet," *HLQ*, 19 (1956), pp. 301–305.
9 Adamson, *Noble Revolt*, p. 487.
10 TNA, SP 16/488/45.
11 TNA, SP 16/488/47.
12 *A True Relation of the unparaleled Breach of Parliament* (London, 1642), p. 4.
13 TNA, SP 16/488/59; BL, Add MS 40883, fol. 12r.
14 LMA, MS COL/CC/01/01/041, fos. 14r–15v.
15 BL, Add MS 21935, fol. 163v.
16 See Sears McGee, *An Industrious Mind: The Worlds of Sir Simonds D'Ewes* (Stanford, 2015).
17 BL, Harley MS 162, fol. 318r; Pearl, *London*, p. 145.
18 Lawson Nagel, "'A Great Bouncing at Every Man's Door': The Struggle for London's Militia in 1642," in Stephen Porter (ed.), *London and the Civil War* (London, 1996), p. 65.
19 Conrad Russell, *The Fall of British Monarchies, 1637–1641* (Oxford, 1991), p. 299.
20 Walter, *Covenanting Citizens*, p. 239.
21 *Protestation* (London, 1641).
22 *A Bloody Massacre Plotted by the Papists intended first against the City of London* (London, 1641), p. 1.
23 *A Discovery of a horrible and Bloody Treason and Conspiracie* (London, 1641), sigs. A2r–v.
24 *The Attachment Examination and Confession of A French-man* (London, 1641), sigs. A2r, A4r.
25 See Peter Lake, "Anti-Puritanism: The Structure of a Prejudice," in Kenneth Fincham and Peter Lake (eds), *Religious Politics in Post-Reformation England: Essays in Honour of Nicholas Tyacke* (Woodbridge, 2006), pp. 80–83; Peter Lake, "Antipopery: The Structure of a Prejudice," in Richard Cust and Ann Hughes (eds), *Conflict in Early Stuart England* (London, 1989).

26 See Lindley, *Popular Politics*, pp. 104–105; Steven R. Smith, "Almost Revolutionaries: the London Apprentices during the Civil Wars," *HLQ*, 42 (1979), pp. 313–328: for note of Lunsford's alignment with "popish plotters," see Mark Stoyle, "The Canibal Cavalier: Sit Thomas Lunsford and the Fashioning of the Royalist Archetype," *HJ*, 59 (2015), pp. 305–306.
27 Anthony Fletcher, *The Outbreak of the English Civil War* (New York, 1981), p. 124.
28 James Salmon, *Bloody News from Ireland* (London, 1641).
29 J. L. Malcolm, *Caesar's Due: Loyalty and King Charles, 1642–1646* (London, 1983), p. 16.
30 M. Perceval-Maxwell, *The Outbreak of the Irish Rebellion of 1641* (Quebec, 1994), p. 261. See in particular Conrad Russell, *The Fall of British Monarchies* (Oxford, 1991). For a recent wider contextualization of the events, see Jane Ohlmeyer and Micheál Ó Siochrú (eds), *Ireland, 1641: Contexts and Reactions* (Manchester, 2013).
31 Adamson, *Noble Revolt*, p. 513.
32 See in particular Bethany Marsh, "'Protestant Martyrs or Irish Vagrants?': Responses and the Organisation of Relief to the Irish in England, 1641–1651" (unpub. Ph.D. thesis, Nottingham University, 2019); see also Bethany Marsh, "Lodging the Irish: An Examination of Parochial Charity Dispensed in Nottinghamshire to Refugees from Ireland, 1641–1651," *Midland History*, 42 (2017), pp. 194–216.
33 See S. L. Adams, "The Protestant Cause: Religious Alliance with the West European Calvinist Communities as a Political Issue in England, 1585–1603" (unpub. D.Phil. thesis, Oxford University, 1973); see Lake, *Bad Queen Bess?*, pp. 468, 481–483.
34 *The Papists Designe Against the Parliament and Citie of London discovered* (London, 1642), A2r.
35 TNA, SP 16/488/58.
36 *The Black Box of Roome* (London, 1642), pp. 3, 9, 12, 18.
37 GL, MS 5570/3, fos. 565–567.
38 Clothworkers' Company Library, Orders of Court, 1639–1649, fol. 53r.
39 John Venn, *A True Relation* (London, 1642), pp. 1–5.
40 HL, HA Correspondence Box 16/5554, 3 January 1642.
41 Venn, *A True Relation*, pp. 5–6. Venn was later paid more than £7 for efforts made in October and December. LMA, MS COL/CA/01/01/059, fol. 383r.
42 *A complaint to the House of Commons* (London, 1642), p. 13.
43 Clarendon, *History*, Appendix 2, n. 375; see also Brenner, *Merchants and Revolution*, p. 370; Brian Manning, *The English People and the English Revolution* (London, 1979), p. 156.
44 Edward Walker, *Historical Discourses upon Several Occasions* (London, 1705), p. 271.
45 Diggs, *An Answer*, p. 55.
46 See in particular Ethan Shagan, "Constructing Discord: Ideology, Propaganda, and English Responses to the Irish Rebellion of 1641," *JBS*, 36 (1997), pp. 4–34.

47 Keith Lindley, "The Impact of the 1641 Rebellion upon England and Wales, 1641–5," *Irish Historical Studies*, 18 (1972), p. 144. Shockingly, 32 percent of material obtained by Thomason in February dealt with Ireland. By April this had increased to 37 percent. Londoners were not simply interested, but rather were positively enthralled by the news; more than a third of the printed material circulating in London dealt with the issue. By July, however, the number of references to Ireland dropped dramatically to just 4.4 percent, and never rose again past 10 percent.
48 Although closer, Edinburgh was estimated to have a population of close to 40,000 at this time.
49 LMA, MS P69/STE1/B/001/MS04458/001/001, fos. 143–145.
50 LMA, MS P69/ALH7/B/001/MS00819/001, fos. 143–145.
51 LMA, MS P69/JNZ/B/014/MS00590/001, fol. 184v.
52 LMA, MS P69/PAN/B/014/MS05018/001, fol. 38v.
53 LMA, MS COL/CA/01/01/059, fos. 454r, 372v–373r, 383v, 390v.
54 *Propositions Made [...] for the speedie and effectuall reducing of the Kingdom of Ireland* (London, 1642).
55 See TNA, SP 63/288–300 for an extensive record of contributions and receipts. In July, members of the Committee for Irish Adventurers would "lend" £100,000 of the money to help fund parliament's war effort. See below, pp. 74–75.
56 See Brenner, *Merchants and Revolution*, pp. 400–408. The effort was led by Lord Brooke and other future parliamentarian leaders. Hugh Peter acted as chaplain. Counted among the leading contributors from London were Richard Shute, Edmund Harvey, Richard Turner, Samuel Harsnett, Francis Webb, and Hogan Hovell.
57 LMA, MS P69/ALH8/B/013/MS00823/001, unfol.
58 LMA, MS P69/LAW1/B/008/MS02593/002, fol. 29.
59 LMA, MS P69/OLA2/B/004/MS04409/001, fol. 274v.
60 LMA, MS P69/MRY9/B/007/MS02596/002, fol, 86r.
61 LMA, MS P69/JNZ/B/014/MS00590/001, fol. 186r.
62 LMA, MS P69/PET4/B/006/MS00645/002, fos. 77r, 78v, 81r.
63 LMA, MS P69/MIC7/B/003/MS00524, fos. 63v–64r.
64 LMA, MS P69/JS2/B/005/MS04810/002, fol. 97v.
65 Camden Local Studies and Archives Center, MS VOL P/GF/M/4, unpaginated.
66 City of Westminster Archives Centre, MS 5 E23, unfol.
67 Southwark Local History Library, MS St. Mary Newington Churchwardens' Accounts, 1632–1734, unfol.
68 TNA, SP 28/170 part 2, fol. 6r.
69 LMA, MS P69/ALP/B/006/MS01432/004, unfol. See also LMA MS P69/ALB/B/003/MS07673/002, unfol. for sums "paid to the Treasurer of the City for the maintenance of Queene Elizabeths maimed Souldiers."
70 For the lesser amount, see LMA, MS P69/Tr13/B/004/MS04835/001, unfol.; for the larger sum, see LMA, MS P69/ANL/B/004/MS01046/001, unfol.; churchwardens at St. Botolph Without paid £1 6s. See LMA MS P69/BOT4/B/008/MS04524/002, fol. 74r.

71 See for instance, LMA, MS P69/ALH6/B/008/MS04956/003/001, fos. 103, 112, 119, 239, 249, 157, 165, 179; LMA, MS P69/BAT1/B/006/MS04383/001, fos. 416r, 426r, 429v; LMA, MS P69/CLE/B/007/MS00977/001, fol. 31v.
72 LMA, MS P69/MIC1/B/008/MS02601/001/001, fol. 174v.
73 TNA, SP 28/170 part 2, fos. 1–58.
74 LMA, MS COL/CA/01/01/059, fol. 384v.
75 Stephen Marshall, *Meroz Curse* (London, 1641), pp. 2, 7. See Jordan S. Downs, "The Curse of Meroz and the English Civil War," *HJ*, 57 (2014), pp. 343–368.
76 Stephen Marshall, *Reformation and Desolation* (London, 1642), p. 52.
77 Edmund Calamy, *England's Looking-Glasse* (London, 1642), pp. 1, 51.
78 Blair Worden's work on political providentialism paved the way for the more systematic analysis provided by G. C. Browell, who, in an unpublished Ph.D. thesis, provided an important consideration of the systematic ways in which both royalists and parliamentarians interpreted providence. See Blair Worden, "Providence and Politics in Cromwellian England," *Past & Present*, 109 (1985), p. 59; Blair Worden, *God's Instruments: Political Conduct in the England of Oliver Cromwell* (Oxford, 2012), pp. 33–62; G. C. Browell, "The Politics of Providentialism in England, c. 1640–1660" (unpub. Ph.D. thesis, University of Kent, 2000). For royalist uses of providentialism see Richard Cust, "Charles I and Providence," in Kenneth Fincham and Peter Lake (eds), *Religious Politics in Post-Reformation England: Essays in Honour of Nicholas Tyacke* (Woodbridge, 2006), pp. 194–195.
79 Hugh Trevor-Roper, "Fast Sermons of the Long Parliament," in *Essays in British History* (London, 1965); John F. Wilson, *Pulpit in Parliament: Puritanism during the English Civil Wars, 1640–1648* (Princeton, 1969).
80 See Stephen Baskerville, *Not Peace But a Sword: the Political Theology of the English Revolution* (London, 1993); Glenn Burgess, "Was the English Civil War a War of Religion? Evidence of Political Propaganda," *HLQ*, 61 (1998), pp. 173–201.
81 Ann Hughes, "Preachers and Hearers in Revolutionary London: Contextualizing Parliamentary Fast Sermons," *TRHS*, 24 (2014), p. 59.
82 For more on this subject, see Achsah Guibbory, *Christian Identity, Jews and Israel in Seventeenth-Century England* (Oxford, 2010).
83 Calamy, *England's Looking-Glasse*, p. 14.
84 Edmund Calamy, *God's Free Mercy to England* (London, 1642), sig. A2r; pp. 1, 5, 7, 21–23, 50.
85 Henry Hammond, *Of Resisting the Lawful Magistrate Under Colour of Religion* (Oxford, 1644), pp. 57–58.
86 Alexandra Walsham mentions the figure "sixty" twice. See Alexandra Walsham, *Providence in Early Modern England* (Oxford, 1999), p. 316; Alexandra Walsham, *Charitable Hatred: Tolerance and Intolerance in England, 1500–1700* (Manchester, 2006), p. 138. For a less specific but nonetheless telling estimate, see Trevor-Roper, "Fast Sermons of the Long Parliament," p. 99.
87 Stephen Marshall, *Meroz Curse* (London, 1642). [ESTC R180387, ESTC R19516, ESTC R204373].
88 William Laud, *The History of the Troubles* (London, 1695), p. 196.

89 BL, Add MS 18781, fol. 110r. This is almost certainly Daniel Dyke, the godly and active lecturer whom Tai Liu has identified with St. Martin Ludgate in 1643–4. Yet even Liu cautions that Dyke's identity is "tentative" in *Puritan London: A Study of Religion and Society in the City Parishes* (London, 1986), pp. 108–109, 121. Dyke's name is not recorded in the vestry minutes for St. Martin Ludgate, 1579–1649: LMA, MS P69/MTN1/B/001/MS01311/001/001.
90 TNA, SP 63/260/230, "The Proposition of the Com[missione]rs for Ireland," 17 June 1642.
91 *To the Right Honourable the Lords [...] The humble Petition of many thousands of the Inhabitants of Norwich* (London, 1642).
92 Walter, *Covenanting Citizens*, p. 240; See also David Cressey, who suggests that the Protestation had become a marker of "a partisan political position" between the king and parliament in "The Protestation Protested, 1641 and 1642," pp. 267–268. According to Conrad Russell, the Protestation had for "many Parliamentarians" become a "title to be in arms" against the king. Conrad Russell, *Fall of the British Monarchies, 1637–1642* (Oxford, 1991), pp. 294–295.
93 Thomas Wilson, *Jerichoes Downfall* (London, 1643), pp. 31–32; Thomas Case, *God's Rising, His Enemies Scattering* (London, 1644), pp. 21, 42; Charles Herle, *A Payre of Compasses* (London, 1642), p. 35; John Ley, *The Fury of War and Folly of Sin* (London, 1643), p. 16. See Downs, "The Curse of Meroz and the English Civil War," pp. 352–353.
94 See Arnold Hunt, *The Art of Hearing: English Preachers and Audiences, 1590–1640* (Cambridge, 2010), chapters 2, 7.
95 Hughes, "Preachers and Hearers in Revolutionary London," p. 68.
96 *A Compleat Collection of the Lives* (London, 1661), p. 158. Thanks are due to Tom Cogswell for bringing this valuable source to my attention. This was likely not John Arrowsmith, who came to the parish in 1645.
97 Jeremiah Burroughs, *Sions Joy* (London, 1641), pp. 1, 40–41, 51. *The Souldiers Catechisme: Composed for Parliaments Army* (London, 1644), title page and p. 15. For other examples of the contemporary propensity to compare the nation to Israel and London to Jerusalem, see Edward Reynolds, *Israel's Petition in Time of Trouble* (London, 1642); John Milton, *Areopagitica* (London, 1644).
98 Hugh Peter, *The Case of Mr. Hugh Peters* (London, 1660), p. 3.
99 William Hall, *A Sermon Preached* (London, 1642), sig. A2r, pp. 1, 32.
100 Thomas Morton, *The Presentation of a Schismaticke* (London, 1642), pp. 2, 4, 24.
101 LMA, Ms COL/CA/01/01/059 Court of Aldermen Repertory 55, fol. 445.
102 Butler, *A Letter*, p. 26.
103 Ian Green, "The Persecution of 'Scandalous' and 'Malignant' Parish Clergy During the English Civil War," *EHR*, 94 (1979), pp. 518–520.
104 Lindley, *Popular Politics*, pp. 50–55, 265–267. See especially A. Argent, "Aspects of the Ecclesiastical History of the Parishes of the City of London 1640–49 (with Special Reference to the Parish Clergy)" (unpub. Ph.D. thesis, University of London, 1984), pp. 45–48.

105 Lambeth Palace Library, MS 4247, fos. 1r–v, 3r. It was later claimed that "he hath publikely in his Sermons affirmed, *the Papists to be the Kings best subjects*." See John White, *The First Century of Scandalous, Malignant Priests* (London, 1643), p. 25.

106 *Articles Exhibited in Parliament against John Squire* (London, 1641); John Squire, *An Answer to a printed paper entitled Articles exhibited in Parliament* (London, 1642). See also Lindley, *Popular Politics*, p. 54. For a valuable discussion of Squire's misery, see Isaac Stephens, "The Politics of Clerical Ejections in London, c. 1640–1662," forthcoming.

107 A brief note is made in the churchwardens' accounts regarding 8s 6d paid for "charges aboute mr Cheslin." See LMA, MS P69/MTW/B/005/MS01016/001, fol. 191r.

108 Tai Liu suggests that his time at Friday Street came to an end in 1634 in *Puritan London: A Study of Religion and Society in the Parishes* (Newark, 1986), p. 114. This view, however, seems to miss Burton's inflammatory sermon at the parish from 5 November 1636.

109 *The Private Journals of the Long Parliament*, vol 2, p. 95 [D'Ewes on 28 March 1642].

110 *CJ* vol. 2, p. 826; see Bodleian Library, Tanner MS 63, fol. 6; Lindley, *Popular Politics*, pp. 53–54, 265.

111 *Mercurius Rusticus* (Oxford, 1643, E.70[26]), p. 122; see Liu, *Puritan London*, p. 127.

112 Robert Chestlin, *Persecutio undecima* (London, 1648), pp. 1, 44–50; C. M. Clode, *London during the Great Rebellion: being a memoir of Sir Abraham Reynardson* (London, 1892), p. 15.

113 Thomas Swadlin, *The Soveraignes Desire Peace* (London, 1643), sigs. A2r–v, A3r.

114 Ibid., pp. 48–50.

115 Bodleian Library, Tanner MS 62, fol. 211v. See William Stampe, *A Sermon preached before his Majestie at Christ-Church in Oxford* (Oxford, 1643).

116 *His Majesties Declaration* (London, 1642), pp. 3, 5.

117 *CJ* vol. 2, pp. 650, 652, 669, 683. See also Merritt, *Westminster*, pp. 49–50.

118 *A Petition of the City of Westminster and the Parishes of Saint Clement Danes and St Martins in the Fields* (London, 1643), p. 5.

119 *A Catalogue of sundry Knights, Aldermen* [...] (London, 1642). I have been unable to identify "Dr Shelly" and "Mr Grosse," two of the seven men. Grosse was perhaps Alexander Grosse of Ashburton, Devon. See Lindley, *Popular Politics*, p. 266 n. 52.

120 Ephraim Udall, *The Good of Peace and Ill of Warre* (London, 1642), pp. 2, 38.

121 Matthew Griffith, *A Patheticall Perswasion to pray for Publick Peace* (London, 1642), p. 43.

122 LMA, MS COL/CC/01/01/041, fol. 42r. The list includes "Mr John Geeringe [Gearing] Mr Theophilius Riley Mr Deputye [William] Taylor Mr Deputy [Richard] Turner Mr Deputy [William] Hobson Mr Michaell Herringe Mr [William] Kendall Mr [William] Greenehill, Mr [Christopher] Nicholson, Mr Alexander Jones, Captaine [Edward] Hooker, and Mr Thomas Brightwell."

123 See Liu, *Puritan London*, p. 71.
124 Lindley, *Popular Politics*, p. 142.
125 *CSPI, 1642–1659* (London, 1908), p. 83.
126 Bruno Ryves, *Mercurius Rusticus* (London, 1685), p. 147.
127 Thomas Morton, *England's Warning Piece* (London, 1642), title page, pp. 1, 3, 5–6. For two classic studies, see Geoffrey Parker, *The Thirty Years' War*, 2nd edn (New York, 1997), and J. H. Elliott, *The Revolt of the Catalans: A Study in the Decline of Spain, 1598–1640* (Cambridge, 1963).

2

Mobilizing the metropolis

While preachers were busy finding and deploying scriptural evidence "to stir up" their auditors, militant Londoners were moving ahead with preparations for war. By June it was clear that the City, which was inundated by refugees and news of the deteriorating relationship between the king and parliament, was sinking into a defensive posture. Writing to his son-in-law on 15 June, Thomas Tyrrell, a deputy lieutenant in Buckinghamshire and later a colonel of horse for parliament, took note of the rapid changes that were taking place all around him. It was, he observed, as if "some suddayne storme will falle upon ye kingdome." "Citizens" were daily delivering "theire mony & Plate roundly according to the propositions" recently made by parliament.[1] The "propositions" that Tyrrell referred to were not the same ones that had been issued for Ireland in February, but were instead a set of nine new proposals that had originated with parliament and passed as an ordinance on 9 June. A committee of six peers and twelve MPs delivered these new propositions to the City the following day.[2] Once printed, parliament's new *Certaine Propositions* were readily available for purchase at the bustling "Hospitall Gate in Smith-Field." These called upon Londoners to bring "Mony or Plate" to the Guildhall to help fund the raising of "Horse, Horse-men, and Arms for the preservation of the publike Peace." All of names and sums loaned were to be recorded and it was assumed that the money would eventually be repaid "with the Interest according to 8 pound *per cent*," and guaranteed by the public faith.[3] Ten days later, an expanded version of the propositions was printed "together with divers Instructions concerning the same," and available for purchase at bookshops in Middle Temple "and next door to the Kings-head" on Fleet Street.[4]

Unlike previous calls for "peace," parliament's new propositions named an aggressor outright, claiming that it was the "*King*" who had been "*seduced by wicked Councell*" and subsequently had every intention "*to make War against his Parliament.*" "Civill War" thus seemed imminent.[5] Indeed, parliament's June propositions came amidst a period that saw the prospect of war shift from being a distinct possibility to an all too probable reality. The drift began in earnest after parliament passed their militia ordinance on 5 March, but far clearer lines were drawn when the king responded with the commission of array on 11 June. By the end of the month, counties began to divide, with men mustering and drilling in preparation for war.[6] Soon thereafter a coup saw London's loyalist Lord Mayor, Richard Gurney, arrested, jailed, and replaced by the energetic opponent of the Crown and leading architect of metropolitan mobilization, Isaac Pennington. With the new Lord Mayor came new galvanizing efforts; along with renewed attacks on church loyalists came a series of targeted precepts, ordinances, and propositions that would help to move metropolitan men, money, and supplies for parliament. The first order of the day was assessing and accessing the City's vast wealth. Naturally, this meant London's liveries. If the ancient trade associations once stood as dependable lenders to the king, they might now readily be expected to bolster parliament's cause.

The "suddayne storme" that Tyrrell anticipated in the middle of June finally broke over Edgehill in October. War had arrived, and with it came new challenges and a new landscape of mobilization; emerging in place of hopes for a relatively bloodless and quick conflict was a terrain of incremental and targeted mobilizations, of sustained efforts to access the wealth and supplies of the City and the nation. While the terms of parliament's *Certaine Propositions* remained intact throughout the autumn of 1642, other practical concerns and questions arose: how might parliament's delving roots better tap metropolitan resources? How, more specifically, might Londoners be encouraged to tighten their belts further to lend toward parliament's war in the wake of their already generous giving for Ireland's relief? And how, finally, might those who failed to respond to the *Certaine Propositions* be persuaded – or, perhaps even coerced – into action?

Emerging in the autumn of 1642 were some of the first coordinated efforts between parliament, City leaders, and parochial administrators to move men and money for civil war. These early topographies of mobilization reveal spaces where, on the one hand, concerted and distinct efforts were made to silence Crown loyalists, and where, on the other, novel efforts for assessing and collecting resources from the capital were implemented and streamlined.

Faced with these collective challenges, Londoners began to ponder more critically the costs of war, and indeed soon the merits of engagement altogether. Matters of mobilization thus became less clear as the seasons shifted; the electric excitements of summer gave way to the cooling apprehensions of winter. All the while, divisions continued to intensify so that by the end of the year large segments of London were petitioning for both peace and a renewed and vigorous war. London's belligerents, as we shall see, would meet these challenges head on.

Mayor Pennington, the propositions, and the people

Overseeing collections for parliament's war effort at the Guildhall during the summer were four leading aldermen with close military and financial ties to parliament's cause. They included John Wollaston, a well-respected goldsmith and colonel of the City Yellow regiment who would take up the mayoralty at the end of 1643, John Towse, later colonel of the Orange regiment, John Warner, colonel of the Green regiment, and Thomas Andrews, an important financier of parliament's war effort.[7] As we have seen, both Towse and Andrews had already acted as collectors for the Irish Adventure. Collections were managed by ward, and counted among the collectors was an overwhelming number of military men, including several leaders from the City trained bands. Captains George Langham, Matthew Sheppard, and Richard Hacket, for instance, made up a third of the collectors from Vintry Ward. Three of the seven collectors in Cheap Ward were also captains, including William Underwood, Edmund Harvie, and Randall Mainwaring, an activist, agitator, and dedicant of war who was later promoted to colonel.[8] Three of the thirteen collectors in Farrington Without were also captains, including Browne, Cuthbert, and Camfield. Captain Robert Mainwaring (Randall's brother) was counted among the seven collectors in the small ward of Cripplegate Without, while Captain Caleb Cockroft served in the same capacity in Coleman Street. All said, at least twenty-one of the collectors in London's central wards were also captains, a dynamic which certainly helped to characterize the task at hand.[9]

London MPs led the charge to donate by example. Captain John Venn agreed to give £100 and a horse; Alderman Pennington pledged £200; Alderman Thomas Soame, a longtime opponent of the Crown, supplied two horses fully equipped for war.[10] Like their London counterparts, other MPs pledged copiously, offering up what they could in terms of weapons, plate, horses, and even fully outfitted riders. On 10 June, John Pym agreed to outfit two horses and give £100 in plate or coin; William Waller offered to bring in four horses and £100; Arthur Goodwin pledged four horses and £100; Henry Marten agreed to bring in and maintain six horses.[11] Sir Arthur Heselrig, whose substantial wealth allowed him to raise and outfit his own troop of London soldiers, provided sixteen horses valued at £200. Although their contributions were at times more modest, other parliamentarians were no less forward in their support. Sir Robert Harley gave two horses, "one bay geldinge with a bald face and one fleabitten gelding" that were together valued at £18 5s. Sir Philip Skippon, who enjoyed a considerable annuity of £300 from the City, gave "one grai gelding with a hackney sadle and bridle" worth £8. One of Pym's two horses turned out to be an impressive "bright bay horse" valued at £15. Peers, as could be expected, pledged on average far more than MPs. The earl of Holland, for instance, "registered thirty faire horses" worth £1,200, while the earl of Essex gave "twenty horses" and "riders" worth a total of £560, a fitting show of support from the future Lord General. Viscount Mandeville paid for "tenn horses" and "their Riders" worth some £380. Lesser means obviously made for smaller contributions. Viscount Saye and Sele, no matter his commitment to the cause, pledged horses valued at £147.[12] All said, 150 members from the two Houses pledged nearly 200 horses and more than £8,000 – offerings that might also inspire Londoners to give liberally toward the cause.[13]

Remaining in the way of collections was Lord Mayor Richard Gurney. Gurney's loyalism was well known and widely commented upon by contemporaries, but the extent of his commitment was not brought into full focus until 10 June, the same day that the *Certain Propositions* became available in print, and when, more importantly, Gurney agreed to issue the king's Commission of Array.[14] In less than a month, a coterie of radical common councilors made their move in the shape of a petition calling for Gurney's removal and replacement with someone of clearer "integrity." Official impeachment proceedings began on 5 July. On 9 July, a group of sixty-six councilors lodged their complaints against the Lord Mayor, who in a moment of frustration stormed away from the day's meeting carrying the City's sword, which along with its partner mace stood as symbols of the office and its authority. Unsurprisingly, the complaints came from a group of leading activists, including Randall Mainwaring, John Venn, Owen Rowe, Theophilus Riley, Richard Turner, Thomas Brightwell, and Richard Warner.[15] Two days later, Gurney was "brought in a delinquent" and committed to the Tower.[16] Within a month a Common Hall was called for a new election; John Wollaston and Isaac Pennington were nominated, with the latter being chosen under the expectation that the prior would become mayor the following year.[17] Had the selection gone in the opposite direction – had Wollaston, in other words, been nominated to be mayor first – London's wartime mobilization would have taken a remarkably different course. On 17 August Gurney's house was ransacked, so that all of the mayoral effects, including swords, a "capp of maintenance," the "Collar of Esses," and the "greate mace belonging to the City" were passed on to Pennington, who signed his receipt for the goods as "mayor elect."[18]

In the months that followed, Pennington came into his full capacity as London's leading proponent of the war effort against the king. Charles and his allies were quick to point out that his rise to the mayoralty did not follow regular procedure and that he was therefore "the pretend Lord Mayor" or "usurper Major."[19] Others, meanwhile, noted his close connections to leading members of the war party in parliament, and the hope that he might flee the kingdom.

> New-England is preparing a pace
> To entertaine King Pym, and his grace,
> And Isaac before him shall carry ye Mace
> For Roundheads old Nick stand up now.[20]

Pennington's name soon became synonymous with mobilizing efforts. Another contemporary song shifted seamlessly between mockery of parliament's military leadership to ridicule of Pennington's efforts to goad citizens:

> Then prithee good Essex forbeare
> and leave these valiant fitts,
> And warne Isaack Pennington Mayor
> To tie up his warlick Citts.[21]

Indeed, Gurney's fall marked a critical turning in London's relationship to the war. More than an opportunity to streamline donations, Gurney's replacement cleared the way, as Lindley has suggested, "for enlisting the resources of the City for war." For Pearl, Pennington's election to the mayoralty "by the City parliamentary puritans" marked a turning point in efforts to mobilize the metropolis.[22] From August onwards, Pennington focused indefatigably on ways in which he could coerce London into supplying parliament's war effort. Rather than simply promote voluntary giving toward the cause suggested by the *Certain Propositions*, the new Lord Mayor issued precepts and approved ordinances. Indeed, over the coming year, Londoners would encounter an unprecedented series of assessments, loan requests, and calls for open participation in the construction and maintenance of City fortifications. In many cases these bore the italicized signature of the Lord Mayor.

Elsewhere, preparations for war continued. On the afternoon of 2 July, the Commons adjourned until Monday so that members could walk to the nearby Tothill Fields to view 800 mounted soldiers who were "very well appointed with Pistolls and Carbines" and had been "voluntarily raised neere and about London" and were "to be at an houres warning for the good and safety of the Kingdome."[23] While efforts to remove Mayor Gurney were under way, parliament forwarded a proposal to the Common Council for "speedily" raising 5,000 "in the City of London." These new forces, which would make up half of the 10,000 they hoped to raise in total, would receive payments of "eight pence by the day" and be made "ready to ma[r]ch into any part of the kingdome."[24] The speed with which Londoners responded bred a sense of optimism among proponents of the war. "We have the City and we have the hearts of the people," exclaimed Henry Marten. The people, he went on, "are ready whensoever we shall hold up our finger."[25] While staying in Covent Garden, Arthur Goodwin reported buoyantly that "a multitude of Volunteers" had flocked to join Essex in Moore Fields, and that the throng professed to "live and dye with him." Londoners, "they say," were preparing to "raise 5000 men for him, and will maintaine them for 3 months at their owne charges."[26] Two weeks later, Goodwin was entrusted to lead sixty-three horses for parliament.[27] According to *A Perfect Dirunall*, "neere upon 3000" men had gathered at the Artillery Garden by the afternoon of Thursday, 28 July, to serve under Essex.[28] Many more apparently arrived by the end of the weekend. When recalling "how forward and active the *Londoners* were to promote this Rebellion," William Dugdale, who may well have been present to witness matters first-hand, estimated that there were some "five thousand" who had enlisted "themselves under the Earl of Essex" at Moore Fields on 26 July. By the start of August, the number of "voluntiers, then in readiness" had expanded "to near ten thousand men, being forthwith committed to Officers and distributed into Regiments."[29] London's volunteer army had coalesced within a matter of weeks. Together with the trained bands, some 20,000 soldiers had mobilized.

Londoners meanwhile continued to give according to their ability. Captain Robert Mainwaring gave £140 9s for "divers" things needed to outfit soldiers in September and October, including "ash elme and beech timber," blankets, locks, candles, wages to pay for a drummer, and enough to outfit thirty men for twenty-four days.[30] Alderman Thomas Andrews pledged to outfit a rider and a horse valued at £26.[31] Records extending from October 1642 to July 1643 provide numerous other examples when money and supplies were collected for the "horse and Armes listed under severall Captaines of the Cittye of London." The months from October to December are particularly well documented, revealing the forwardness with which "middling sorts" of Londoners gave toward the cause. On 11 October, the pewterer Edward Heath "listed one gray gelding furnished with a Carbine, a Case of pistols, a buffe Coate a sword" that were together valued at £24 and sent on to serve in Captain Washborne's regiment. On the following day, James Melcott, a dyer, met with commissioners "att the blackbow nere Paulswharfe in Thamestreet" to contribute "one gray trotting gelding furnished with a Carbine pistols, buffe Coate & sword" which were also valued at £24. One "Rushwroth, Esq." – likely the parliamentarian lawyer and historian John Rushworth – met with commissioners "att the goldenbale in Sheerelane" to give a "bright bay horse with a starr" that was valued at £14. The horses brought in by Melcott and Rushworth were destined to serve under Richard Browne of the Orange regiment. Thomas Andrews, High Sheriff of London, gave an "able white and gray pied gelding" that was fully equipped with a rider, Thomas Jones, and "armed with a sadle and furniture, a Carbine a case of pistols, a buffe Coate & a sword." These were together valued at £27 and sent on to be used by Captain Mainwaring.[32] Andrew Kendrick, a Mercer from Coleman Street, furnished a "dapple gray gelding" with pistols and arms for Skippon that were valued at £22, while the skinner Richard Bateman provided the same with two horses and arms valued at an impressive £60.[33]

London's women were equally forward when it came to giving for the cause. On 22 October, Ann Sacheverill of Aldergate Street "listed two bay horses" and riders "armed with Carbines, pistols, buffecoates, and swords" and valued at £60. Elizabeth Fant, Sacheverill's neighbor, gave horses on numerous separate occasions; she initially gave one bay gelding and equipment worth £25 and an additional two bay horses and goods worth £65. Both Sacheverill and Fant returned to the cause on 28 October; Sacheverill offered two more horses worth £50 and Fant gave two more with equipment worth an additional £60. Sacheverill gave another £74 worth of horses and equipment on 31 October, and another £60 on 3 November; her individual contributions thus reached a value of at least £244. On 7 November, commissioners recorded a joint contribution from both Sacheverill and Font, who as "widdowes listed two black browne geldings, one bay baled gelding and one gray gelding their riders Armes compleate" worth £108. Fant returned yet again to give horses worth £48 on 8 November. The widows had given more toward parliament's cause than Pym and a number of other parliamentary leaders. Indeed, City women were pledging up significant sums elsewhere. On 28 October, Mary Coxe of Coleman Street donated a white gelding and equipment worth £12, while on 22 November one Sara Bridges gave "one white fleabitten gelding" valued at £18.[34] One account book ultimately reveals 323 separate occasions between October and December 1642 when horses and arms worth a total of £7,576 16s were transferred to parliament.[35] Londoners of middling and substantial means remained highly active in their support of the cause; it might be assumed with some reason that other account books reveal similar levels of commitment.

Countless other inhabitants made modest but nevertheless important contributions to parliament. Preachers, for instance, sometimes put their money where their mouths were. "Doctor [Cornelius] Burges of Watford" provided "one brown bay gelding" valued at £18 to parliament's cause on 31 October.[36] Burgess had already forwarded the substantial sum of £700 between 3 March and 19 July toward the Irish Adventure.[37] Numerous single donations arrived in the wake of the *Certain Propositions*, and much of what came in was from people who might be counted among the City's "lower sorts." Writing some years after the war, William Dugdale recalled that the extent of contributions could "hardly be imagined" with "people of all sorts pouring out their Treasure, as if it had been for the most advantageous purchase in the world; throwing in with their Plate and Rings; and not sparing their very Thimbles and Bodkins."[38] Clarendon described a scene in which the treasurers at Guildhall could not keep up with the "vast proportion of plate that was brought in." Wollaston and his colleagues had "hardly enough men" to keep up with the money that arrived over the span of ten days in June. It soon became apparent that they also lacked a sufficiently large enough "room to lay it in."[39] When assessing parliament's ability to wage and win the war, Bulstrode Whitelocke concluded that success was owed due to "the indeavours of sundry Ministers and others," and the many "poore women" who gave up their "their wedding rings and bodkins."[40]

Fielding and maintaining an army were costly affairs. After initial rounds of contributions were made, and indeed as personal finances depleted, proponents of war turned their attention from money to commodities. Londoners brought in sundry goods that were deemed either useful or of value. Thomas Hall, for instance, brought £10 7s 4d worth of wooden mallets, cases, lanterns, and even "50 trunkess for fireworks."[41] Goods from ladles to tongs were collected and forwarded, each in its own way to become a part of the apparatus of war. Others, meanwhile, turned their attention to caches that could be sequestered. Unsurprisingly, bishops' estates made enticing targets. William Laud recalled the arrival of "Captain Royden and his company" at Lambeth on the evening of 19 August. The men "stayed there all Night, and searched every Room." When "any Key was not ready," the soldiers would "brake open Doors." Their efforts proved fruitful; by "the next Morning they carried … Arms away in Carts to [the] *Guild-Hall*." Laud was relieved to conclude that they made off with "not enough for Two Hundred" arms, a mere fraction of what would be needed to outfit the "Ten Thousand Men" proposed for parliament's army.[42] Londoners were prepared to support the cause by any means possible.

Apart from the 5,000 volunteers raised for Essex, it was also hoped that the City might maintain a steady stream of new recruits. On 2 September the Common Council, headed by Pennington, agreed to raise two regiments of foot, a total of 2,400 men, four troops of horse consisting of a total of 240 horses and riders, and additional officers. "It is very probable," claimed councilors on 2 September, "that the Inhabitants of the said Citty will cheerfully subscribe to lend money and Plate upon the Proposicions beside what they have done already."[43] Collections, as we have seen, had been under way since early June, and there was little to suggest that Londoners' enthusiasm was flagging.

On 13 September, a letter from Essex reached Common Council in which he requested that the City, which had shown outward "affection both to the cause, and to my selfe" might consider loaning £100,000 to help "bring this busines to a quick and happy conclusion." After some "serious Consdieracion," councilors agreed that the "iminent danger" to the City merited action and they therefore ordered that Londoners should be called upon to subscribe again according to parliament's propositions so that those who had "not allreadye contributed" to the cause might do so and that those who already did might "inlarge their Subscriptions."[44] Four days later, on 19 September, parliament's propositions were ordered to be reprinted as *Certain Propositions of Both Houses of Parliament, concerning the raising of Horse, Horsmen and Arms* along with "instructions concerning the same."[45] The collection proved to be an unqualified success. The entire loan, as Ben Coates has pointed out, was raised "in just four days," a remarkable feat for the times.[46] The ability to raise £100,000 in so short a time remains a testament to the popularity of the cause and the efficiency of the machinery of the City and the state. Days later, the newsbook *Speciall Passages* reported that "two wagons laded with money went from the Guildhall" on "to his Excellency" the Lord General. So much "plate and money comes still very fast to Guild-hall," *Speciall Passages* went on, that it was fortunate that "great heaps of money and Plate do not decay."[47] London's ability to finance war seemed boundless.

Livery companies and the politics of lending

Deteriorating relations between the king and parliament did little to change the fact that Ireland's Protestants were in need of aid and by June 1642 it was clear that another large sum of money would be needed to help fund a relief expedition. London's livery companies seemed a natural answer to the problem. Wealthy and politically independent, the City guilds had long served the Crown with loans at times of need.[48] As recent as October 1640, £50,000 was demanded by the king as an emergency loan until the Long Parliament could meet. With the king gone, parliament turned to the companies in early June to request a loan for Ireland. In one of his final acts as Lord Mayor, Richard Gurney called a Common Hall for 2 June and issued orders for City livery companies to meet at their respective halls on the following Tuesday at two o'clock in the afternoon.[49] Once gathered, companies were expected to read out orders and instructions for the collection of a loan of £100,000. Each company was assessed according to their stores of grain and promised repayment at the standard rate of 8 percent per annum, which was guaranteed by "public faith." Nearly all companies paid forward what they could out of their own resources, but many could not immediately fulfill their assessments, and subsequently borrowed from company members at various rates of interest. London's twelve great companies were assessed the lion's share of the £100,000, leaving the City's other companies to contribute the remaining sums proportionately.[50] Collections, which took place over two months before the outbreak of civil war, reveal dynamics of London's contentious political landscape; much less a clear-cut matter of supplying a loan to assist the king and parliament for Ireland's recovery, it soon became apparent that the loan might instead be used to help parliament in their incipient struggle against the king.

Gauging the political outlooks of livery companies is notoriously difficult. Like London's many parochial communities, livery companies were politically heterogeneous and included members with a wide range of political, financial and religious concerns. As guilds, companies maintained numerous prescribed working relationships between masters and apprentices who lived both inside and outside of the City's walls.[51] Financial matters remained paramount for most, and stemming from these matters came closely related questions about status, reputation, and precedent. While the political affiliations of particular companies were not always clear-cut, there were occasions when majority votes, or proclaimed concerns, might be taken to suggest political leanings. But again, untangling politics from the often coded language of precedent and procedure can be difficult. Ironmongers, for instance, were the only company to "resolutely refuse" their portion of the October 1640 loan to Charles, a move that might seem to suggest that they were as concerned over the circumstances of the loan as they were with breaking precedent set by their peers. Yet later that year they agreed to pay a reduced sum. It was again "only by absolute compulsion" that the company agreed to loan £3,400 for Ireland in 1642.[52] Their concerns might obviously be assumed to be less about politics than they were about finances.

Nevertheless, parliament's request for £100,000 on the eve of civil war affords some moments in which we might confidently gauge the political leanings of London's companies. This is foremost due to the fact that the loan which was ostensibly requested for the relief of Ireland was, in fact, upon the outbreak of war, diverted to pay for parliament's war against the king. In the transition from a unified effort to relieve Protestants in Ireland – which gained widespread support from both loyalists to the Crown and future supporters of parliament's war effort – to the start of civil war at home, London's livery companies were presented with unique occasions when they could make explicit statements about their views about lending. In the language of their answers we find a sort of quiet and coded opposition not only to the rules of precedent, but also to parliament's purposes.

The speed with which companies responded to the orders for money varied significantly. Wardens from the Grocers' Company, for instance, immediately agreed that the "summe of 9000¹ should be lent by this company for and towards the defence and relief of that distracted kingdome of Ireland," and paid their entire loan on 14 June.[53] Fishmongers, meanwhile, "assented unto" the precept "from the right honorable Lord Maior of this Citty" that called for the "raysinge" of £6,200 and was "assented unto by the Liverey of the Severall Companyes of this City att the Common hall."[54] Fishmongers, as Lindley has suggested, were one of several companies that raised "objections" to the loan.[55] They nevertheless paid in parts, sending £2,200 on 25 June, £1,000 on 1 July, £1,000 the next day, £800 on 8 July, and another £700 on 4 August. The payment of £5,700 of their £6,200 assessment seems to have appeased collectors well enough.[56]

Matters of precedent afforded a direct means for voicing objections. Early complaints therefore made mention of the method of the request for the loan; having come to companies by way of a parliamentary request to Common Hall, the loan did in fact break with previous examples. Wardens from the Drapers' Company were assessed £7,500, and on 10 June they recorded that "it was thought fitt for this time by this assembly not to deny but to condescend to the perfomance of the furnishing of the foresaid" loan, but they made note that "they doe utterly protest and disavowe" to "the manner of the grant made by the Com[mon]hall." But there were other issues at play. The company also made note of the "divers ... members of the howse of Commons [who] came in person to this Company for the furthering and effecting of the said business of the loan."[57] Lacking the £7,500 of their assessment, the Drapers made requests for loans from their own members at rates that sometimes surpassed the standard 8 percent. George Garrett, the company's master, was promised £32 on his £400 by 20 June 1643. Yet other loans were made at far less favorable rates. Alderman Thomas Adams expected £1,500 for his loan of £1,080, a return of 28 percent, while Thomas Arthur was promised £400 for his contribution of £270, a staggering return of 32.5 percent. Accounts show that the company intended to return a total of £9,730 for loans of £6,902 made by forty-seven members. Concern over the debt led the Drapers to forego "their lardge Feasting upon" the "election of new M[ayo]r and wardens," which was normally a time of considerable celebration.[58] Their unprecedented efforts nevertheless allowed them to raise their full portion of the loan by 17 June.[59]

After being assessed £3,400, ironmongers took a similar tack to the drapers. "Upon reading" of the Mayor's "letter and ordinance," they fell to "debate" and concluded that they and other "Companies of London ought not for matter of loane for mony to be bound to obye [sic] the order and direction of the Common Hall which hath not bin the custome of antcient tymes." However, they, like the drapers, concurred that they should be "willing to furnish and lend such monye as they Can rayse" for the sake of providing "aide and assistance" to "the Parliament."[60] Six members of the company agreed to immediately lend £1,100 toward the relief of Ireland. By the middle of the month their records show that they had only raised an additional £600 toward their total assessment. Parliament issued an additional order in July asking that funds be paid forward due to the "generall and urgent necessitie of Ireland" and to see "the Rebells subdued." A terse entry in their accounts shows that they acquiesced to the orders on 29 July, agreeing that "the some [sic] of £2,400" would be paid into the Guildhall "according to the said order for the service of Ireland only."[61] The money was delivered three days later with the stipulation that the funds should be limited to use for campaigns in "Ireland only," a condition which suggests their growing awareness and concern that the money might be used elsewhere. The company did not pay in their final £1,000 until 6 October.[62]

Vintners followed suit, stipulating that their loan was made under the conditions, "given not as bound thereto by that generall consent or com[mon]hall at the guild-hall but of the freewill of the company for relefe of a supply of the urgent necessities of the kingdome of Ireland." By 1 July they had delivered in £2,500 from loans made by twenty-nine company members, which amounted to only half of their £5,000 assessment.[63] Following Gurney's arrest, money came in much more slowly. As a result, parliament took matters into their own hands, issuing a new request for the payment of their outstanding loan. On 23 July, the company agreed under pressure to pay the remaining half, but collections went very slowly, with a final payment of £1,000 made on 15 September.[64] Although they were ultimately more compliant than the Vintners, Mercers ran into similar problems when attempting to pay their £6,500 assessment. The company had already sent off "two peeces of Iron Ordinance" to be used "for the relief of London Derry."[65] Parliament responded to their slow payments with a letter requesting money "forthwith" unless they hoped to watch the "great army" for Ireland "be disbanded, & the kingdone indangered."[66] This appears to have had the desired effect since the company sent in their full £6,500 no later than 23 July.[67]

By 27 June, Goldsmiths had paid £5,700 for their assessment of £7,000. Members debated about the remaining £1,300 and whether or not they "should paye in the rest & accomplish their full com[mitment]e or deferr the payement longer." Once again, they considered the state of their fellow livery companies, noting that "the Mercers Ironmongers nor Clothworkers" had not "paid any parte of their allottment towards the Loane." In the end, they determined that it would be best to pay the remaining £1,300 in order to "protect the leave of the said 7000l."[68] The final £1,300 was paid in on

22 July.⁶⁹ Other pressing matters were at hand. Around the same time that debate was under way about what to do about the final portion of their loan, liverymen agreed to admit "Captaine John Bradley of the Citty of London" to consider whether or not their granary at Bridewell might provide a fitting place to store gunpowder for parliament's use. Several other companies had already agreed to store powder for parliament, but in the wake of the violent protests of the previous winter, and in light of their hall being in a place "more dangerous for the Citty to dispose of such a quantity of powder," the Goldsmiths decided to offer their granary "gratis w[i]thout any rent or reward."⁷⁰ Loaning money was, in their case, just one of several compounding pressures surrounding a conflict that had begun to spill over from Ireland into England.

Several companies had already agreed to help Ireland by other means. On 3 May, the Haberdashers' Company was ordered to lend 770 quarters of wheat for an expedition across the Irish Sea. In June, the company noted that they were "not furnished with mony" to pay their £7,700 assessment.⁷¹ "Severall members of the Company" made loans so that they could pay the outstanding £700 of their assessment by 7 July.⁷²

The Salters' Company, one of four liveries that Lindley identified for taking issue with the loan, "unanimously conceived and consented" that £4,800 "was fitt to bee lent." Prior to lending cash they were apparently "pleased to furnish & bestow a peece of Ordnance to bee sent for the Irish service."⁷³ They sent their full £4,800 on to parliament on 27 June. Skinners, likewise, paid their "proportion of 4200l" on 23 June with no record of opposition.⁷⁴ The reluctance shown by individual members was seldom enough to prevent compliance.

Merchant Taylors were apparently hampered in their efforts to raise £10,000, the largest sum assessed to any company. Nigel Sleigh-Johnson's detailed study of the company reveals that they initially paid £7,000, but that they then just barely "scraped together" an additional £600 over the five following weeks. It was not until August when Alderman Abraham Reynardson, the company's master, pledged £2,400 that the company could finally claim to have paid in full.⁷⁵ Lump sums of £1,200 were paid on 13 August and again on 22 August.⁷⁶ Reynardson's loan, which was made after the outbreak of war, may have owed as much to his desire to see the company avoid trouble as it did for his realization Ireland's troubles had come closer to home.

Clothworkers did little to hide their opposition to their £5,500 assessment. After they failed to respond to the Common Hall's orders, parliament wrote to them directly, demanding that they come to Westminster "to attend the Commons in Parliament" so that they might "retorne" an "answere." Marmaduke Rawdon, a leading merchant and later royalist colonel, was sent on as the company's representative. His reply left little to be gleaned about the Clothworkers' sentiments regarding the loan: "That the Company did never yett Inscribe to lend the said proporcion of 5500¹ neither doth this Company Conceive that they are bound to lend the same." "Nevertheless," he went on, should parliament produce some legal grounds for the loan, then the company would stand "ready to yeild all possible assistance for the raisinge of the same with all Convenient speede." Exacerbating matters was the arrest of Mayor Gurney, a veteran of some forty years with the company. The stalemate finally broke on 24 August when "the Beadle of the Livary of this Company" received orders to "repaire to" the houses of liverymen in order to "request them forthwith to bring their moneyes to the Hall."[77] Intimidation made for a limited success. On 6 November, the company paid a final sum of £120 "in further part of" their assessment, making their total payment £2,120 of £5,500.[78]

All said, the twelve great companies paid a total of £76,800, a substantial part of the £100,000 total assessed to City liveries. £23,200 remained to be raised by London's other guilds. Although company records outside of the twelve tend to be less robust, they nevertheless tell a similar story of precedential deference, limited recalcitrance, and coercion. Smaller loans were, on the whole, more easily collected and paid. Glaziers, for instance, paid their small assessment of £80 on 14 June. Waxchandlers paid their £250 the following day.[79] Cordwainers "consented unto" and paid their loan of £100 on 17 June.[80] On 10 June, a proposed loan of £170 was "assented unto by all of the livery" of the Turners' Company. The money reached collectors on 1 July.[81] Assessed the relatively small sum of £200, Blacksmiths "paid unto the chamber of London" by 16 June. Four members paid £50 each, enough to cover the entire loan.[82] Three members of the Painters-Stainers raised the entire £150 loan.[83] Likewise, four plumbers paid £50 each, enough to cover £200 of their company's £250 assessement.[84] The ability of some wealthy members to pay the majority of assessments did not mean that companies were altogether free from financial strain.

Like the twelve "great" companies, several of the smaller liveries experienced difficulties raising money. Saddlers gave £20 "to the poore protestants in Ireland" in March, well before they were assessed £1,200 in June. Wardens agreed to pay £1,000 and immediately ordered that £100 "worth of plate" was to be sold to help pay the loan. The remaining £900 was borrowed directly from members. Edward Cropley loaned £500, while Thomas Potter gave £200 and William Pease and Josua Sheppard stepped in to provide £100 each.[85] Their full £1,200 was not paid until 15 September.[86] Wardens from the Tallow Chandlers' Company agreed to pay "the whole 1300l imposed upon this Companie by the Lord Maiors precept." Like many others, they were forced to turn to the largesse of individual lenders. £700 was raised by one John Woods upon the mortgage of property in Bankside, but the company found it difficult to raise the remainder, with only "small summes of money" coming in. They nevertheless delivered £1,000 of their £1,300 "into the Chamber of London" on the afternoon of 21 June. Their final £300 reached collectors on 5 July.[87] Orders were next made for the entire company to gather at their hall on 20 July to hear parliament's ordinance read aloud. An abysmal turnout followed with "a verie small appearance of the livere" that included "but five in nomber."[88] Tilers and Bricklayers appear to have avoided their assessment of £250 entirely by agreeing to appear at a "generall Court soe to bee called" at an unspecified date.[89] If they did attend, there appears to be no record of the session. In the end, companies paid what they could. Precedent, as we have seen, remained the main impediment to lending.

Yet a far more distressing matter came into view on 28 July, when the parliament's newly established Committee of Safety sent a letter to the Committee for the Irish Adventurers to request that they consider "publick necessity" and "if it may bee spared from the present and urgent affayres of Ireland," that they would be willing to "Loane One hundred thousand pounds for the defence of ye King Parliament and Kingdome upon the publick faiyh." The letter contained the signatures of several high-profile committee members and wartime activists such as Bedford, Essex, Saye and Sele, Sir Philip Stapleton, John Hampden, William Waller, Denzil Holles, and Holland. Remarkably, their request was approved.[90] Thus, £100,000, which had been stipulated for the use of Ireland, was made available for war in England. News of the transfer doubtless did little to ease the nerves of lenders who had hoped to make sure that their money would be used for "the effectuall reducing of the Kingdom of Ireland."[91] Indeed, this eleventh-hour development may help to explain why the Ironmongers used their 29 July letter to specify that their loans should be used "for the service of Ireland only." Likewise, we might speculate that this move motivated wardens from the Vintners to stipulate that their loans be used for the "supply of the urgent necessities of the kingdome of Ireland."[92] Between the arrest of Gurney, and the appropriation of £100,000, loyalists had just grounds for apprehension.

More reason to pause came in August. Besides evidence of earlier contributions of money, arms, corn, and ordnance, London's companies had organized to pay for their own martial representatives who would serve in Ireland. Captain Thomas Church, who acted as "agent in Ireland" for the Ironmongers' Company, petitioned in August to ask that the leading twelve companies might "worke with ye Parliament" to make sure that he should "receive the arreres due unto him for service done in Ireland in the raysing arming & mainteyning 200 foote & 50 horse." If parliament could not pay his arrears, he hoped liveries might intervene and "leave him" the

£167 16s 2½d "which he oweth the Company & their Accociates."[93] After some consideration, Mercers agreed that he should be paid his arrears; on 19 August, "the Associate Companies" forwarded funds.[94] Naturally, this raised further questions about what, exactly, would be done with the £100,000 loan. Should companies still be expected to pay for intervention in Ireland, regardless of the large sums that they had agreed to raise by order of the Lord Mayor and parliament? Further, what, exactly, would be done with the money that was already paid? These questions were complicated further on 22 August when Charles I raised the royal standard at Nottingham.

Parliament all the while continued to exert pressure on uncooperative companies. By December, London's liveries had paid in £91,770 of the £100,000.[95] The few companies that still owed money – and now only ostensibly "for suppressing the Rebells in Ireland" – were dealt with by a new Committee for the Advance of Money, which was established in late November and, as we shall see, was concerned foremost with assessing and extracting money from individuals for parliament's use. With £3,380 of their £5,500 assessment outstanding, the Clothworkers' Company had the most "monies yet unpaid." Smaller sums were in arrears from the Barber Surgeons, the Painter-Stainers, the Masons, the Plumbers, the Founders, the Cooks, the Tilers and Bricklayers, the Scriveners, the Brownebakers, the Inbraiders, the Musicians, and the Girdlers.[96] On 6 December, orders were issued so that "the officers of the severall halls" might "take the best and speediest course they can for the bringing in of these arrears." Two days later, the Committee for the Advance of Money ordered Vintners to bring £1,500 "before Monday next in the Afternoone or otherwise appeare before the said Committee."[97] Records of payments fizzle at this point, suggesting that the remaining sum may have been forgiven. Doubtless, the companies without outstanding payments remained under the scrutiny of parliament's new committee.[98]

Significant changes had taken place between the time when the company loan for Ireland was first proposed and collected. Not least was Mayor Gurney's ejection and replacement Pennington, the outbreak of war, and the implementation of new influential parliamentary wartime committees. With these major changes and political realignments, parliament gained unprecedented access to the resources of London's livery companies. By giving in to parliament's demands, and thus ultimately breaking with precedent, companies ensured that they would remain instrumental components of wartime finance. For the next two years, parliament, working in close cooperation with City leaders, would repeatedly turn to livery companies in order to fulfill wartime financial and military needs. As we shall see, lending on the scale demanded by parliament not only hampered daily company operations, but it eventually drove some companies to the brink of insolvency.[99]

With cash secured, attention next turned to the implements of war. On 25 August, Lord Saye, Lord Wharton, Sir Gilbert Gerard, and John Glynne delivered a new message from the Committee of Safety to Common Council regarding their pressing need for the "sinewes of Warr." They praised "the forwardnesse and assencion of the Cittye of London" for following the *Certain Propositions*, but they also wished to make them aware of the "6000 Musketts" that they hoped for daily, but which apparently remained "beyond the Seas." In the meantime, parliament's new recruits could neither drill in the capital, nor hope to march out against their enemies. It was thus the Committee of Safety's hope "that the Citty would lend unto them 6000 Musketts and 4000 Pikes to furnish the forces who are Presently to march with the Lord Generall." All that could be raised, they assured, would be assessed so that the "vallew thereof should be returned unto the owners as they shall think fitt." Common Council agreed immediately, and Mayor Pennington next issued requests as precepts that were printed and delivered to London's wards.[100]

Livery companies were once again expected to play a part. The descent into open war doubtless added a sense of exigency to the lending process. Some companies were again quick to respond, but others moved more cautiously, waiting to observe the actions of their peers. Drapers copied out Mayor Pennington's precept and request for what "may be spared towards ye making upp of ten thousand armes whereof there to be sixe thowsand musketts and fower thowsand Cosletts."[101] Having noticed that the "Fishmongers had allready condescended unto the furnishing & delivering in of one hundred and fifty armes," wardens from the Drapers' Company agreed on 30 August to offer "forty Cosletts & pikes and Threescore Musketts furnished out of the Companies armes."[102] Likewise, in light of their observation that "many of the Companies of this City have already out of their store furnished good quantities," the Haberdashers' "Court being unwilling to be behind," decided to loan "one hundred armes." The eagerness with which they hoped to emulate their peers was apparent; on 3 September, Haberdashers readily agreed to have "the said M[aste]r and wardens" inspect and "make up the said number."[103] Grocers decided the same day to lend "twenty muskets and forty pikes and Corslets," stipulating that they expected "the sure returne of the same againe indeminished or the like in kind of ye value thereof in money if any shalbee lost or endamaged."[104]

Despite the difficulties that they were experiencing with the loan, Clothworkers concluded that it was "thought fitt and so ordered that there shalbe lent unto the Parliament for their present use Forty Musquetts and Twenty Pykes with Twenty Corsletts and Threescore Swords, Forty payre of Bandiliers and Forty Rests."[105] Receipts were drawn up to ensure that supplies of equal value would be returned to their armory. After the "reading of a Copy" of the precept from Pennington, members of the Mercers' Company agreed to loan "forty musketts and Twenty Corslets" for the "march away with the r[ight] ho[nora]ble the Earle of Essex Lord Generall hereof for the defence & safetie of this Kingdome."[106] Emptying armories to defend the kingdom seems to have been a less controversial matter than raising money to intervene in Ireland.

Like their peers, the Fishmongers had already outfitted forces for Ireland. In April, they equipped sixty men with pikes, helmets, and chest pieces, and another 140 men with muskets, belts, and bandoliers. A member, Mayor Pennington personally attended the 30 August meeting when the company read his precept. Fishmongers subsequently agreed to loan "fifty Pikes Corsetts and headpeeces and one hundred Musketts Belts and Bandeleeres," along with "wormes and Scowrers" for cleaning. Pennington's presence may have influenced members again on the following Thursday when the company agreed to send on an additional 150 arms – fourteen pikes and breastplates, thirty-six muskets, fifty helms, and fifty swords – to the Guildhall "for the service aforesaid." All present, save for one "Mr. Andrewes," agreed that the extra arms should be loaned.[107] Fishmongers thus sent seven hundred items to help equip parliament's new army.

As with cash loans, smaller companies were once again assessed and expected to contribute according to their means. Modest but important contributions came from Brewers who brought "5 Corsletts, 5 Pikes, 5 Swords and 2 Belts, and also 5 Musketts, 5 rests, 5 bandeleers and 5 swords" to the Guildhall on 6 September for use by "the Earle of Essex Lord Generall of the Parliaments Forces."[108] Weavers provided a similar share, delivering in "two new Cosletts with headpeeces and pikes" to outfit two men and "one old Coslet & headpeece with a new pike" to ready another. Three pairs of bandoliers, three muskets and rests, along with six swords, completed the loan. Turners gave twenty-four pieces of armor and arms – enough to outfit six soldiers.[109] If humble by comparison, supplies, like money, nevertheless added up. Shortly after they delivered their arms and armor, turners "ordered that the money which should be spent on the fifth of November" celebrations "shall not be spent but shall be imployed to the buying of arms for the use of the Commonwealth."[110]

Although the quantity of arms and armor loaned remains unknown, it is clear that London's companies played an important role outfitting some of the first armies to take to the field in the fight against the king. The speed with which liveries loaned arms and armor raises a number of questions, not least about the nature of their commitment to the war effort. Whereas Clothworkers had previously expressed concern over the payment of loans that were ostensibly for the relief of Ireland, they did nothing to impede the delivery of arms and armor. This may ultimately indicate that London's livery companies faced predominantly financial, as opposed to political, strains – although it should also be noted, again, that lending of supplies was logistically easier than procuring loans. An equally likely scenario, however, seems to be one in which companies were increasingly brought to heel by the combined efforts of the new Lord Mayor who was working in unison with new parliamentary committees, a testament to the degree to which the alignment of interests in London and Westminster could serve to move the resources of the capital. In agreeing to lend £100,000 along with arms and armor, companies signaled both their compliance and their willingness to set aside precedent. Once completed, corporate loans successfully supplied the requisite cash and supplies needed to field parliament's first armies. Alongside the countless individual Londoners who delivered plate, bodkins, and other offerings to the cause, livery companies had helped to set the stage for war.

Marching out

On Monday, 15 August 1642, a troop identifying themselves only as "London prentices" entered the parish church in the small town of Marsworth, Buckinghamshire. While there they "broke the rayles at the upper end of the Chancill where formerly the Communion Table stood, and beat downe all the painted glass in the windowes." Their efforts did not end there; they soon reached the house of the local minister, Roger Wilford, who they ordered to hand over his "service booke and surpliss." Failure to do so, they warned, would give them reason to "pull down his house over his head." Upon discovering that the book and vestments were not with Wilford, the men turned their attention back to the church, where further searching turned out not one, but two "service books." They "tore" the first book "all to pieces," scattering its leaves "about the streets." They then tore and hoisted the remaining book "upon the pointes of their swords" as trophies. Having finally located the surplice, one Londoner put it on and "marcht away to Alisbury triumphing in contempt and derision." The actions of London's apprentices were by no means unusual. Participants engaged in acts of ritualized iconoclasm that were one part an expression of youthful excitement for war, and another part a well-rehearsed display of godliness. Indeed, behavior like that seen at Marsworth had become commonplace among soldiers marching out from the capital for the first time.[111] The letters of Nehemiah Wharton, an officer who served under Essex in the autumn of 1642 and who frequently wrote home to his master, George Willingham, at the Golden Anchor in St. Swithin's Lane, provides remarkably similar reports of zealous young Londoners looting churches and households to destroy objects deemed "popish" or superstitiously affected. On Tuesday, 9 August, Wharton recalled the pillaging of a home of a "papist" and the enthusiasm with which soldiers "defaced the antient and sacred glased picure and burned the holy railes." On the following day, City soldiers burned altar rails they found in Chiswick. They did the same again at Uxbridge, where they tossed rails and a service book into a bonfire. Wharton's fellow troopers energetically continued their search for "papists" and "malignants" as they marched westward, imposing their metropolitan sensibilities upon what Wharton otherwise took as "the sweetest Country that ever I saw."[112]

Parliamentary chaplains played a part in stoking the fires of iconoclasm.[113] Their eagerly anticipated sermons helped to maintain resolve and, on occasion, perhaps even inspire action. Before burning altar rails on 10 August, Wharton's men took in "a famous sermon" given by "Mr [Christopher] Love," a staunch puritan who would later take up preaching in London at Aldermanbury and St. Lawrence Jewry.[114] By late August, Wharton revealed that he was "exceedingly" hopeful for a fresh "supply of faithfull able ministers."[115] In the coming days, some of London's most capable and celebrated preachers gave their sermons in the field. Obadiah Sedgwick of St. Mildred Bread Street delivered what seemed "a worthy sermon" to the soldiers in September. Sedgwick's preaching was widely anticipated and Wharton recalled that his "company in particular marched to heare him in ranke and file." On the following afternoon, a Saturday, Wharton and his men enjoyed "a famous sermon" by John Sedgwick of St. Alphage in Cripplegate. Also preaching at camp was "Mr Marshall that worthy champion of Christ" and "Mr [Simeon] Ash." Wharton was unable to hear Ashe preach, but he assured his London contact that he hoped to make time to do so. Although there is scant evidence to directly link listening to action, it might still be assumed that effective preaching stood to influence newly fielded Londoners. Love, Marshall, Ashe, Calybute Downing, and both Sedgwicks apparently gave stirring sermons to soldiers who were far away from their homes in the capital. Wharton, for one, maintained "great hopes" for the good achieved by the presence of so many capable parliamentarian preachers. He at one point proclaimed to Willingham that their "sermons" had "subdued and satisfied more malignante spirits amonst us than 1000 armed men could have done."[116]

Capable preachers, Wharton believed, were essential to the success of parliament's mission. Some of the weaker Londoners were said to possess "malignante spirits" that eroded resolve. When called to muster in early September, several soldiers refused outright. Some demanded the payment of five shillings each, revealing what Wharton believed to be "their base ends in undertakinge this designe."[117] But flagging enthusiasm may have owed to any number of issues. Payments quickly fell into arrears, and idealized notions of war were easily dispelled by long days of marching. The autumn campaign, moreover, provided many new soldiers with their first exposure to the horrors of war. A brief skirmish near Coventry cost fifty lives. In addition to the number of the slain, which included "one drummer," were terrible scenes of horses with "their guts beaten out on both sides."[118] Downtime led to drilling that was itself not without risk. While in Worcester in October one soldier mistakenly discharged his rifle and "shot one of his fellow soldiers through the head."[119] Inspired preaching offered welcomed relief to what could be gruesome wartime realities.

But early engagements served another important purpose. Marching out in the autumn also provided many young apprentices with valuable experience, offering familiarity with the sounds of "the drumms beatinge and the Trumpets sounding."[120] Time in the field prepared recruits for later skirmishes, pitched battles, and sieges. Wharton again recalled the trying conditions one night in Warwickshire when it "rained hard" and no shelter could be found. His response, after more than a month of campaigning, gave way to a poetic sympathy for a time when "our foode was fruite for those who could get it [and] our drink water." "Our beds," he went on, were "the earth" and "our canopy the clouds."[121] If a means to expose "malignant spirits," experience also hardened Londoners for the realities of war.

A long-standing commitment to martial practice meant that the capital was already home to some of the best-trained officers in the nation. Although many of the recruits who joined Essex on the march out were inexperienced young apprentices, most were held to the high standards set by their commanders, leaders who had participated in war themselves, or at least had some training. Some parliamentarian commanders brought sensibilities of leadership that were forged in the extreme violence and protracted campaigns of the Thirty Years' War. Philip Skippon, for instance, had earned a reputation for his leadership after serving in both the Palatinate and the siege of Breda. Others had obtained knowhow from years of training in local militias. Problems with pillaging led Lord Brooke, the lord lieutenant of Warwickshire, to proclaim in late August that "whosoever should affront" would face "martiall law."[122] The initial enthusiasm for war shown by many Londoners can, on the one hand, be understood as part of a long history of civil participation in the drilling and pageantry of war, and a popular fascination and familiarity with military culture. London, as David Lawrence has suggested, served as a center for the printing of manuals on military instruction. Consuming such books and pamphlets were members of the City's Honorable Artillery Company and other military clubs, fraternal organizations that served as "incubators of military ideas" and provided spaces "where the gentlemen and merchants of London trained, talked, and eventually wrote about the martial arts."[123] Fashionable military clubs were a fixture of metropolitan life. Although military companies were "scattered through England," and could be found in most large towns and cities, London was unmatched for its ability to provide an "advanced education" in martial training.[124] Interest in "advanced" military matters helped to pave the way for more general booklets and manuals covering the fundamentals of war. In early September 1642, Londoners could obtain *Lawes and Ordinances of Warre*, a booklet for the "better conduct" of soldiers in parliament's armies. The booklets were distributed to troopers and officers with the expectation that they might help to spread order and godliness throughout the ranks of fresh volunteers. *Lawes and Ordinances of Warre* revealed aspects of soldierly conduct that ranged from matters spiritual to practical, and were at times as draconian as they were brief: blasphemers could expect to have their "tongue[s] boared with a red-hot iron," while the display of "armes unfixt of undecently kept" might lead to "arbitrarie Correction."[125] Doubtless these orders kept some from stepping out of line, making readily clear what would be expected and tolerated in the field.

The condition of London's soldiers sometimes contrasted sharply with their provincial counterparts. The latter, as Charles Carleton has suggested, often ranged from being "of value" to "worse than useless."[126] As Tom Cogswell has shown, country musters had devolved into "increasingly casual matters" over the course of the 1630s, so that significant improvements were needed by the 1640s.[127] Buckinghamshire's disorganized and inexperienced troops revealed the scope of the problem when they mustered in preparation for deployment to Ireland in 1642. The solution, Sir Thomas Tyrrell recalled, came with "Mr Cottefore," a military man "from London" who arrived "to discipline the foote."[128] Indeed, the knowledge of war afforded in the metropolis contrasted sharply with what could be found in some counties where inhabitants had become strangers to mustering. From the outset of war, London's commanders demonstrated the benefit of their martial training, achieving early successes as they funneled out of the capital behind Essex in the west and Captain Richard Browne in the southeast. Browne, who royalists often mocked as a lowly born "Woodmonger," ended up a great favorite among Londoners.[129] On 12 October, Mayor Pennington, along with a group of leading sheriffs and common councilors, appointed Browne a captain of a troop of City horse consisting of "threescore horsemen" who were to "muster" regularly and "trayne and Exercise" and be equipped "with Brest, pistoll proofe, Backe and Pott, Carbine, a Case of Pistolls and a sword, all good and serviceable."[130] Browne's popularity persisted throughout the war and by the end of the following year he obtained the rank of major-general. If easily exhaustible, or even obstinate, many London recruits found their place on the battlefield. Their first encounters, which included mostly minor skirmishes and the capture of magazines and arms, won extensive praise in London's press.[131] Larger engagements, like those that took place on 23 August at Southam and Long Itchington, Warwickshire, could be celebrated as decisive parliamentarian successes. These left figures like Colonel Hampden celebrated as a "valiant Champion," and affirmed that Lord Brooke and the parliamentary cause that he supported enjoyed "the protection of God."[132] Such optimism had only to be tempered.

Edgehill and Turnham Green

The first major turning point in the war came on 23 October 1642 near Kineton, Warwickshire. Previous engagements had been small by comparison and left little space for debate over outcome. The long day of fighting at Edgehill, which lasted from the early afternoon until the evening, opened up significant space for interpretation. Londoners undoubtedly played an important part in the battle, serving in regiments under Lord Brooke, Sir Henry Cholmley, Denzil Holles, and Lord Wharton.[133] It was here that they found themselves at the center of the first pitched battle of the civil war, a struggle between what Anthony Fletcher called "a citizen army led by Puritan gentry," and a royalist "army of tenantry led by conservative squires."[134] If ultimately indecisive, with each side losing several hundred men, the outcome of the battle was nevertheless hotly contested; both royalists and parliamentarians were eager to set the record by claiming victory.[135] First reports were hastily printed in London with "ink smudges and typos" on 25 October, just two days after the battle ended. Reports mistook – or perhaps deliberately cast – the day as a parliamentarian victory down to the misreported assumption that Prince Rupert had been captured.[136] A letter, written at two o'clock in the morning and "sent from a worthy Divine to the Right Honourable Lord Ma[yor] of the City of London," arrived two days later and told of parliamentary "valiantnesse" that was so apparent that "every common soldier" could walk away "with the honour of [a] Commander."[137] Days later, a letter addressed to Pym from Holles, John Meldrum, and four other parliamentarian officers was available in print. This offered a more detailed and balanced account of the engagement; yet the author(s) could scarcely resist the need to boast about a Garter badge that was bought for twenty shillings from a "common Souldier" who found it on the field of battle.[138] Another account revealed the importance of London's new recruits. While all but eighty of Cholmley's men "used their heels" and were soon followed by some of Wharton's men, other actions were worthy of praise and celebration. Holles's "red-Coates, under God did most gallant service, every one fighting like a Lion," while Lord "*Brookes* purple-Coats" were the ones who "won the field" that day.[139] No matter the outcome, accounts seemed to confirm what was previously assumed: parliament's commanders and soldiers fought well.

London's preachers reinforced these views with the aid of scripture. Thomas Case weighed in with a fast-day sermon preached to the Commons on 26 October, and in which he drew from Psalm 68:1–2, "*Let God arise, and let his enemies be scattered, let them that hate him, flee before him.*" Although his sermon was not printed until 1644, those who heard it at St. Margaret would have little trouble gleaning that the retreat of the king's forces after Edgehill was the result of God's great awakening – a momentary flight that amounted to the scattering of God's enemies. When the royalist foot broke rank, parliament's army pursued them, so that "the Armies of *God*" could set to "slaying and beating them down with great destruction."[140] Like Lord Brooke's rumored ability to dodge bullets, Case's theme helped to reinforce the growing sense that God's providential favor would see to an eventual parliamentarian victory.

Others, meanwhile, took the news of the battle as an overwhelming confirmation of the need to continue mobilizing. Preaching on the same fast-day as Case, John Goodwin addressed "the Right Honourable the Lord Major, the Sheriffes," and "the worthy Inhabitants of this great and famous City." In his sermon, *The Butchers Blessing*, Goodwin laid out a series of arguments for continuing the fight against "*Romish Cavaliers.*" Goodwin's stated purpose was "to engage you all as one man, to rise up at once in your might, for the preservation and defence of your selves, as of your City, against that whirlewind of cruelty and blood" that had been produced on the king's behalf. If "other parts of the Land have bin punished seven-fold," he went on, then it was clear that "*London* (doubtless) shall be punished seventy times seven fold." Goodwin surmised that there were ultimately five main reasons to maintain the fight. The City was, foremost, "the great Bulwark" and "sanctuary" that had served to protect the kingdom from "prelaticall invasions" that extended well into the past, but had manifested most recently with Ireland. London, he went on, provided "the chiefe protection and safeguard of that Honourable Assembly and Court of Parliament." Third, London served as the metaphorical parent of the nation; all of England looked to the capital for "inward principle" and for "animating others." Fourth, the City acted as a defense against the rise of prelacy, a holdout from "the sweet bread of Romish superstitions and Doctrines." If London fell to the cavaliers they might use the City as "their footstoole" to carry out their "rage and crueltys" and secure other "thrones." The City, Goodwin concluded, acted as the nation's "great Magazine of wealth, riches, & treasure"; it was nothing less than a metaphorical "garden of the *Hesperides*," out of which grew the "golden apples" of immortality. Londoners, "more than all the Kingdome besides," should meditate on how they might "do or give for the advancement of the great service that hath been recommended unto you." Edgehill was not, by Goodwin's auxesis and measure, the first battle of an English civil war; it was instead a much more significant affair in which the inhabitants of a Protestant capital were expected to "rise up" against the dangerous designs of international Catholicism.[141]

On balance, the sermons and reports that came in the wake of Edgehill left Londoners more concerned than relieved. If his concerns were decidedly closer to home, Nehemiah Wallington nevertheless suffered from "many distempered thoughts" on the fast day; in particular, he recalled "the sad newes" from days earlier about the "twenty thousand slaine" at Edgehill.[142] If obviously exaggerated, Wallington's anxieties reveal the sensibilities of a Londoner who had spent the better part of a year anticipating foreign invasions and armed uprisings. Terrible news had become so widespread that one pamphleteer proclaimed "each hour is a herald of homicides, each day a messenger of mischiefs, each week a Diurnall of dangers, each month a Motto of misery."[143] There was no end in sight. On the day after Case and Goodwin preached, parliamentary war-party leaders traveled to the Guildhall to deliver their own rousing speeches in support of mobilization. Wharton, Strode, Pembroke, Holland, and Saye took turns urging London's leaders to consider how they might advance the cause. Saye suggested that each and every Londoner should "shut up his shop" and "take his musket" and "offer himself readily, and willingly" to parliament's war effort. "Remember what was said," he warned ominously, in "*Curse ye Merosh*."[144]

Such dire warnings came amidst more discouraging news. Few things were more disconcerting than reports that followed the royalist attack on parliament's infantry at Brentford, a small town less than ten miles west of London. On the evening of 12 November, reports reached the capital where it was discovered that Prince Rupert had successfully defeated "two of the best Regiments of the Parliaments forces," those of Lord Brooke and Denzil Holles. Their forces were surrounded and scattered, with many drowning "most inhumanely" as they attempted to cross the Thames.[145] Some of the very soldiers who were recently celebrated as "lions" at Edgehill had been either slain or captured. Among those taken prisoner was John Lilburne, the future Leveller who would remain in royalist hands until the following year. Losses were made worse by the fact that they appeared to be avoidable; days earlier, the Committee of Safety had sent a letter to the Lord General in which they expressed their hope that he might deploy cavalry to assist the infantry. Essex's refusal, many assumed, was the main reason for defeat. Worse yet, royalists had opened a direct path to London.[146]

That night, the trained bands "stood all upon their guard and secured the Citie."[147] On the following morning, thousands of Londoners responded by heeding Saye's advice from two weeks earlier; they closed up shops, boarded windows, grabbed what weapons and implements they could find, making their way to Chelsea Field. From here they marched west to stop the king's push toward the capital. By the mid-morning, Londoners had reached Turnham Green, a small town eight miles west of the City. After failing to prevent a crushing defeat at Brentford the previous day, the Lord General ordered his army of 12,000 to march on and rendezvous with the Londoners. Numbers swelled further as reinforcements arrived from the London's trained bands and the trained bands of Essex, Herefordshire, and Surrey. Standing on the field by the afternoon were upwards of 24,000 people, the largest force to ever oppose the king.[148] The trained bands marched out under Philip Skippon's banner, *ora et pugna*, "pray and fight." Bulstrode Whitelocke, who trailed a pike out of the City with Sir John Hampden, recalled first-hand the rousing speech given by Skippon to his soldiers on the field:

> Come my Boys, my Brave boys, let us pray heartily and fight heartily; I will run the same fortunes and hazards with you; remember the cause is for God, and for the defence of yourselves, your wives and children: come, my honest brave boys, pray heartily and fight heartily, and God will bless us.[149]

These words, cast in recognition of fraternity, providential favor, and the preservation of family, would have a lasting impact on the hearts and minds of Londoners. If stirring, Skippon's speech could do little to prepare Londoners for the sight of 13,000 royalist troops. Some who had marched out that day came with little more than household tools, grasping tightly to their spades and rakes. Others were simply unprepared to fight. Whitelocke recalled the "two or 300 horsemen who came from London to be spectators," but turned to flee "as fast as they could ride" when the king's army began shouting out. Their hasty retreat proved discouraging to "the Army & divers of the soldiers" who remained in place. Despondency soon gave way to joy when carts of ale and food arrived from the City. Volunteers, soldiers, and spectators alike were thereby "refreshed & made merry." Rather than risk bloodshed, the king eventually withdrew for Reading, a move that left some Londoners to prematurely assume that they had won the day. Less sure about the result, others nevertheless left with the sense that they had preserved their "honor" and secured "safety enough" for their families and "the parlement."[150] The day thus ended without violence and only a handful of shots fired by some of Essex's men.[151]

Turnham Green did little to advance notions of a swift parliamentarian victory. Rather than finding a day of glory on the battlefield, Londoners partook in hours of posturing and stalemate against an army that was smaller but still sizeable; few doubted that more conflicts lay ahead. Charles ultimately fared little better. Historians readily agree that the king's decision to abandon the field amounted to a decisive moment in the history of the war. Had a battle ensued the war may have ended. Gardiner ultimately saw the day as "the Valmy of the English Civil War," an engagement that was largely bloodless but served to invigorate the parliamentarian cause. Much more recently, Charles Carlton claimed that the king's departure meant that he "lost his best chance of capturing the capital and seizing the rebel's heartland."[152] In retrospect, we can see that the stalemate at Turnham Green provided the king with a highly fraught opportunity, a moment when he had to decide between raising a sword against the inhabitants of his capital city, or departing in hopes that loyalist sentiment would eventually win out. The risk proved too great; none could know it at the time, but Turnham Green would remain the closest Charles I came to London before his capture, trial, and execution.

Clear to participants who lined up that day was the spectacle of a "whole Army of Horse and Foot" that "consisted of above 24,000 Men." The gathering at Turnham Green on 13 November stood out as the single largest mobilization in more than a generation. Far from a sorry sight, one observer recalled seeing "stout, gallant, proper Men, as well habited and armed, as were ever seen in any Army."[153] Beyond simply a matter of "defeating" the king, Londoners had outnumbered his forces by nearly two to one, revealing both their collective size and suggesting their vast potential. Observers would recall the display over the coming years, taking note of the men who were willing to take up arms when "the cause is for God, and for the defence of yourselves, your wives and children." The gathering augured later developments. Militants in both London and parliament would readily point out the size and spirit of the resistance at Turnham Green when proposing new measures for mobilization, using the event as a template for a rising en masse against the king in 1643, and again with measures to remodel parliament's army in 1644 and 1645. Prior to these developments, in the aftermath of Edgehill, Brentford, and Turnham Green, parliament had to tackle the pressing matter of diverging opinions over how best to move forward, both in terms of outcries for peace and fracturing notions of how best to wage war.

London committees, dividing opinions, and the establishment of parliamentarian wartime finance

Whilst thousands of inhabitants engaged in a spectacular display of popular mobilization by closing up shops and marching out to oppose the king on the field of Turnham Green, a group of "gentlemen of the City of *London*" traveled the much shorter distance from the City to "the door" of the House of Commons. They brought with them a petition. Led by "one Mr. [Richard] *Shute*, a Merchant," they revealed their desire to both "speak" and share "a Petition of Ten Particulars" on behalf of "many Thousands" of their fellow Londoners. In light of the pressing matters of the king's recent victory at Brentford and London's subsequent peril, the petitioners proposed the creation of a new army made up of soldiers, "Captains and Officers" who could be trusted to "live and die with the House of Commons, and in the Defence thereof." Such an army, the petitioners went on, would stand ready with "our Persons, Purses and Estates, all at your Command" and to "do with us at your Pleasure."[154]

Taking the matters into close consideration, the Commons invited the "Gentlemen" petitioners to depart and return to the House later in the day. Once back, Shute and his associates clarified their positions, and expressed particular concern over "the Coming of the Lord General's Army into the City of *London*, and staying there so long as they did." The failure at Brentford, they insisted, fell squarely on Essex and his second in command, Sergeant-Major-General Sir John Meyrick. Soon thereafter, parliament appointed a committee to take the petitioners' requests into consideration; having met, the committee forwarded the popular view that Philip Skippon should be appointed as commander of any new "forces" that the "Gentlemen shall raise." Well aware of Skippon's godly disposition and the courage recently shown by London's "brave boys" at Turnham Green, parliament accepted the proposal, making way for a new committee tasked with raising a new volunteer army. Incensed by the threat to his sole leadership as Lord General, Essex at first deliberated only to later agree to appoint Skippon as Sergeant-Major-General at the cost of his close associate, Meyrick; the celebrated leader of London's trained bands was not, then, to become the leader of a newly raised and independent City army, but would instead fall directly under Essex's command. This outcome, which frustrated Shute and his fellow London petitioners, made apparent some of the first cracks that were forming in the parliamentary coalition. With Skippon lost to the controversial structure of parliamentary command, Londoners were forced to look elsewhere for their new army leader.

Taking Skippon's place in the petitioners' estimation was Richard Browne, the one-time "woodmonger" who was to become "Collonell and Commander in Chief" over City Dragoons.[155] It was scarcely a coincidence that Richard Shute found himself at the head of an extra-parliamentary committee tasked with supplying money and supplies for Browne's new position. His fellow committeemen, as David Como has suggested, were "leading city activists" who met at the infamous Nag's Head Tavern on Coleman Street, a space that remained crucial to the committee's operations.[156] The program for raising dragoons appears to have enjoyed moderate success.[157] Browne had already been appointed a "Captaine of one of the fower Troopes of Horse" on 20 October, a position which granted him "such power within the Citty of London" as "the Lieutenants have in the severall Counties." The position came with sixty riders, fully armed and equipped with "breast, pistoll, proofe, backe and pott, carbine, a Case of pistols and a sword."[158] These may have come to use in his new capacity as Colonel and Commander in Chief. Supply contracts and payments reveal that Mayor Pennington was among a group of Londoners who stood behind Browne's efforts. On 13 December, Pennington signed off on a warrant to transfer £3,400 from the City subcommittee for weekly subscriptions "unto Mr Richard Shute."[159] An additional £1,200 reached the committee again by way of the Lord Mayor in January and February.[160]

Pennington and his fellow activists were busy elsewhere. Two days after Turnham Green, the Lord Mayor appointed "a generall Committee" of twenty-seven members who would meet at Weavers' Hall and "collect and receive all such subscriptions" of money and arms that could be raised for a new army. Pennington, as Lindley has suggested, "made sure that like-minded men were appointed" to the committee.[161] Indeed, appointees were selected by ward and of the twenty-seven members, eleven were Irish adventurers and no fewer than nine had, or would soon, play a part in radical metropolitan politics.[162] Robert Sweet, the appointee from Langbourn Ward, went on to be a treasurer for the London sequestration committee the following year; John Bellamy of Cornhill became a member of the City Militia Committee. Vintry Ward's member, William Walwyn, scarcely needs introduction. He later joined the radical committee for the general rising and went on to become a leading Leveller. Hogan Hovell, a grocer from Breadstreet Ward, maintained numerous ties to separatists; Christopher Nicholson of Castle Baynard signed the Lunsford petition and was a prominent root and branch activist; Walter Boothby of Cripplegate was a leading supplier of arms to parliament's war effort; Robert Meade of Walbrook Ward was a radical activist and another promoter of the general rising; John Kendrick of Tower Ward was a known radical and war financer; Lindley notes that Edward Vaughan of Farringdon was engaged as a "radical activist" between the years 1641 and 1642.[163] It stands to reason that other members were engaged on behalf of parliament's cause, even if they left less clear trails of their activities.[164] Accounts from the committee, which predate to cover the month of November, reveal that they had "subscriptions" from 103 parishes that included 1,450 arms, 6,900 men, and 24 horses. These forces would require "weekely pay" of £1,664 15s 4d. By 3 December, the collectors noted being in possession of £1,450 "or thereabouts."[165] Although they held less than a week's worth of money for fielding such a large army, they had nevertheless established "the organizational basis for a monthly tax on the City to support parliament's army." Much more than a short-term solution, their efforts would have significant and lasting implications for parliament's wartime finance and administration.[166]

For the time being, what mattered most was the fact that London's belligerents had implemented urban programs for mobilization. Backed by the Lord Mayor, Richard Shute and his fellow petitioners had successfully established two new committees tasked with recruiting and financing new City forces. Already, then, London's radicals had gained a taste for the successes that could be secured through popular petitioning and agitation – efforts that were almost certainly coordinated and aided by a sophisticated print campaign that spanned from the chambers of Westminster to the streets of London, and which helped, as Jason Peacey has argued, to keep "radical parliamentarianism at the front of people's minds." Importantly, a part of this campaign saw efforts to characterize parliament's new financial expedients as "gentle borrowing" and justified the "disposal" of property in light "of imminent danger," blunted language used to justify novel forms of taxation and forced lending.[167] Although plans to create a new army were of limited scope (and indeed success), the design, which sought to create an army beyond the reach of the Lord General, raised pressing questions about the future shape of parliament's command, about the shape of the cause at hand, and about how the prospect of peace might eventually be handled. Questions of this nature presaged troubles to come.

If only tacitly aware of these matters, London's masses remained eager for news out of the west. Demand was readily met, and readers soon found descriptions of a war that looked dramatically different than their day out at Turnham Green. Holles's report of the battle at Edgehill reached booksellers' stalls in the Middle Temple and Fleet Street on 28 October. Two weeks before the terrible news of Brentford, Londoners read of the "bitter night," the "extreme want of Victualls," and the "push of Pike."[168] News from Kineaton revealed that Essex was forced to abandon "200 miserable maimed soliders," who suffered "without relief of money or surgeons."[169] Two unfortunate "souldiers, there maymend" were left in Warwickshire for years to be cared for "night and day."[170] Other suvivors made their way back to London where they hoped to be cared for by family, find charity, or simply pick up the pieces. After he "lost the use of both his hands in the Battaile att Edgehill," Richard Andercon made his way back in the metropolis. Andercon petitioned the Court of Aldermen for a pension, which he finally received in January 1644. One Thomas Robins, "a poore man that was wounded at Edgehill," had sixpence given to him by the churchwardens of St. Ethelburga Bishopsgate in July 1644.[171]

Growing need led parliament to establish a new Committee for Sick and Maimed Soldiers on 2 November. Twelve days after its creation, the committee took full control over the Savoy Hospital on the Strand, designating the facilities and staff for parliament's use. Collections for the operation of this new facility were made in London's parishes. Mayor Pennington, as Eric Gruber von Arni noted in his important study of care for the wartime maimed, played a significant role promoting parochial collections that would be used to care for parliament's sick and wounded.[172]

Maimed soldiers added a troubling dimension for those who feared a protracted conflict. Sir William Drake meditated on these matters in a private parliamentary journal. "Consider the Unexpresable calamities," he asked, "that the most plentifull and flourishing Countries have bin brought unto by an Intestine war." Composed under the heading "for speech in Parlement," he outlined his plan to alert his fellow MPs about the disastrous outcomes that might come as a result of a prolonged civil war. Foremost, England might suffer from an immediate "lack of trade." An initial slump would open the way to more systemic troubles. Not least, economic hardship might "breed a manner and mislike among the kings sort," which, he went on, would in turn "have a dangerous influence uppon the poorer sort." Widespread enmity, Drake feared, could act as an "invitation" to foreign nations that sought to "attempt uppon us when they shall find us throughly weak[e]ned." Civil war, in other words, might open the door to foreign invasion. Frightening as this all seemed, Drake remained most concerned about long-term damage that would come as a result of disrupted trade. A "stupendious debt" might accrue and thus "lay a Foundation of misery for the child unborne," leaving future generations to pay the price for an unnecessary and detrimental war.[173]

Drake was not alone in his fears and in the coming months members of a growing faction that would increasingly be identified as a "peace party" in both parliament and the City expressed similar concerns.[174] Indeed, politicians, petitioners, and pamphleteers repeatedly touched on the same matters as Drake did when explaining their growing opposition to war. Simonds D'Ewes proved an outspoken proponent of peace. D'Ewes spent the first eight months of the war arguing with a cohort of war party leaders in parliament who he identified as "fiery" and "violent spirits."[175] D'Ewes played an important role during the winter of 1642–3, a time when moderates – headed by John Maynard, John Glynne, Bulstrode Whitelocke, and increasingly Denzil Holles – became outspoken in their criticism of the brand of military escalation proposed by men like William Strode, Henry Vane, and Henry Martin.[176] If well-known, the high political narrative of the period, the narrative of an ascendant parliamentary peace party in opposition to a war party, has persisted; David Wootton, who looked at the politics of the winter of 1642 to 1643 two decades ago, has largely supported Jack Hexter's analysis of fifty years prior, claiming that "the peace party held the upper hand in the House of Commons from 21 November 1642 until 11 February 1643." This "peace party" majority, as the narrative goes, began to falter in February once it became apparent that Charles would be unwilling to accept terms for settlement put forward by parliament in what is known as the Oxford Treaty, and lost yet more crucial ground in April when the king made excessive demands that prompted parliament to recall their peace commissioners to Westminster.[177]

If an admittedly small sample of "elite" political opinion, the voices of Drake, D'Ewes, and others nevertheless help to establish the contours of an emergent party politics in parliament, of opposing views that would become entrenched. Parallel concerns to those of Drake and D'Ewes were being shared throughout the metropolis, where the aftermath of Edgehill, Brentford, and Turnham Green had stirred many to share their concerns from the pulpit and in print. By the end of the year, Londoners could pick and choose to hear from either side of the equation. By early January 1643, Richard Williams, a preacher from St. Martin Vintry, articulated the matter in *Peace, and No Peace* as a dialogue between "*Phil-eirenus*, A Protestant, *A lover of peace*" and "*Philo Polemus*, A Separtist, *An Indendiary of War*." For Williams, who clearly favored peace, "malignants" had "raised a party within the City among themselves," and their opponents, who were "religious, loyall, and true-hearted Protestants," had simply expressed their hope "to bring the Olive-branch of peace." *Peace, and No Peace* concludes with both parties agreeing that "prayer is the only means to obtaine" a reconciliation and "the peace of *Jerusalem*."[178]

The king, for his part, sought ways to extend his own olive branch to his subjects in the capital. The first of these came after Edgehill. On 27 October, Charles issued a royal proclamation to the City in which he offered his "gracious Pardon to all the Citizens and Inhabitants of" London and Westminster. All would be excused, "except" for the original five members and a handful of opponents who had already been singled out in a royal declaration from 12 August, including "Doctor [Calybute] *Downing*," "Captain [John] *Venne*," and "Alderman [Isaac] *Pennington*." Added to the growing cast of unforgivables were "Alderman [John] *Fulke* and Captaine [Randall] *Manwaring*." Pardons awaited all but this handful of "Traytors and Stirrers of sedition." "Since the encounter" at Edgehill, the king's message continued, parliament's claims to be fighting for the king's safety had lost all credibility. Edgehill had exposed parliament's "malice" and overt desire "to have destroyed Us."[179] In the aftermath of Turnham Green, the king tried a different tactic, turning his aims for peace from the people to the parliament that he had so recently accused of "malice." While a slim majority of the Commons were willing to entertain the prospect of "drawing up such propositions as may tend to peace," others were less eager to see the conflict ended prematurely. Eleven hours of debate saw proposals narrowly advanced. However, on the next day, the Commons once again found Richard Shute and "divers Citizens at the Door." This time they had come to express opposition to "accommodation" and "a Peace more feared than their Power." With their concerns heard, they delivered the most enticing case yet made for war. Not only would they "freely lend to the Parliament all the plate belonging to the severall Halls of the City of London," but they would agree to a "cess throughout the City of London by order of Parliament" so that "every man" could "contribute monethly towards the charge of this war according to their severall abilities."[180] The extent to which Shute and his fellow Londoners were permitted to make such offers on behalf of Londoners and the livery companies was perhaps dubious. Yet their proposal proved irresistible. In a desperate last-minute gamble to stay peace, militants were offering up the city's purse strings on a platter. This was not, moreover, a baseless proposal; Shute and his fellow petitioners were banking on their ability to extend the terms of Pennington's program for general committee at Weavers' Hall to parliament; the extent to which parliament would use this newfound license can be seen in their establishment of a new committee tasked with assessing and collecting metropolitan resources.

The Committee for the Advance of Money, Mayor Pennington, and the £30,000 loan

Few developments proved more divisive during the autumn than parliament's establishment of the Committee for the Advance of Money. The Committee, which first met on 26 November at Haberdashers' Hall on Gresham Street, a stone's throw from the Guildhall, was responsible for investigating individuals' wealth and extracting funds for parliament's use, and included a bicameral cast of war party leaders including Brooke, Manchester, Saye and Sele, Pym, Strode, Vane (the younger), and Samuel Vassall.[181] A wide latitude was granted to the committee, including the "power to call such persons of the City or others whome they shall thinke fit to their Assistance for the Advance of Money upon the late Ordinance passed by both howses."[182] Nearly three weeks prior to the committee's establishment, parliament had already printed a list of fifty-six "Knights, Aldermen, Doctors" and "Ministers and Citizens" who had refused "to contribute Money for the publicke safety" and who were being held in custody in various makeshift jails throughout London. Listed detractors covered the social gamut from leading royalists such as Sir Kenelm Digby to more obscure figures such as the bookseller "cod-pice-Ned."[183] Granted its wide latitude, the committee wasted little time seeking out and "procuring of Monies or other necessaries for the Army aswell within the City as other parts of this Kingdome." Loans obtained by the committee were set to the standard interest rate of 8 percent, which was determined by the Lord Mayor and City sheriffs. Detailed accounts for the committee's proceedings are recorded for the period spanning the committee's appointment on 26 November 1642 until 25 May 1643.[184]

On 26 November – the committee's first official meeting – Mayor Pennington issued requests to London's parishes for the collection of a £30,000 loan. Pennington's orders were remarkably detailed and suggest considerable coordination with the committee, which had informed Common Council and the mayor that they "desired" to see £30,000 raised in the City. Churchwardens were asked to deliver their funds by the following Tuesday afternoon and travel to the Guildhall to "give an Account of what Moneys they have raised." Further, it was expected that wardens would arrange for "an Assembly of the Parishioners," so that "the Ministers of every Parish" could work "publickly to stir up" attendants for lending. Repayment for the new loan was to come from collections of the twentieth part, a newly established tax that fell on anyone with more than £100 who had not given more than a twentieth of their estate.[185] The architecture of the assessment for raising money in the City related directly to that of the general committee at Weavers' Hall (which was from this point forward to be a subcommittee of the Committee for the Advance of Money).

The response to the request once again proved overwhelmingly positive; records of collections provide us with some of the best-preserved evidence of wartime financial mobilization. Parochial returns list the names of some 1,127 inhabitants from thirty-one parishes which contributed £15,822 10s. Beyond these precise figures were an unknown number of contributors from Christ Church and St. Mathew Friday Street. "Well affected" parishioners from the latter gave a total of £170.[186] To these figures can be added the 111 accounts worth some £37,000 tabulated by Ben Coates. Together, these corroborate the claim that Londoners overpaid significantly toward the £30,000 November loan.[187] With these figures in mind, some of the vastly exaggerated claims made by the London newsbook *Speciall Passages* become slightly more plausible. Londoners, boasted *Speciall Passages*, maintained such "resolution of the Cause" that "they brought in and subscribed for about 40000" within a day. By the following week, "above 60000 pound[s]" of the £30,000 had been made available. Moreover, inhabitants agreed to maintain 60,000 soldiers a month, "and hope ere long to make them 100000." Even if the suggestion of 100,000 soldiers tested credulity, the reports spoke to the overall optimism that surrounded the £30,000 loan and to the remarkable speed with which collections were made. "The City," concluded *Speciall Passages*, "rests not."[188] A closer look at some of the parochial returns reveals a healthy landscape of support for parliament's war effort, and indeed illuminates a handful of London communities where the cause was championed.

St. Pancras Soper's Lane was one such community. Home to activists who regularly supported parliament's war, its inhabitants had first set about reforming their church in October 1641 by stripping away "inscriptions on grave stones," along with "all the Crosses left upon the walls and on the Candlestick by the pulpit," all "images over the Church porch" and even their "Silver flagon for the marke on it being superstitious and Jesuiticall." Parishioners readily gave toward relieving Ireland and later recorded the names of those who responded to parliament's requests. In late October, twelve parishioners agreed to outfit thirty-eight "men at armes" for an expedition of three months, while an additional twenty-two parishioners promised to pay up to £3 weekly to support others. Joseph Parker, a godly member of the parish and councilman, gave money to equip seven men. Three widows from the parish made contributions that totaled £4 and 12s. More support was offered as the year went on. When presented with the Lord Mayor's November precept for £30,000, twenty-three parishioners loaned outright. Joseph Parker gave £50, while one "Mrs Highlord Widdow" gave £100. All said, the twenty-three parishioners contributed a total of £568.[189]

Unsurprisingly, many of the parishes that loaned outright toward the £30,000 were also home to leading parliamentarians and wartime activists. Counted among the contributors were numerous well-to-do individuals who had signed the July petition against Gurney, or showed their support through other means. Civic leaders from Coleman Street, for instance, gave extensively. Owen Rowe, a captain in the trained bands, member of the City's militia committee, and later regicide, loaned £100. Following not far behind him was James Russell, a fellow activist and member of the militia committee who gave £80. The skinner Caleb Cockroft did his part by delivering £80. Samuel Avery, Mark Hildesley, Samuel Jones, and Richard Ashurst gave £50 each. Russell, Cockroft, and Avery could be counted among a group of "new" radicals who recently joined Common Council, while both Rowe and Russell had petitioned for Gurney's removal. Other activists loaned according to their ability. Henry Overton, for instance, gave £6, John Goodwin gave £5, and Thomas Goodwin gave £6. Nearly half of St. Stephen's loan of £1,310 19s came from identifiable activists, but many of the ninety-seven recorded contributors remained unnamed. Three spinsters and two widows gave £5 each. The smallest sums came from "three particular men" who together gave 19s.[190] If wealthy parochial activists led by example, the "lowly" in some instances followed their lead.

Similar patterns emerge in other City parishes known for activism. The relatively poor parish of St. Mildred Bread Street was home to several leading lenders. Thomas Brightwell, who signed the petition against Gurney in July, gave £50. Trailing closely behind him was Samuel Crispe, who gave £40; three unidentified men gave £30, while another three gave £20. £240 of St. Mildred's £330 loan came from just eight men, but the remaining £90 came from twenty-five others.[191] At St. Stephens Walbrook, Alderman John Warner gave £200, followed by the militants Samuel Warner and William Thomson, who each loaned £100, and William Underwood who managed £50. Arthur Juxon and his wife offered £50, while John Greensmith brought in the same. The £953 collected in Walbrook also came from numerous smaller loans, including some made by one husband "and partner."[192] £763 was raised at All Hallows on Lombard Street. £100 came from Thomas Cullum, who would later partake in radical committee action in 1643; £50 came from Richard Waring, who also signed the July petition against Gurney. The goldsmith Robert Cordell, the ironmonger Joshua Foote, and Captain Edward Clegatt each pledged £10.[193] Foote had already delivered £17 10s 6d worth of goods "for the waggons" that were to leave London with Essex.[194] Contributors toward the £758 collected in St. Mathew Friday Street included £140 from three councilors and an additional £170 from an unknown number of "well affected" parishioners. Individual contributions of £40 came from the radical petitioner Edward Parks and £50 from James Smith, a salter who had already loaned generously in support of the Irish Adventure.[195]

At St. Andrew Undershaft, Alderman Thomas Atkins gave £200, nearly a quarter of the entire parish return. Following close behind were Abraham Chamberlain and William Hawkins, who each gave £100. Seven others gave £50, including Robert Gayer, son of the future Lord Mayor, and Abraham Cullen of the Honorable Artillery Company.[196] Alderman John Fowke topped the list at All Hallows Barking with a pledge of £100, more than double that of any other contributor.[197] One of the seven leading lenders from the wealthy parish of St. Mary Aldermanbury was Walter Boothby, the Weavers' Hall collector, who loaned £50. The vast majority of the remaining parishioners gave between £1 and £10 toward a total contribution of £924.[198] In the wealthy parish of St. Lawrence Jewry, which raised an impressive £1,840, Lady Elizabeth Camden provided £200. Following her lead were Alderman George Clarke, Thomas Stone, and William Besley, who each gave £100. Alderman John Cordell, an opponent of parliament's earlier propositions, is listed with a contribution of "nothing."[199] Forty-nine parishioners loaned £525 13s 4d at St. Mary Le Bow, with some of the leading contributions coming from Theophilus Riley, Captain Francis Roe, and Thomas Haselrige. If St. Mary was home to parishioners who, as Liu suggests, "were clearly divided among themselves," they nevertheless loaned generously toward the requested £30,000.[200]

This is not, of course, to suggest that Londoners were uniformly pleased by the prospects of lending to support armed conflict with their king. Along with the £758 collected at St. Mathew Friday Street were the names of several refusers: Roger Stonghton was noted as "a sufficient man" who would "lend no thing," and Samuell Vainford was "a Rich man" who would "lend none to this business."[201] Alarmed by the recent commotions, the community at St. Mary Newington, Southwark, decided to take their own precautions, which included buying "a muskett for the Church" at £1 and hiring an outfit of soldiers to keep the peace, which cost £2 16s for a month's service. Another 9s 9d was spent on "three feathers for Church soldiers," presumably meant as markers to differentiate between soldiers in service to the church and the many other soldiers who were about London.[202]

Some Londoners, meanwhile, sought more direct means to help their sovereign. Unlike the ample parochial records of loans made for parliament, evidence of money loaned and services rendered toward the king's cause in London tend leave fainter traces. At least eighteen members of the Lords "voluntarily" provided subscriptions to the king to match those given toward parliament in June. Counted were some obvious supporters such as the king's two sons. Others would rally to support the king on the field of battle, including the peers Richmond, Southampton, Northumberland, and Montague. Altogether, eighteen men did "severallie ingage" themselves "to assist his Majestie in defence of his royall person, the two houses of Parliament the protestant religion, the laws of the Land, the liberties and properties of the subject and privileges of his Majestie" with a total of £940. This was a mere fraction of what was raised by the king in London, but it was again an important case of loyalists leading by example.[203]

Some Londoners remained outspokenly sympathetic with the Crown, while others apparently wished to avoid the business of lending altogether. It should be noted that recalcitrance could in its own way amount to a form of passive support. Churchwardens noted the names of parishioners who were unable to contribute, who were conspicuously "out of town," or who simply refused, on numerous occasions. St. Andrew by the Wardrobe returned just £109 5s from twenty-three contributors. Thirteen of their parishioners were noted for refusing with the words "will not" give, despite being "very able."[204] £195 10s was given by forty-three parishioners from St. Andrew Hubbard. Five, however, "refused to contribute according to their ability."[205] Singled out from St. Benet Sherehog, which gave £307 10s, were "Mr Wadeworth," a man who was "willing but not able," and "Mr Wige," who "hath now money." One "Doctor Oxsenbreage Wedowe will Leand nothing," claimed one account in response to the mayoral precept.[206] Three refused from St. Peter Westcheap, while eighteen did the same at St. Olave Silver Street.[207] Apart from records of the small sums that went unpaid, collectors were taking note of several large "sufficient Estates" with outstanding payments based on assessments. Within the parish of St. Mary Axe were John Goare, a "marchant in Limestreet" who failed to pay £100 on his £500 assessment, Robert Gaire of "Leaden-hall-street" who had yet to pay £200, and Rice James, a sugar-baker in Billiter Lane who owed some £40.[208]

Yet more examples of passive support for the king can be found in the recorded names of parishioners who refused to contribute toward the 26 November loan. Records contain hundreds of names for those who had yet to be assessed, who had not yet paid, or who were conspicuously absent. Refusers were regularly summoned to answer for their recalcitrance. Thirty-seven parishioners from Aldgate were ordered to appear before the Committee for the Advance of Money at Haberdasher's Hall for failing to pay toward the loan. Hundreds more were subject to similar summons, with written lists noting groups of Londoners who were "all rich," or individuals who might simply be identified as "a very able man," or "a very rich man." Some were deemed worthy of single mention; John Wells of St. Clement Lane was "conceived" to have a "worth" of £15,000; Peter Langley, meanwhile, was "reputed to be worth £20,000." Together, their twentieth parts might produce an impressive £1,750. Others might have legitimate reasons for missing the payment. Robert Tichborne could not pay since he was "at sea," while the Lady Courtopp had been "gone these 2 yeares."[209] As with the efforts to remove "scandalous" and "malignant" ministers, efforts would continue to target and coerce Londoners who refused to support the cause.

It remains to be seen if subscriptions towards the £30,000 loan approached the £60,000 suggested by *Speciall Passages*. No matter the case, collections reveal that Londoners were overwhelmingly supportive of parliament's efforts in late 1642. Like war-party leaders in parliament, civic leaders used the November contribution as a means to lead by example, to reveal both their "forwardness" for parliament's cause, and to inspire their fellow parishioners. Despite widespread support, considerable segments of the metropolis avoided lending altogether; in their choices can be found a sort of passive loyalism, or perhaps even an active resistance. By the end of November, lists of "non-contributors" were being compiled, affording proponents of war in the City and parliament a clearer picture of how they might better coerce the population and realize their ambitions. In a stunning turn of events, Pennington's proposal for the Weavers' Hall subcommittee had, by way of Shute's offering of a "cess throughout the City of London by order of Parliament," been implemented as a loan request for £30,000. Overpayment suggested that radicals might continue their push for an independent army. The next step would be to extend the legal reach of the

Committee for the Advance of Money to put additional pressure on London's many "non-contributors."

Ward assessments for non-contributors

In light of the early successes of the £30,000 loan, parliament ramped up efforts to assess and collect what money remained with "non-contributors." On 1 December, parliament printed an ordinance in which they required "the assessing of all such as have not contributed upon the Propositions of both Houses of Parliament." Collectors were once again granted wide latitude including the "power to distrain" the property of those who "refused to pay" and the authority to imprison "persons, and families of such disaffected persons."[210] A subsequent "Assessment book for non-contributors in London and Southwark" reveals both the expectations of payments on the "20th part of the Estates of the persons" in London and the sums "as have not Contributed or not in proportion."[211] The book offers an unparalleled record of assessments and payments made throughout London's wards between late November 1642 and early 1643, and which amounted to £72,007 12s 11d. These detailed accounts provide a snapshot of the amounts collected for parliament in each ward, sums that can in turn be mapped as percentages to reveal a topography of financial mobilization.[212] When considered in close connection to London's parishes, this topography of support provides an important means to link local activism to parliament's wider war effort; in the case of ward assessments for non-contributors we can see how radical efforts that began with Pennington's proposal for the Weavers' Hall subcommittee were, by way of Shute's offer to parliament, implemented as official parliamentary collections made by the Committee for the Advance of Money. More than simply shedding light on the parts of London that paid the most by order, this topography suggests links between ideology and action – it exposes, in short, the extent to which radical ideas translated into popular localized mobilization.

In an attempt to gain a better handle on collections and improve yields, the City added sixty-nine new collectors, a move that added 39 percent to the original force and increased the total number of collectors to 245. Entries made in the committee's assessment book between November 1642 and early 1643 show dated contributions made in cash and in kind, and note overall discrepancies between assessments and payments. Figures range significantly from the 26 percent collected in Portsoken Ward, to the much more impressive 72 percent that was collected in Bread Street Ward. The highest returns as percentages were made by a core group of City wards that stood southeast of St. Paul's Cathedral. Wards situated outside of central London often returned significantly less than their centralized counterparts.

Farringdon Within, for instance, brought in an impressive 65 percent of their assessment, while Farringdon Without paid only 32 percent. Wards adjacent to Bread Street (including Farringdon Within) also returned relatively large sums; Candlewick Ward paid 60 percent; Castle Beynard retuned 58 percent; Queenhithe, meanwhile, brought in an impressive 68 percent. A second concentration of payments took place slightly downriver; Dowgate returned 69 percent; Candlewick some 60 percent; and Billingsgate 63 percent. These relatively high percentages stand in notable contrast to the capital's average collection of just 47 percent, a contrast that sharpens further when we consider that the central wards of Bassishaw, Cheap, and Walbrook returned only 37 percent, 33 percent, and 34 percent, respectively.

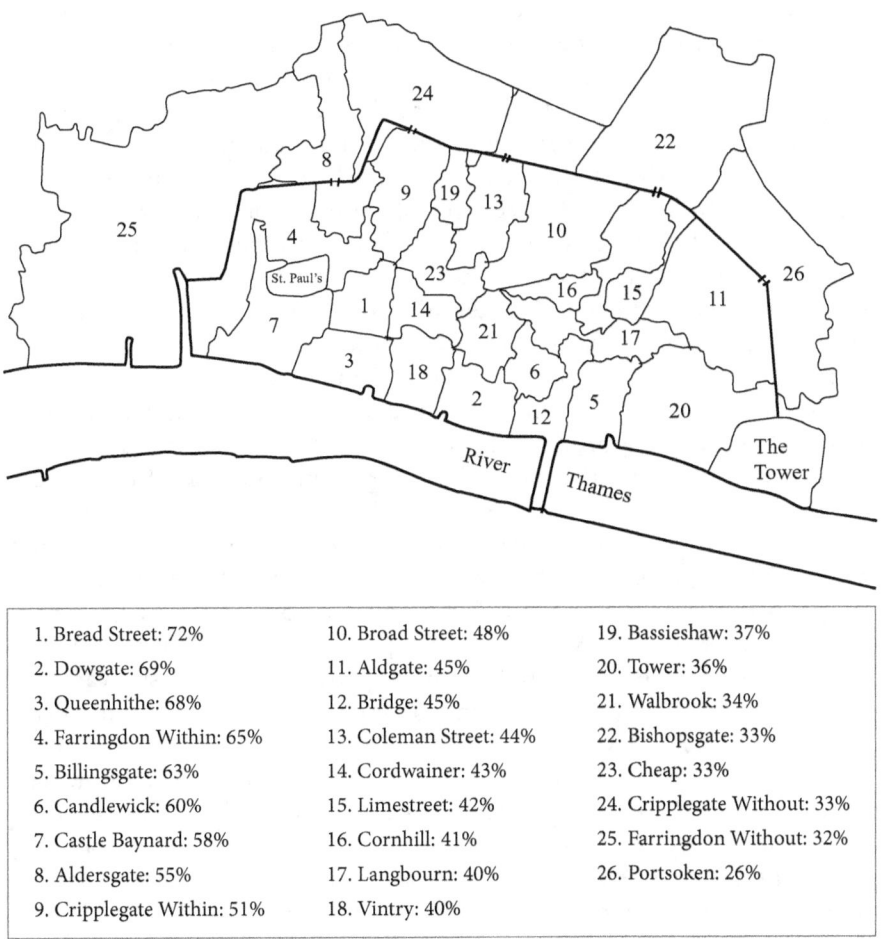

1. Bread Street: 72%
2. Dowgate: 69%
3. Queenhithe: 68%
4. Farringdon Within: 65%
5. Billingsgate: 63%
6. Candlewick: 60%
7. Castle Baynard: 58%
8. Aldersgate: 55%
9. Cripplegate Within: 51%
10. Broad Street: 48%
11. Aldgate: 45%
12. Bridge: 45%
13. Coleman Street: 44%
14. Cordwainer: 43%
15. Limestreet: 42%
16. Cornhill: 41%
17. Langbourn: 40%
18. Vintry: 40%
19. Bassieshaw: 37%
20. Tower: 36%
21. Walbrook: 34%
22. Bishopsgate: 33%
23. Cheap: 33%
24. Cripplegate Without: 33%
25. Farringdon Without: 32%
26. Portsoken: 26%

Figure 2 The London assessment of November 1642 and payments by ward.

Wards with the highest returns tended to share a number of characteristics in common. Most, again, were centrally located, and most contained parishes that paid significant sums toward earlier collections for parliament, including, importantly, areas that oversubscribed to the £30,000 loan. As the end of the year approached, parliament's new committee began wielding their authority in earnest; on 23 December, churchwardens received orders to "use their best diligence" to collect remaining assessments and forward the names of any parishioners who "refuse to pay."[213]

Above all else, the success of collections depended upon the presence of a sympathetic laity and ministry. Bread Street, with its return of 72 percent, contained the parishes of All Hallows Bread Street, and the connected St. John the Evangelist, St. Margaret Moses, St. Mildred Bread Street, and part of St. Mary le Bow. Bordering to the north side of the ward was St. Mathew Friday Street, the parish where Henry Burton served as rector. Breadstreet Ward's parishes hosted a number of leading wartime activists and preachers who were outspoken supporters of parliament. Thirty-six parishioners from All Hallows Bread Street had already petitioned in September to have their dying rector replaced by the presbyterian Lazarus Seaman. William Kendall, Tempest Milner, and John Venn were among the petitioners.[214] Adjacent to All Hallows was Margaret Moses of Friday Street, the parish where Richard Culverwell held the parsonage.[215] Obadiah Sedgwick had served as curate and lecturer at St. Mildred since 1630. Meanwhile, George Walker held the parsonage of St. John the Evangelist.[216] Together, these parishes constituted a core of popular metropolitan puritanism and militancy. Each of the above ministers enjoyed a history of opposition to Archbishop Laud and in some instances they went on to become leading proponents of his removal and the war. Burton had suffered mutilation by the archbishop's order in 1637; Laud once called Culverwell "the greatest troubler in London."[217] The parishes were also home to leading wartime activists. Bread Street, as Lindley has suggested, was one of the areas of London where "support for the Lunsford and militia petitions was strongest."[218] The ward also contained a large portion of St. Mary Magdalene Milk Street, the parish where Thomas Case regularly preached. One would be hard-pressed to find a more stalwart supporter of the war than Pennington's own chaplain who, as John Walter notes, had preached two sermons on the Protestation in 1641 and acted as "one of the City's representatives in the Commons and a key intermediary between the parliamentary leadership and City radicals."[219] Bread Street thus affords a valuable example of an intersection between a politically active laity, a particularly vocal ministry, and a place where a sizeable contribution was made for parliament's war effort. Similar – if also less distinct – patterns arise elsewhere in the City.

Queenhithe and Dowgate Wards returned the second and third largest sums of cash toward the November assessment, respectively. The wards did not feature prominently in either the Lunsford or militia petitions, but, like Bread Street, they contained parishes that provided livings for godly preachers and parishioners, some of whom openly sympathized with parliament's cause. Queenhithe sat just to the south of Bread Street, in what has been described as a densely populated and "overchurched area of the old City." The ward was home to some relatively poor populations that included St. Mary Somerset, St. Mary Mounthaw, St. Nicholas Olave, and St. Michael Queenhithe. Liu observed that St. Nicholas Olave contained "many poor people in it but few substantial or well-to-do tradesmen," while St. Mary Somerset and St. Michael Queenhithe had similar demographics that included "an overwhelming number of poor and a very low proportion of well-to-do inhabitants."[220] If impecunious, the inhabitants of St. Michael Queenhithe nevertheless managed to raise £214, some 68 percent of the November assessment.[221] Further, sixty-nine parishioners contributed £72 5s 6d toward "the monethlie payment for the mayntayninge of soaldiers" on 31 December, while forty-nine gave an additional £58 12s 4d on 1 March 1643.[222] In the case of Queenhithe, some of the City's poorest inhabitants were paying the largest proportions of their assessment to help fund the war.

Dowgate included the parishes of All Hallows the Great and All Hallows the Less, and contained portions of the bordering parishes of St. John the Baptist, St. Michael Paternoster Royal, and St. Laurence Pountney. John Downham served as rector at All Hallows the Great, which was an enclave for Fifth Monarchist preachers including Christopher Feake and John Simpson.[223] Meanwhile, All Hallows the Less was home to a number of civic wartime leaders including Captain William Coulson of the City's Blue regiment. The parish had no settled preacher, but instead regularly invited ministers to give sermons. Churchwardens happily paid 3d "for halfe a pinte of Sacke" to help quench one preacher's thirst.[224]

The adjoined and centrally located wards of Bassishaw, Cheap, and Walbrook returned money well below average. Each of these wards, importantly, could be said to be religiously and politically heterogeneous. Bassishaw Ward contained only St. Michael Bassishaw, a parish north of the Guildhall that Liu counted "among the most prominent and influential parochial communities in Puritan London." If relatively wealthy and important, the parish was also home to a mixed lot that included the expelled loyalist common councilor Robert Alden, along with a number of proponents of war, including the presbyterians Edwin Browne, George Dunne, and Walter Pell.[225] Bassishaw in the end returned only 37 percent of its assessment. Likewise, both Cheap and Walbrook contained parishes with disparate compositions. The latter, which was made up mostly of

St. Swithin Stone, and portions of seven other parishes, returned just 34 percent. Fifty-one of St. Swithin's parishioners nevertheless loaned £468 toward the £30,000 loan.[226] St. Lawrence Jewry, which sat adjacent to the Guildhall and returned the impressive sum of £1,184 toward the £30,000 request, fell partially within Cheap Ward, which returned a total of only 33 percent toward the assessment.[227] The low figure is best explained by the presence of All Hallows Honey Lane, St. Mary Colechurch, St. Martin Ironmonger Lane and St. Mildred Poultry. Each of these parishes, save for St. Mary Colechurch, which was home to a number of City leaders, were relatively small and unremarkable. The clearest signs of support for war came from single acts of giving.[228] One "Lady Rumney" of St. Martin, for instance, "did voluntarily and freely send" £2,000 to support parliament's cause, more than four times the total raised in St. Swithin.[229]

Ward returns for the November assessment were, again, rarely clear-cut matters. The politico-religious outlooks of ministers and parishioners varied significantly from parish to parish – and indeed, as importantly, from person to person – making it extremely difficult to garner clear impressions about the how money moved in the metropolis. No parish highlights this fact better than St. Stephen's Coleman Street of Coleman Street Ward, a hotbed of puritanism and nonconformity in the 1640s that scholars recognize as the "most notorious" in the City.[230] Occupying St. Stephen's pulpit was John Goodwin, a firebrand who preached Meroz and openly urged his auditors to "consider the cause" and to "engage yourselves to the utmost."[231] But no matter how "radical" or forward St. Stephen's parishioners were in their support for parliament's cause, the parish was, after all, just one of several in the wider Coleman Street Ward. As a whole, the ward returned 44 percent of the November assessment – a figure that fell just slightly below the capital's average of 47 percent returned per ward.[232]

This relatively low return is explained by the makeup of Coleman Street Ward, which extended from the wealthy area around the Guildhall to crowded and poor neighborhoods near to Moorfields to the east. Any "forwardness" shown by the parishioners of St. Stephen's was easily offset by the relative recalcitrance or inability to give of the ward's numerous other inhabitants. Parishioners from neighboring St. Olave Old Jewry were decidedly less enthusiastic about contributing. St. Olave was home to a number of loyalists including Oliver Neve, Moses Tryon, Edmund Right, and the former Lord Mayor, Richard Gurney.[233] Although St. Olave's parishioners gave readily toward Ireland in early 1642, and despite their appointment of the presbyterian lecturer Ralph Robinson in October of the same year, there is little in their account books to suggest that they contributed on the same level toward the November assessment.[234] Coleman Street Ward's makeup offers an obvious explanation for the relatively low return rates and thus helps to explain why the home to Mayor Pennington and Richard Overton's printing press returned significantly less than neighboring wards of Dowgate, Bread Street, and Queenhithe. Further, it suggests that wards must not serve as the final category of inquiry when mapping mobilization, but that they are best used as indicators for exploring the makeup of their constituent parochial communities.

Coleman Street Ward's third parish, St. Margaret Lothbury, fell under the jurisdiction of collectors from Coleman Street, but was also partially within Broad Street Ward.[235] Lothbury's minister, Humphrey Tabor, had "absented himself from his said Cure sometimes Six Months together," and was known to be outspoken "against such as take up Arms for the Defence of the Parliament."[236] "Att a generall meeting att the parish" on 27 November 1642, "parishioners" came together and "did there agre[e] and lend for a p[re]sent supply for the use of the kinge and parlyment uppon the parlyments proposytion."[237] Sixty-five individuals pledged sums ranging from 10s given by "widdow Thompson" to £25 given by one Peter Pheasant. It was not, then, the minister, but rather the parishioners who led in the effort to raise money for parliament. Moreover, these figures once again belie the relatively low returns made by Broad Street and Coleman Street wards, and further caution against the over-simplistic assumption that parishioners adopted the religio-political outlooks of their ministers.[238] Clearly, Coleman Street Ward's returns varied significantly. A lingering recalcitrance among the parishioners from St. Olave, along with the curate's vacancy at Lothbury, might also be taken into account when attempting to explain the low returns from a ward containing London's parish most frequently identified with radical rebellion.

Regardless of the specific reasons for poor or robust returns, ward assessment figures help to underscore important aspects of London's topography of mobilization: apart from Bread Street, Dowgate, and Queenhithe, City wards were home to parochial communities with largely heterogeneous politico-religious outlooks. Returns for the November assessment suggest that monetary contributions toward parliament's late 1642 war effort varied throughout the metropolis; as a general rule, the handful of concentrated areas where Londoners paid proportionally more toward the assessment were centrally located areas in which there were discernible concentrations of godly civic activists and sympathetic preachers. More surprising, perhaps, is the fact that economic and demographic divisions seemed to have had little bearing on the overall frequency of contributions. Ward returns thus add another layer to an emerging topography of metropolitan mobilization, revealing that the strongest concentrations of parliamentarian support in late 1642 depended on factors that were not strictly socio-economic. Again, the highest rates of return came from the core of the City, from the wards and parishes clustered west of the Guildhall and the densely populated areas to the east of St. Paul's and around the bookseller's stalls of the churchyard and on to spaces connected around the thoroughfare of Cheapside. These were bustling locales where popular agitation was rife, where livery halls hosted parliamentary committees, and where godly preachers reached godly auditors.[239] In the case of Billingsgate, we find a ward that loaned above average and was defined as much by its busy "water-gate" harbor to the east of London Bridge as it was by its constituent parishes. If we are to maintain, as some historians have, that Coleman Street became London's "Faubourg St Antoine of the English Revolution," then we might also suggest that Bread Street had become its Faubourg St. Marcel.[240] Assessment records from the Committee for the Advance of Money may ultimately provide a cautionary tale against too readily reifying London's political geography by ward. Indeed, the collection figures reviewed here suggest that mobilization was, at its very core, a process that relied upon the efforts of the very women and men who navigated and imposed meaning upon their City, parish by parish and street by street. Ward boundaries fade yet more under the light of the "spatio-temporal rhythms" described by Henri Lefebvre, and what comes into focus instead are urban networks that developed as a result of engagement between daily routines, ideas and representations.[241] Mobilization could all the while be as demanding for the City's poor and middling sorts as it was for the civic leaders who possessed the means to make large contributions. It just so happened that the wards with the highest rates of return also maintained discernible relationships between an active laity and a zealous ministry. These were the same centralized wards where, perhaps unsurprisingly, parishioners oversubscribed to the £30,000 loan.

The December petitions

On 1 December – the same day that parliament's ordinance for assessing non-contributors was printed – an ominous petition claiming to represent "many of the Citizens of London" reached the House of Commons. Delivered by Sir David Watkins, Richard Shute, and the preachers Hugh Peter and John Goodwin, the petition made ten specific requests that revolved around the hope that accommodation with the king would be avoided and that parliament might instead pursue "a more speedy and effectuall prosecution of the Warres." Petitioners hoped "that life" might also "be given to such Ordiances" that would allow for the "seazing and securing of malignant persons and estates" as a means for raising "six thousand Horse" and ensuring "that his Excellency [the earl of Essex] may instantly goe forth" to fight against the king. Funding for these efforts was to come from sequestered estates and the pocketbooks of the very Londoners who had shown themselves disaffected toward parliament's cause – a request that clearly aligned with, and also hoped to expand upon, the 26 November ordinance for collecting from non-contributors.

Upon presentation of the petition, the Commons promptly notified the deliverers that they could not take their requests into consideration without direct support from the Lord Mayor and Common Council. Rebuffed, Watkins, Shute, and their godly attendants therefore made the short journey back to the Guildhall to gain the approbation of Pennington and other sympathetic civic leaders. While Common Council's journal makes no direct reference to the petition, the contemporaneously printed *The True and Originall Copy* reveals that Pennington was in fact eager to have the petition heard. Upon a first reading of the petition, many councilors put forward arguments both "*pro & contra.*" Ultimately, the "said petition was rejected and throwne out of the Court." Even if supported by the Lord Mayor, the petition was too radical to be tenable and could not gain majority approval.[242] Londoners, meanwhile, remained on edge. On 3 December, orders were made for City regiments to be at the ready and "repair to their Colours" upon the sound "the Beating of Drums in the City." Failure to act promptly, they were warned, would lead to punishment set by "the law of Arms."[243] Many still feared an attack by the king.

News of the radical petition spurred otherwise peaceable Londoners into a frenzy. Shortly after the petition was read in Common Council, 300 inhabitants gathered "with Torches, and Linkes" at Haberdashers' Hall on Staining Lane to demand that members of the Committee for the Advance of Money consider a new peace petition to counter the one put forward by Watkins and Shute. Calling out "A Petition, A Petition," the crowd was eventually greeted by Lord Wharton, who suggested that they might instead proceed to the House of Commons, where they "should receive sufficient satisfaction concerning their desires." Well aware that doing so would cause their petition to follow the same course as the previous radical one, they set out instead for the Lord Mayor's residence. Their time outside of Pennington's was short-lived as a troop of the trained bands soon arrived. The clamorous crowd next turned their attention to the Guildhall, which they soon reached and entered in order to read their requests aloud. Their hopes for peace purportedly met with "great Humme, and applause" and led to additional subscriptions. Two companies of trained bands and a troop of horse next dispersed the crowds for the evening.[244]

City officials were understandably concerned. Most were eager to avoid tumults on the scale of the previous winter. As it turned out, they had more than disgruntled and potentially violent petitioners to contend with. On 9 December, Laurence Whitaker read a report to the Commons in which he noted that a dangerous number of soldiers refused to march with Essex and were instead idle in the capital. His figures, "from 4 parishes" alone, included "100 horsemen & above 300 foot." More alarming yet was the rumor that they "were here lurking and lying up and downe in Alehowses Taverns & other byplaces." Many soldiers may have enlisted but refused to march and fight; others were almost certainly troops who were still awaiting pay for their service during the Bishops' Wars; some were likely soldiers of fortune who were waiting for the same after returning out of Ireland. Frightened by what Whitaker found in just a few parishes, D'Ewes noted in his journal that "it might [only] be guessed [at] what the number would bee when a Generall certificate should be returned in."[245]

If droves of recalcitrant, armed, and inebriated soldiers in the capital were not worrying enough, City officials soon found more reason for alarm. On 11 December, Common Council took into consideration yet another peace petition signed by "divers" Londoners. The "humble" petition presented this time warned of "stronge and violent parties" that were gaining ground in the metropolis and "prove of very dangerous consequence if not speedily prevented by the wisdome and care of the magestacye of this Cittye." The means by which magistrates might hope to "quench this Flame" was obvious to the petitioners: The Court of Aldermen and Common Council should draw up their own City petition to present to "his Majestie and both howses of Parlyament," which would make "such a peace as may give unto Ceasar the things that are Ceasars and to God the thinges that are Gods."[246] While Common Council sat to consider the petitioners' appeal, the haberdasher Robert Osboldston delivered yet another copy to the Court of Aldermen. Osboldston and his fellow petitioners were determined to be heard. His petition urged London's leaders to "consider the effects of a Civill warr, as the destrucc[i]on of Christians, the unnaturall effusion of bloud, fathers against Sonns, brothers by brothers, friends by friends slaine then famine and sicknesse then followes." In order to avoid further bloodshed, diminished trade, and a reduction of the population, City leaders should seek "a speedy peace and happy Accomodac[i]on" with the king. Taken together, London's various peace petitions articulated a message that was strikingly similar to the one recorded by Drake, D'Ewes, and others.[247] For Ian Gentles, such petitions suggested that Londoners were "more lukewarm towards parliament than received accounts would lead us to believe."[248]

While Common Council deliberated over the petitions, "a great multitude of people" gathered outside of the Guildhall to "promote" and "understand what successe" their petition "should receave."[249] Where conflicting, accounts nevertheless make clear that matters quickly escalated out of control. According to *The Image of the Malignants Peace*, an anonymous news account, the gathering turned violent after some of the peace petitioners called a man "Round-head Rogue, and then beat him." But this was just the beginning of the day's trouble. When Captain Edmund Harvey arrived with a troop of City horse he found "a great multitude in the Porch and yard of the said Hall with their swords drawn fighting." Upon noticing that the trained bands had arrived, a group of the petitioners stormed the Guildhall, barricaded themselves in, and set about banging on the door of the chamber where Common Council was in session. Refusing to leave, the petitioners remained barricaded in the hall until members of the trained bands wheeled up two cannons and threatened to blow down the Guildhall's doors.[250] Faced with the prospect of being fired upon, the men finally relented and agreed to unbar the door. The "tumult" thereafter dispersed, leaving behing a few men who were arrested as ringleaders. Two days later, the Commons ordered that Pennington and the two sheriffs of London should seek to "prevent any [further] tumultuous Gatherings" and inquire into the causes of the recent disturbance. Within a week, Pennington had delivered the names of thirty-one Londoners whom he suspected of plotting with the peace petitioners to free prisoners and seize the Tower.[251]

On 17 December, just six days after the unsettling affair at the Guildhall, Common Council returned to the matter of drawing up petitions that would be suitable for presentation to both the king and parliament. One would reflect calls for peace; the other was to frame reasons for war. Two days later, their paired petitions were delivered for consideration by the Commons. When D'Ewes arrived to the House at around eleven o'clock in the morning he noted "the two Sheriffs of London" were present, including "Alderman [John] Fowke" along with "divers of the Cittizens." Also present in the chamber was "the Lord Mayor of London" whom D'Ewes made special note of as he "came this morning into the howse (being a member thereof) and sate there before the delivery of the said petition and sate there during the reading of it."[252] Fowke and his companions received "hearty thanks" for their petitions. But whilst this was all going on, a purported crowd of 5,000 Londoners poured into Westminster's Palace Yard to deliver their own unsanctioned peace petition.[253]

The new petition boasted signatures that had been collected throughout the metropolis. When informed that the Lord Mayor had refused to add his own signature to a peace petition, one "Mr Banks" from Cheapside claimed "My Lord Maior, my Lord Fart: I know no Lord Major there is; for the King said there was none, and he did believe the king." One unnamed minister had decided to use his time in the pulpit on Sunday to "make a Speech, inciting Parishoners to subscribe the same." Another "Mr Clay," also a resident of

Cheapside, signed the petition under duress; Clay's apparent reluctance to sign was met with the threat of having his ear sliced off if he refused.[254] The use of such coercive tactics was almost certainly the exception rather than the rule, but evidence of this type makes estimating the actual number of "peace" petitioners difficult. One surviving copy of the petition contains at least 1,380 signatures, evidence of at least some support, if not the 5,000 claimed by the royalist newsbook *Mercurius Aulicus*.[255]

When it came time to discuss the peace petition in the Commons, Sir Henry Vane the Younger proposed an outright rejection. Opposing Vane in their speeches were D'Ewes and others.[256] After some debate, it was finally agreed on 26 December that the petitioners' proposals should be taken forward, a decision that would, as we shall see, have important ramifications on peace and war interests the following year. Some MPs mave have moved forward under the assumption that the king would reject their terms outright. If true, they were correct to be so concerned; a full cessation of arms was too much to ask of the Crown, and Charles himself would later claim that the men who "penned" the first round of peace propositions must have "had no thoughts of peace in their hearts, but to make things worse and worse."[257] Indeed, what would soon become the Treaty of Oxford, a series of official peace talks between parliament's commissioners and the king, lasted from the end of January to the middle of April.

Save for some passing comments by Pearl, little to no attention has been paid to the fact that the decision to move forward with the peace treaty was the direct result of popular petitioning, or indeed that the petitioners' actions led to decisive political maneuvering by London's leading militants.[258] Well aware of the dangers that might come from a peace settlement, councilors, headed by Pennington, decided to deliver their own petition to Oxford. This, they claimed, might ostensibly "give unto Caesar the things that are Caesars and to God the things that are Gods."[259] Thus, in late December 1642, while both Houses were busy discussing whether or not to draft propositions based on London's peace petitions, councilors and the Lord Mayor had already seized the initiative and nominated a party of Londoners to travel to Oxford to present their own "affections" to the king. Their decision, both remarkable and unprecedented, was to have wide-ranging implications for metropolitan and national politics. It led the king to make a political mistake that amounted to "a pivotal contribution to radicals' efforts" and, as one historian has claimed, unwittingly made him "the best friend of the parliamentary junto."[260] Much more than a boon to parliament's belligerents, Charles's mistake "reunited a divided City" by polarizing popular opinion and escalating London's stake in the civil war.[261]

Notes

1. HL, STG Box 67/9.
2. *CJ* vol. 2, p. 617.
3. *Certaine Propositions of Both Houses of Parliament* (London, 1642), sigs. A2r, A3r.
4. *Certain Propositions [...] Together with divers Instructions* (London, 1642), title page [E1275].
5. *Certaine Propositions*, sig. A2r; TNA, SP 16/491/30–33; See pp. 68–70 and 74 regarding *Propositions Made [...] for the speedie and effectuall reducing of the Kingdom of Ireland* (London, 1642).
6. See in particular Ann Hughes, *Politics, Society and Civil War in Warwickshire, 1620–1660* (Cambridge, 1987), pp. 114–168.
7. *Certaine Propositions*, sig. A4r.
8. Although PA, HL/PO/JO/10/1/132 #378 retains the name "Mannering," this was almost certainly Randall Mainwaring.
9. PA, HL/PO/JO/10/1/132 #378.
10. BL, Tanner Ms 66, fol. 51; Pearl, *London*, pp. 209–210. These sums were given in early June. See Anne S. Young and Vernon F. Snow (eds), *The Private Journals of the Long Parliament: 2 June to 17 September 1642* (Dexter, 1992), p. 469.
11. *The Private Journals of the Long Parliament*, pp. 466–480; Bodleian Library, Tanner MS 66 fol. 61v.
12. TNA, SP 28/131/3 fos. 7v, 46v, 70v, 75v, 102r, 117r, 121r–v. Skippon was awarded £300 for life for his service as Major General of London's forces. This sum increased to £600 by Act of Common Council on 2 May 1648. See LMA, MS COL/CHD/MV.03/003.
13. F. Kyffin Lenthall, "List of the Names of the Members of the House of Commons that Advances Horse, Money and Plate," *Notes and Queries*, 12 (1855), pp. 358–360. These are approximate numbers as some members offered to keep horses "in readiness" or pledge money or maintain horses at rates of £50 or £100. If horses are valued at the upper estimate, the total was worth approximately £15,000 more, bringing the full value of contributions to approximately £23,000.
14. Thomason's copy of *Certaine Propositions of Both Houses* is dated "10 June." See E.151[5], title page.
15. PA, HL/PO/JO/10/1/127–128; Lindley, *Popular Politics*, pp. 213–215; Brenner, *Merchants and Revolution*, p. 373.
16. *LJ* vol. 5, p. 198; Pearl, *London*, pp. 156–157. Gurney remained in the tower until his death in 1647.
17. LMA, COL/CC/01/01/041, fol. 34v; Pearl, *London*, p. 157.
18. PA, HL/PO/JO/10/1/131, #337.
19. BL, Harley MS 987, fol. 7v.
20. HL, Hastings MS 16522, "Poems and Ballads," p. 73; This poem is also listed in Alexander Brome, *Rump or an exact collection* (London, 1662), p. 95.

21 HL, Hastings MS16522, p. 140.
22 Lindley, *Popular Politics*, p. 215; Pearl, *London*, p. 158.
23 *Some Speciall Passages from London* 3–10 July (London, 1642), sigs. G4r–v.
24 See PA, HL/PO/JO/10/1/128.
25 BL, Add MS 14827, fol. 169v. Quoted in Anthony Fletcher, *The Outbreak of the English Civil War* (New York, 1981), p. 338.
26 HL, STG Box 65/43.
27 TNA, SP 28/131/3, fol. 46r.
28 *A Perfect Diurnall of the Passages in Parliament*, 25 July – 1 August (London, 1642), p. 6.
29 William Dugdale, *A Short View of the Late Troubles in England* (London, 1681), p. 99.
30 TNA, SP 28/131/2 fos. 33v–34v.
31 TNA, SP 28/131/3, fol. 100v.
32 TNA, SP 28/131/5, fol. 1.
33 Ibid., fol. 2.
34 Ibid., fos. 6, 7, 9, 11, 12, 16, 20, 21, 26.
35 Ibid., fos. 1–26.
36 Ibid., fol. 12.
37 TNA, SP 63/300/123–125.
38 William Dugdale, *A Short View of the Late Troubles in England* (London, 1681), p. 99.
39 Clarendon, *History*, vol. II, pp. 226–227; Coates, *Impact*, p. 55; Lindley, *Popular Politics*, p. 218.
40 BL, Add Ms 37343, fol. 253r.
41 TNA, SP 28/131/2, fol. 11r.
42 William Laud, *The history of the troubles* (London, 1695), p. 196.
43 LMA, COL/CC/01/01/041, fol. 36r.
44 LMA, COL/CC/01/01/041, fos. 38r–v.
45 PA, HL/PO/JO/10/1/133 #116.
46 Coates, *Impact*, p. 55.
47 *Speciall Passages* (London, 1642, E.119[2]), p. 55.
48 Sheilagh Ogilvie, *The European Guilds: An Economic Analysis* (Princeton, 2019), p. 59.
49 Mercers' Company Library, Acts of Court, fol. 38r.
50 See Coates, *Impact*, pp. 70–74.
51 See Joseph P. Ward, *Metropolitan Communities: Trade Guilds, Identity, and Change in Early Modern London* (Stanford, 1997), esp. chapter 2; see also Joseph P. Ward, *London's Livery Companies and Metropolitan Government, c. 1500–1725* (Stanford, 1992).
52 William Herbert, *The History of the Twelve Great Livery Companies of London* (London, 1836), p. 577.
53 Grocers' Company Library, Grocers' Court Minutes, fol. 51; for the date of payment see TNA, SP 16/493/79r.
54 GL, MS 5570/03, fol. 592.

55 Keith Lindley has suggested that the salters, drapers, fishmongers, and goldsmiths were the main companies who raised "objections" to the loan. I have found little direct evidence to support his claim and he does not furnish direct evidence for this assertion in *Popular Politics*, p. 166 n. 39. See also Pearl, *London*, pp. 208–209.
56 TNA, SP 16/493/79v.
57 Drapers' Company Library, Court Minutes and Records, 1640–1667, fol. 17r.
58 Ibid., fos. 18v–19v.
59 TNA, SP 16/493/79v.
60 GL, MS 16967/4, fol. 371.
61 Ibid., fol. 311v.
62 TNA, SP 16/493/80r.
63 GL, MS 15201/1, fos. 84–86.
64 GL, MS 15201/1, fos. 89, 96; SP 16/493/80r.
65 Mercers' Company Library, Acts of Court, fos. 25r–v.
66 Mercers' Company Library, Acts of Court, fos. 40v–41r.
67 TNA, SP 16/493/79v.
68 Goldsmiths' Company Library, Court Minute Book W, fol. 10r.
69 TNA, SP 16/493/79v.
70 Ibid., fos. 11v–12r.
71 GL, MS 15842/1, fol. 311r.
72 GL, MS 15842/1, fol. 311v; TNA, SP 16/493/79v.
73 Salters' Company Library, Minute Book, 1627–1684, fos. 237, 239; TNA, SP 16/493/79v; Lindley, *Popular Politics*, p. 166 n. 39.
74 GL, MS 30708/3, fol. 197r; SP 16/493/79v.
75 Nigel Victor Sleigh-Johnson, "The Merchant Taylors Company of London, 1580–1645" (unpub. Ph.D. thesis, University of London, 1989), pp. 220–221.
76 TNA, SP 16/493/80r.
77 Clothworkers' Hall, London, Orders of Court, 1639–1649, fos. 63r, 68v, 69r.
78 TNA, SP 16/493/79v–80r.
79 TNA, SP 16/493/79r.
80 GL, MS 7353/1, unfol.; TNA, SP 16/493/79r.
81 GL, MS 3297/1, unfol.; TNA, SP 16/493/79v.
82 GL, MS 2881/5, fos. 102–103.
83 TNA, SP 16/493/79r; GL, MS 5667/1, fol. 168.
84 GL, MS 2208/1, unfol.
85 GL, MS 5385, fos. 228v, 229v, 230r. The plate sold for £109 15s 8d. 132 Spoons alone brought in £62 3s.
86 TNA, SP 16/493/80r.
87 TNA, SP 16/493/79v.
88 GL, MS 6153/1, fos. 206r, 208r–v, 212r.
89 GL, MS 3043/2, fol. 145v.
90 PA, HL/PO/JO/10/1/130 #268. Listed at the bottom of the letter, in what appears to be Saye's hand, is the simple note: "read 31 July 1642 & assented."
91 *Propositions Made ... for the speedie and effectuall reducing of the Kingdom of Ireland* (London, 1642).

92 GL, MS 15201/1, fol. 84; GL, MS 16967/4, fol. 377.
93 Mercers' Company Library, Acts of Court, fol. 44r.
94 Ibid., fol. 46r.
95 TNA, SP 16/493/80r.
96 Ibid.
97 TNA, SP 19/1 pp. 34, 36. "Monies yet unpaid."
98 GL, MS 15201/1, fol. 96; SP 16/493/80r makes no note of further payments.
99 The Salters' Company, for instance, were still waiting on the repayment of £8,000 "for the service of the kingdome upon several ordinances" in August of 1650. Salters' Company Library, Court Minute Book, 1627–1684, pp. 252, 276.
100 LMA, MS COL/CC/01/01/041, fol. 35r.
101 Drapers' Company Library, Court Minutes and Records, 1640–1667, fol. 22r.
102 Ibid.
103 GL, MS 15842/1, fol. 313r.
104 GL, MS 11588/4, fol. 56.
105 Clothworkers' Company Library, Orders of Courts, 1639–1649, fol. 70r.
106 Mercers' Company Library, Acts of Court, fol. 49r.
107 GL, MS 5570/3, fos. 585, 625.
108 GL, MS 5445/17, unfol.
109 GL, MS 4655, fol. 116r.
110 GL, MS 3297/1, unfol.
111 HL, EL 194/7765.
112 TNA, SP 16/491/265–266, 345. For a valuable exploration of the application of "malignancy," see Thomas Leng, "The Meanings of 'Malignancy': The Language of Enmity and the Construction of the Parliamentarian Cause in the English Revolution,' *JBS*, 53 (2014), pp. 835–858.
113 See A. Laurence, *Parliamentary Army Chaplains, 1642–1651* (Woodbridge, 1990).
114 TNA, SP 16/491/265.
115 TNA, SP 16/491/345.
116 TNA, SP 16/492/49. See John Sedgewick, *England's Condition Parralleled with Jacobs* (London, 16432) FIND; Calybute Downing received more than £25 in December for his expenses on campaign, see TNA, SP 28/4/176. See above for Downing's sermon to the artillery company from 1640. See Jacqueline Eales, "Provincial Preaching and Allegiance in the First English Civil War (1640–6)," in Thomas Cogswell, Richard Cust, and Peter Lake (eds), *Politics, Religion and Popularity* (Cambridge, 2002), p. 196.
117 TNA, SP 16/492/9.
118 TNA, SP 16/491/310.
119 TNA, SP 16/492/87.
120 TNA, SP 16/492/68.
121 TNA, SP 16/492/69.
122 TNA, SP 16/492/266.
123 Lawrence, *The Complete Soldier*, pp. 156, 376–392.

124 Donagan, *War in England*, pp. 55–60.
125 *Laws and Ordinances of Warre* (London, 1642), title page, sig. B3r. The same laws were reprinted for Warwick on 19 November. See Donagan, *War in England*, pp. 148–149.
126 Charles Carlton, *Going to the Wars: The Experience of the British Civil Wars, 1638–1651* (London, 1992), p. 24.
127 Tom Cogswell, *Home Divisions: Aristocracy, the State and Provincial Conflict* (Manchester, 1998), pp. 194–196.
128 HL, STG 67/17.
129 Josiah Ricraft, *The Civill Warres of England* (London, 1649), sig. B1v: "*they called that galland soudier Generall* Brown *a* Woodmonger, *a tearme very suitable to their sufferings, or they know very well, that this* Woodmonger *hath oftentimes cudgeled their Militia from the* Generalissimo *to the* Corporall."
130 TNA, SP 19/144 Part 2 fol. 18.
131 Samuel Pecke, *Certaine Speciall and Remarkable Passages* (London, 1642), sig. A4r.
132 *A True and Perfect Relation* (London, 1642), pp. 4, 6; Samuel Pecke, *Certaine Speciall and Remarkable Passages* (London, 1642); *A true and exact relation* (London, 1642).
133 Christopher Scott, Alan Turton, and Eric Gruber von Arni, *Edgehill: The Battle Reinterpreted* (Barnsley, 2004), p. 44.
134 Fletcher, *Outbreak*, p. 346.
135 Peter Gaunt suggests losses were "probably fairly equal, with each losing a few hundred men" in *The English Civil War: A Military History* (London, 2014), p. 78. Ian Gentles, "The Civil Wars in England," in John Kenyon and Jane Ohlmeyer (eds), *The Civil Wars: A Military History of England, Scotland, and Ireland 1638–1660* (Oxford, 1998), p. 133.
136 Carlton, *Going to the Wars*, p. 231.
137 *A True Relation* (London, 1642), sigs. A3r–v.
138 *An Exact and True Relation of the Dangerous and Bloody Fight* (London, 1642), p. 7.
139 *Speciall News From the Army* (London, 1642), sig. A2r.
140 Thomas Case, *Gods Rising His Enemies Scattering* (London, 1644), pp. 1, 32. See Laura Knoppers (ed.), *The Oxford Handbook of Literature and the English Revolution* (Oxford, 2012), p. 12.
141 John Goodwin, *The Butchers Blessing* (London, 1642), pp. 1–2, 5–6. See John Coffey, *John Goodwin and the Puritan Revolution: Religion and Intellectual Change in 17th Century England* (Woodbridge, 2006), pp. 91–93.
142 BL, Add MS 40883, fol. 47v.
143 *Englands Division, and Irelands Distraction* (London, 1642), sig. A2r–v. See also Carlton, *Going to the Wars*, p. 230, in which the same passage is quoted.
144 *Eight Speeches Spoken in Guild-Hall* (London, 1642), pp. 18–19.
145 Robert Wood, *A Continuation of certaine Speciall and Remarkable Passages* (London, 1642), pp. 2–3. Como gives an excellent account in *Radical Parliamentarians*, pp. 137–138.

146 In the weeks that followed, Brentford's inhabitants created a petition to parliament to complain that had been "plundered and bereaved" by the king's forces and had lost property and goods worth thousands of pounds. See *The Humble Petition of All the Inhabitants* (London, 1642), sig. A2r.
147 *A Continuation of certain Speciall and Remarkable passages* (London, 1642), p. 2.
148 Braddick, *God's Fury*, pp. 248–249.
149 Bulstrode Whitelocke, *Memorials of the English Affairs* (London, 1682), p. 62.
150 BL, Add MS 37343, fos. 261v–262r.
151 Braddick, *God's Fury*, p. 249.
152 Gardiner, *History*, vol. I, p. 69; Carlton, *Going to the Wars*, p. 118.
153 Whitelocke, *Memorials*, p. 62.
154 *CJ*, vol. 2, p. 847.
155 TNA, SP 17/17F, fol. 11.
156 See Como, *Radical Parliamentarians*, p. 143. Members included Arthur Dewe, William Pennoyer, John Pocock, Edward Story, and Joseph Vaughn. These committeemen are listed in TNA, SP 28/144, part 2, fol 28v.
157 See Como, *Radical Parliamentarians*, p. 142; TNA, SP 19/1/54.
158 TNA, SP 28/144, part 2, fol 18r.
159 TNA, SP 19/1/54–55. Accounts from "the subcommittee for weekly assessment" show that £4,652 was collected between 13 December 1642 and 9 February 1643. See TNA, SP 19/144, part 2, fol. 28v.
160 TNA, SP 28/144, part 2, fol. 28v.
161 See Lindley, *Popular Politics*, p. 230. The following analysis draws extensively from Lindley.
162 TNA, SP 19/1/30–31; *A Declaration of the Lords and Commons Assembled in Parliament* (London, 1642).
163 See Lindley, *Popular Politics*, pp. 131 n. 134, 138–139 n. 159, 193 n. 175, 194 n. 181, 230, 316, 360 n. 22. Lindley seems to have also identified Vaughan as one of the leading promoters of St. Dunstan in the West's 22 December 1642 peace petition on p. 193.
164 See *CSPI* vol. 4, p. 2. David Como identified Coleman Street's Mark Hildesley as a "radical" due to his leadership and association with "John Goodwin's gathered flock." *Radical Parliamentarians*, p. 143. Hildesley may indeed have leaned toward "radicalism" at this point. He was a member of the Weavers' Hall subcommittee and had previously loaned toward the relief of Ireland. But opinions on the matter differ. John Coffey, for instance, has suggested that Hildesley was in fact a parliamentarian "of the middling sort." See Coffey, *John Goodwin and the Puritan Revolution*, p. 83.
165 Bodleian Library, MS Carte 80, fos. 106r–107r.
166 Lindley, *Popular Politics*, p. 229.
167 Jason Peacey, "'Fiery Spirits' and Political Propaganda: Uncovering a Radical Press Campaign of 1642," *PH*, 55 (2004), pp. 15, 21. *A Discourse Betweene A Resolved, and a Doubtfull Englishman* (London, [3 December] 1642, E.128[41]), sig. A4r; *The Way of Reconcilement* (London, [December] 1642), pp. 3–4. See also *Answer to the London Petition* (London, [14 December]

1642), p. 7. I wish to thank John Collins for his stimulating consideration of the legal parameters of "imminent danger" in 1642, a talk without which I would not have considered the above point.
168 Denzil Holles, *An Exact and True Relation of the Dangerous and Bloody Fight* (London, 1642), pp. 6–7; Carlton, *Going to the Wars*, p. 146.
169 Thomas Carte, *A Collection of Original Letters and Papers Concerning the Affairs in England, 1641–1660*, vol. 1 (London, 1739), p. 13.
170 TNA, SP 16/539/3 fos. 168–169.
171 LMA, MS COL/CA/01/01/061, fol. 34r; LMA MS P69/ETH/B/006/MS04241/001, p. 389.
172 See Eric Gruber von Arni, *Justice to the Maimed Soldier: Nursing, Medical Care and Welfare for Sick and Wounded Soldiers and their Families during the English Civil Wars and Interregnum, 1642–1660* (Aldershot, 2001), pp. 64–68.
173 HL, MS HM 55603, fos. 41v–42v.
174 Michael Mendle, "A Machiavellian in the Long Parliament before the Civil War," *Parliamentary History* 8 (1989), p. 116. For an extensive discussion of Drake's journal and notebooks, see Kevin Sharpe, *Reading Revolutions: The Politics of Reading in Early Modern England* (New Haven, 2000), especially pp. 121–163. As Sharpe points out, Drake departed England apparently "for his health" on 4 February 1643 (see p. 71).
175 For a valuable discussion of D'Ewes's political hiatus and return, see McGee, *An Industrious Mind*, pp. 381–385.
176 See, for instance, Braddick, *God's Fury*, pp. 247–248.
177 David Wootton, "From Rebellion to Revolution: The Crisis of Winter 1642/3 and the Origins of Civil War Radicalism," *EHR*, 105 (1990), p. 659; Hexter, *The Reign of King Pym* (Cambridge, MA, 1941), pp. 49–51, 67–72. For an earlier example of this trajectory, see Gardiner's *History*. See also, David L. Smith, *Constitutional Royalism and the Search for Settlement, c. 1640–1649* (Cambridge, 1994), pp. 112–114; Braddick, *God's Fury*, pp. 256–258. For the machinery of party propaganda at this time, see Peacey, "'Fiery Spirits' and Political Propaganda," p. 19. For a recent and subtle reevaluation of party dynamics and a convincing criticism of Hexter's original claims about party dynamics, see David Scott, "Politics in the Long Parliament," in George Southcombe and Grant Tapsell (eds), *Revolutionary England, c. 1630–c.1660: Essays for Clive Holmes* (London, 2016), pp. 32–55.
178 Richard Williams, *Peace, or No Peace* (London, 1643), sigs. A1r–v, A4v.
179 *His Majesties Declaration to all His loving Subjects* (Cambridge, 1642), pp. 38, 55, 69, 70, 78. Thomason's note shows that it was printed at York prior to Cambridge. *By the King. His Majesties fractious proclamation to the Cities of London and Westminster* (London, 1642).
180 *CJ* vol. 2, pp. 858–859; *A Continuation Of certain Speciall and Remarkable passages* (London, 1642, E.242[22]), pp. 1, 7; *Perfect Diurnall* (London, 1642, E.242[26]), sig. Z2r. See Como, *Radical Parliamentarians*, pp. 144–145.
181 TNA, SP 19/1/21. The Members included Sir William Brereton, Lord Brooke, Baron Howard of Escrick, Walter Long, the Earl of Manchester, Sir Thomas Middleton, Edmond Prideaux, William Purefor, John Pym, Lord Saye and

Sele, Sir Thomas Soame, William Spurstowe, William Strode, Sir Henry Vane junior, Samuel Vassall, and Lord Wharton. See M. A. E. Green, *Calendar of the Proceedings for Advance of Money, 1642–1656*, 3 vols (London, 1888), vol. 1, p. 1.
182 TNA, SP 19/1/21.
183 *A Catalogue of Sundry Knights, Aldermen* (London, 1642).
184 TNA, SP 19/1/21.
185 John Rushworth, *Historical Collections*, vol. 5 (London, 1721), pp. 52–77. A printed copy of the order can be seen in George Goring, *The Discovery of a great and wicked Conspiracie* (London, 1642), sig. A4v; Coates, *Impact*, pp. 23, 59.
186 TNA, SP 16/492/201, 203, 205, 207–208, 210–212, 215–217, 219–221, 223–224, 226, 228, 230, 232–233, 235, 237, 239, 241, 243–245, 247, 249, 251–252, 254, 256–258, 260.
187 Coates, *Impact*, pp. 59–60.
188 See ibid., p. 60; *Speciall Passages*, 22–29 November (London, 1642 E.128[28]), p. 138; *Speciall Passages* (London, 1642 E.129[5]), pp. 139, 143.
189 LMA, MS P69/PAN/B/001/MS05019/001, fos. 76, 83–84.
190 TNA, SP 16/492/215–16; see Coffey, *John Goodwin and the Puritan Revolution*, p. 82; Lindley, *Popular Politics*, p. 193; Pearl, *London*, pp. 324–325; Brenner, *Merchants and Revolution*, pp. 372–373. Avery invested £300 in the Irish Adventure. TNA, SP 63/290/151–152.
191 TNA, SP 16/492/232.
192 TNA, SP 16/492/212.
193 TNA, SP 16/492/219–220; LMA, MS COL/CC/01/01/041, fol. 67r; PA, HL/PO/JO/10/1/127–128. See Brenner, *Merchants and Revolution*, p. 455 n. 112.
194 TNA, SP 28/131/2 fol. 28r.
195 TNA, SP 16/492/235. See Brenner, *Merchants and Revolution*, p. 544. On 16 July 1642, Smith made the last part of his £200 investment for the Irish Adventure, TNA, SP 63/298 fol. 287.
196 TNA, SP 16/492/223. See G. A. Raikes (ed.), *The Ancient Vellum Book of the Artillery Company, being the Roll of Members from 1611–1682* (London, 1890), p. 66.
197 TNA, SP 19/78 fol. 96.
198 TNA, SP 19/78 fol. 102.
199 TNA, SP 16/492/207; SP 19/78 fol. 141v. The parish was assessed £1,184 and thus overpaid by £656.
200 TNA, SP 16/492/233; Liu, *Puritan London*, pp. 199–200.
201 TNA, SP 16/492/235.
202 Southwark Local History Library, St. Mary Newington Churchwardens' Accounts, 1632–1734, unfol.
203 TNA, SP 16/491/29. For more on the subject of loyalty to the king, see Richard Cust, *Charles I and the Aristocracy, 1625–1642* (Cambridge, 2013), chapter 5.
204 TNA, LMA MS P69/AND1/B/009/MS02088/001, illegible pagination; TNA, SP 16/492/24.
205 TNA, SP 16/492/221.

206 TNA, SP 16/492/249.
207 TNA, SP 16/492/208; SP 16/492/254.
208 TNA, SP 19/78 fol. 106.
209 TNA, SP 19/78 fol. 106r–121r.
210 TNA, SP 16/492/271–274, *An Ordinance and Declaration Of the Lords and Commons ... For the assessing of all such as have not contributed upon the Propositions* (London, 1642). The ordinance was dated 29 November 1642.
211 TNA, E179/147/577, fol. 2r.
212 TNA, E179/147/577, fol. 86r, which shows a total of "£72006-12-11." See also Coates, *Impact*, pp. 51–52. For the original plan, see Bodleian Library, MS Carte 80, fos. 106r–107r.
213 TNA, SP 19/1/57.
214 See Tai Liu, "Seaman, Lazarus," *ODNB* (2004); Liu, *Puritan London*, p. 157.
215 For Culverwell's godly preaching, see William Andrews Clark Memorial Library, Clark MS B8535 M3, 1625–1665.
216 See David Como, "Walker, George," *ODNB* (2004).
217 TNA, SP 16/500/6, fos. 35–38.
218 Lindley, "London's Citizenry in the English Revolution," in R. C. Richardson (ed.), *Town and Countryside in the English Revolution* (Manchester, 1992), p. 27.
219 St. Mary Magdalene Milk Street fell between Cripplegate Ward and Bread Street Ward. Thomas Case was apparently first to sign the Protestation of 5 May 1641, and on 8 May 1643 he received £20 to serve the parish over the course of 1643–4. See LMA, MS P69/MRY9/B/001/MS02597/001, fol. 59; LMA, MS P69/MRY9/B/007/MS02596/002, fol. 88r. See Walter, *Covenanting Citizens*, p. 88.
220 Liu, *Puritan London*, p. 118.
221 Ibid., pp. 37, 136. See TNA, SP 19/78 fol. 91.
222 LMA, MS P69/MIC6/B/005/MS04825/001, fol. 61.
223 LMA, MS P69/ALH7/B001/MS00819/001, fol. 145r.
224 LMA, MS P69/ALH8/B/013/MS00824/001, unfol.; see Liu, *Puritan London*, p. 31.
225 Liu, *Puritan London*, pp. 33, 81.
226 TNA, SP 16/492/210.
227 TNA, SP 16/492/207.
228 The above paragraph draws from Liu, *Puritan London*, pp. 25–29, 30–31.
229 John Vicars, *God on the Mount* (London, 1643, E.73[4]), p. 128.
230 Adrian Johns, "Coleman Street," *HLQ*, 71 (1998), pp. 33–34.
231 John Goodwin, *Anti-Cavalierism* (London, 1642), sig. A3r. See also Section I: Ireland's Cause.
232 TNA, E179/147/577.
233 See Liu, *Puritan London*, pp. 76–77.
234 LMA, MS P69/OLA2/B/001/MS04415/001, fos. 106r, 107v.
235 See Bodleian Library, MS Carte 80, fol. 106r; Broad Street returned only 48 percent of their assessment.
236 *LJ* vol. 5, p. 616.

237 LMA, MS P69/MGT1/B/001/MS04352/001, fol. 150v.
238 Ibid., fol. 149v. Six men loaned £20, including Edward Chard, Anthony Beninfield, Robert Lowther, William Librey, Edward Hopgoode, and William Downall. Richard Cox gave £15, while eight others gave £10.
239 See Peter Blayney, *The Bookshops of Paul's Cross Churchyard* (London, 1990).
240 This is an often-repeated comparison, first made by Christopher Hill, *Economic Problems of the Church from Archbishop Whitgift to the Long Parliament* (Oxford, 1956), p. 255; Pearl repeated the sentiment in *London*, p. 183. John Coffey has been the most recent to deploy the phrase in *John Goodwin and the Puritan Revolution*, p. 2.
241 Henri Lefebvre, *The Production of Space* (Oxford, 1991), pp. 116–119.
242 *The True and Originall Copy of the first Petition* (London, 1642), sigs. A1r–A4r. Thomason acquired his copy on 15 December.
243 *CJ* vol. 2, p. 875.
244 *The True and Originall Copy of the first Petition* (London, 1642); *The Lord Whartons Speech to the Petitioners for Peace* (London, 1642); Pearl, *London*, p. 255; Brenner, *Merchants and Revolution*, pp. 439–443.
245 BL, Harley MS 164, fol. 245. 9 December 1642.
246 LMA, MS COL/CC/01/01/041, fol. 43v.
247 Ibid., fol. 43r–v.
248 Ian Gentles, "Parliamentary Politics and the Politics of the Street: The London Peace Campaigns of 1642–3," *PH*, 26 (2007), p. 140.
249 LMA, MS COL/CC/01/01/041, fol. 43r–v.
250 *Image of the Malignants Peace* (London, 1642), sig. A4r. George Thomason's Ms note shows that he acquired his copy on 17 December 1642.
251 *CJ* vol. 2, pp. 884, 894; Lindley, *Popular Politics*, p. 246.
252 BL, Harley MS 164, fol. 265r. *CJ* vol. 2, p. 894.
253 *Mercurius Aulicus*, 16 January; *CJ* vol. 2, p. 894.
254 *Mercurius Aulicus*, 16 January, A3r–v.
255 PA, HL/PO/JO/10/1/139, "Peace Petitions from 22 December 1642." See Lindley, *Popular Politics*, pp. 340–342.
256 BL, Harley MS 164, fol. 270v.
257 *LJ* vol. 5, p. 590; see Bodleian Library, Clarendon MS 1654, Charles I to Ormond.
258 Pearl, *London*, pp. 256–257.
259 LMA, MS COL/CC/01/01/041, fol. 43r.
260 Brenner, *Merchants and Revolution*, p. 442; Gentles, "Parliamentary Politics and the Politics of the Street," p. 146.
261 Pearl, *London*, p. 256.

3

A third house of parliament

Six Londoners reached Oxford by way of carriage between one and two o'clock in the afternoon on Monday, 2 January 1643. Their intended purpose was to deliver directly to the king the petitions that had been approved by the Lord Mayor and Common Council. Although the travelers found that they could "gett no lodging before night," they persisted; the purpose of their mission was too pressing to be stalled.[1] Two of the six men, Sir George Garrett and Sir George Clark, were City aldermen, and with them went Peter Jones, George Henley, Richard Bateman, and Barny Reames.[2] The king knew Garrett personally as he had dined at his residence in the City before fleeing for Oxford the previous January. The other five men had varying political outlooks. Clark and Henley were both involved with the second Root and Branch Petition from December 1641 and might safely be labeled as radicals. Henley had directly opposed the king again in that month when he joined Lilburne, Overton, and Walwyn by signing the Lunsford petition. Jones sat as a "lone conservative" on the Council in 1642, and Bateman, who Lindley described as a political "trimmer," sat on both the Committee for the Fortification of the City and the London Militia Committee. Tai Liu has suggested that Reames was simply one of a number of "well-heeled parish zealots" from Saint Martin Orgar.[3] Taken together, then, the group was politically heterogeneous, an important point that should not be overlooked when considering their appointment as City delegates. Common Council was at this point committed to a fair hearing for both respective war and peace petitions.

The six men obtained an audience with the king shortly after five o'clock in the evening. Charles provided the travelers with a written answer to their petition on the following Wednesday and requested that they might be accompanied back to London by Henry Herne, a messenger who was to read the king's response to their petitions at a Common Hall.[4] Charles hoped that calling such an assembly, which included all City liverymen and which could include upwards of 4,000 attendees, might ensure that his message would reach well beyond the confines of Common Council and maintain "faire play above Board."[5] The king, in other words, believed that a large audience would be best suited to hearing his request.

Historians have by and large focused on the winter of 1642–3 in terms of war and peace party interests in the House of Commons and the failed peace negotiations between parliament and the king that collapsed in April and left the end of war nowhere in sight.[6] Decidedly less attention has been given to the London mission to Oxford, the king's response, and the aftermath of these crucially important developments, which, as we shall see, fundamentally rearticulated London's relationship to the king's position and parliament's cause. The king's response, which singled out a group of seven leading Londoners as treasonous, served to further cleave divisions in the City but it also renewed a sense of urgency for the need to support parliament's efforts. Spearheaded by the accused Londoners and their militant allies in parliament, the king's "attempt on the seven" ushered in a period of unparalleled coordination between parliament and the City. Stemming from these efforts would be radical new propositions, alliances, and oaths, the establishment of coordinated iconoclasm, the introduction of new policing methods, the raising of auxiliary City forces, new demands for loans, and the construction and maintenance of the Lines of Communication, metropolitan fortifications. London thus embarked on a new phase of wartime mobilization over the winter of 1642–3 and the following spring, a time when the Lord Mayor and Common Council began acting as "a third house of parliament" in order to extract money and resources from London. Before this all could happen, however, six Londoners had to escort the king's messenger back to the City. It is to the outcome of this fateful conveyance that we must now turn.

The attempt on the seven Londoners

Charles had good reason to assume that the vast majority of Londoners remained sympathetic to his position. December's widespread peace petitioning afforded some reason for optimism; so too did printed books and pamphlets, which were rife with anti-war sentiment. Works such as *A Plea For Peace* and *Accommodation Cordially Desired* left little doubt about the extent of popular loyalist sympathies in the capital.[7] Efforts, as we have seen, were already well under way to target and extinguish loyalist preaching and popular intransigence in the metropolis. One need look no further than a single sheet printed in November to show the names of fifty-six prominent "Knights, Aldermen, Doctors: Minister and Citizens" who were being held in Gresham College and Crosby House for "misdemeanors" and included their refusal to contribute toward the cause.[8] Others had been jailed in the Fleet since July for reasons that ranged from "readeinge a declaracion of the Kinge in P[ar]ishe of St Gyles in the Fields" to "levying war ag[ains]t the Parliam[en]t."[9] Where divisions existed, the king espied opportunity.

But even if this was so, Charles miscalculated the extent to which he might take advantage of these divisions; and in so doing he played directly into the hands of his militant opponents. At the very least, he seems to have conflated a handful of displays of loyalism and demands for peace with a willingness among them to take action – a mistake that he made again months later when backing Edmund Waller's foiled attempt to secure London for the king.[10] If not simply obtuse in tone, the king's letter, which was printed in Oxford on 5 January, was in places positively alienating. In this he complained that London's "Brownists, Anabaptists, and all manner of Sectaries" had all been busy preaching "seditious Sermons against his Majestie," and ordered that contributors toward parliament's war "must expect the severest punishment the Law can inflict." By far the most problematic demand, however, came next in the form of a request that seven prominent citizens be arrested immediately on charges of high treason. Four of these men were well known civic leaders including Mayor Pennington, Alderman John Fowke, Captain John Venn, and Colonel Randall Mainwaring. The other three were less prominent, but nonetheless important military men: Richard Browne, as we have seen, was recently placed in charge of City dragoons, while Edmund Harvey led a City troop of horse, and Robert Tichborne served as commander of the City Yellow regiment. Of the four leaders accused of treason, Pennington was singled out in the king's letter as the "pretended Lord Maior" and "the principall author of those Calamities which so nearly threaten the ruine of that famous City." "Ven, Foulke, and Mainwaring" fared little better; they were lumped together as "persons notoriously guilty of Schisme and high Treason."[11] Charles had singled out a handful of London's most respected public figures as patently guilty, as *personae non gratae*. More perplexing yet, he had done so in a manner that closely resembled his infamous attempt on the five members the previous year.

Admittedly, Charles had good reason to be suspicious of the seven accused, and this was particularly true of Pennington, Fowke, Venn, and Mainwaring. Whitelocke for one noted that the king "could willingly pardon all, except Pennignton, Ven, Fouke & Mainwaring."[12] Amerigo Salvetti, the Tuscan agent in London, recalled that the king had suspected "l'artifice" on the part of Pennington and his allies for some time, and that it was his intention that his letter should be read at a Common Hall with the hope that it might bypass their tampering in particular.[13] Pennington, for one, frequently demonstrated that he would use any means possible to promote parliament's cause in London, no matter how controversial. He was a leading member of the Militia Committee, and one of the original architects of the July 1642 motion to start weekly voluntary contributions toward the war. He was, as we have now seen, closely involved with early efforts to remove ministers who preached opposition or were lukewarm toward parliament's cause.

Although somewhat less outspoken, the other accused citizens nevertheless enjoyed their own reputations for radicalism. Alderman Fowke was a fellow member of the London Militia Committee and had grievances against customs duties and the king that dated to the 1620s. These made him, as Pearl explained, one of "the crown's most persistent opponents." John Venn had been a prominent activist in City politics for two years. A close ally of Pennington, Venn played a leading role in the push to remove the royalist mayor Richard Gurney, and from October he had served as the parliamentarian governor of Windsor where he defended firmly against royalist attacks. One contemporary letter account in which "Pennington and Venn" were singled out, claimed they were as "two banquerot – Citi[z]ens white & Proud a paire of 10 groates Petty foggers."[14] Mainwaring, who was appointed as deputy to Mayor Pennington in August, soon thereafter gained the sobriquet "the crased Mercer." His regiment of Redcoats earned a reputation for bravery at Edgehill, but they had since turned their efforts to policing the metropolis through crowd control, house raids, and the seizure of goods belonging to known and suspected detractors.[15] If less well known than their fellow accused, Robert Tichborne, Edmund Harvey, and Richard Browne had each found an important part to play in City or parliamentary affairs.

Four days after the king's letter was available in print, Common Council reported to the Commons that "a printed book now lately published as a pretended answere to the aforesaid Peticion" was also available.[16] George Thomason acquired the self-proclaimed "true Copie" of *His Majesties gracious Answer* on 11 January.[17] The next day, "Richard Hearne confessed at the Bar that he had printed *His Majesties gracious Answer*" and that he received his copy from Henry Glapthorne, a playwright "who lived in Fetter Lane."[18] Hearne, who was no stranger to censors, landed himself in the Fleet for his part in the printing of the "pretended answere," but there is no evidence for punishment of Glapthorne, the purported author.[19] If *His Majesties gracious Answer* was not the king's official response to the City petition, why did it draw such attention? One possible reason is that the pamphlet depicted a far more amenable royal position. The king, by this reading, was not simply interested in arresting the seven, but was instead "verie willing and concurrent to any propositions," and that he believed "subjects" to be the "kings best inheritance, the flower of his Crowne, and glorie of his Scepter." Charles, according to Hearne and Glapthorne, never found himself "in more or better security, then when guarded with the faithfull hearts and valiant hands of those courageous and well-experienced Citizens" of London.[20] These irenic remarks, it should be added, made no mention of the "pretended answer," London's seditious ministers, the need for aboveboard dealing, a threat to the king's person, or indeed of any of the seven accused. Hearne and Glapthorne both knew that any mention of the king's concerns and accusations would cast the king in a negative light and thus stymie peace negotiations. They had, in short, put forward an amenable – albeit fake – version of the king's response.

Printing about parliamentary affairs without a license of course meant that both men had broken censorship laws.[21] But this alone does not explain the haste with which Common Council delivered the "pretended answere" to Westminster. Again, one plausible explanation for their quick action is that Pennington and his allies, like Glapthorne and Hearne, recognized that a conciliatory version of the king's letter posed a contradictory narrative, one that isolated their militant position and, worse yet, eroded the pressing need for mobilization. If ostensibly less dangerous to the accused, the "pretended answere" threatened to do irreparable damage to wider belligerent interests. Pennington and his allies therefore had little choice but to seek the censorship of the "pretended answer." This view is supported by the fact that the king's original hostile response remained widely available in London, while copies of *His Majesties gracious Answer* were confiscated. Eight unexpurgated editions of the king's letter circulated over the course of January, and at least one edition claiming to be printed in Oxford had in fact been printed in London.[22] In an ostensibly self-damaging move, then, Pennington and his fellow zealots actually preferred to heighten public awareness of the king's charges of treason; doing so bolstered support for their cause. The treatment of the king's answer thus sheds light on some of the new and sophisticated ways in which partisans began to use print as propaganda in their efforts to sway popular opinions and shape mobilization.[23]

On 12 January, the same day that the Commons ordered Glapthorne's book to be censured, they agreed that the king's "answer to the City Petition should be read in Common Hall" in order "to see if it was the same that was printed [and] which contained 'Matter very scandalous to the Parliament, dangerous to the City and whole Kingdome.'"[24] That afternoon, parliament established the aptly named "Committee for the Vindication of the Parliament from the Aspersions thrown on them in the King's Answer to the London Petition," which was to meet in the Painted Chamber at eight o'clock the following morning to determine what answers would be made to the king's letter.[25]

Meanwhile, Pennington ordered extra precautions for London's defenses, including a "substanc[i]all double watch" and extra attention for guarding the City's "gates & landing places."[26] On the following afternoon, Mainwaring and his Redcoats stood guard at the Guildhall while Common Hall commenced. The king's letter, read according to plan by his messenger Henry Herne, proved to be the same as that which was circulating in London, and not Glapthorne and Hearne's conciliatory "pretended answer." According to one chronicler, Herne's reading was uninterrupted apart from a single cry of "No Lord Maior," which came from a royalist who snuck into the meeting under alderman's robes. More telling to the effect of the reading were the declarations of the many attendants who shouted out that "they would all live and dye with" the seven accused.[27]

After Herne's speech, it was time to hear from the two men chosen by the parliamentary Committee for the Vindications. They were none other than the earl of Manchester and John Pym. Both were stalwart, if obvious, supporters of the war effort, but they shared another important distinction: They, too, had been accused of high treason by the king. It just so happened that their accusation came almost exactly a year earlier as part of the debacle over the five members. They had narrowly escaped arrest when Charles marched on Westminster with 400 soldiers and entered the House to make their arrest. Manchester and Pym were not just important parliamentary leaders – they stood as stark reminders of the king's willingness to transgress the law, to infringe upon parliamentary privileges, and to use military force to obtain his ends. One would be hard pressed to find better suited speakers.

Although relatively brief, their speeches left little to be guessed about the dire state of affairs, and in particular the injustice that threatened London's leadership. Manchester spoke first, acknowledging the "many wounding Aspersions [that had been] cast upon Persons of very eminent Authority in your City, and upon others of very great fidelity and trust among you." He then promised that members of both Houses "will never desert you, but will stand by you with their lives and fortunes for the preservation of the City in general, and those persons in particular, who have been faithful." Pym followed with a slightly longer speech in which he noted especially the "great aspersion upon the proceedings of Parliament, and very scandalous and injurious to many particular Members of this City." Rather than simply allude to the four "eminent" City leaders, Pym named them directly, claiming "*That the King demands the Lord Major, Master Alderman Fowke, Colonell Ven, and Collonell Manwaring, to be delivered up as guilty of Schisme and high Treason.*" "Concerning which," he went on,

> I am commanded to tell you, as the Sense of both Houses of Parliament, That this demand is against the priviledge of Parliament (two of them being Members of the Commons House) most dishonourable to the City, That the

Lord Mayor of *London* should be subjected to the Violence of every base fellow, be assaulted, seiz'd on, without due process or warrant, which the Law doth afford every private man.[28]

These terms bore a striking resemblance to those that accompanied the king's attempt on the five members in 1642. Pym's words agreed with Manchester's, making it clear that parliament's military leadership would maintain political solidarity with well-affected Londoners. He reminded those gathered "that the King is drawn by the ill councell now about Him," and "that Religion, the whole Kingdom, this glorious City, and the Parliament, are all in great danger." The best means for staving off the threat would be to provide "a further contribution, whereby this Army may be maintain'd for all your safeties." To conclude, Pym returned to the matter of "my Lord Major here, and those worthy Members of your City, that are demanded," declaring that parliament planned to stand by them, "that you should express it your selves likewise," and that similar protection would be granted "to all others that have done any thing" to help the cause. "Such an acclamation" thereafter erupted that it could "have drown'd all the former," giving way to a chant of "we will live and dye with them, We will live and dye with them."[29]

The very next day, Fowke arrived at the House to express thanks for Pym's speech and to request that his words "might be printed for satisfying the people."[30] The diarist Sir Simonds D'Ewes noted soon thereafter that the speeches were available "in print with that which was spoken against it in the Guild hall by Edward Earle of Manchester and Mr Pym."[31] The *Two Speeches* were readily available to underscore solidarity and remind Londoners that regular financial contributions were needed to maintain defensive forces. If the request to have the speeches printed was telling, so too was the passing of an ordinance on the same day that allowed "the Lo[rd] Mayor & Comittee for the Militia in London" to disarm anyone who had refused to provide money according to the assessments of the previous November.[32] On 15 January, Mainwaring and his Redcoats began to raid the houses of any who had failed to contribute to assessments. A second ordinance passed both Houses just two days later and called "for stopping all carriages waggons, and other conveyances going to or from Oxford without leave of Parliament or of the Earl of Essex." These were the first in a series of targeted efforts that followed in the wake of the attempt on the seven.

Indeed, polemicists and pamphleteers soon voiced their own opinions regarding the king's attempt. Edward Bowles, a chaplain to Colonel John Meldrum's regiment, offered his own assessment of the occasion in *Plaine English*, a tract that echoed opinions from Manchester's recent speech at the Guildhall.[33] Bowles expressed bewilderment at the king's recent order to arrest the seven, observing that "we now see instead of those 6. at least 26 accused of treason for the same cause that they were, that is, being forward and active for the preservation of the Kingdome from the Kings *Guard*." Bowles went on, urging readers to note the uncanny resemblance between the events of January 1643 and January 1642. "It is," he went on, "the same season of the yeare." But was it not, he asked, "a more unquestionable cause, where are your pikes and protestations? Your courage and resolution? Do you conceive your danger more, your enemies more formidable, should not your valour encrease with your danger, if it were so, when the cause remains the same?"[34] The cause was, in short, more pressing than ever. The same attempt that threatened leading politicians in parliament in January 1642, and which led members of the City trained bands to accompany the five members back to Westminster with copies of the Protestation affixed to their muskets and pikes "like a little square banner," had since come to threaten citizens of London.[35]

Of course, Bowles was not the only one to exploit the opportunity afforded by these heightened political tensions. Emboldened, petitioners resurrected, altered, and resubmitted their December petition that called for the use of sequestered estates to fund the City's war effort.[36] Their new petition was almost exactly the same as the copy that was delivered by Watkins and Shute, but it dispelled any question about the significance of recent political developments, noting in a proviso that their purpose had become even more relevant in light of the "pressing dangers upon this City and Kingdome" and the "conditions" that were recently "expressed by Master Pym at *Guild Hall* in the City of *London*."[37] Unlike their previous attempt to have the petition read, which, as we have seen, led to a prompt dismissal by the Commons, their new effort made considerable headway. On 26 January, John Blakiston raised the matter of the petitioners' request in the Commons and suggested that the Committee for the Advance of Money should produce new "instructions for raisinge and conductine [*sic*] of an army of volunteers for suppression of ill affected parties." Further, Blakiston proposed that the Commons should nominate members for a "Committee of Association" that would oversee the direction of men at arms from England, Ireland, and Scotland, and who would "leade their forces where they seeme fitte." Alexander Rigby, a "war party man," was nominated to appoint a committee that would "treate with some of the citie for some course for raisinge of a constante army of 20000 men."[38] Although there is in the end no evidence to suggest that the "humble petition" gained serious traction, the fact remains that the failed petition from the previous December made new headway in the wake of the king's charge against the seven.

These developments alarmed the king's supporters. On 10 February, Sir Edward Nicholas wrote to Henry Hastings, earl of Huntington, in the hope that he might assuage his friend's anxiety over rumors that a powerful army of 20,000 was being raised in the metropolis. "In London," Nicholas assured, "the prentises will not suffer ye Parliam[en]t Drums to beate for Recreuts, but say that they will have peace."[39] Writing eleven days later, Nicholas clarified his meaning, adding that Huntingdon "neede not to apprehend ye Lo[rd] Brookes Comming to Staffordshire or out of London." Brooke's hands were, he claimed, still tied in the capital, where he was "very earnesrtly labouring there against any Treaty for an Accomodac[i]on." Further, Nicholas assured, "the truth is they in London owe soe much to their Souldiers as they are reddyer to mutyeny, then to march." Should it not be Brooke, he went on, but another commander, such as Philip "Skippon (the Roundheads God of warre)," then there was still little reason to worry; Skippon sat "sick at Windsor" while the City waited in limbo for "want money to rayse or send any considerable forces."[40]

Nicholas was doubtless correct. No matter how much traction militant petitioners had gained, the majority of Londoners were unprepared to finance and enlist a new army of 20,000. But this fact alone should not obscure the other important developments that were taking place in the metropolis. Indeed, City militants had recently hardened their resolve in light of the king's charge of treason against the seven Londoners. Well aware of the fact that there would be little "hope for pardon" and further that "a Cessac[i]on and Treaty for an Accomodation" would almost certainly lead to the need "to make upp their Trunks & be gonne," zealous Londoners pushed harder than ever to transform their City.[41]

Leveraging the king's attempt

London's radical leadership, in close association with members of parliament's war party, leveraged fears about the king's accusation to gain control over London's press and secure the metropolis. On 22 January, *Aulicus* reported that "none of His Majesties Subjects of that City are to submit to any Orders, Directions, or Commands" from the Lord Mayor, and further that the king was "once more requiring, as well the Sheriffes as other the Magistrates thereof, to cause the said *Pennington*, *Foulke*, *Ven*, and *Manwaring*, to be apprehended and committed to safe custody, that so He might proceed against them as in case of Treason." Mentioned again with the four leading traitors were "*Browne*, *Tichborne*, and *Harvey*."[42] Repeated discussion of the arrest orders guaranteed that the king's actions would remain at the forefront of public concern. Indeed, contemporaries remained transfixed by the entire episode, which compelled pamphleteers and propagandists to churn out yet more material that claimed to be the king's answer, or at the very least offered a reinterpretation of the course of events. Difficulty discerning the king's original message from fabricated responses became so widespread that some feared "the whole citty" might erupt "in a combustion."[43] On 23 January, the Committee of Safety ordered that all livery companies were "directed to forbeare to publish" any material relating to the printed versions of the king's answer and that they were "required to bring the said lettres with the messengers thereof to this Committee." The delivery of any such material would be received by the Committee as "an argument of their good affection to the Parliament." The architects of the order, which included Pym, Manchester, and Saye and Sele, wished to maintain tight control over the narrative of the king's charge against the seven.[44]

As with the censorship of "the pretend letter," controlling print remained a top priority for belligerents in Westminster and London alike. Yet, over the course of the month, numerous tracts sought to weigh in on the attempt on the seven. These ranged from novel interpretations to politically explicit commentaries. *The Bloody Game at Cards* offered an interesting view of the recent struggle, which was "Shuffled at London, Cut at Westminster, Delt at Yorke, and Plaid in the open field," and in which the king of hearts faced off against the "Citty-clubs."[45] *An Humble Remonstrance* offered a decidedly less veiled interpretation, urging "your most excellent Majesty" to reconsider his charge against Pennington, Venn, Fowke, and Mainwaring, and instead "think on them as innocent, and cleare from all suspition of treason or treachery."[46] More explicitly condemning tracts followed soon thereafter. One of these, *A Briefe Answer to a Book Intitled His Majesties Letter*, offered sympathy for the efforts of Pennington and his fellow belligerents, and condemnation for Charles's actions. The author of *Animadvertions upon the Kings Answer*, meanwhile, concluded that it was "cunning and deceit" on the part of the king's meddling ministers – "his pernitious, pestilent, and desperate seducers" – that had robbed the king of reason and made the Crown a "stalking horse to pernicious ends."[47] Acquired by Thomason on 30 January, *A Brief Answer* questioned the king's own "power over His Rationall Faculties" and challenged the claim that Pennington was a "pretended Lord Maior." *A Brief Answer* not only suggested that the City would remain "as zealous for the Parliament as ever they were," but also that Pennington's appointment as Lord Mayor was legitimate due to the fact that he was "chosen by the *major* part" in parliament.[48] Doubtless, the seven accused welcomed – if not actively promoted – such printed votes of confidence. The presence of *A Brief Answer* provided an important counter to the king's cause in London. Fowke, meanwhile, was busy writing his own response to the king's accusation. Printed on 11 February, *The Declaration and Vindication* asserted that their purpose was to "safeguard" London to protect both "the subjects liberties, and the security of the true Protestant religion."[49]

The shift in popular opinion was important, but the king's fateful charge had another altogether more significant impact on the war effort: it steeled proponents of the cause and energized efforts by the accused to mobilize the metropolis. Indeed, in the wake of the king's attempt, Pennington, Fowke, Venn, and Mainwaring spearheaded efforts to transform London through aggressive policing, the collection of loans, and the construction of eleven miles of defensive fortifications.

Londoners genuinely feared the threat of royalist attack in the aftermath of Turnham Green, and tensions remained high throughout the winter of 1642–3. Weekly reports warned of "suspitious dangerous and idle p[er]sons" who resided in the "out p[ar]ishes" and of countless "malignants" who lurked in the City.[50] The sinful City was always threatened by the prospect of divine reprisal, moreover; London ministers hurled daily warnings upon the lukewarm, the recalcitrant, and the "neuter." If London did not suffer the fate of Magdeburg, it might just as soon become like the cities of the plain, a Sodom and Gomorrah, or still yet maybe a Meroz.

The accused eagerly promoted this pessimistic view. They took the king at his word, which meant that a peace would almost certainly lead to their trial for treason. Contemporaries readily recognized and spoke of the danger that awaited the original five members and the newly added seven. Well aware of this prospect, the seven promoted the cause that would best preserve their lives and livelihoods. Mainwaring and his Redcoats worked diligently to search out and seize upon any and all goods that could be used to support their cause. Joined by Captain Harvey on 21 January, Mainwaring confiscated £300 that belonged to Sir Nicholas Crispe, a merchant taylor who, if his later biographers are to be believed, had been busy delivering gold and supplies to the king in Oxford while "disguised as a butter-woman on horseback."[51] One month later, *Aulicus* claimed that Mainwaring and his men had disrupted a meeting of the vestry at St. Giles Cripplegate after their Sunday sermon to "demand to have the Church stock delivered to them for the use of the Parliament." When it became clear that they had no money, the troop decided to relieve the parishioners of their "*poores money*." Mainwaring and his associates became so successful and feared that the press could soon claim that the "*Redcoates*" had "in effect become Masters of the Citie."[52] Meanwhile, feverish efforts were under way to raise more money and men. Richard Browne worked diligently to post "up tickets every where to signifie that he will give four shillings six pence *per diem* to such as will bring Horse and Armes of their owne to serve under him as Dragoneers."[53] The seven accused Londoners who stood to lose the most from peace showed no signs of backing down. They wrote tracts, issued precepts, policed the metropolis, and worked outright to raise a new army. Their range of efforts encapsulated the metropolitan war effort.

On 18 February 1643, members of both Houses travelled to the City to request a new loan of £60,000 to "keep ye Army from disbanding." On the same day that the request for the loan arrived, London militants delivered a collection of propositions to Common Council "to be considered on for the reforming right ordring and contracting of the Army."[54] Fowke vetted the proposal and was asked to decide whether or not their request was fit to be delivered on to parliament. On 20 February, Fowke made the short trip to Westminster with Alderman Gibbs, Abraham Chamberlin, Theophilius Riley, James Russell, and John Kendrick to express the "cheerfulness and alacrity" with which they agreed to lend the £60,000. They immediately offered a show of support in the shape of £6,000 and declarations of the amounts that the "Lord Maior Aldermen and Comons" of the Council would lend "respectively." In return, however, they had set out nine specific requests that would shape London's relationship to the war effort going forward. These included the expectation that parliament might agree to reduce the total weekly assessments on the City, that MPs might themselves pay a surety into the Guildhall as a means "to incourage others" to loan money, and that assessments "may not wholy lie uppon the willing." Further, it was expected that parliament would give no "credit" to the "private persons" who were responsible for spreading "misinfomacions" about the City, and finally that if a peace be settled the king's forces would "goe to their severall habitacions" rather than to London where they might cause a "disturbance of the peace safety and welfare of the said Citty." Their request seemed reasonable enough; in exchange for the £60,000, they would be better placed to protect their inhabitants – including the accused – by pledging to deny false claims and keep the king's disbanded armies well away from the metropolis.

Yet there were "further humble desires" that Fowke considered fit to pass on for consideration.[55] Appended to the nine initial requests were three additional points drawn directly from the propositions regarding parliament's army. Each of these went well beyond matters of financial sureties and rates of assessment; instead, they revealed Common Council's newfound willingness to weigh in on matters of national importance, to suggest the "preservacion of our Religion Lawes and Liberties" and the "reformacion of what is amisse in Church and Comonwealth." The final three propositions sought to broach the topics of military reform, indemnity for the City officials, and the establishment of a religious and political association – all issues that were at the center of the radical December and January petitions, and which, as we have seen, made considerable headway over the previous two months. The City expected that important reforms would be made to Essex's army, but their most pressing concern was for the establishment of "a religious Governm[en]t and firme associac[i]on" that would legally bind the Commons and the City to mutual defense. Such a "Covenant," they proclaimed, formed the basis of their willingness to loan money.[56]

Short of cash, parliament was in no position to ignore such requests, and on 23 February both Houses issued a letter response to the three key propositions: reform in the Army, indemnity for adhering to parliament, and the proposal for a religious and political association were all thus addressed. The matter of indemnity was readily agreed upon, while "the other two proposicions being matters of great importance and consequence," were put aside with the promise that they would be taken "into a speedy and serious consideracion."[57] Although temporarily tabled, Common Council's decision to weigh in on matters of such "great importance" was in itself significant. It suggests that they were aware of the increased political leverage that came as a result of parliament's pressing need, but also that they were open to using the moment as a means to protect the seven accused and to advance their own stake in determining how the war would be fought. Parliament's access to the nation's greatest concentration of people and wealth would depend, in short, upon their willingness to entertain Common Council's decision to negotiate as a "third house." Having made their case, Common Council next set about drawing up orders for raising the remaining £54,000.

Soon thereafter the "minister of every parish church" in London received instructions to "publish" their request and take pains to preach sermons that would "stirr" parishioners "upp effectually to advance freely." Churchwardens were ordered "to repaire to every Inhabitant and Lodger within their severall parishes and earnestly to perswade them unto the good work."[58] The stationer and printer for the City, Richard Coates, was ordered to print "300 orders for the Speedie raising of 60000ˡ" for distribution throughout London's parishes.[59] Parochial records reveal a spotty but in some cases detailed picture of the collection. Indeed, they present a largely fragmented landscape in which some gave freely and others were disinterested or refused. Fifteen parishioners from poor parish St. Katherine Coleman, Fenchurch Street, for instance, paid sums that ranged from a modest 10s. to the very impressive amount of £50.[60] Returns from the parish make specific note of fourteen individuals who were "able, but would lend nothing." Attendants from St. Stephen Walbrook gave an impressive £901, while those from John the Evangelist gave the somewhat more modest sum of £113.[61] St. Andrew by the Wardrobe produced a list of fourteen contributors who gave a total of £55.[62] Vestrymen from St. Lawrence Jewry agreed to pay "4s. 8d. for 12 weeks" to help pay arrears and keep an army in the field.[63] The churchwardens at St. Mary Abchurch, meanwhile, paid 18s 1d to deal with the "busines of subscription, collection, and payment of money towards the 60000ˡ advanced to the Parliament."[64] Procuring the full £60,000 loan was, in the end, of limited success, with some £23,000 of the total collected.[65] Already, a gradual if general flagging of commitment could be sensed in the poor returns, which obviously paled in comparison to the oversubscribed £30,000 loan. Yet even if Londoners were not so forward as they had been, City leaders had nevertheless assured their own closer proximity to parliament's cause, pledging mutual defense and making their own cases in exchange for the money needed to keep parliament's armies fielded.

The Lines of Communication

On the same day that Fowke reported to Common Council about his delivery of the propositions, Colonel Mainwaring was busy recounting his own meeting with "some skilfull Engeneers" who had assessed the state of London's defenses. Mainwaring's report reveals detailed information about plans for protecting the metropolis, and especially of the many strategically positioned earthworks that needed attention to make the City impregnable. Gravel Lane was to be built up with "one Bulwark and halfe a battery"; at Whitechapel Windmills there was to be "A horne worke with two flancks"; the area between Whitechapel Church and Shoreditch was to have "one Redoubt with flankes." More batteries were to be set in Islington, "a battery and breastwork on the hill neere Clarkenwell towards Hampsteed way," a "redoubt and two flanks" for St. Giles in the Fields. Further fortifications were set for "Tyborne highway and the second turning that goeth towards West[minster]," ending with what was to be "a large forte with flankes on all sides" set for "hide park corner," and earthworks set to defend Westminster at "Tuttlefields." Finally, it was recommended that "at the end of every street" there should be an open space that could be set with "defensible breastworks" that would be "muskett proofe" and allow for turnpikes. When put to vote, councilors approved of all of the proposed fortifications and further appointed a committee of twenty, headed by Mainwaring, which would see to the "speedy proceeding" of the construction.[66] Committee members were permitted to demolish any "shedds and buildings as they shall thinke necessary" and dig up fields – a sort of eminent domain without the financial remuneration – and that their actions would be fully "defended by [the] authority" of Common Council. Mainwaring and his twenty fellow committeemen had, in short, been granted carte blanche to transform London's defenses.

The Lord Mayor and Common Council provided additional and indispensable support for their plans. Work soon began in earnest on fortifications that would come to encompass London, Westminster, and Southwark, and be known collectively as the Lines of Communication. Plans to improve London's defenses had been under discussion since the previous year, and some progress had been made during the autumn when, in the aftermath of Edgehill, trenches were dug and ramparts built, and Skippon and a group of leading officers, including Mainwaring, Richard Browne, and Thomas Player, were sent to devise the best means to fortify the City's entryways.[67] Perhaps more impressive than the sheer scope of the Lines, and indeed the speed with which they were erected, was the fact that they were devised, constructed, and maintained entirely by Londoners. Building efforts were redoubled in the aftermath of the attempt on the seven, and particularly at the behest of Mayor Pennington.[68] *A True Declaration* praised the Lord Mayor for being "courageously bold" in his promotion of the "workes," an undertaking that was said to extend from "Gods Spirit in your heart," and owed to his "piety and constant resolution to defend the Protestant Religion, and your constancie in opposing those malignants that would destroy the King."[69]

Common Council, at the behest of Pennington and Mainwaring, had in fact produced a number of orders to livery companies and parishes, including a tax of "eight whole fifteenths," and requests for tools that could be used to build the Lines.[70] City accounts reveal that "200 ticketts" were to be printed and distributed as a means "to perswade Citizens to send theire Children and servants to worke about the outworks or fortifications."[71] All capable inhabitants were expected to participate in the construction, and where possible it was assumed that they would take pride in their efforts. On 1 March, Colonel Venn delivered Common Council's request regarding the Committee for Fortifying the City to the House of Commons. Six days later, parliament issued orders for "Intrenching and fortifying the City of London."[72] Mayor Pennington played the final critical part in the push to build London's new defenses with a series of orders for the purchase of tools, the contribution of funds, precepts demanding participation.

William Lithgow, a Scottish traveler who was in London during the four months when the Lines were being constructed, and who walked the entire length of the fortifications, reported in unmatched detail on "the daily musters and showes of allsorts of *Londoners*" who marched out

> to the fields and outworks (as Merchants, Silk-men, Macers, Shopkeepers, &c.) with great alacritie, carrying on their shoulders yron Mattocks, and wooden shovels, with roaring Drummes, flying collours, and guilded swords; most companies being also interlarded with Ladies, women, and girles: two and two carrying baskets for to advance the labour.

The sheer scale of participation was staggering; Lithgow was equally astonished by the pride and competition that drove Londoners to their daily work. "Divers wrought till they fell sick of their pains," and "all the trades and whole inhabitants (the Insey Courts excepted) ... went day about to all quarters for the erection of their Forts and Trenches." Of the companies, none was more active than the Merchant Taylors, who "Carrying fourtiesix collours, and seconded with eight thousand lusty men" marched out to work daily. Trailing them were the London Watermen who numbered "seven thousand Tuggers, carrying thirty seven collours." Other companies followed closely behind and included some 5,000 shoemakers and the oysterwives who "advanced from Billingsgate through Cheapside to Crabtree field all alone, with drummes and flying collours."[73] Company members exhibited their usual healthy sense of pride and competition.

On 22 February, Mayor Pennington issued orders for buying tools that doubled for putting out fires and building the Lines. Diligent record-keeping reveals the precise number of tools that were purchased. On 1 March, Mercers paid for "fower dozen of buckets one dozen of pickaxes, three hookes, fower dozen of great birching broomes, one dozen of shovels shod, & halfe a dozen of shovels unshod."[74] Similarly, Goldsmiths inventoried three dozen leather buckets, ladders, and hooks, which were purchased to "fullfill the contents of the precept" that was issued by Pennington. It took just five days for them to "have in readiness att and w[i]thin our Com[m]on Hall 3 dozen of buckett 2. ladders 2 great Hookes wth Chaines 6 Pickaxes 12 Spades & shovels." All of these tools were as useful "for the quenching of fier" as they were for moving soil.[75] Smaller companies contributed likewise, providing what they could to further secure the City according to Pennington's orders. The Turners purchased a dozen spades, shovels, and buckets, along with "six pickaxes" that they could use "for the provision of this City" on 24 February.[76] Three days later, the Plumbers invested in "twelve buckets six shovels one ladder & one hooke the ladder" that extend thirty feet.[77] Brewers refrained from purchasing "bucketss ladders hookes and other instruments" until 16 May, well after they had received "the Lord Maiors precept dated the xxth day of February last." Despite the delay in their response, they had finally agreed to the order for supplies; it was perhaps not a coincidence that their payment was finally made on the same day that thirty-six company members "dyned with Isack Pennington the Lord Maior."[78] Whether to appease Pennington, or in response to a renewed request, the Brewers eventually found the means to support the original precept.

Parishes received the same orders to buy tools. Yet churchwardens offered a wider range of responses to Pennington's letters; in some cases, parochial records offer details about the dual purpose of their newly acquired implements. Churchwardens at St. Mary Aldermanbury, where Edmund Calamy served as curate and where a majority of parishioners maintained unquestionably parliamentarian sympathies, noted the expense of 10s 4d for "for Broomes Shovels and Spades." Such routine expenses would remain nondescript if not for the accompanying entry that mentions an additional 28s paid "for hyring of Carte at 3 severall tymes by order for the carrying of victualls to the Army and for baskets and other charges," and an additional 6s paid "for baskets for the parrish which they when they went out to dig."[79] Parishioners from St. Mary Magdalene, Milk Street, where Thomas Case led the ministry, spent £1 8s 3d "for twenty shovells and Spades and six baskits and markeing Iron" that could be used by any who wished to help build the Lines.[80] It is noteworthy that the two parishes where the most money was spent on tools were led by Calamy and Case; the former was indicted for high treason by Charles earlier in the year and apparently held meetings in his house to promote "the godly cause in Parliament and among the citizens," while the latter, as we have noted, was Pennington's chaplain.[81] Both men pressed forward with their respective efforts to deliver London's more humble inhabitants to parliament's cause. As future leading presbyterians, moreover, Calamy and Case stand as valuable reminders of the fact that parliament's war effort continued to benefit from the efforts of a wide coalition of actors as opposed to those of a single emergent and distinctly radical vanguard.[82]

Parishioners found other means to contribute toward the construction of defenses. St. Michael Bassishaw, on the north end of London, was given £15 by the Committee of the Militia to help "towards the building of a court of guarde and erecting Poaste and makeing chaines for the safeguard of our Warde." The total cost for building defenses, which included "Watchhouse poaste and chaines sett upp" ended up being £23 15s 7d.[83] Construction was one matter; maintenance was another altogether. Once finished, the eleven miles required upkeep and manning. As the year progressed, the Lord Mayor and Common Council issued numerous orders for their repair and defense. Churchwardens from St. Olave Old Jewry noted the "assessment to be leveyed of every Inhabitant" by Common Council on 8 July 1643 and which called "for the finishing of divers Forts and workes for the better defence and safety of the Citty as by the Lord Maiors warrant." Both the collection of the fifteenth and of the eighteenth are recorded together for St. Olave, and the total assessment for sixty-four individuals and households was £22 12s 3d (of which £19 7s 4d was apparently collected immediately).[84] As the war continued, Londoners were repeatedly asked to contribute toward the maintenance of the Lines – to protect inhabitants, as orders often claimed, from any surprise attack by members of the "malignant party," or simply to make regular repairs. St. Bride's churchwardens paid

£1 16s in August 1643 to "Mr Jones in Goate Court for two hoggsheads of beere carried into the fields when Captayne Wilson and his Company went to diggin." £1 8s 2d was paid in October to "Mr Bellamy for bread wyne and Cheese per bill that daie Captayne Wilson and his Company went out to the trench work."[85] Although the cost and effort might be burdensome, the Lines stood as the capital's single greatest defense.

Maintaining the integrity of the Lines was not only essential to London and its environs, but also to parliament. All that was contained within the fortifications was soon put on equal footing. "London," Lithgow concluded after walking the length of the perimeter, "was never truly London till now."[86] Construction continued on through summer as skilled day laborers, liverymen, soldiers, women, and even children all lent a hand.[87] In late May, Gerolamo Agostini, the Venetian secretary to the Doge and Senate, estimated that "more than 20,000" inhabitants were "working voluntarily daily without pay on the fortifications of this city," that some "principal positions" were already being stocked "with guns," and that the project would "be complete in a few weeks."[88] None could be said to be more active in the promotion of the task than the Lord Mayor. As *The True Declaration* praised, it was Pennington who embodied "the daily voice and imagination of the people," and it was Pennington who reminded the people of the threat when "the King and his Cavaliers are coming"; it was, in the end, "Maior" Pennington who set about to make sure that London's own defenses would stand like "the walls of Jerusalem."[89]

The falcon and the eagle: London sermons and the escalating rhetoric of war

Precepts and ordinances were of course essential components of the effort to mobilize citizens, but so too were the many providential warnings that continued to issue from pulpits in the wake of the attempt on the seven Londoners. Throughout 1643, networks of godly ministers redoubled their efforts to incite parishioners, calling upon biblical examples to say why they should seek to support – or alternatively, in some cases, hamper – parliament's efforts. Days of fasting and solemn humiliation remained of great interest to Londoners. These afforded parishioners with opportunities to hear sermons, or even, as Ann Hughes has explained, chances to move around in order to catch "more exciting or more congenial preachers."[90] As Pennington's precept from 26 November suggested, organized days of humiliation and preaching offered important opportunities to encourage or excite parishioners for the cause at hand. Londoners who missed the fast-day sermons of high-profile preachers might hope to hear them repeated, or they might just as soon seek copies in print.[91] Some did both.

George Thomason, for instance, inscribed his copy of John Arrowsmith's fast-day sermon from 25 January 1643, *The Covenant-Avenging Sword Brandished*, with "this sermon I heard preached." Arrowsmith's peroration deserved follow-up reading since he had taken the fiery Leviticus 26:25 as his theme: "I will bring a Sword upon you, that shall avenge the quarrel of my Covenant." "Justice," Arrowsmith proclaimed, "requires that the crie of sin should be answered with an echo of wrath," and divine wrath should be understood by three propositions. First, "warre is a judgement of Gods own bringing"; second, "the sword is an instrument of vengeance"; and third, "that which the sword comes to avenge, is some quarrel of Gods Covenant."[92] War, for Arrowsmith, was not simply sanctioned by God, but it was decreed as a just response for a broken covenant. Recent upheavals seemed to evidence a broken covenant that needed replacing. If stirring in the pulpit, Arrowsmith's words might furnish a similar response as text.

Thomason also "heard preached" Jeremiah Whitaker's equally incendiary afternoon sermon, which was later printed as *Ejrenopojos*.[93] Whitaker, who was known to climb the pulpit "four times a week" in London, followed Arrowsmith's lead – perhaps even coordinating his theme – in order to urge his listeners to seek religious unity and consider closely the cause. "*England*," Whitaker proclaimed, had clearly found its place alongside the other war-torn nations of the age, including "the *Palatinate, Bohemia, Germanie, Catalonia, Portugall,* [and] *Ireland*." Recent developments in these nations were, he warned, little more than previews of the time when "God will shake all Nations Collectively" and all "*elements shall melt with fervent heate*." If less direct in his assessment of the causes of war, Whitaker nevertheless expressed confidence that England's recent upheavals were a mere preview of a coming catastrophe, and that the nation should ponder carefully their recent "shaking" by God.[94]

While parliament pursued a regular fast-day program of preaching to the Commons in St. Margaret and the Lords in the Abbey, efforts were under way to implement another regular program for sermons in the City. Indeed, London's Corporation had taken a special interest in finding a venue for public preaching since the previous summer when Richard Gurney had rushed to stock pulpits with loyalists. The open-air pulpit of Paul's Cross, nestled on the northeast corner of the Cathedral and adjacent to London's many booksellers, provided what many took to be an ideal location. It was, as Mary Morrissey has suggested, "one of the very few large, open spaces in a very overcrowded city," and a venue that had long hosted some of the nation's most memorable and "politically sensitive sermons." These dated back to the reign of Elizabeth and continued on through to the early 1640s.[95] Pennington's first month as mayor coincided with efforts to determine "whome" retained the "right" and "hath byn" in charge of "the appointment of those preachers" in the pulpit at Paul's Cross. The City soon petitioned parliament directly to complain of recent "unsound, unfaithful, and unprofitable" preaching, and with the hope that a new program for preaching might be implemented. Parliament consented on 25 September, agreeing the Lord Mayor and Aldermen should retain "provision of and for all Ministers that preach at *Pawle's* Church, *Pawle's Crosse*, the *Spitte*, and other Places."[96] Under the aegis of Mayor Pennington – and indeed his successors to the mayoralty – the revived "Paul's Cross" sermon program looked as if it might provide an important platform for preaching, and perhaps even a space commensurate to the venues of parliament's fast-day sermons. At the very least, London's Corporation had secured an important open-air venue.

Preachers were of course keenly aware of the interests of their patrons. Although specifics are often unclear, it might be assumed that fast-day preaching was no different, with both sides assuming numerous underlying commitments and responsibilities. Joseph Caryl knew his audience when preaching on 27 March 1643 at Christ Church Greyfriars, Newgate Street, a popular alternative venue to Paul's Cross. Sitting before him that day were the Lord Mayor, aldermen, and numerous other citizens. His sermon, *Davids Prayer for Solomon*, was ostensibly given to commemorate the eighteenth anniversary of the king's inauguration, but when "embolden'd" in print it instead contained a dedication to Mayor Pennington who was praised for "act[ing] (on the Stage of this Ancient City) the part of a Great King."[97] Looking to "the distinct callings" of City magistrates and to their corresponding "abilities," Caryl concluded that London resembled Israel with its "Judges" rather than "a King." The latter was, he proclaimed, little more than "a new Title, but the worke was still the same." Caryl's argument, given his audience and later dedication, could not be clearer: "in that one word (*Iudge*) by a Synechdoche, all the duty and business of a King is comprehended." Pennington and his associates knew well enough what was being said. London's leaders were comparable to the twelve biblical judges who served as military leaders during a time of upheaval and divine punishment. Sitting to hear the sermon with his fellow "*representative kings*," Pennington was fit to maintain his own jurisdiction; the City, so recently surrounded by the Lines of Communication, was undoubtedly Pennington's own "sphere of judgement and righteousnesse." Caryl then added a second historical comparison, proclaiming that the "Senate of *London*" stood sturdy like "the Senate of *Rome*," with aldermen acting as "*an assembly of Kings*," with each member holding the capacity to "*judge with the righteousnesse of God.*"[98] London's magistrates would be hard-pressed to find higher praise or a clearer elucidation of their purpose. From a loyalist's perspective, Caryl's claims were no doubt beyond the pale. These marked an ideological break and a potent reminder of the radicalism shared by the Lord Mayor and his allies, each of whom had been emboldened in their interpretation of the "ancient" and exceptional relationship between the City and the Crown. Like Christ Church Greyfriars offered a viable and appealing alternative to the more restricted atmosphere of Westminster's official fast-day sermons; under Pennington's watch, London's pulpits had become receptive spaces for the sounding of ideologically controversial or sensitive topics, including, as Caryl's sermon made readily apparent, the sticky question of secular authority.

This is not to say that the City had been purged of opposition preaching; indeed, many pulpits remained accessible to loyalists and contrarians. Matthew Griffith, for instance, sought to cool heated tempers with a number of highly controversial sermons framed in support of the king and in opposition to City belligerents. Griffith had been arrested by members of the City trained bands the previous Guy Fawkes's Day and had already suffered the sequestration of his livings at St. Mary Magdalen and St. Benet Sherehog in late February and early March. Yet little could be done to prevent him from getting his words into print. His *A Sermon Preached in the Citie of London* became available in May, and provided Londoners with a diametrically opposed view to the one espoused by Caryl. Griffith chose Ecclesiastes 8:4 as his text: "where the word of a King is there is power, And who may say unto him what doest thou." Taking the opposite tack to Caryl, Griffith proclaimed "kings are not the offspring of man but the generation of God." England's lamentable state, he continued, suggested that its people should "learn more manners towards Kings." Griffith could do little more than pray that his message might reach a wide audience and help convince his readers that Caryl and other opponents of the Crown had assumed a perversion of natural order and law. Indeed, Pennington's perceived role as a "representative king" was akin to that of "the Falcon" who set out "to seize upon the Eagle."[99] Faced with imprisonment and sequestration, Griffith soon fled from the City to join the king in Oxford; left behind for London were words of his sermon.

City officials acknowledged that Griffith's sermon, and indeed the sermons of like-minded loyalists, stood to harm their agenda. Pennington and his allies responded by tightening their grip on City pulpits and redoubling their efforts to restore preaching at Paul's Cross. *Aulicus* made note of their efforts on 20 April, when a printed "paper signed by Isaac Pennington" arrived, revealing his "direction to the Ministers in and about the Cittie of London" with regards to "what they were to pray for, and what to preach." This latest attempt included yet another order "*to stirre up your people to appeare in person, and to joyne with the Army.*" Those who failed to "confrome themselves" to the orders – like "*the parson of S. Laurence Poultney*" – were "committed unto prison." "It seems there is no use of *Bishops*," *Aulicus* went on, "when a Lord *Maior* (though an intruder on that office) takes on him to prescribe the *Clergy* both what they are to *preach* and *pray* for." Parliament seemed all too willing to make Pennington their "*Vicar-generall*" to the City.[100] On 4 May, the Court of Aldermen requested that parliament might allow "the Lord Maior and Aldermen to nominate and appoint such ministers as shall hereafter preach upon the Lords day weekly att the place to be appointed in Paules Churchyard." In the "interim," they intended to retain the authority to appoint and pay ministers for a "convenient place as by them shall bee thought meete." Less than two weeks later, on 16 May, parliament responded, sending Samuel Vassall and John Venn to "to bring in an Ordinance to enable the Lord Mayor to appoint Preachers to preach the Sermons, given by the Chairty of well-disposd People, at *Paul's Cross*, or elsewhere."[101] That same day, London's Corporation sent officials out to the eastern corner of St. Paul's to find "a convenient and fitt place" where they might erect a new "pulpit to stand" for the use of "the Lord Maior Aldermen" and others who could gather "to heare the word of God preached as heretofore hath byn accustomed upon the Lords day."[102] On Whitsunday, 21 May 1643, London's Corporation paid to have both Thomas Goodwin and Edmund Calamy give sermons in the outdoor pulpit.[103] Yet the space where "they should have preached" remained unfit, and the sermons were subsequently given in the Mercer's Chapel on Cheapside.[104] The diarist John Greene noted that "there be sermons every sunday in the afternoon from the first sunday in Michaelmas terme till Easter in Mercer's Chappell."[105] Subsequent sermons, which are recorded in London's Cash Accounts as "Paul's Cross" sermons, were preached nearby in St. Paul's Cathedral.[106]

With parliament's approval, London's political leaders expanded and entrenched preaching for the cause. This would, they hoped, provide the Lord Mayor and the Corporation with the ability to disseminate views like those put forth in Caryl's *Davids Prayer for Solomon*. As Griffith lamented, and as likeminded loyalists doubtless agreed, a new venue might provide yet another means by which City "falcons" could attempt to "seize upon the eagle." With plans for the restoration of London's preeminent open-air pulpit under way, Pennington and his allies could turn their attention to other pressing matters.

Reforming the cityscape

Not least in their sights was the removal of lingering Laudian innovations and other church trappings deemed "popish." As Julie Spraggon's illuminating study of 1640s iconoclasm reveals, the period from early 1643 onwards saw "the mayor and aldermen of the City of London" working alongside leading parliamentary militants who wished see implemented new plans for "reforming London." Their coordinated efforts reached a meridian in April 1643 with parliament's establishment of a new Committee for the Demolition of Monuments of Superstition and Idolatry. Robert Harley, a godly parliamentarian, led the Committee, and with him were fifteen other sympathetic members, including Francis Rous, Sir Gilbert Gerard, and John Blakiston.[107] From its inception, Committee members worked alongside Londoners who sought to destroy lasting visible vestiges of popery, from monuments to stained glass windows – images collectively deemed offensive to God and, by extension, a hindrance to parliament's war effort.

Zealous Londoners were no strangers to iconoclasm. Days before Harley's Committee was officially formed, on 30 March 1643, Henry Marten returned from Somerset House where he had assisted in the arrest of five Capuchin servants from Queen Henrietta Maria's household. All five were given over "to the custodie of the sherifs of London" and later expelled from England. Before leaving, Marten and his peers set about "pulling downe & defacing the Idols in the saied chappell." They proceeded to pile up "idols together with the copes" and other "alter-clothes & other vestments" for burning.[108] Among the more valuable objects destroyed by Marten and the other commissioners was Peter Paul Rubens's *Crucifixion*, an original painting that had been given to the queen by the late duke of Buckingham. John Clotworthy "climbed on top of the altar table and looked at the very valuable painting in its gild frame" and set about striking the painting with his halberd; he first slashed at "Christ's face in contempt" and then delivered a "second blow" to the "Virgin's face" while uttering some "hateful blasphemies." The painting was thus "ripped ... to pieces."[109] The queen's religion had long been a point of contention for the godly; doubtless the opportunity to dismantle her chapel was relished.

London's many churches provided other targets for puritans of tender conscience; ministers and parishioners eagerly pursued any new opportunity to dismantle widely detested Laudian "innovations." Indeed, parliament lost little time making programs for iconoclasm official. "Within weeks" of its opening, the Long Parliament had declared that Laud's 1640s canons were illegal. As Kenneth Fincham and Nicholas Tyacke have pointed out, these attacks included the then infamous "Canon 7," which called for rails to be built around altars and tables set altarwise. By September 1641, the Commons had issued their "own, more radical, order" to see that "Comunion tables were to be moved from the east end of chancels," and that each should "stand without candles, candlesticks, or basins." Accompanying these orders were further instructions that "rails were to be taken away, chancels leveled, imagery of crucifixes, the Trinity, and the

Virgin Mary removed, and bowing at the name of Jesus or towards the altar forbidden." Reforms had thus been under way for more than a year.[110]

If "widely obeyed," parliament's orders also met with resistance in the capital. Fincham and Tyacke identified "at least ten London parishes" in which the "laity as well as clergy opposed the removal of rails in 1641–2."[111] Their figures coincide with other assessments; Lindley, for instance, found extensive evidence to suggest that parishioners were initially driven into "rival factions" over the removal of rails; notable struggles took place in the parishes of St. Saviour and St. Olave, Southwark, St. Thomas the Apostle, and St. Magnus the Martyr. "Some other resistance" can be accounted for in the parishes of St. Botolph Aldersgate, St. Giles in the Fields, St. Lawrence Jewry, St. Martin Orgar, St. Olave Old Jewry, and even the cathedral.[112] If fewer in number than their opponents, there were still Londoners who hoped to preserve the beauty of holiness, or perhaps simply prevent the unnecessary whitewashing of their places of worship.[113]

Voices in favor of such innovations were all but silenced in early 1643. This owed in no small part to the systematic harassment and arrest of the City's remaining loyalist clergymen by Pennington and his allies in Harley's Committee. Many of the targeted clergymen were already jailed, while others, as we have noted, already fled from the metropolis, or had already relinquished under systematic pressure to conform.[114] Some of the parishioners who had responded reluctantly to parliament's attack on the canons in 1641 appear to have embraced the new parliamentary programs for iconoclasm over the course of late 1642 and early 1643. Reformers hoped to lead by example; on 23 March, aldermen "thought [it] fitt" to have "Goodge Mr Callomy Mr Case and Mr Seamen" to come together and "viewe the pictures and figures in the glass windows within Guildhall and in the Chappall" and determine what "they shall finde or conceive to bee superstitious and Idoletrous." Objects deemed dangerous were "to bee forthwith pulled downe."[115] Further efforts were set in motion in April and May. Printed on 17 May, orders of the Committee for the Demolition of Monuments of Superstition and Idolatry required the destruction of stone altars, the rearranging of "altar wise" tables, and accounts made for "all Crucifixes, Crosses, Images or pictures of any one or more persons of the Trinity, or of the Virgin Mary upon the outside of your said Church or Chappel, or in any open place within your parish."[116] Churchwardens were expected to participate and deliver their reports within three days.

The extent to which parishes responded to the orders can be seen, and in some cases precisely dated, in extant churchwardens' accounts. Spraggon's compelling research identifies twenty-nine individual parishes where various acts of iconoclasm were carried out. Among these were St. Olave Jewry, St. Lawrence Jewry, St. Margaret New Fish Street, St. Martin Orgar,

St. Michael Cornhill, and St. Leonard Eastcheap.[117] Incidentally, several of the above parishes fell within wards that contributed significantly toward the parliament's November 1642 assessments. Although characteristically concise, churchwardens' accounts do sometimes reveal how parochial communities responded to orders for reform over the course of 1643–4. March to May of 1643 is particularly well recorded as it corresponds to the period when Harley's Committee began their so-called "campaign against crosses," a series of attacks on monuments and idolatrous images, along with a systematic attempt to alter London's cityscape by removing lead crosses and other figures from church parapets, ridges, and steeples.[118]

Like the Committee's other efforts, their "campaign against crosses" met with what appeared to be general enthusiasm. Regardless of the popular response, logistical and practical issues surrounded the physical alteration of churches, making it somewhat difficult to gauge the overall response to the "campaign against crosses." Chiseling stone and sawing lead, which had a heightened value during the war, required planning and execution. Alterations were undertaken at the expense of the parish and thus required discussion, planning, and preparation among churchwardens and vestrymen who met regularly but sometimes infrequently. The end result of these sometimes lengthy processes, made protracted by external factors, is a fitful scene of targeted iconoclasm. It is nevertheless integral to defining the reshaping of London's cityscape in 1643, a subtle and important part of the program for mobilization.

Some parishes managed to cover expenses associated with removal by selling the lead and other raw materials that were being scrapped. The churchwardens at All Hallows the Great, for instance, paid 18s to a "carpenter for scaffolding and takeing downe the Crosses from the steeple according to an order of Parliament," but they were able to recover £1 8s 4d from "Charles Lawe the Plumer for the lead of the Crosses when they were taken of the steeple."[119] At Holy Trinity the Less, the cost for removing lead crosses came out to 4s 6d, but the sale of lead mitigated the cost with a return of at least 4s.[120] Richard Overton's accounts from St. Peter Westcheap reveal that £5 3s was paid to "Mr Haynes plummer for Lead sodder and workmanshop to mark up the crose of the steeple."[121] All Hallows the Less did not record any costs associated with the removal of their crosses, but they did mention the receipt of 6s "for the lead of the Crosse which stood upon the Church steeple." Churchwardens were nevertheless grateful for the opportunity and happily paid 1s to the official who "brought the Order of the Parliament for demolishing superstitious and Idolatrous Monuments."[122] Churchwardens at St. Peter Cornhill waited until August to approve a payment made for "the charges of taking away of superstitious pictures out of the Church and of repayring and adorning the same."[123] Their compliance came only after parliament officially issued a bill against "Monuments of Superstition and Idolatry" on 26 August.

Delayed efforts might understandably raise questions. Foremost, it must be asked if slow responses were solely a matter of logistical constraints, or if they owed to latent opposition? Given the sparse nature of accounts, we must rest upon assumptions. Some parishes, such as St. Margaret Pattens, did not record specific dates, but instead only made note of sums received and paid, such as the £2 8d that was "paid for taking downe the Crosse from the Steeple."[124] Similarly, expense accounts from St. Laurence Pountney reveal only that masons were afforded 2s 6d for "cutting the stones where the crosses stood."[125] Complicating matters further is the fact that some parishes expressed preferences for the removal of some specific objects over others. Churchwardens from St. Lawrence Jewry, a parish adjacent to Guildhall, nominated one "Mr Sutton" to assess the idolatrous elements in their church windows. Members of the parish eventually agreed to pay £1 to have two men pull "downe the greate East Windowe." Their efforts to destroy the glass came shortly after parliament's orders were received, but it took several more months for them to pay 1s to the messenger who brought the "Order of Parliament sent for the pulling downe of Crucifixes and other thinges."[126] Stained glass may well have piqued consciences more than exterior lead crosses, thus causing the removal of windows to take precedence over the mending of the steeple. Other parishes displayed similar idiosyncratic approaches to the removal of images, which again might suggest that the anxieties and concerns of daily worship dictated how parishes responded to parliament's orders. The churchwardens at St. Mary Woolchurch Haw, for their part, recorded nothing about the mending of crosses, but nevertheless wrote detailed notes about the seventy-seven pounds of "old brass taken out of superstitious monuments in the Church."[127] Officials at St. Mary Abchurch, meanwhile, paid 3s "for Cutting down the Crosses" and an additional 2s 6d for "taking up the Superstitious monum[en]ts."[128] Like other parishes, their records can be read to suggest parochial priorities, but they cannot, on balance, be taken as confirmation of wider attitudes toward Harley's program for reform.

Some parish records offer up more clear-cut examples of enthusiasm for iconoclasm. For example, St. Botolph-without-Bishopsgate was home to a godly community that had pursued parochial reforms since well before the outbreak of war. Churchwardens from St. Botolph recorded a payment of 12s 6d to "Mr Pennington and his Assistantes" who apparently oversaw efforts for "taking downe the Crosse" more than a fortnight before official orders were printed. Churchwardens had already paid 1s 6d the previous year for "takeing downe the rayles and carying them away," and an additional 1s 6d to bell "ringers when the Bishops were rooted out of the house of Lords."[129] Parishioners from St. Michael Bassishaw were also quick to respond to orders for removing offensive images, having "paid the Plumber the 10th of Maie 1643 for leade and workemanshipp donne upon the topp of the Steeple att the taking downe the Cross there." Their commitment to reform was matched by enthusiasm for the war. On the following day, churchwardens paid 5s 6d to have meat delivered out to parliament's army.[130] Again, it is worth keeping in mind that accounts of this nature cannot be used to perfectly gauge the extent of interest in iconoclasm; but they do, nevertheless, afford opportunities to observe an important dynamic of parochial mobilization. When taken in aggregate, seemingly small-scale efforts could have a large impact.

Not least, the "campaign against crosses" dramatically altered London's physical appearance. As contemporary journals and etchings reveal, the removal of numerous lead crosses reshaped the cityscape. The diarist John Greene observed alterations first-hand, noting in particular the striking change that came with the removal of "the crosses" that once stood "upon Paul's and the tops of other churches."[131] As *Aulicus* could report, "the Crosse upon the top" of Westminster Abbey was already "tooke downe" by order of parliament.[132] Details of this nature were not lost on Wenceslaus Hollar, the Czech-born artist who made every effort to represent the City accurately in his etchings. Hollar's view of London from 1647 contrasts sharply with Claes Visscher's rendition of the City from three decades earlier. The latter's work reveals the one-time prominence of lead crosses and weathervanes, while the prior's work shows a notable absence of crosses. In no place was this absence more apparent than St. Paul's Cathedral, which, as Greene suggested in his diary, gave up four massive lead crosses from ridges of its transept and nave and several smaller crosses from pinnacles. By late 1643, London's cityscape was indelibly altered, its once skyward crosses sawn and sold.

Other iconic monuments were under attack. Cheapside's medieval cross, with its "idolatrous and superstitious figures" of apostles, saints, and bishops had long earned the ire of zealous Londoners. But it had also, in recent years, become an important rallying point for agitators and discontents. Londoners famously met to destroy the so-called "Dagon cross" in February 1642, but an equally large crowd met them to defend the monument. Richard Overton blamed the cross that same year for the part it played in seducing "his Majesties liege Subjects from the true Protestant Religion, to the Romish Caholike faith, to the utter subversion and ruine of the Kingdome by civill warre."[133] Cheapside Cross was finally toppled on 2 May 1643. Orders for demolition came this time from Harely's Committee and the "*Lord Major of London*," who, along "with the Aldermn and Citizens," gathered to watch as the monument was scaled and attacked

146 Civil war London

Figure 3 Claes Visscher, *The Visscher Panorama of London*, etching from 1616.

Figure 4 Wenceslaus Hollar, *Long View of London from Bankside*, etching from 1647.

with hammers and chisels. No opposing party came to the defense of the cross that day, but instead "brave Bands of Souldiers" gathered around, "sounding their Trumpets, and shooting off their peeces, as well as shouting-out with their voices."[134] The demolition played out according to plan, making for a moment that Spraggon likened to a well-rehearsed "exercise in propaganda, with parliamentarian authorities aiming to stir up anti-Catholicism and to promote the godly cause."[135]

The toppling of Cheapside Cross kicked off several days of excited popular iconoclasm. Fervor saw Londoners gathered in the streets again on 10 May to burn copies of the king's detested Book of Sports. Enthusiasm spread as godly activists sought out "the destruction of [other] crosses and figures." Agostini witnessed with horror when "a great concourse" gathered "to pull to pieces the royal monuments in the church of Westminster." He ruefully reported that their success saw ruined "one of the finest ornaments of this city, admired by all foreigners for its antiquity and the perfection of the beautiful marble carving."[136]

Proponents might voice their approval, while opponents were forced to witness in silence. Preaching during the solemn fast-day in June, Herbert Palmer expressed his concern over enemies abroad and at home, from "*By-standers, and Neuters*" to the king's new "*Army raised ... by Papist-counsels.*" The "nations [sic] sins," Palmer assured, was "the provoking Cause of all these Judgements." If peccant men wished to stem further reprisals from the Almighty, they should seek to follow the example of 2 Kings 18, and of King Hezekiah of Judah who set about to "pull down all the high-places, even superstitious, as well as idolatrous." Following Hezekiah's lead might help to stay "Gods *heavy wrath*." What better place to start than the City, the place where "*Idolatry*" stood out as "the sinne that is most *formall high treason against God*"? Palmer was no stranger to parliament's cause; his *Scripture and Reason Pleas for Defensive Armes* had already been printed in April at the behest of parliament's Committee for Printing. His plea for an "active endeavour of reformation" added yet another voice to the growing chorus that was the "campaign against crosses."[137]

Men like Overton and Palmer could conjure any number of reasons for attacking idolatrous images and opposing profane practices. Overton believed in earnest that idols were in part to blame for the recent struggles between parliament and the Crown; dangerously powerful, monuments stood to entice and corrupt, to pervert beliefs, and eventually even drive men to take up arms. Palmer expressed similar views; idols, claimed Palmer, could be like the golden calf and plunge the nation into superstition and conflict. How might men rest while these dangers stood in plain sight? Behind such acts and assumptions – behind official orders and agitating efforts – were Pennington, Harley, and likeminded leaders who believed that

God and the cause stood to benefit from their efforts. Heeding their calls to action were pamphleteers and preachers, men like Overton and Palmer, who were poised to motivate auditors and readers alike. At the forefront, all the while, were the countless Londoners who took calls to action seriously, who hoped to reform their city as a means to spiritual salvation and providential favor – and by extension, perhaps, victory in war. Standing in the way in May and June of 1643 were fewer opponents, but some loyalists remained, and so too did empty cures that could be put to better service.

Replacing malignant ministers

Efforts to finally rid London of its disaffected clergy also reached a high point in early 1643. As the reader may recall, Pennington's replacement of Gurney led to the first concerted and systematic push to root out London clergymen deemed "ill-affected" to parliament's cause. Indeed, many who were initially accused had already fled the capital or been jailed.[138] Efforts showed little sign of slowing in the autumn and winter; by December 1642 a committee of ten councilmen was appointed to sit at Camden House to collect information about the City's "disaffected." Their findings were to be reported to the Lord Mayor, who would then pass information on to parliament. Members of the new City committee included, in some cases, now familiar activists such as William Kendall, William Greenhill, Theophilus Riley, and Richard Turner.[139] In March, the committee was granted authority to pursue and arrest "delinquents" under official sequestration orders. The nature of complaints and accusations leveled against clergymen varied considerably, with charges ranging from misbehavior and negligence to the more serious matters of corruption, incompetence, and absence. Tarred as "malignant," "seditious," "scandalous," and "disaffected," such ministers could now officially be sequestered.

Sequestration offered solutions to issues that had long plagued parliament. For one, it provided help with perennially depleted wartime coffers.[140] Equally beneficial in the eyes of many was the prospect of restocking vacant cures with proponents of the cause. In some instances, ejections allowed for the vindication and promotion of individuals who had old scores to settle; this was particularly true for clergymen who had suffered in the past under Archbishop Laud. Emerging by early 1643, then, and following on from Pennington's initial push for parochial reforms, was a series of new coordinated efforts to remove clerical opposition. These efforts revealed a growing interdependence that spanned between parochial activists, London's committee at Camden House, the Lord Mayor, and established parliamentary committees like the one for Plundered Ministers, a body that was established at the end of December 1642 to hear cases made against clergymen in London and by various county subcommittees.[141] Working in lockstep during a relatively short period in early 1643, Londoners coordinated with the Committee for Plundered Ministers to silence parochial opposition and elevate sympathetic replacements.

Ejections at St. Margaret Lothbury, St. Martin Vintry, and St. Nicholas Olave were largely matters of formality; charges were officially made so that cases could pass on quickly for formal judgment by the Lords. All three sequestration charges dealt with individuals who were absent from their cures and had since fled the capital. Lothbury's parishioners had been key contributors toward parliament's November assessment, and on 21 February they openly declared their opposition to Humphrey Tabor, their "double-beneficed" parson who had been absent "sometimes Six Months together." Tabor had briefly espoused the royalist cause at St. Margaret; charges against him included his refusal to read orders from parliament to inveighing "against such as take up Arms for the Defence of Parliament, declaiming against them as Rebels, and as led therein by the evil Spirit that works in the Sons of Disobedience." Parliament ordered that Leonard Cooke, the vicar of Walton-upon-Thames who had been "plundered by the King's soulders," should replace the tardy Tabor.[142] The ejection order for St. Martin Vintry proved similar; nothing needed to be done to remove one Dr. Bevin Reeve, who had "deserted and forsaken his Cure" the previous June, having "betaken himself to the Army of Cavaliers" where he eventually joined Charles's Council of War. Arthur Sallwey, "a Learned and Orthodox divine," was appointed in his place.[143] Oliver Whitby's removal from St. Nicholas Olave was an equally routine matter; Whitby's cure had sat vacant since 23 October of the previous year.

Pennington remained a decisive figure in the removal and replacement of "malignants." His part is evidenced by way of a letter sent to the Speaker of the House in late March, and which reveals how he helped to apprehend three preachers suspected of delinquency. One was "a dangerous fellow" named Thomas Cheshire who preached "twise or thrice at Pauls very seditiouslye," and who had subsequently fled from London to be "newly returned from the kings army." Detained around the same time was Matthew Griffith, a loyalist who was beneficed at St. Benet Paul's Wharf, was rector of St. Mary Magdalene and St. Benet Sherehog, and stood accused of "inveighing against ye parliament." The third man taken into custody was Thomas Tuke, a vicar from "old Jury." Pennington sent Griffith and Tuke to Newgate, yet both managed to post bail. "If not some course be taken to make some of them examples," Pennington bemoaned to the Speaker, "I know not what it may come to."[144] The mayor's sentiments regarding Tuke and Griffith were not altogether surprising; Griffith had already preached *A*

Patheticall Perswasion to Pray for Publick Peace at St. Paul's on 2 October 1642 and went on, as we have seen, to print *A Sermon Preached in the Citie of London*, in which he explicated about "the power of a King."[145] Cheshire, meanwhile, had given a sermon at St. Paul's on 10 October in which he confessed to being "perswaded" of his obligation "to bow."[146] Like most proponents of war, Pennington was eager to see all loyalists and prelates replaced by equally stout supporters of parliament's cause, and, like other puritans, he abhorred genuflection. Griffith's parsonage at St. Mary Magdalen was sequestered at the end of February and given to Ithiel Smart, a godly minister from Wombourne, Staffordshire who had run afoul of Laud's reforms in the 1630s.[147] Days later, Griffith's second parsonage at St. Benet Sherehog was filled by Edward Roode, the one-time vicar of St. Helen's in Abingdon-on-Thames, Berkshire.[148] Like Smart, Roode had suffered under Laud; an imposition that saw him replaced by an Arminian in 1629, but Roode found his way back to the vicarage of St. Helen's in 1640, only to once again be driven away again by royalist soldiers in early 1643. Replacing Griffith with Roode must have seemed a fitting retribution, then.[149]

Pennington, meanwhile, warned explicitly about Tuke's "more insolent" mode following his release from Newgate. Tuke had enjoyed his living at St. Olave Old Jewry since 1617; since the outbreak of war, Tuke revealed himself to be a vocal and persistent supporter of the king. He regularly refused to read out parliamentary orders and at one point purportedly shouted from the pulpit that he hoped to see "the Devil confound all Traitors, Rebels and turbulent Spirits."[150] Tuke's sequestration made way for William Hignell, a godly man who John Greene recalled "pracht" on the final Sunday of March.[151]

Coordinated efforts to remove and replace clergymen continued throughout February and March. Parishioners from St. Mary Abchurch proved instrumental in the dismissal of Benjamin Stone, their parson. On 9 March, the Commons agreed that Stone was "a Person very scandalous," and hence that he should lose both the parsonages of Abchurch and St. Clement Eastcheap.[152] Walter Taylor replaced Stone at St. Clement and his position at Abchurch was given to John Rawlinson, a man who might be trusted to toe the parliamentarian line because he had recently been "driven from the City of York by the Cavaliers."[153] Other parishes followed suit. The inhabitants at St. Michael Cornhill were delighted by the opportunity to present charges against William Brough, their own "doctor in divinity." The prestigious Dr. Brough, who had once flourished under Laud and served as a chaplain to Protestants in Henrietta Maria's household, had also been the subject of numerous complaints by parishioners. These ranged from the charge of "publique preaching" to the serious allegation that he promoted "Popish and superstitious doctrines" such as "bowing to or before the Alter worshipping toward the East, Washing away of originall Sinne by Baptisme, Children dying without Baptisme to be damned, and the error of Arminianisme of universall Grace, and Freewill in man fallen, and the Apostacy of the Saints." Replacing Brough was Thomas Mall, a man of obscure origins, but one approved of as "a godly, learned, and orthodox Divine."[154] On the following day, orders were passed for sequestering the parsonage at St. Giles in the Fields and the vicarage at St. Olave Old Jewry. Dr. Heywood's parsonage at the former passed to Henry Cornish, while Tuke's position, as we have seen, went to Hignell.[155]

On 17 March, John Squire, the vicar of St. Leonard Shoreditch who had long been the subject of controversy, was formally removed and replaced by Matthew Clarke.[156] Later that day, orders were made so that profits from St. Margaret New Fishstreet would be paid to Thomas Froysell, another "godly and learned Divine."[157] Concerted efforts to purge London's parishes were by no means complete at the end of March, but the month's closure did coincide with a notable slackening of efforts. Attention turned temporarily instead to Somerset House and the removal of the Queen's Capuchin friars. Efforts resumed once again in April when Pennington ordered London's ministers

> to commend to God in your Prayers, the Lord Generall, the whole Army imployed in the Parliaments Service, and the Designe undertaken by them, As also in your Sermons, effectually to stirre up your people now to appeare in person, and to joyne with the Army, to stand up for our Religion and Liberties, as is desired and expected by the said Army, and the Committee for the *Militia*, in this City.[158]

Aulicus copied the order out verbatim after noting that "this day came to Towne in print, a paper signed by Isaac Pennington, containing a direction to the Ministers in and about the Cittie of London, both what they were to pray for, and what to preach." Failure to comply with the order, *Aulicus* went on, led to jailing: "all that doe refuse to conforme themselves to these *directions*, or *commands* (call them what you will) are forthwith committed unto prison; as amongst others the Parson of *S. Laurence Poultney* (a Church neare *Guildhall*) for that reason onely."[159] Royalists once again surmised that Pennington was at the heart of the matter.

On 15 April, the same day that the Lord Mayor's orders were printed, William Cooper, the parson of St. Thomas the Apostle, was replaced with James Moore.[160] The next sequestration order arrived just two weeks later when Nehemiah Rogers was ordered to vacate St. Botolph-without-Bishopsgate, in order to make way for John Vincent, the new rector.[161]

Soon thereafter, on 12 May, Richard Wollaston and George Henly of St. Peter Cornhill were granted authority by the Commons to "appoint such orthodox Divines, as they shall think fit, to preach and officiate" due to the removal of their own "Dr. [William] Fairfax."[162] Fairfax held on until official sequestration orders were made in August; the rectory thus appears to have sat vacant until the presbyterian William Blackmore arrived in 1656.[163]

On 20 June, the rectorship of St. Ethelburga was sequestered from John Clarke and given to Edward Archer, while Bryan Walton was stripped of his position as rector of St. Martin Orgar and replaced by Richard Lee.[164] Clarke was known "to corrupt his auditory with the leaven of Popish doctrine," and was reportedly "a common haunter of Tavernes and Alehouses" who "exprest great malignity against the power and proceedings of Parliament."[165] The next parochial ejection was not made until nine days later when Ephraim Udall of St. Augustine by St. Paul was "branded" as "*Popishly affected*." Officials carted Udall off to jail, but a scene came when they attempted to remove his wife, Philippa, who, despite being "infirm" and "lame," was infamously carried out of her house on a chair and left "to the mercy of the Wind and Weather."[166] Udall had produced a number of controversial works in 1642, including the anti-war sermon *The Good of Peace and Ill of War*, and *Noli me tangere*, a pamphlet in which he proposed that cathedral lands and tithes should be maintained indefinitely and further warned that rule by a national assembly would almost certainly cause God to punish the nation.[167] Udall's subsequent summertime sequestration on 29 June marked the unofficial end to the phase of coordinated efforts to rid London's pulpits of "ill-effected" clergymen. In a period of just over three weeks that spanned from the end of February to the middle of March, ten London clergymen had been removed from their livings. Five more clergymen were removed between April and June. In several cases, as we have seen, the replacements brought with them a history of mistreatment by Laud, and in a few instances encounters with royalists. Sequestrations of course continued after this period, but the targeting of London's clergymen became far less frequent and systematic. Silencing parochial opposition was an integral component of mobilization. Although the reasons behind sequestrations often varied from allegations by parishioners to more official charges leveled by the Camden House Committee, the end result was the same: loyalists (or those suspected of loyalism) were ejected in favor of appointees who could be entrusted with the promotion of parliament's cause. Collectively, this helped to rid metropolitan parishes of lingering loyalism and further stifle communications between supporters of the king. If not driven from the metropolis or arrested, the removal of men like Griffith helped to further transform London into a "parliamentarian" stronghold, a capital that was admittedly looking more and more like the "rebellious City" described by Clarendon. Efforts to counter loyalist activism may have "peaked in 1643," as Lindley suggested.[168] But the task of rooting out sympathies for the Crown could scarcely be considered complete. Moreover, limited success sometimes came with unintended consequences. Deprived of curacies and pulpits, efforts on behalf of the king were driven further underground and forced to rely upon clandestine letter networks, secret meetings, and illicit printing. This all came as parliament's war effort faced new strains and uncertainties, matters that paved the way for a climate in which secret plotting would become the assumed instrument of loyalist opposition.

Raising London's auxiliaries

In the wake of the king's attempt on the seven Londoners, and in light of the failed negotiations at Oxford, London's belligerents revitalized their efforts to establish a volunteer army. *Aulicus* chimed in with news that London's radicals had devised a plan to charge "every Housekeeper in the Citie to maintain one of his Apprentices with Armes" so that they might be "ready on all occasions to defend the Citie, or to go forth against the enemie." Rumor spread that efforts were under way to raise "an Army of 10,000 men," who would be "maintained and armed without" the need to "charge" parliament. Less than two weeks later, on 10 April, *Aulicus* suggested that Londoners sought "to perswade their fellowes, not onely to contribute money, but to give away their shirts, shooes, and stockings for maintaining and clothing of their Souldiers."[169] If ambitious, the possibility that London was raising a new army was cause for alarm amongst loyalists.

On 12 April, parliament passed an ordinance authorizing the creation of a subcommittee of the Militia Committee that would sit at Salters' Hall on Bread Street, the heart of the ward, and oversee the raising of new London auxiliary regiments. At least five of the new colonels were selected from the trained bands and these included Robert Tichborne, one of the seven accused Londoners, along with Thomas Gower, Edward Hooker, Christopher Whichcott, and William Willoughby.[170] As Lawson Nagel suggested in a hitherto unpublished dissertation on the City militia, accounts of the size and ability of the new regiments conflicted and it therefore remains unclear "how quickly the ranks of Auxiliaries were filled." At least "three Regiments of stout men" could muster as early as 13 April. And while all nine complete regiments of 2,000 may never have materialized, later evidence suggests that incomplete regiments nevertheless entered the field. Three incomplete regiments marched out with William Waller at the end of August 1643, and some of the auxiliary forces destined for service were claimed to be "all complete" by October.[171] As with many volunteer armies, the total number of auxiliaries fluctuated due to desertions and losses. Ben Coates and others have concluded that the total may have reached upwards of 8,000 men.[172] One contemporary list accounts for 4,716 "additions to the Trayned Bands" in the shape of the Tower Hamlets regiment, the Westminster Liberty regiment and the Southwarke regiment, and a total of 7,200 men in the Red, White, Blue, Yellow, Green, and Orange auxiliaries.[173]

The new forces were comprised mostly of volunteer apprentices and non-householders. Once raised, the regiments were divided into ten companies of "about 40 up to a maximum of 66 soldiers." A contemporary muster role from Captain Moses Meare lists the names of volunteers, their masters, and the location of their living. Among the new men was "Thomas Gilforde" who was "Mr Andrewes man in Love Lane," "Samson Haris Mr Terones man in Holborne," and "John Carter" from "Holborne." Meare's roll lists recruits who came almost exclusively from the north and the east ends of the City. Enlistees were listed as carpenters, shoemakers, and chandlers, among other professions. Some were likely long-time residents who had adopted the names of their masters, or perhaps even sons, such as "Arter Johnson Thomas Johnsons man" and "Frances Ballye Mr Ballyes man at the Brig."[174] Less than two weeks before the plans for auxiliaries were implemented, vestrymen from St. Botolph-without-Bishopsgate made complaints about rampant "povertie" due to "deadnes in, And lake of trading," and the fact "that divers of" their "parishioners have listen themselves for Souldiers." So many had gone that their scavengers "could not receive the Assessment."[175] For some, enlisting apparently served as a pathway to pay.

Funding for the auxiliaries was to come from a controversial plan whereby London's "well-affected" would voluntarily forgo a weekly meal and in turn deliver the value on to collectors appointed by the Salters' Hall subcommittee.[176] An extant list of voluntary contributions made by "severall Parishes in London & Parts adjacent toward the providing of Armes and other necessaries for the Auxiliaries raised in those parts" reveals that some £1,647 4s 6d reached collectors, a small sum given what was needed to field and maintain an army, but nevertheless an indicator of some initial support for the program. The largest collections came by way of St. Stephen Coleman Street (£76), St. Margaret Moses (£42), St. Giles

Cripplegate (£198), and St. Bride's on Fleet Street (£84). £1,598 7s 4d of the collected funds went to cover the cost associated with recruiting and outfitting recruits. Money was spent to repair arms and get new bandoliers, swords, muskets, drums, belts, and other necessary goods. £2 was given "to Laborers for setting up 2 pulpitts in the Artilery garden & bringing formes & other necessaries about the same." Damage to the documents obscures the amount paid "to the Printer" who was involved in recruitment.[177] By May, official orders for the "great Worke" were printed and distributed in London so that "persons and Families sensible" might "abstaine and forbeare some one Meale in the Weeke, and on every *Munday* ... pay and deliver the true value thereof" to collectors for the auxiliaries.[178] As Coates notes, the relatively low returns for the program meant that "the weekly meal had to be turned into a compulsory tax."[179] After months of dealing with various parliamentary military expedients, most Londoners seemed inclined to keep the value of their meals.

Arming auxiliaries required innovative efforts on the part of City authorities. Peter Edwards's work on the arms trade during the civil wars estimates that some "30,000 pikes, 102,000 swords and 111,000 firearms" were contracted between parliament and London "between August 1642 and September 1651." As impressive as these figures are, the fact remains that contracts took time to fill and it would still be some time before London's "manufacturers" could "gear up to meet extra demand." Contract receipts reveal that a great deal of what was being produced in London was being sent out to the counties. As Edwards suggests, London's gunmakers did not regularly fulfill their autumn contracts with the Committee for Safety until the spring, which means that the auxiliaries might be at least a year out from outfitting.[180] Rather than rely on contracts, the Salters' Hall subcommittee sought to cobble together what could be purchased, donated, and found.

Doubtless, many Londoners saw the program as an additional and unwelcomed burden. Like foregoing a meal, the prospect of arming yet more young and unruly Londoners may have seemed more trouble than it was worth. Interactions with armed soldiers had already led to tense or hostile situations. On 20 February, inhabitants from Lambeth complained to the Commons about a group of enlisted men from Captain Andrewes's company, which served under Colonel Mainwaring, who had entered their church on the Sabbath "with their hatts on, & takeing Tobacco." After "disturbing the minister," and disrupting the service they were "reproved," a move that led them to draw their swords and set about "slaying one of our parishioners, & sorely wounding an other."[181] Equally troubling were the growing number of sick and wounded soldiers who continued to stream into the metropolis. Their presence had become so distressing that parliament requested in April that "all those parishes that are mentioned within the weekly Bill of *London*" along with the counties of Middlesex and Surrey collect money on the following fast day and deliver it to the Committee for Maimed Soldiers.[182]

Plans nevertheless moved forward, and on 25 May parliament's Committee for the Advance of Money sought a means to help, ordering that "the Committee at Weavers hall" should emulate "the care & industry of the Committee sitting at Salters hall in Bread Street" by seeking "moneyes still in arreres [sic] and unpaid" and what "may be gotten in and imployed for the arming of the auxiliary souldiers."[183] If, as *Aulicus* claimed, backers of the plan might hope to acquire shirts and stockings through the generosity of "their fellowes," more expensive equipment still needed to be found by other means. The largest boon to the process of arming auxiliary forces came by way of "severall persons of the Committee of Weavers Hall." The subcommittee, which, as we have seen, was first established in the wake of the loss at Brentford and by order of Mayor Pennington, and which was initially meant to raise funds to help create its own volunteer army, was now fully committed to providing for the auxiliaries project. A delivery of 342 muskets, 321 rests, 352 bandoliers, 366 swords, and 346 belts thus reached new leaders such as Colonel Thomas Gower of the Orange auxiliaries and Colonel Christopher Whichcote of the Green auxiliaries.[184] An additional 525 muskets, 525 rests, 525 bandoliers, 500 swords, and 500 belts were accounted for with the note that they were given to the Salters' Hall subcommittee by the "Committee Sitting at Weavers Hall."[185] With the end goal being the expansion of the army, parliament's Committee for the Advance of Money saw no issue ordering one subcommittee to deliver supplies on to the next. Advocates were not averse to cannibalizing resources if it advanced the greater cause; committee action surrounding the establishment of London's auxiliaries was, on balance, not wholly unlike developments of the previous June when loans made by livery companies for Ireland were scooped up to fund civil war. As was increasingly becoming the case, committees and committeemen were behind innovative, and by some estimates, radical efforts to move men, weapons, and money.

Supplies for the auxiliaries arrived piecemeal from throughout London. Five hundred pikes came from "the magezine in Tower street," for instance. Arms were in some cases purchased outright, including the 237 muskets and 282 rests bought by "Captayn Shambrooke and mr Tomsen." Colonel Tichbrone brought in nine muskets, eight rests, ten bandoliers, fourteen pikes, and nine swords "from the drapers Hall being armes seized on." Pennington brought in seventeen muskets and pikes which "were seized and wer Imperfect and wer repyared." After delivering stray repaired arms, the Lord Mayor and Common Council turned yet again to London's dependable liveries. On 27 April, requests were issued "to all the sev[er]all companies of this Citty," with the hope that they might "lend their Armes to be used and ymployed at present for the necessary use defence & safety of this Cittye."[186] Like the previous year, companies responded to the requests at various speeds. Goldsmiths took Pennington's letter into consideration on 3 May and immediately supplied what they could. Their accounts reveal the nature of Pennington's letter, which made specific reference to "imminent danger" and the need "for the better securinge & safety of this Cittye." It was, the letter continued, the Lord Mayor's "desire" that companies might loan "all the Armes of ye Companye."[187] Soon thereafter, the Goldsmiths responded, declaring that it "is thought fitt agreed & soe ordered to deliver such Armes." Within two days they had taken inventory of supplies worth £38 16s. The Salters' Hall subcommittee next accounted for the delivery of sixteen muskets, rests, bandoliers, and pikes along with thirty-two swords.[188] Clothworkers followed suit, lending an unspecified number of pieces worth £64 12s.[189] On 3 March, members of the Haberdashers' Company sent in 150 swords, 149 belts, 100 muskets, ninety-eight bandoliers, and six corsets, supplies worth £178 14s 4d.[190] Vintners, who at first agreed to "deliver onely 30 muskets and 20 pykes furnished," eventually gave thirty rests and bandoliers, along with fifty swords and belts.[191]

Few companies could claim to be more forward with loans than the Skinners. After reading Pennington's request "that all Companyes shall send all their Armes to furnish the auxillarye forces," they agreed "accordingly," giving six muskets, rests, and bandoliers along with four pikes and ten swords and belts. If less in quantity than some other "great" companies, their decision left Robert Thurlebye, their resident armorer, with "not soe many Armes for him to looke unto as formerly." It was subsequently decided that poor Robert might retire; after submitting to the court his "humble peticion," and in light of the fact that he was "an ould man and hath bine an ancient servant to the companye," members agreed to pay him a pension of 5s 8d.[192]

Requests for arms and armor came with little indication of how or when the said goods might be returned. Fishmongers, for instance, did not seek to have their goods replaced until May of 1645, well after the creation of the New Model Army and at a time when they became concerned over "all such of this Companyes Armes formerly lent unto this City." Liverymen made note of twenty-four corsets that were eventually returned from the Salters' Hall by Colonel Hookes. It was agreed that they should be "made cleane and emended" and "putt upp into this Companyes Armory in lieu of" ones that were "lento [sic] the City the Tenth of May 1643."[193]

Several companies voiced concern over the burden of lending arms and armor. Grocers complained about previous unfulfilled loans, citing the £4,500 "paid at the beginning" of the Long Parliament for "removing" Scottish forces, and the additional £9,000 loaned "towards the charges of reducing the kingdome of Ireland into obedience." With payments outstanding they rightfully wondered what else might be "borrowed by this Company upon the security & seale thereof." The extent of their outstanding debts, which they estimated to be "£4000 more at the least" than the £13,500 that they had already loaned, proved deeply disconcerting. They proceeded "deliberately & sadly" as they took into consideration what means might be used to remedy their debts. "Being forced to borrow money at interest to pay interest for the summes formerly lent to the Parliament" led them to the difficult conclusion that they should sell £1,000 worth of plate on 8 May. Doing so, they concluded, might see them avoid insolvency.[194] Requests for arms and armor did little to help such matters, but it also did not stop the company from sending in eight pikes and twenty swords.[195]

Although their wardens never record specific quantities, Drapers made note of loaned equipment worth £77 5s. This figure becomes more generous in light of their concurrent orders that "plate shalbe sold" to cover debts, save for "spoones for the Companies use."[196] Mercers scarcely fared better. Having loaned "forty muskets and Twenty Corselets with pikes for the arming of the auxiliary forces raysed by this Citty," they also had to sell off plate worth £699 7¾d to help cover "payment of the Companies debts."[197]

Nine leading companies – the Skinners, Goldsmiths, Vintners, Drapers, Merchant Taylors, Salters, Fishmongers, Grocers, and Leathersellers – loaned at least 207 muskets, 157 stands, 137 bandoliers, 152 pikes, 340 swords, 208 belts, and 90 helmets for outfitting London's auxiliaries.[198] Receipts from the Salters' Hall subcommittee reveal that "other Armes" were also "delivered by Severall Companies."[199] Although they inevitably delivered fewer items, smaller livery companies nevertheless contributed to the effort. Carpenters, for instance, agreed to give "2 of the best coslettes" along with "twoe pikes and five swords."[200] Turners paid £1 14s to secure "4 swords & 4 belts" which were likely loaned or used as replacements after fulfilling Pennington's request.[201] Smaller companies suffered similar fates to their larger peers who were forced to sell plate while concurrently emptying their armories. At a court held in May, members of the Innholders' Company determined that they would need to sell off £100 worth of plate to cover their debts on account of the interest and loans made to parliament.[202] "After longe debate" the painters-stainers agreed to sell plate to cover outstanding debts of £42 5s 7d.[203] Apart from some minor disappointments and delays, London's companies managed, altogether, to deliver 1,300 pieces of equipment; if just over a tenth of the 12,790 pieces of arms and armor recorded by the Salters' Hall subcommittee, the supplies nevertheless helped to outfit the new City forces.[204] Less important than the total number of pieces loaned was the speed with which the supplies could be delivered – unlike contracts, liveries kept stores of readily usable armes and armor. In a similar fashion to lending money, then, company supplies acted as a crucial stopgap, as a means to secure resources before fully realized programs for supply could be implemented. In the end, the collection for London's auxiliaries amounted to a minor yet important victory for belligerents; Pennington had once again effectively wielded the authority of his office to coerce livery companies to lend resources; in this case, these efforts meant delivering arms and armor directly to the radical Salters' Hall subcommittee on Bread Street.

New financial expedients

Grim reports from the battlefield prompted other military and financial expedients. On 13 April, news of royalist successes at the Battle of Ripple Field sent new shockwaves through the metropolis. The following month brought equally devastating news of heavy parliamentarian losses at Stratton, followed days later by accounts of the failed siege of Worcester. A growing mood of despondency and uncertainty settled over the City as some turned their attention to the progress made toward raising auxiliaries, and others began seeking alternative projects whereby the wealth and manpower of the City might be moved. Militant Londoners were soon made painfully aware of the gulf that existed between their expectations and reality. Indeed, much of London's initial enthusiasm for war seemed to evaporate in response to the string of parliamentary defeats. Compounding matters was the fact that parliament was still waiting for the fulfillment of assessments and requests from the previous year. The 15 November entreaty for "a thousand light Horse, and three thowsand dragoons" to supply Colonel Browne, for instance, and which was to be overseen by the subcommittee at Weavers' Hall, was still being collected in early 1643.[205] Other proposals fared little better. In May, a proposed £50,000 loan for the "reducing of Newcastle" and capture of much-needed coal generated a mere £6,848 in London.[206] Eager to see progress, a handful of leading parliamentarians and wealthy citizens took it upon themselves to outfit and equip new recruits.

One such regiment belonged to Sir Arthur Haselrig, one of the original five members and a parliamentary commander who outfitted his cuirassiers with weapons and polished plate armor. Like other City recruits, Haselrig's men were apparently enthusiastic but inexperienced. Nearly fifty of Haselrig's so-called "lobsters" nevertheless gave their lives to hold ground at the Battle of Ripple Field on 13 April. More brave acts were recorded months later at the Battle of Lansdowne, but tragedy struck at Roundway Down on 13 July when Haselrig's cuirassiers fell backwards, broke their line, and retreated. Their retreat earned scornful and lasting remarks from royalists who saw similarities to crustacean locomotion. Samuel Butler made light of their retreat years later in *Hudibras*, a poem celebrating when the royalist commander Ralph Hopton took "crabs and oysters prisoners, And lobsters, 'stead of cuirassiers."[207] Despite suffering heavy losses during the campaigns of 1643, Haselrig's ranks were eventually replenished by new London recruits who would go on to play decisive roles in the siege of Arundel Castle in December, at Cheriton in March 1644, and the second Battle of Newbury that October. The trials and tribulations of war hardened the unit. Royalists who met with Haselrig's "formidable" cuirassiers in December 1643 were left pondering their own "naked and unarmed" condition. Some, claimed Clarendon, "could not bear their impression."[208] The "London lobsters" serve as a reminder of one of the ways in which personal efforts could generate unique moments of mobilization. Lord Brooke's tireless efforts to recruit and outfit Londoners for service in Warwickshire provides another example.[209]

Efforts were seldom as successful as those of Haselrig and Brooke. The radical parliamentarian Henry Marten often entertained hopes that he might lead his own troop of City horse. On 19 May, the Commons agreed that "money Plate and Jewells seised" by Marten and his officers from the royalist earl of Holland could be used "towards the raising of his Regiments."[210] Captured treasure seemed an auspicious start to Marten's efforts, but his plans soon derailed. Marten apparently spent an inordinate amount of time wandering the City in search of horses and riders, efforts that did little more than annoy his enemies and allies. On one occasion, he seized six coach horses belonging to Elizabeth Savage, Countess Rivers. Marten gave little thought to his actions at the time, but Savage's family ties to the queen and court ran deep enough to make an issue of the affair. Laurence Whitaker recounted that Marten took the horses with the knowledge that they belonged to "a knowne Papist through the Wife of a peer." Marten thus crossed a line, broaching the increasingly sensitive matter of parliamentary privilege, and was ordered by his own House to make amends.[211] It was not a lack of enthusiasm that kept Marten from the battlefield; indeed, he was still busy rounding up horses and promoting other military ventures up to the time of his ejection from the Commons on 16 August 1643. It remains to be seen if his horses or men went on to join other parliamentary commanders upon his dismissal, but his efforts had, for the time being, laid bare deepening tensions between the Commons and Lords.[212]

If a lingering concern for parliamentarians, horse conscription had become a persistent burden for war-weary Londoners. Only the wealthiest of citizens could afford to pay the £14 to £32 that it cost to outfit a horse and rider. Far more animals were secured early in the war, at a time when enthusiasm was widespread and supplies readily available. Indeed, a staggering 3,757 "horses geldings and mares, with what Armes was listed with them" were raised in 1642, which were worth £54,772 18s 4d.[213] Once conscripted, horses were rapidly assigned to London's regiments. In September 1642, ninety-nine horses went to Captain Heriot Washborne; eighty-eight went to Philip Skippon; forty-seven to Richard Browne; ninety-five to Edmund Harvey; sixty-six to Robert Mainwaring; [Peter?] Willett, meanwhile, received fifty-four horses.[214] Decidedly fewer horses were procured in early 1643. Accounts show that at least 459 horses were provided by the City between the months of October 1642 and July 1643. Once equipped, they had a total value of £9,309. Efforts to raise and outfit horses still depended largely on individual efforts of eager leaders like Marten, or indeed of military men like Colonel Edmund Harvey. The latter managed to raise twelve horses and armor worth a total of £393 in Cornhill Ward, no small feat.[215]

While some wealthy Londoners could easily afford to outfit and loan several horses at once, the loss of just a few animals could spell disaster for the less fortunate. George Searle of Middlesex pled for restitution in a petition to parliament after the Lord General's men seized his cart and four horses. Searle requested the repayment of their value so that he could care for "himself his wife and seaven small children."[216] Others meanwhile found opportunity in the heightened demand. Thomas Pittman welcomed parliament's request that he assist the driving of an artillery train for forty-nine days from early November to December 1642. On 3 January Essex wrote to Gilbert Gerrard, Treasurer for the Army, to request that Pittman receive a payment of £17 17s for his service. Pittman was paid in full by 8 February.[217]

Persistent demand and slow supply led Pennington and Common Council to petition on 22 June for the passing of "an ordinance of Parliament" that would allow "for the lifting and fitting for service all horses in and about the Citty of London, and Twelve Miles Compasse." Maintaining a supply of horses to parliament apparently required both a wider area of focus and the ability to "lift" what was needed. London's leaders did "pray that the said Ordinance" for securing more horses would be "forthwith passed."[218] In all likelihood, the areas within the Lines had simply exhausted their supply, forcing attention to the wider areas within twelve miles of the City.[219]

Other supply issues were coming into focus, and not least was the problem of money. "Mony," Sir Edward Nicholas noted on 3 May 1643, remained the leading concern "which troubled" most parliamentarians. Countless individual donations, an already robust program for taxation, and *ad hoc* lending by livery companies propped up the cause. But more was needed. Money that reached parliament's coffers, Nicholas went on, was "very hardly gotten & slowly at London by ye 2 houses."[220] Making matters worse was the fact that London's appetite for lending continued to flag. Clearly, other financial expedients were needed.

Sequestrations, followed by options for compounding, offered one solution. On 27 March 1643, parliament passed a general sequestration ordinance so that the "estates of such notorious Delinquents ... or instruments of the publike calamities ... should be converted and applied towards the supportation of the great charges of the Common-wealth." Sequestrations within the capital fell under "the Jurisdiction" of the Lord Mayor, aldermen and councilmen who appointed a committee to carry out the orders.[221] The six new committeemen were William Kendall, Richard Morrell, William Perkins, William Pitchford, Robert Sweet, and George Willingham, a group that Lindley identified as "worrying examples of newly risen militants."[222] One would be hard-pressed to challenge this assessment. Kendall, as we have seen, was an active radical petitioner and close associate of John Venn.[223] Pitchford joined with Randall Mainwaring and John Towse as a leading parochial activist in St. Mary Colechurch.[224] Sweet, meanwhile, was a member of the Weavers' Hall subcommittee. Willingham was Nehemiah Wharton's London contact as he marched off to war in 1642. Of these men, Perkins, a tailor, maintained the least conspicuous record as an agitator and activist.[225] London's sequestration collectors brought in a total of £33,268 2s 2d between July 1643 and June 1647, with the largest sums collected between the years 1643 to 1644. As Coates points out, contributions from London were substantially larger than any other part of the country, save, that is, for Suffolk, where treasurers raised £40,826 11s. Suffolk's treasurers, it should also be noted, actively maintained records past 1647 and on to June 1649. London's sequestration treasurers brought in proportionally more than any part of the nation, adding nearly a sixth of the total £209,547 18s 5-3/4d that was collected. Treasurers from Westminster recorded £5,433 3s 11d collected between July 1643 and March 1645, while Middlesex's brought a total of £10,649 12s 4d between June 1643 and September 1649. "The majority of the receipts from sequestration," as Allan Everitt first observed, "failed to reach the central treasury."[226] So while London's sequestration collectors ultimately accounted for more money collected than in any single county, it may well have been the case that much of what was sequestered was hived off for local use.

Other efforts for raising money were well under way. On 20 February, Samuell Gosse and deputies of his choosing were appointed by the

Committee for the Advance of Money to "daily attend at the warehouse in guildhall & take into their Custody all such goods hosehold suff wares marchandize and Commodities as shallbe seized of distreyned by the severall collectors." By early March, the Committee was ramping up their pursuit of outstanding collections, arrears of the twentieth part, and any large unpaid sums assessed to known royalists and other detractors. Assistance came from London's trained bands, including Randall Mainwaring's infamous "redcoats" and other City forces that would "sack the houses and shops of everything without any reference to the amount due."[227] On 4 March, the Committee ordered the disposal "and sale of the goods distreyned" from "the houses of Mr Thomas Massan Marchant in Milkestreet London, and of Sr William Acton" of Woodstreet. Massam may have been an obvious target; Glapthorne's *His Majesties Gracious Ansvver* bore a dedication in his name. On 5 April, goods from Thomas Fownes's house in St. Mary Axe were delivered for parliament's use. Ten days later, the Committee sent Colonel Walter Long to "recover" and compound rents to a total of £1,500 still owed for the assessment by Alderman George Whitmore, an ardent supporter of the king who sat imprisoned in Crosby House. Two days later, the Committee froze £500 due to the royalist Marmaduke Rawdon, who "may be liable for satisfaction of his said assessment." That same day, Samuell Gosse was asked to deliver in £1,500 of goods distrained from Daniel Harvey and another £500 from Ellial Harvey. Over the coming months, the Committee continued to compound and liquidate estates. Orders arrived on 21 April to have "the hay oates and other goods and howsehold" items belonging to Sir Nicholas Crispe and Sir Thomas Abbey "forthwith distreyned appraised and sold towards satisfaction of their severall assessments." The Committee was informed on the same day about "divers person" seeking "warrants to seize goods which malignants endeavor to convey away" from London. In response, the Committee for the Advance of Money requested that the Lord Mayor issue warrants to the same end. Ten days later, the Committee sent collectors by boat to Hammersmith in order to seize "all such goods" that remained in Crispe's estate. Captain Peter Willett had his own orders to seize plate, chattels, and "horses and Armes" belonging to Sir John Gore, son of the late Lord Mayor of the same name. The next day it was Thomas Browne of Bassishaw who was targeted for failing to pay his £120 assessment, and Thomas Hutchinson of Aldersgate who had not accounted for the £300 he was assessed. After them it was Sir Thomas Abbey, who owed £800. Rumors that William Gore was planning to have trunks of goods "transported beyond the seas" led to swift action with the seizure of goods that might cover his £700 assessment.[228]

Affronts continued unabated, and on 7 May parliament passed a new ordinance for the "speedy raising & levying of Money throughout the whole kingdome ... by taxing such as have not at all contributed or lent or not according to their estates & abilities." Nine days later, the Committee's jurisdiction expanded to include "Twenty Miles Compasse" around London, and "such persons before them that have not contributed proporconably [*sic*] upon the propositions."[229] Efforts thereafter continued with the pursuit of outstanding payments such as the £86 owed by Tobias Lisle and the £100 required of Dr. Thomas Turner, rector of St. Olave Southwark.[230] If, as Coates has suggested, "sequestration proved much less productive in London than other parts of the country," it nevertheless provided another piece of the sprawling equation that was parliamentary finance in early 1643.[231]

On 24 February, an ambitious new program was enacted for weekly assessments. Payments varied by county, but the largest sums by far were requested from Londoners, who were expected to bring in £10,000 a week for a period of three months.[232] Pym's first attempt to introduce a tax on "superfluous commodities" – an excise – was made that same month, but it was initially voted down. It was not until 22 July, some four months later, and a month after the weekly assessments were scheduled to end, that the proposal for an excise passed. Excise was widely discussed and hotly debated from the time of its introduction to its eventual "approval." A version of the tax had already been implemented on 17 May when the Commons agreed to charge one shilling per barrel of beer, ale, cider, or perry sold to "the first buyer." One week later, a tax of one farthing per pound was imposed on raisins, figs, and currants. Taxes on sugars and cloths followed on 27 May.[233] Deeply unpopular with London's trade associations, the excise on "superfluous commodities" was a matter of national interest. "They are setting upp ye exacting of excises upon all provisions at London," wrote Edward Nicholas in early April. It would be a surprise, he added, "yf they can prevail," since it was clear that "they will ther find great opposic[i]on." Parliament's need for cash was, as always, urgent, and Nicholas went on to reveal that "the truth is that they are in London in great distrac[i]on for want of money & cannot hold out long unlesse excises be paid."[234]

Once fully implemented, the excise would provide a 5 percent charge on imported goods that included "groceries, drugs, silks and other fine fabrics, linen textiles, haberdasheries, paper, glass and earthenware, leather and upholstered goods." Outraged, butchers and brewers took to the streets in protest, but their efforts failed to stop what would soon be understood to be the "most important new form of taxation of the Civil War." Some estimates suggest that half of the money collected for the excise during the war came from Londoners; well beyond any other form of wartime taxation, the excise would become a cornerstone of parliament's financial apparatus.[235] Excise, as D'Maris Coffman has argued, was thereby an essential component of state formation.[236] For the time being, in the spring of 1643, it was one of several novel, if also controversial, components of parliamentary wartime finance.

Popular concerns over the recent increase in taxation soon boiled over. On Saturday, 18 March, "Captain *Mainwaring* (he whom His Majesty hath branded for his seditious courses, both in his Proclamations, and other writings)" broke up a group of nearly 1,000 apprentices who had gathered in Southwark to protest the assessment of a twentieth part.[237] On 29 March, the day after Pym first proposed the excise, an ordinance passed to extend assessments to London's non-contributors. John Fowke was one of several men appointed to nominate collectors by ward. A little more than a week later, on 7 April, Common Council issued an act calling for the collection of an additional tax of fifteenths, and shortly thereafter 300 copies of the ordinance were printed with the stipulation "that it shall be lawfull" for the Lord Mayor "to make a Warrant or Precept unto any Collector (requiring the same) to Distraine the Goods and Chattels of every person or persons refusing to pay the said fifteenths."[238] Disillusioned Londoners had little recourse for opposing the new fifteenths – save, that is, for their collective ability to petition, agitate, and take their protests to the streets.

The aftermath of the "Christmas gamboyle"

It would perhaps be easy to dismiss the attempt on the seven Londoners as an insignificant affair, as one of a number of minor developments lost in the fast-moving political currents of early 1643. Yet, to dismiss (or simply fail to account for) the event is to lose a central component of the calculus of metropolitan mobilization, an explanation for the urgency with which Londoners helped build the Lines, for the speed with which Pennington and his allies helped to purge City pulpits, raise auxiliaries, and indeed implement new financial expedients. The entire affair was, as Peter Heylyn lamented months later, an "odious" construction, "a *Christmasse* gamboyle" that began with "Alderman and others" travelling to Oxford and ended with "Master *Pym* in the *Common-Hall*."[239] But the gamble, no matter how repulsive it may have seemed to loyalists, had paid off; Pennington and his allies had thereby shifted the political narrative in London, redrawing how the capital would respond to parliament's war, and by extension how parliament might continue its effort. And by April it was clear that the war would continue – perhaps, as some lamented, indefinitely – and that the fate of London, with its mended steeples, unadorned glass windows, and newly erected fortifications, would remain tied to the prevailing interests in *both* parliament and Common Council.

Given all of this, it might be wise to reevaluate the prominent place afforded by scholars to the Oxford Treaty; while clearly a matter of import, contemporaries did not necessarily see it as a single overarching determinant for the course of the war. It was perhaps not, then, as John Morrill suggested, a prevailing fear that "if the treaty failed" those stuck in the capital "would have to fight for Parliament," or indeed that the "collapse" of the treaty, as Barry Coward surmised, signaled "a definite end of the first phase in the war."[240] Myriad other concerns were equally at play. Como, for instance, has suggested that "fear of accommodation with the king continuted to vex hard-line parliamentarians," and that concerns of this nature were becoming "acute" by March 1643.[241] Doubtless these were the same concerns that prompted the City to send their own representatives to the king in the first place, and it seems entirely possible that the "threat" of a peace accommodation was a motivating factor that led several of the accused seven to redouble their efforts to mobilize the metropolis. Peace, to put it another way, meant different things to different people.

Not least, the attempt paved the way for an important moment of ideological escalation – a time when petitioners, polemicists, and pamphleteers disseminated new radical ideas in print.[242] This episode surely might stand alongside other critical moments, and some of which have recently been delineated with precision by Como.[243] Indeed, as David Wootton originally suggested, the winter of 1642–3 was a time of central importance, a period when later "Levellers' views" were "foreshadowed" in political and religious writings.[244] Bowles' *Plaine English* was, of course, just one of several important printed polemics to ratchet up political rhetoric by suggesting that the king was subject "to the Laws" of the nation. Other "radical" claims were being proposed at the end of March. London's *Remonstrans Redivivus*, for instance, framed ten requests to parliament by reason of *salus populi suprema lex esto*, the notion that the "safety of the people is the Supreme Law." Concerned foremost with legal authority, the *Remonstrans Redivivus* petition drew attention to parliament's right to sit annually according to statute of Edward III (and not every three years as the Long Parliament's Triennial Act of February 1641 had established), to their right to check the authority of magistrates (including the king), and to their ability to pass laws for "the safety and freedom of the people."[245] Although reportedly available in March, the petition was not in fact printed until July, when tensions in the capital and the parliamentary coalition escalated yet further. According to the pamphleteer Henry Parker, royalists had meanwhile come to show particular disdain for "*Pennington, Ven, Foulk*, and *Mannering*, as notoriously guilty of Schisme." It was "the Lord Major," however, who garnered the greatest ire. Pennington was "railed at" for being the arch-agitator who "*stiled the stifling of peace in the womb.*"

Aiding Pennington's effort were his fellow accused Londoners, and alongside them were the "City Preachers" who put forth their best efforts to rally inhabitants to *"fight against the King in the feare of God"* and transform their own *"spirituall Milita into weapons of the flesh."*[246] Through a process of distilling royalist polemics Parker had, in essence, uncovered the zeitgeist of early 1643 and thereby laid bare the king's same narrative in which the City had been corrupted by the efforts of a coterie of militants. This was, if plainly obvious, an echo of earlier narratives surrounding the king's attempt to arrest the five, just as it would in time become part of the king's perennial attempt to blame opposition on a handful of discernible offenders.

And like the earlier attempt on the five, the king's attempt on the seven Londoners ultimately energized his opponents. From January onwards, militants worked at a feverish pace to mobilize the metropolis. It was in the short few months after the attempt that the Lines of Communication were developed and completed, when Pennington and Harley's Committee coordinated to remove offensive images, when the City's auxiliary regiments were raised, and when, importantly, new financial expedients were implemented. With these developments came renewed considerations of the religious and political reasons for war, made readily available in tracts, pamphlets and petitions.[247] These developments owed in no small part to Common Council's decision to send envoys to Oxford and the king's misguided response. Charles's critical misstep, and indeed the diligence of the accused, fundamentally transformed the terms of the civil war. It was by no means a coincidence that contemporaries began calling Common Council as "a third house" of parliament, a body that gained so much influence that "it was in vain for the Faction in Parliament to *contrive* unless the Faction in the Common-Councell in London would *execute.*"[248] Nor, it should be added, was it a coincidence the accused members would remain some of the most active supporters of London's war effort. Four of the seven later became regicides.[249] As with the attempt on the five members in 1642, the attempt on the seven Londoners in 1643 created stalwart and lifelong opponents to the Crown. Heylyn thus felt confident that his readers would agree with his assessment in late August 1643 that "Lord *Say*, or *Pym*, or *Isaac Pennington*" should be expected to oppose peace "in any of the three Houses wherein they are leaders."[250]

Politics thus polarized further for all walks of metropolitan life, a matter than ensured that the tensions of the winter would spill over into the spring and summer. Adding to this atmosphere and spurring on radical efforts were troubling dispatches from the west. Little could be done to conceal the miserable start to parliament's spring campaign.[251] The sink toward a low point began on 2 March, when Lord Brooke was shot through the eye in Lichfield by a royalist sniper, a rebuke to many champions of parliament's cause. By the following month, Sir Edward Nicholas could write with confidence to his fellow royalist, Henry Hastings, that the Lord General was up against insurmountable difficulties at the Siege of Reading; having lost "700 of their men, & broken thereby their 2 best Regim[en]ts of Blew, & Red coates," matters looked dire. Rather, Nicholas went on, "it is conceived wee might have a very fine opportunity to destroy their Army." With such failures in plain view, new rumors began circulating in the capital, including suggestions that the Lord General refused to pursue the enemy, and instead that he was busy trying to deal with soldiers who "run away dayly by great numbers."[252] Other parliamentarian generals could claim little better; although he secured Hereford in April, William Waller was repelled from Worcester the following month, forced to retreat in the dark toward Tewkesbury like a "night owl." Brewing amidst parliament's few pyrrhic victories and its growing tally of losses were rivalries that would shape politics for years to come.

Notes

1 LMA, MS COL/CC/01/01/041, fol. 46r.
2 These six men are first recorded in ibid., fol. 45v as "S[i]r Georg Garrett and Sir Georg Clark knights and Ald[e]r[m]en Mr Peter Jones Mr Georg Henley Mr Richard Bateman and Mr Barny Reames."
3 Lindley, *Popular Politics*, pp. 67, 138–139, 188, 191. For Bateman, see Liu, *Puritan London*, p. 201.
4 Pearl, *London*, p. 50. Herne is at times referred to in contemporary accounts as "Heron."
5 LMA, MS COL/CC/01/01/041, fol. 46r.
6 For an estimate of contemporary concern over the negotiations, see John Morrill, *Reactions to the English Civil War, 1642–1649* (London, 1982), p. 40. Ian Roy, for instance, claimed that the negotiations came in the wake of a "political softening-up campaign" in "'This Proud Unthankfull City': A Cavalier View of London in the Civil War," in Stephen Porter (ed.), *London and the Civil War* (London, 1996), p. 159. See in particular Braddick, "History, Liberty, Reformation and the Cause," pp. 117–118.
7 *A Plea For Peace* (London, 1642); *Accommodation Cordially Desired* (London, 1642).
8 *A Catalogue of Sundrie Knights, Aldermen, Doctors: Ministers and Citizens* (London, 1642).
9 PA, HL/PO/JO/10/1/139, "A Schedule of names of such persons as are and have been committed to the Fleete," 30 December 1642.
10 For a nuanced interpretation of Charles's political tactics, see R. Cust, *Charles I: A Political Life* (Harlow, 2005), *passim*.
11 *The Humble Petition of the Major, Aldermen, and Commons of the Citie of London and His Majesties Gracious Answer the fourth of January 1642* (London, 1643), pp. 7–8, 10.

12 BL, Add MS 37343, fol. 262v.
13 BL, Add MS 27962 K(i). 9 January 1643.
14 BL, Sloane MS 1467, fol. 130r.
15 Pearl, *London*, pp. 187–189, 316–320, 323. For mention of "the crased Mercer," see *An Honest Letter to a Doubtful Friend* ([London], 1642 [1643], E.87(4)), sig. A3r.
16 LMA, MS COL/CC/01/01/041, fol. 46v.
17 Henry Glapthorne, *His Majesties Gracious Ansvver* (London, 1643, E.84[41]), title page; S. R. Gardiner recognized that this copy was in fact a fake.
18 D. McKenzie and M. Bell (eds), *A Chronology and Calendar of Documents Relating to the London Book Trade*, vol. I (Oxford, 2005), p. 80. Another short example of the king's message was printed at the end of *A Most Joyfull Declaration Made by Colonell Skipon* (London, 1643), sig. A4v.
19 D. Freist, *Governed by Opinion: Politics, Religion and the Dynamics of Communication in Stuart London, 1637–1645* (London, 1997), p. 40.
20 Glapthorne, *His Majesties Gracious Ansvver*, pp. 4–5, 7.
21 See J. McElligott, *Royalism, Print and Censorship in Revolutionary England* (Woodbridge, 2007), pp. 21–22; Freist, *Governed by Opinion*, p. 41.
22 These figures are based on data from the English Short Title Catalogue.
23 For the extent to which wartime print functioned as propaganda, see Hughes, *Gangraena*; J. Peacey, *Politicians and Pamphleteers: Propaganda During the English Civil Wars and Interregnum* (Aldershot, 2004). For a contemporary example of falsified print in action, see Edward Hyde's forged speeches for the Earl of Pembroke and Lord Brooke in December 1642. Edward Hyde, earl of Clarendon, *Two Speeches Made in the House of Peers* (London, 1643, E.84(35)).
24 McKenzie and Bell, *A Chronology and Calendar*, vol. I, p. 80.
25 The ten committee members from the Lords included Northumberland, Pembroke, Sarum, Holland, Warwick, Manchester, Saye and Sele, Baron Howard of Escrick, Baron Grey of Warke, and Denbigh. See *LJ* vol. 5, p. 551. The twenty-one Commons included Sir John Hampden, Henry Marten, John Pym, Sir Philip Stapilton, Sir William Strickland, William Strode, Sir Peter Temple, Sir Henry Vane, Sir Peter Wentworth, John Ashe, Sir Gilbert Gerard, Henry Ludlow, Walter Erle, Robert Long, Thomas Jervoise, Richard Knightley, John Corbett, John Glynne, John Francklyn, Edward Dunch, and Anthony Nicoll. See also *CJ* vol. 2, p. 925.
26 LMA, Ms COL/CN/01/01/001, fol. 27r.
27 Vicars, *God on the Mount*, p. 248.
28 *Two Speeches Spoken* (London, 1643), pp. 14, 17–18; see also *Two Speeches Delivered* (London, 1642 [1643]), pp. 14, 18; Vicars, *God on the Mount*, p. 248.
29 *Two Speeches Spoken*, pp. 21–22.
30 *CJ* vol. 2, p. 927. 14 January 1643.
31 BL, MS Harley 164, fol. 276r. In his excellent study, *An Industrious Mind: The Worlds of Sir Simonds D'Ewes*, Sears McGee marks this as the time when D'Ewes lost a great deal of faith in Pym, claiming that Pym along with

"'Mr. Hampden' had maneuvered 'to interrupt the treaty of peace'" (p. 393). It is also worth noting that Ian Gentles, in his *ODNB* entry for "Montagu, Edward, second earl of Manchester" (2004) misdated this speech to the year prior, to the time just after the king had made the attempt on the five members. This error supports the view that too little is known about City politics in early 1643.

32 PA, MS HL/PO/JO/10/1/142, fol. 115, 14 January 1643, "all such in the Cittie of Westm[inste]r and the Liberties & the Counties of Midd[lesex] as refuse to Contribute uppon the propositc[i]ons and that the Lo[rd] Mayor & Comittee for the Militia in London doe forthwith disarme such in the Cittie of London & Suburbes & Liberties as refuse to Contribute uppon the proposic[i]ones according to the foremer order."

33 A. Laurence, *Parliamentary Army Chaplains, 1642–1651* (Woodbridge, 1990), pp. 49, 173.

34 Edward Bowles, *Plaine English: Or, A Discourse concerning the Accommodation, The Armie, The Association* (London, 1643), p. 26.

35 BL, MS Harley 162, fol. 318r. For the political significance of the Protestation, see John Walter, *Covenanting Citizens: The Protestation Oath and Popular Political Culture in the English Revolution* (Oxford, 2017).

36 *The True and Originall Copy of the first Petition* (London, 1642).

37 *To the Right Honourable The Lords and Commons assembled in Parliament* (London, 1643), sig. A2r. The earlier petition from December 1642, *The True and Originall Copy*, includes the phrase "expressed by Master *Pym* in Guildhall," yet this did not refer to his speech given alongside Manchester from 13 January, but instead referred to his speech from November 1642 recorded in *Two Speeches Delivered by the Earl of Manchester and Mr Jo[hn] Pym* (London, 1642).

38 BL. Add MS 18777, fos. 133r–133v. Yonge pointed out that the following men were to sit on the committee: Alexander Rigby, John Rolle, Sir Peter Wentworth, William Cage, Sir Henry Mildmay, "Mr [Michael?] Noble," "Mr [Roger?] Hill," John Blackiston, Sir Henry Vane, and Sir Thomas Barrington. An alternative list of eighteen men is provided in *CJ* vol. 2, p. 943: Alexander Rigby, John Rolle, John Blackiston, Sir Peter Wentworth, Sir Henry Heyman, Sir William Strickland, William Cage, Edmund Prideux, William Heveningham, Sir Henry Mildmay, William Strode, Cornelius Holland, Godfrey Bosevile, William Purefoy, Henry Marten, John Gurdon, Sir Thomas Barrington, and Sergeant John Wilde. See also, Brenner, *Merchants and Revolution*, pp. 443–444; Hexter, *Reign of King Pym*, p. 110. For Rigby, see Malcolm Gratton, "Rigby, Alexander, (bap. 1594, d. 1650)," *ODNB* (2004). Brenner notes that seven of the above committee members were considered "revolutionaries" by David Underdown in *Pride's Purge* (Oxford, 1971), p. 210 and appendix. For Brenner's note, see again *Merchants and Revolution*, p. 444 n. 95.

39 HL, Hastings Correspondence, Box 16/9681.

40 HL, Hastings Correspondence, Box 16/9682.

41 Ibid.

42 *Mercurius Aulicus*, 22–28 January 1643 (Thomason E.246[9]), p. 1.
43 GL, MS 15201/1, fos. 100–101.
44 GL, MS 16967/4, fol. 386. The letter was signed "Pembroke, Montgomerie, Say and Seale, Jo: Pym, Manchester, Edw^a: Howard, Auck: Nicoll, Bolingbrooke, J: Evelin." A copy of the same request for "pretended" letters is recorded in GL, MS 15201/1, fos. 100–101.
45 *The Bloody Game at Cards* ([London], 1643). Thomason acquired his copy on 10 February 1643.
46 *An Humble Remonstrance ... in vindication of the honourable Isaak Pennington ... Alderman Foulkes ... Captaine Venne ... [and] Captaine Manwaring* (London, 1643), p. 4.
47 *Animadvertions upon the Kings Answer* (London, 1643), pp. 1, 6.
48 *A Briefe Answer to a Book Intitled His Majesties Letter* (London, 1643), pp. 2, 5.
49 John Fowke, *The Declaration and Vindication of Issack Pennington now Lord Mayor of the Citie of London of Colonell Ven, Captain Mainwaring, and Mr Fowke* (London, 1643), p. 3.
50 LMA, MS COL/CC/01/01/041, fol. 48v.
51 *CJ* vol. 2, p. 938. J. Burke, *A genealogical and heraldic history of the extinct and dormant baronetcies of England* (London, 1861), p. 141. See also Brenner, *Merchants and Revolution*, pp. 442–443; Ward, Lock and Co., *Ward and Lock's Pictorial Guide to the Environs of London* (London, 1878), p. 29.
52 *Mercurius Aulicus*, 19 February 1643, sigs. P3r–v. E.246[41].
53 *Mercurius Aulicus*, 17 February 1643, sig. N4r. E.246[39].
54 LMA, MS COL/CC/01/01/041, fos. 47v–48r.
55 Ibid., fol. 49v.
56 Ibid., fos. 49v–50r.
57 Ibid., fol. 51r.
58 LMA, MS COL/CC/01/01/041, fol. 48r.
59 LMA, MS COL/CHD/CT/01/004, fol. 223v. I have been unable to locate a printed copy of this order.
60 For an account of the financial status of the parish, see Liu, *Puritan London*, p. 38.
61 See Mary Anne Everett Green (ed.), *Calendar of the Proceedings of the Committee for Advance of Money, 1642–1656*, 3 vols (London, 1888), part I, p. 15.
62 LMA, MS P69/AND1/B/009/MS02088/001, illegible pagination.
63 LMA, MS P69/LAW1/B/001/MS02590/001, fol. 334.
64 LMA, MS P69/MRY1/B/006/MS03891/001, unpaginated.
65 The loan was intended to be paid in three parts on security of the weekly assessment, with £20,000 coming in monthly. *CJ* vol. 2, pp. 983, 999; see Coates, *Impact*, p. 60.
66 LMA, MS COL/CC/01/01/041, fos. 52r–v. Committee members are listed as "Colonell Mannering, Peter Mills, Christopher Nicholson, John Harley, Thomas Foot, Richard Bateman, Alexander Jones, Thomas Noell, Christopher

Pack, Tobias Dixon, George Willingham, John Bellamy, Thomas Arnold, John Kendrick, Samuell Langham, Richard Hunt, William Beck, Richard Young, James Storey, William Wyborne and Joseph Parker." See also LMA, MS COL/AD/01/041, fol. 66.

67 Simon Marsh, "The Construction and Arming of London's Defences 1642–1645," *Journal of the Society for Army Historical Research*, 91 (2013), pp. 276–278. The other two officers were Marmaduke Rawden and George Langham.

68 See V. Smith and P. Kelsey, "The Lines of Communication: The Civil War Defences of London," in S. Porter (ed.), *London and the Civil War* (London, 1996), pp. 117–148.

69 *A True Declaration and just Commendation of the Great and Incomparable care of … Isaac Pennington* (London, 1643; Thomason E.99(27)), pp. 4–5.

70 LMA, MS COL/CC/01/01/041, fol. 53r.

71 LMA, MS COL/CHD/CT/01/004, fol. 223v; Peacey, *Print*, pp. 337–338.

72 *LJ* vol. 5, pp. 641–642. 7 March 1643. *An Ordinance and Declaration Of the Lords and Commons* (London, 1643).

73 William Lithgow, *The Present Surveigh of London and Englands State* (London, 1643), sigs. A4v–Bv. Further companies included the "Feltmakers, Fishmongers and Coupers" who marched out on 17 May, and many other trades, including the "Goldsmiths, Ferriers, Bakers, Bruers, Butchers, Cooks, Candlemakers, Smiths, Cutlers, Carpenters, Shipwrights, Joyners, Boxmakers, Wheelwrights, Turners, Carmers, and foure thousand Weavers, Braizers, Dyers, Imbrouderers, Horologiers, Watchmakers, Engravers, Tinkers, Haberdashers, Feathermakers, Clothiers, Tanners, Curriers, Glovers, Spurriers, Painters, Printers, Stationers, Bookbinders, Gunmakers, Glaziers, Masons, Tecturers, Brickmakers, Plumbers, Vpholsters, Combemakers, Girdlers, Coblers, Chimney-sweepers, Jackfarmers, with many more that I can not recollect." Smith and Kelsey suggest that "a degree of exaggeration and superficial observation may have crept in" to Lithgow's account, but there is no real way to test their claim ("The Lines of Communication," p. 123).

74 Mercers' Company Library, Acts of Court, 1641–1645, fol. 69v.

75 Goldsmiths' Company Library, Court Minute Book W, fos. 44r, 49v.

76 GL, MS 3295/2, unfol.

77 GL, MS 2208/1, unfol.

78 GL, MS 5445/17, unfol.

79 LMA, MS P69/MRY2/B/005/MS03556/002, unpaginated.

80 LMA, MS P69/MRY9/B/007/MS02596/002, unpaginated.

81 LMA, MS COL/CA/01/01/060, fol. 23r makes note of Case as Pennington's chaplain and plans for Case to preach in the Guildhall; see Pearl, *London*, p. 232.

82 See Como, *Radical Parliamentarians, passim*, but especially pp. 101–103, 224–225; Elliott Vernon, "The Sion College Conclave and London Presbyterianism during the English Revolution," pp. 77–111.

83 LMA, MS P69/MIC1/B/008/MS02601/001/001, fos. 170v, 173v.

84 LMA, MS P69/OLA2/B/001/MS04415/001, fol. 117r.
85 LMA, MS P69/BRI/B/016/MS06552/001, pp. 123, 125. The said "captayne Wilson" was most certainly Rowland Wilson, who continued to support the war effort and went on to command the City's Orange regiment at the first battle of Newbury in September. L. C. Nagel, "The Militia of London, 1641–1649" (unpub. Ph.D. thesis, King's College London, 1982), pp. 57–58, 316 on Rowland Wilson and pp. 125–134 for the role of London regiments at Newbury.
86 Lithgow, *The Present Surveigh*, sig. B4v.
87 For skilled laborers, see LMA, MS COL/AD/01/041, fol. 94v.
88 *CSPV* vol. 26, pp. 267–278. Lithgow noted "two hundred twelve pieces of Cannon" in *The Present Surveigh*, sig. B4v.
89 *A True Declaration* (London, 1643), p. 6.
90 Hughes, "Preachers and Hearers," p. 62.
91 Arnold Hunt provides a very interesting discussion of the ways in which printed sermons, or even "the same sermon" might be read from the pulpit and thus repeated "many times," *The Art of Hearing*, pp. 179–186.
92 John Arrowsmith, *The Covenant Avenging Sword Brandished* (London, 1643), title page and pp. 1, 2, 4. Hugh Trevor-Roper noted that Arrowsmith was nominated to preach his 25 January fast-day sermon by Francis Rous, John Pym's kinsman. See Trevor-Roper, "The Fast Sermons of the Long Parliament," p. 287.
93 Jeremiah Whittaker, *Ejrenopojos* (London, 1643), title page. For the note regarding his preaching in London, see Joseph Hirst Lupton, "Whitaker, Jeremiah," *DNB* (Oxford, 1885–1900), vol. 61, p. 17.
94 Whittaker, *Ejrenopojos*, pp. 1, 9, 21.
95 Mary Morrissey, *Politics and the Paul's Cross Sermons* (Oxford, 2011), pp. 1, 4, 34.
96 *CJ* vol. 2, p. 782.
97 Joseph Caryl, *Davids Prayer for Solomon* (London, 1643), sig. A2r–v.
98 Ibid., pp. 7–10.
99 Matthew Griffith, *A Sermon Preached in the Citie of London* (London, 1643), pp. 1–2, 11, 13.
100 *Mercurius Aulicus*, p. 203. E.100[18].
101 *CJ* vol. 3, p. 82.
102 LMA, MS COL/CA/01/01/060, fos. 168v, 173v; *CJ* vol. 3 p. 105. See Morrissey, *Politics*, p. 225.
103 LMA, MS COL/CHD/CT/01/004, fol. 215v.
104 Morrissey notes that sermons intended for Paul's Cross were instead given at the Mercers' Chapel "on 11 June and 18 June 1643" in *Politics*, pp. 224–225.
105 E. M. Symonds, "The Diary of John Greene (1635–59)," *EHR*, 43 (1928), p. 391.
106 Morrissey, *Politics*, p. 227.
107 Spraggon, *Puritan Iconoclasm*, pp. 84, 108, 144.
108 BL, Harley MS 164, fol. 349r.

109 Translated and quoted in Albert J. Loomie, "The Destruction of Rubens's 'Crucifixion' in the Queen's Chapel, Somerset House," *Burlington Magazine*, 140 (1998), pp. 680–682.
110 Kenneth Fincham and Nicholas Tyacke, *Altars Restored: The Changing Face of English Religious Worship, 1547–1700* (Oxford, 2007), pp. 275–278.
111 Ibid., p. 278.
112 Lindley, *Popular Politics*, pp. 39–44.
113 Fincham and Tyacke, *Altars Restored*, p. 279.
114 See pp. 47–52 and 148–153.
115 LMA, MS COL/CA/01/01/060, fol. 140r.
116 Spraggon, *Puritan Iconoclasm*, p. 258.
117 Ibid., p. 144.
118 Ibid., pp. 86, 149.
119 LMA, MS P69/ALH7/B/013/MS00818/001, fos. 153r, 154r.
120 LMA, MS P69/TRI3/B/004/MS04835/001, unfol.
121 LMA, MS P69/PET4/B/006/MS00645/002, fol. 80r.
122 LMA, MS P69/ALH8/B/013/MS00823/001, unfol.
123 LMA, MS P69/PET1/B/001/MS04165/001, fol. 268.
124 LMA, MS P69/MGT4/B/004/MS04570/002, p. 143.
125 LMA, MS P69/LAW2/B/010/MS03907/001, unpaginated.
126 LMA, MS P69/LAW1/B/008/MS02593/002, fos. 30, 68. Anthony Burgess officially replaced Thomas Crane as vicar of the church in January 1645. He had, however, been acting as "vicker" of the parish since 13 December 1643, a date when the vestry agreed to pay him "twentie five poundes every quarter." See LMA, MS P69/LAW1/B/001/MS02590/001, fol. 331.
127 LMA, MS P69/MRY14/B/006/MS01013/001, fol. 184r.
128 LMA, MS P69/MRY1/B/006/MS03891/001, unfol.
129 LMA, MS P69/BOT4/B/008/MS04524/002, fos. 61r, 63r, 78v.
130 LMA, MS P69/MIC1/B/008/MS02601/001/001, fol. 178v. See also, Saint Michael Cornhill, which paid thirty shillings to "Mr Robinson for takeing downe the Fowre crosses on the steeple." LMA, MS P69/MIC2/B/006/MS04071/002, fol. 143r. Nineteen shillings were "paid for taking downe the crosse upon the steeple and mending the vayne" at Saint Pancras Soper Lane, LMA, MS P69/PAN/B/014/MS05018/001, fol. 41v.
131 Symonds, "The Diary of John Greene (1635–59)," p. 392.
132 *Mercurius Aulicus*, p. 131. E.102[1].
133 Richard Overton, *Articles of High Treason Exhibited against Cheap-Side Crosse* (London, 1642), p. 3.
134 Vicars, *God on the Mount*, pp. 326–327.
135 Spraggon, *Puritan Iconoclasm*, p. 119.
136 *CSPV* vol. 26, p. 266.
137 Herbert Palmer, *The Necessity and Encouragement* (London, 1643), pp. 10–11, 13, 17–18, 36–77; Herbert Palmer, *Scripture and Reason Pleases for Defensive Armes* (London, 1643).

138 See Lindley, *Popular Politics*, pp. 266–269. Lindley found that "ten clergymen were among the principal citizens rounded up and imprisoned on 29 October for failing to contribute towards parliaments war effort."
139 Committee members included Thomas Brightwell, John Gering, William Greenhill, Michael Herring, William Hobson, Edward Hooker, Alexander Jones, William Kendall, Christopher Nicholson, Theophilus Riley, William Taylor, and Richard Turner. See Lindley, *Popular Politics*, p. 267 n. 55. See also TNA, SP 28/252/1 fol. 46r. Collectors from neighboring Middlesex included William Palmer, Sir Gilbert Gerard, and Sergeant Wilde. TNA, SP 20/1 fol. 5v.
140 See Coates, *Impact*, pp. 40–46. Coates reveals that £27,953 was accounted for in 1643. A very small proportion of this money came from clerical sequestrations.
141 I. M. Green, "The Persecution of 'Scandalous' and 'Malignant' Parish Clergy during the English Civil War," *EHR*, 44 (1979), pp. 515–516. See also Lindley, *Popular Politics*, pp. 256–257. It is worth mentioning that Camden House was also the meeting place for parliament's Sequestration Committee, a proximity that suggests communication between these important committees.
142 See John Nicholl, *Some Account of the Worshipful Company of Ironmongers* (London, 1866), p. 243.
143 *LJ* vol. 5, p. 616.
144 PA, HL/PO/JO/10/1/146, #233.
145 Griffith, *A Sermon Preached in the Citie of London*.
146 Thomas Cheshire, *A True Copy of That Sermon Which Was Preached at S. Pauls* (London, 1642), p. 25.
147 John Walters notes that Smart stands as an "Example of the godly and political networks by which early taking of the Protestation might be secured in the country in 1641." *Covenanting Citizens*, p. 137.
148 *LJ* vol. 5, p. 997.
149 See Manfred Brod, "Doctrinal Deviance in Abingdon: Thomasine Pendarves and her Circle," *Baptist Quarterly*, 41:2 (2005), p. 93.
150 Tai Liu makes note of Tuke's actions on p. 129 of *Puritan London*, quoting A. G. Matthews, *Walker Revised* (Oxford, 1948), p. 60; see also J. F. Merritt, "Tuke, Thomas (1580/81–1657)," *ODNB*.
151 Symonds, "The Diary of John Greene (1635–59)," p. 392.
152 *CJ* vol. 3, pp. 6, 12. Orders for the sequestration of Abchurch were taken up to the Lords by Robert Harley on 17 March, while official sequestration ordinance for St. Clement Eastcheap passed on 22 March.
153 *CJ* vol. 2, p. 996; *CJ* vol. 3, p. 3.
154 LMA, MS P69/MIC2/B/001/MS04072/001, unpaginated. See also, *CJ* vol. 3, p. 3.
155 The *Commons' Journal* claims that the sequestration was for Thomas Tuke of St. Olave's Southwarke. Tuke held the parsonage of St. Olave's Old Jewry, but I have been unable to find any records to confirm that he also held the position in St. Olave's Southwarke. See *CJ* vol. 3, p. 4.

156 Clarke ran into troubles of his own with St. Leonard's parishioners in January 1647. See Robert Ashton, *Counter Revolution: The Second Civil War and its Origins, 1646–8* (New Haven, 1994), pp. 231–232.
157 *CJ* vol. 3, pp. 6–7.
158 *Apill [sic] 15, 1643 You are required to commend to God* (London, 1643).
159 *Mercurius Aulicus*, p. 203. E.100[18].
160 *CJ* vol. 3, p. 51.
161 Ibid., p. 67.
162 Ibid., p. 83.
163 See E. C. Vernon, "Blackmore, William (1616–1684)," *ODNB* (2008).
164 *CJ* vol. 3, p. 136.
165 White, *The First Century*, p. 25.
166 *Mercurius Rusticus*, p. 154.
167 Ephraim Udall, *Noli me tangere* (London, 1642), pp. 10–11, 25. See also Ephraim Udall, *The Good of Peace and Ill of Warre* (London, 1642); Ephraim Udall, *Directions Propounded, and Humble Presented to the High Court of Parliament* (London, 1642). See also Arnold Hunt, "Udall, Ephraim (*bap.* 1587, *d.* 1647)," *ODNB* (2004).
168 Lindley, *Popular Politics*, p. 265.
169 *Mercurius Aulicus*, 29 March and 10 April 1643.
170 Willoughby was from Tower Hamlets.
171 Nagel, "The Militia of London," p. 83. Nagel quoted "three regiments of stout men" from *A Perfect Diurnall*, 10–17 April (London, 1643).
172 Coates, *Impact*, p. 48.
173 H. A. Dillon, "On a MS List of Officers of the London Trained Bands in 1643," *Archaeologia*, 52 (London, 1890), p. 144. See the National Army Museum, MS 6807-53, "The Enseigns of the Regiments in the rebellious City of London both of Trayned Bands and Auxiliaries"; LMA, Ms CLC/270/MS03342, "London in Armes Displayed."
174 TNA, SP 28/121A Part 5, fol. 620r–v; Nagel, "The Militia of London," pp. 83–84.
175 LMA, MS P69/BOT4/B/001/MS04526/001, fol. 60r.
176 See Pearl, *London*, pp. 260–269; Lindley, *Popular Politics*, pp. 311–314; Como, *Radical Parliamentarians*, p. 158.
177 TNA, SP 28/198, part 1, pp. 4–5.
178 *A Declaration and Motive of the Persons trusted, usually meeting at Salters Hall in Breadstreet* (London, 1643).
179 Coates, *Impact*, p. 57.
180 Peter Edwards, *Dealing in Death: The Arms Trade and the British Civil Wars, 1638–52* (Stroud, 2000), p. 71.
181 PA, HL/PO/JO/10/1/114, fol. 188r.
182 *Another Order for Contributions for Maymed and diseased soldiers, who have been employed under the Command of his Excellencie the Earl of Essex* (London, 1643), p. 5.
183 TNA, SP 19/1, p. 155.
184 TNA, SP 28/198, part 1, p. 6.

185 Ibid., p. 8.
186 LMA, MS COL/CC/01/01/041, fol. 58v.
187 Goldsmiths' Company Library, Court Minute Book W, fol. 56r.
188 Ibid., fos. 58v–59r; TNA, SP 28/198, part 1, p. 8.
189 Clothworkers' Company Library, Orders of Courts, 1639–1649, fol. 80v.
190 GL, MS 15842/1, fol. 314v.
191 GL, MS 15201/1, fol. 110; TNA, SP 28/198, part 1, p. 8.
192 GL, MS 30708/3, fos. 204v–205r; TNA, SP 28/198, part 1, p. 8.
193 GL, MS 5570/3, fol. 833r.
194 GL, MS 11588/4, fos. 72, 74.
195 TNA, SP 28/198, part 1, p. 8.
196 Drapers' Company Library, Court Minutes and Records, 1640–1667, fos. 26v, 27v, 57r. Order from 8 May.
197 Mercers' Company Library, Acts of Court, 1641–1645, fos. 74r, 79r.
198 TNA, SP 28/198, part 1, p. 8.
199 Ibid.
200 GL, MS 5204/5, fol. 7v.
201 GL, MS 3297/1, unfol.
202 GL, MS 6649, p. 13.
203 GL, MS 5667, p. 176.
204 TNA, SP 28/198, part 1, pp. 6–7.
205 PA, MS HL/PO/JO/10/1/137, fol. 96.
206 LMA, MS COL/CC/01/01/041, fos. 60r, 117r; see also Coates, *London*, p. 57.
207 Samuel Butler, *Hudibras* (London, 1678), p. 215.
208 Clarendon, *History*, vol. 3, p. 347.
209 See Hughes, *Politics*, pp. 148, 181.
210 TNA, SP 28/7, fol. 159v.
211 BL, Add MS 31116, fol. 48v.
212 See Sarah Barber, *A Revolutionary Rogue: Henry Marten and the Immoral English Republic* (Stroud, 2000), pp. 8–9.
213 See above account and TNA, SP 28/131/3, fol. 131v: a book of London horse conscriptions.
214 TNA, SP 28/131/5, p. 35. Peter Willett was a parliamentarian captain who died later that year.
215 Ibid., p. 34.
216 TNA, SP 28/6/110–111.
217 TNA, SP 28/5/23.
218 PA, MS HL/PO/JO/10/1/152.
219 Again, see Robinson, *Horses, People and Parliament, passim.*
220 HL, Hastings Correspondence Box 17/9688.
221 *A&O*, pp. 106–117.
222 Lindley, *Popular Politics*, p. 331 n. 134.
223 Ibid., p. 331 n. 133.
224 See Liu, *Puritan London*, p. 78.
225 As Coates notes, he ended up "imprisoned for debt by April 1647." *Impact*, p. 154.

226 TNA, SP 28/216, part 5, pp. 1–3, 11–14, 20; Coates, *Impact*, p. 40; Alan Everitt, *The County Committee of Kent in the Civil War* (Leicester, 1957), pp. 160–161.
227 *CSPV* vol. 27, p. 252.
228 TNA, SP 19/1, pp. 110, 115, 122, 125, 127–128, 131, 134–139, 142.
229 TNA, SP 19/2, fol. 1r contains a copy of the ordinance that was printed on 11 May 1643.
230 TNA, SP 19/1, pp. 151, 155.
231 Coates, *Impact*, p. 40.
232 TNA, SP 19/1, p. 148.
233 *CJ* vol. 3, pp. 89–90, 101, 107–108.
234 HL, HA Correspondence Box 17/9686, Sir Edward Nicholas to Henry Hastings, 5 April 1643.
235 Coates, *Impact*, pp. 30, 32, 35. As Coates points out, there are no excise records for the early years of the war. The approximation of half is based on his figures for the period from 1647 to 1650, when London provided £487,656 of the total £853,345 collected, a figure that amounted to "fifty seven per cent."
236 Coffman, *Excise Taxation*.
237 *Mercurius Aulicus*, 19–25 March 1643, p. 146.
238 *An Act of Common-Councell concerning the Collecting of the Fifteenes Granted for the necessary Defence of the City of London* (London, 1643); LMA, MS COL/CHD/CT/01/004, fol. 223v.
239 Peter Heylyn, *Lord have mercie upon us* (Oxford, 1643), p. 17.
240 See Morrill, *Reactions to the English Civil War*, p. 40; Barry Coward, *The Stuart Age: England, 1603–1714* (Abingdon, 2012), p. 194.
241 Como, *Radical Parliamentarians*, p. 157.
242 Christopher Hill, *The World Turned Upside Down: Radical Ideas during the English Revolution* (London, 1972); Penry Williams, "Rebellion and Revolution in Early Modern England," in M. R. D. Foote (ed.) *War and Society* (London, 1973), pp. 225–40; Quentin Skinner in "Classical Liberty and the Coming of the English Civil War," in Quentin Skinner and Martin van Gelderen (eds), *Republicanism: Volume 2, The Values of Republicanism in Early Modern Europe: A Shared European Heritage* (Cambridge, 2002), pp. 9–28. For a thought-provoking, if at times contradictory consideration of the utility of "radicalism" as a category of inquiry, see Glenn Burgess, "Radicalism and the English Revolution," in Glenn Burgess and Matthew Festenstein (eds), *English Radicalism, 1550–1850* (Cambridge, 2007), pp. 62–86 and especially p. 65, where Burgess speculates that future approaches to the topic of radicalism might "be *pointillist*, extensively multi-causal, explicitly anti-deterministic and non-hierarchical." For more recent treatments, see Braddick, "History, Liberty, Reformation and the Cause," pp. 117–134.
243 Como, *Radical Parliamentarians*, pp. 149–155 in particular.
244 David Wootton, "From Rebellion to Revolution: The Crisis of the Winter of 1642/3 and the Origins of Civil War Radicalism," *EHR*, 105 (1990), p. 657.

245 *Remonstrans Redivivus: An Account of the Remonstrance and Petition Foormerly presented by divers Citizens of London* (London, 1643), pp. 4–5. Pearl claims that a printed copy of the petition and remonstrance was presented to the Common Council on 30 March 1643. LMA, MS COL/CC/01/01/041, fol. 57, however, does not indicate that this was the case. *An Account of the Remonstrance* only briefly mentions a "Petition of Lords and Commons, 14 Dec. 1641." William Walwyn was involved with the "Remonstrance presented to the Common Council" during the time "when Alderman Pennington was Lord Mayor." See William Walwyn, *Walwyns Just Defence* (London, 1649), p. 8. David Como notes this connection in "Print, Censorship, and Ideological Escalation in the English Civil War," *JBS*, 51 (2012), p. 838.

246 Henry Parker, *Accommodation Cordially Desired* (London, 1642), pp. 11, 30–31. Parker makes clear that his writing is intended as a response to "a late Pamphlet, pretended to be Printed at Oxford; a Reply to the Answer of the London Petition for Peace." Further, he makes frequent references to the author of the pamphlet as "the Replicant." See Michael Mendle, *Henry Parker and the English Civil War: The Politics of the Public's "Privado"* (Cambridge, 1995), p. 112.

247 See in particular, *Touching the Fundamentall Lawes* (London, 1643), p. 7; *Remonstrans Redivivus* (London, 1643), p. 4; Jeremiah Burroughs, *The glorious name of God* (London, 1643), p. 30; John Bramhall, *The Serpent Salve* (1643), pp. 35–37, 63, 200.

248 Butler, *A Letter*, p. 9.

249 These four were Isaac Pennington, John Venn, Edmund Harvey, and Robert Tichborne.

250 *Mercurius Aulicus*, 29 August 1643, p. 475.E.67[7].

251 John Greene made note of the "very cold Spring" that frequently saw "dry northerly winds." Symonds, "The Diary of John Greene (1635–59)," p. 392.

252 HL, Hastings Correspondence Box 17/9687 Sir Edward Nicholas to Henry Hastings, 19 April 1643.

4

London's *levée en masse*

By summer 1643, few Londoners could claim to be unaffected by the war. Even those who remained within the confines of their parishes during the months of "civill and intestine" fighting were subject to the distressing spectacles of conflict, and not least the steady arrival of maimed and injured soldiers who required care. Readers could meanwhile pick and choose between newsbooks and pamphlets that reported in titillating detail about parliament's "miraculous" victories – and, increasingly, its "lamentable" defeats.[1] Like many of his fellow godly parishioners, Nehemiah Wallington continued to agonize over the details of parliament's successes and its failures, portents of God's judgement.

By July, Wallington had come to focus on six particularly troubling matters. First, he lamented, was the issue of the "trust in ye Earle of Essex with his greate Army and how littel hath he done." Second was the sad news "that worthy Lord Brooke" had been "slaine in battil like good King Josia" in Lichfield. Third, and not least, were the Scots, who had failed "to come to helpe us in this our greate nessissyty." Fourth was "the Lord Fairfaxe" who was recently "overthrowen by the enemie" on 30 June at the Battle of Adwalton Moor. Fifth were Sir John Hotham and his son, both of whom were captured after making "perfidious & Treacherous" plans to deliver up Hull to the earl of Newcastle. Last, and perhaps most disconcerting of all, was the matter of "worthy Sir William Waller whom our God hath prospered to wine so many greate victories," but who had just been dealt a crushing defeat at the Roundway Down on 13 July 1643.[2] Although recorded privately in his personal journal, Wallington's "vaine outward hopes" hinted at just some of the most apparent issues that plagued parliament's commanders in the field.

Scholars have commented extensively about parliament's abysmal spring and early summer campaigns in 1643. According to Brenner, early summer 1643 "probably" marked "the very lowest point in the war for the parliamentary forces." Adamson likewise discerned that the summer was a time when parliament's "fortunes" were decidedly "at their lowest ebb." The "military fortunes" of Fairfax, like other parliamentarian commanders, claimed Gentles, had "reached their nadir."[3] Politicians and pamphleteers played no small part shaping this gloomy outlook. London's militants were acutely aware of the fact that the recent string of defeats strained wider efforts to mobilize. Reports "of the great defeate given by His Majesties Forces to *Sir William Waller*" at Roundway Down did little to encourge Londoners who were being asked to entertain new measures for taxation and lending.[4] Enthusiasm waned further in June when reports of the excise "upon divers Commodities, for the raising of mony to maintain the Parliaments Army" arrived.[5] Bemused by what might come next, Londoners began asking fundamental questions about how, if war persisted, they could sustain both their families and livelihoods.

Concerns over Waller's "miserable rout" in distant Wiltshire were brought closer to home in early June.[6] Londoners grew clamorous for any and all information that could be found about developments on the last Wednesday of May, a fast-day when Andrew Perne's morning sermon at St. Margaret was interrupted by the Speaker's "Macebearer" who had been sent "into the Church, to desire some of the Members to come speake with him" regarding some "intercepted letters" that revealed details about "a horrible plot against the Parliament, and the City of London."[7] According to the *Mercurius Aulicus*, the disruption allowed "some 50" members of the Commons to delegate "the whole power of the House to Master Pym" and a group of fellow committeemen who were tasked with investigating and responding to the conspiracy. Since then, London had been "filled" with more "noyse and clamour" than could be "before remembered." The trained bands were alerted and ordered to "seize upon such persons as they thought were likely to crosse their purposes," while some selected City "ministers" were "plundered of ther Sermon-notes, under pretence of looking for suspected Papers." On 2 June, John Glynne reported the full scope of the plot to the Commons on the behalf of the Committee of Safety, revealing that they had narrowly escaped "a Treason of such dangerous consequence that the Powder-plot, the *Sicilian Vespers*, [and] the massacre at *Paris*, were not to be compared unto it."[8]

On the afternoon of 8 June 1643, Pym and four other members of the parliamentary Committee of Safety, Sir Gilbert Gerard, Oliver St. John, Sir Henry Vane Junior, and John Glynne, arrived at the London Guildhall to speak in front of a packed Common Hall. Pym had once again been appointed to relay parliament's sentiments of good will and hope for unity to the City; but only on this occasion, he was also bearing pressing and dangerous news. Similar to the previous January when parliament sent Pym to address the City, attendees at the assembly were already aware of the subject of his impending speech – even if, that is, they were not fully sure of the details. In the wake of Pym's revelation came new demands for oaths of loyalty, renewed considerations of a possible peace settlement, and efforts to create yet another volunteer army, and in this case one made up of all able-bodied Londoners. This swift succession of interconnected developments, traditionally seen by scholars to have culminated with the petition efforts to create a volunteer army of the "general rising" on 20 July, would finally bear fruit on 7 August, the date when Pennington and his allies called upon Londoners to join together and march to Westminster's Old Palace Yard to protest against propositions for peace being floated in the House of Lords.[9] The actions of the subsequent mass gathering – a "multitude" of thousands – created what Simonds D'Ewes could only call "one of the saddest of daies that happened since the beginning of this Parliament." It was, D'Ewes concluded, a time when "seditious & scismaticall persons in the City of London" managed to subvert "all the priviledges" of parliament, and shake the institution to "the very root."[10] As we shall see, London's "seditious" conspirators and the resulting mob did much more than threaten violence against royalist sympathizers and impede upon parliamentary privilege: rather, they steered the nations course from that of potential peace to continual war.

Waller's plot

Six days passed before Londoners could read about the "mischievous Design."[11] Renditions of the plot's main points, as conveyed by copies of Pym's speech to Common Hall, were made ready for purchase by 9 June.[12] The details were chilling. According to one account, the conspirators received a commission from the king that ordered royalists in London to rise up on "a night where most part of the Trained Bands that kept the Courts of guard should be their friends." Their first move would be to "seize upon the Magazine in London" and then move on to take "the [out]workes." With the Lines of Communication captured, the plotters were then to signal 3,000 of the king's men who would be waiting "within 15 miles of London" and were ready to ride in and arrest "the L[ord] Major and all the Committee of the Militia of London" along with "Members of both Houses, viz the L[ord] Say L[ord] Wharton Mr Pym, Sir Philip Stapleton, Col[onel] Hampten and Col[onel] Strod." A specialized "regiment of 100 desperate rogues from Oxford" would next be let in to the City so that they could be "imployed in cutting the throates of the chief Round heads." Distinguished by white ribbons and equipped with clubs and halberds, the uprising would then meet at Guildhall before setting out to retake the entire City. The total size of the force could only be guessed at, but some hinted that it was 20,000 strong since as many as one in four loyalists might be expected to rise up within the City walls, while three out of four might hope to do the same "in the out parts."[13]

Edmund Waller was identified as the plot's ringleader. Alarmingly, he had co-conspirators that ranged from City liverymen to peers. Waller was tasked with delivering a commission of array from the king to discontented Londoners. It was purported that Katherine Stuart, Lady d'Aubigny, smuggled the king's commission into the City while ostensibly on business for her late husband, and that she had in fact delivered a commission from the king to Sir Nicholas Crispe, the wealthy merchant taylor who, as noted earlier, transported gold and other supplies from London to Oxford in disguise.[14] Crispe allegedly brought the commission from d'Aubigny to Waller, who was in turn expected to rally City loyalists for the coming fight. The circuitous plot – soon thereafter simply referred to as Waller's plot – confirmed suspicions and fears that were reminiscent of the long nights of January 1642. The severity of these accusations led to the courts-martial, trial, and the public execution of Waller's co-conspirators, Nathaniel Tompkins and Richard Chaloner.

Waller's plot has long held a place in accounts of the civil war period. Most often, the "murky" or "muddled" affair has been described in relation to Pym's leadership in the Commons. For Geoffrey Smith it was quite clearly a "plot by Pym," which afforded him with "a marvellous propaganda opportunity" that ultimately "demoralised and rendered ineffective two potentially powerful and overlapping movements in London: popular royalism and the peace campaign."[15] Braddick concluded that the plot was "revealed theatrically," and that it was "deliberately withheld until the fast day on 31 May," and was thus part of a grand political maneuver.[16] For Hexter, who was admittedly concerned foremost with Pym's "reign," Waller and his plot exemplified one of two extremes: Waller stood at one end of a political spectrum that contained devout royalists on one side and "fiery spirits" such as William Strode and Henry Marten on the other.[17] Pearl believed that the plot, no matter how influential, was "unearthed" long "before it had time to mature."[18] It was for most, then, an important but passing crisis in a year of crises, a moment when Pym could again take up his place as the prime mover in parliament, as an "elegant English Cicero, or sweet-tongued Seneca."[19]

But it was Hexter who saw clearest that the plot was part of something bigger for London, and that it was Pym who "took advantage of" the plot as a means to "impose a vow and covenant" on the City. And this without question was the single most important aspect of Waller's plot, and one that has, despite Hexter's observation, garnered little more than passing comment by historians. Once reintegrated into the narrative of the summer, the relationship between Waller's plot and the Vow and Covenant helps, on the one hand, to explain how a "City conspiracy" managed to "induce" the Houses to finally agree to implement a deeply unpopular oath – an oath which had been proposed in various iterations by London petitioners since the previous autumn but had to this point been consistently rejected.[20] On the other hand, it casts new light on a wider strategic program for radical metropolitan mobilization. More than an opportunity for Pym to remind his colleagues and the nation of the need to remain steadfast to the parliamentary cause, the revelation of Waller's plot afforded an opportunity for Pennington and his allies to implement plans to mobilize Londoners en masse.

Contemporaries of course had their own opinions about the nature and purpose of the plot. Bulstrode Whitelocke recalled observing Waller from the previous February when they had travelled together to Oxford as peace commissioners for parliament. Whitelocke remembered in particular how Charles spoke to Waller, who was the final commissioner to kiss the royal signet, along with the king's comments: "though you are last, yett you are not the worst, not the least in my favour." Whitelocke and his companions were puzzled and "wondered att the meaning of these words, till afterwards the discovery of a plot then in hand in London to betray the Parliament."[21] Agostini, always the skeptic, reported that the entire "conspiracy rests upon nothing but the report of an ordinary individual sent to some members of parliament while they were at church on the fast day."[22] Salvetti found much the same, writing home at length about the "uno commissione militare ad uno de deputati della camera inferiore," and the rampant rumors that plotters planned to open up the City and capture the Tower.[23] Royalists took similar if decidedly more cynical views of the plot, exploiting the revelation and subsequent theater of politics as an extreme example of parliament's propaganda machine in action. *Aulicus* at first exclaimed that the plot was little more than a specious matter, a thing concocted by "Master *Pym* and his accomplices," and thus by those "who were both the authors and discoverers." The "pourpose of the distraction," *Aulicus* went on, as "any understanding man may see," was "to affright the poore people with an apprehension of horrible danger, on purpose to make them lend some present money to be eased of this imaginary destruction."[24] It was, in short, another sham aimed at emptying pocketbooks for parliament.

"Wariness," Conrad Russell reminds us, had by this time become "an entirely justified reaction with any Long Parliament plot." Yet such "wariness," he went on, should "stop short of incredulity."[25] Indeed, regardless of Waller's intentions, his namesake plot became – even if only briefly – the *cause célèbre* among Londoners of all sorts and stations. As such, the plot ended up being much more than a means to silence "popular royalism and the peace campaign" in the City. Indeed, as we shall see, it coincided with the need for a new oath of loyalty to parliament's flagging war effort, and with a fundamental revitalization of the City's commitment to war against the king. A mere month after first reporting on the plot, *Aulicus* revised its assessment, declaring that the Waller affair was not simply Pym's design, but instead was part of a much larger orchestration that included "Kimbolton" and a handful of the usual suspects such as "Mainwaring, Ven, the Devill, and a few others." "The Devill," as Mayor Pennington had come to be known in some circles, would indeed make use of the plot.[26] If it can be assumed with some certainty that Pym had tuned the plot in parliament, it might also be surmised that Pennington played a similar part in the City. To fully understand the metropolitan dimensions and significance of Waller's plot – and indeed its aftermath – we must first recount its reception and its immediate byproduct: the Vow and Covenant.

Competing covenants

Initial doubts over the legitimacy of Waller's plot, like those expressed in *Aulicus*, were countered by an outpouring of support for parliament's cause. On 3 June – five days before a Common Hall in which Pym revealed the full scope of the threat – George Thomason acquired a copy of *A Declaration of the Loyalty of the Citizens of London*. Printed anonymously, the short pamphlet provided an unmistakable expression of devotion to parliament. Cast in the familiar language of mixed constitutionalism, the tract identified parliament as an inseparable third of a Gordian knot, the legislative strand of a "triple object" that depended "upon their Prince, upon religion, and upon law." More than simply suggest the unbreakable nature of the "threefold Cord," *A Declaration* praised London's "heroick Companies of trained souldiers, [who] daily exercised for the security both of Parliament and City," and which built London's "fortifications, bulwarks and trenches." "Thousands," claimed the author, had rallied "in a warlike manner with their Commanders Colours, Drums and weapons of war in one hand, and instruments of labour in the other" to see that the City was both secured and defended. To make certain that such efforts were not done it vain, *A Declaration* proposed "searching out and rejection of the disloyall hearted" in London. Once found, they should be subjected to "exemplary punishment."[27]

Although important in its own right, *A Declaration* was just one of several tracts that tied the discovery of Waller's plot to Londoners' wider commitment to a continuation of war. Laurence Whitaker, who was present in the House when Pym reported the plot, noted the unusual uproar that followed the account of plans "to seize the Lord Say, and Lord Wharton and 5 of the house of Commons, viz, the Lord Mayor, Mr Pym, Sir Phillip Stapleton Coll Hamden, and Mr Stroed."[28] The list of arrests read like a recurring nightmare; most in the chamber recalled the attempt on the seven Londoners months earlier, and none could forget the events of January 1642. For a third time, then, the king called for the arrest of specific targeted opponents. Following Pym's report, "divers notes were passed in the house" and several important proposals were put forward.[29] It was decided that a public thanksgiving would be held on 15 June, and that parliament should seek to establish "a more firm Bond and Union" that would serve "for Uniting all together" in support of the war.[30]

The resulting Vow and Covenant, drawn up that same day, advanced numerous proposals that had been dismissed in previous months for being too "radical." Foremost, the proposals were meant "to distinguish the good Party from the bad: and to unite faster together the good Party." Members of the "good party" were expected to show "sorrow" for individual "sins, and the Sins of the nation," which were readily understood to be the cause of "the Calamities and Judgements that now lie upon" England. Repentance was to be followed by a military declaration to never "consent to the laying down of Arms, so long as the Papists, now in open War against the Parliament, shall, by Force of Arms, be protected from the Justice thereof." To conclude, the covenant clarified yet further the military role of each and every oath taker, to "assist" in accordance with "power and Vocation" all of "the Forces raised and continued by both Houses of Parliament, against the Forces raised by the King without their Consent." These were unmistakable terms: affirmers would be bound not only to prove their loyalty to parliament's cause, but also to fight on its behalf.

Remarkably, the Vow and Covenant was "forthwith taken by the Speaker, and all the Members" save for fifteen who refused only so that they might take "some time to Consider of it." These few dissenters were given until the following Friday morning.[31] On the same day it was ordered that the Committee of Safety should meet "to prepare this Covenant in a fit Manner to be taken by the whole Kingdom." On 9 June, three days after the Commons had subscribed, sixteen peers agreed to the terms of the oath. It was determined that all who were absent would be given the same "when they come to the House."[32]

Word of the Vow and Covenant spread rapidly. On 13 June, Sir Edward Nicholas wrote to Hastings to share his concerns about parliament's new oath. Even if "London" could "levy noe money" and "not men considerable," he claimed, the City had nevertheless "lately made a rebellious Covenant against the King."[33] Between the time when the Lords took the oath and the day of public thanksgiving set for 15 June, a flood of pamphlets with information on Waller's plot became available. Resolute Londoners sought any shreds of news they could find about their recent "delivery" from the conspiracy. Pym's 6 June speech at the Guildhall was subsequently printed as *A Discoverie of the Great Plot*, and went into three editions.[34] On 13 June, Thomason acquired *A True Discoverie Of the late intended Plot*,[35] and on the same day picked up *A Copie of the Commission sent from his Majestie to The Conspirators of the Citie of London*.[36] Each of these corroborated Pym's report, driving home popular concerns over safety. On 14 June, the day prior to the public humiliation, Pym reported to the Commons that "divers Preachers about London had Enformed us that the People were not sufficiently satisfyed of the Truth of ye Plott" and that it was therefore necessary that a "declaration to be made to be published to morrow in all Churches in and about London," and which explained the imminence of the late threat.[37] On the same day appointed for public thanksgiving, Thomason acquired a *A Brief Narrative of The late Treacherous and Horrid Designe*, a copy of Pym's speech from Guildhall that included with it a copy of the king's commission.[38] Any doubts over the plot's legitimacy might thereby be dispelled.

On 15 June, the same day that the "brief narrative" was "read in all Churches and Chappels, in the Cities of London and Westminster, and the Suburbs thereof," four prominent ministers climbed Westminster pulpits to preach fast-day sermons.[39] Stephen Marshall and Obadiah Sedgewick were appointed to preach to the Commons at St. Margaret, while Charles Herle and Edmund Calamy were selected to give sermons to the Lords in Westminster Abbey. Each of these ministers was widely known and respected, and each took special pains to urge humility in light of London's providential delivery from ruin. Marshall left his audience with no shortage of vivid imagery, praising "the good hand of God in Crushing this cockatrices egge, before it brake out to be a fiery flying serpent." More than merely offering thanks to the Almighty for delivering Londoners from the plot, he cautioned that the nation would be "brought under the curse of God, if you perform not this solemn Covenant."[40] Sedgewick next beseeched his audience to never fall "*flatt*," but rather "*raise* and *quicken*" to action.[41] Sermons in the Abbey carried a similar tone. Herle offered thanks to God for "blasting the Plots of traiterous enemies," while Calamy launched into a lengthy discussion of the dangers that came from "the great breach of *Oaths and Covenants*." "One great reason why the Sword is now drawne in *England*," Calamy went on, was that the "Nation" was already "deeply guilty of" breaking past oaths and covenants. It was, he proclaimed, his duty "to remind you, that in this Covenant you have also vowed" was the promise "*to assist the forces raised by the Parliament, according to your power and vocation, and not to assist the forces raised by the King, neither directly nor indirectly.*"[42] Few could have departed without reflecting on the gravity of their commitment.

Similar exhortations were heard throughout the capital. Nehemiah Wallington awoke early on the morning of 5 June and soon found himself "walkeing alone to & froe in the Kichin meditating of God grat mercy in discovering of that devilish plot." The next day he went on to St. Matthew Friday Street to hear Henry Burton preach "a day of Thanksgiving" to commemorate the recent discovery and "great deliverance from that hellish ploot (of fiering of the City)." Following the sermon, Wallington could not help but to wonder "what the Spainyards in 88 would have done and the hellish gunpowder plott and a thousand plots more sence." He concluded with certainty that the "grat plot of fiering of the City" was "prevented" so that Londoners "may know the righteousnesse of the Lord." On 15 June, the "day of Thanksgiving over the whole City," he again took to pondering "the grat deliverance from that hellish plot (of fiering the City and to put to death all the people of God)." After engaging in some "privat thoughts" relating to Esther Chapter 9, he went to his parish church of St. Leonard Eastcheap to hear Henry Roborough preach on Psalm 121:5 and why "the Lord is the keeper & protecter of his children."[43] Four days later, on 19 June, the Venetian ambassador observed that "all these things" had exacted "confusion and alarm among the people" and thereby "irritate[d] them more against the king and to encroach upon his authority."[44]

More than fifty miles away in Oxford, Charles and his advisers could scarcely afford to leave these matters unchecked. Newsbooks, as we have seen, already cast doubts over the legitimacy of the plot, but a more serious response was needed in light of parliament's new oath. Thus, on 24 June, royalists countered with the *A Sacred Oath or Covenant*, a single sheet that instructed subscribers to maintain "his Majesties just Rights" and resist "the Forces, under the conduct of the Earl of *Essex*."[45] Although a clear and obvious response to parliament's Vow and Covenant, the Sacred Oath never fully gained the traction that was hoped for. The royalist oath was likely produced with more modest intentions in mind; foremost, it served as a counter-oath and an important means to mitigate the damage done by parliament's new Vow and Covenant. By this measure, the royalist plan was something of a success. Whereas *A Sacred Oath or Covenant* left no outward signs of support in London in terms of subscriptions, it did offer an ideological counterpoint and alternative path to parliament's new covenant.

If the Sacred Oath was printed in haste in Oxford with the intention that it might reach a wide audience in London, the Vow and Covenant was already gaining ground as a result of its systematic distribution throughout the capital.

The Vow and Covenant in London

The first printed editions of the Vow and Covenant were made available for purchase at the Middle Temple on 12 June. Each of these contained a self-endorsement in the shape of a list of the names of each member of the Commons who had subscribed.[46] Official orders for taking the oath were distributed a fortnight later, and just two days after *A Sacred Oath or Covenant* was printed in Oxford. These stipulated that the new oath was to be distributed "unto every Parish Church or Chapel" and taken "in all fortified Cities, Towns, Castles, and Forts, or other Garrisons" held by parliament. Londoners were expected to hear the oath read aloud in church, so that they could subscribe and be accounted for by churchwardens. Lists of confirmed oath-takers were to be delivered to parliament "within Six Dayes," while lists of any who refused or were absent during the reading were to be recorded and delivered to parliament "within Twenty Days." All refusers were to be immediately "disarmed" and marked as opponents to parliament's cause.[47] Refusal was seen as implicit support for "His Majesties command." Londoners were thereby presented with an ostensibly simple task: take the Vow and Covenant and "binde themselves" to fight "against the Forces raised by the King," or be tarred as supporters of the king, and subject to disarming, arrest, and sequestration.[48] Notwithstanding the practicality of their demand, parliament had necessitated that inhabitants commit to one of two sides of the conflict.

Measuring the extent to which Londoners subscribed to either the Sacred Oath or the Vow and Covenant remains challenging. Any potential lists relating to the Sacred Oath – which might obviously be clandestine matters in the City – are gone. Our records are somewhat better with regards to the Vow and Covenant. In his study of civil war oaths, Edward Vallance suggested that "as a political test the Vow and Covenant's life was short-lived" and that it was simply "too divisive" to be widely accepted.[49] This assessment is supported by the contemporary account of Agostini, who reported on 12 July that the "oath of the covenant," which had been appointed for "the day of general fast" on 28 June, "was not done, as they are somewhat afraid of proposing it since many leaders of the army have refused to take it." And "yet," Agostini went on, "they have printed the order to be observed by every parish, and say that it will take place on

Sunday next." "Many," he believed, were "trying to escape" from London and thus "avoid being forced against their wills and consciences."[50]

Agostini's remarks suggest awareness of the oath's divisiveness. Apart from overt loyalism to the king, which came with its own problems for inhabitants of the capital, there were, admittedly, some very good reasons for avoiding the Vow and Covenant. Soldiers, for instance, might claim that they could not swear to the terms of the oath on the grounds that doing so would contradict and thus break previous oaths. Swearing to a second oath, as Vallance points out, could put them in breach of "earlier oaths of loyalty, including the Protestation." Others waffled when pressed with the opportunity, employing "tactics of equivocation" that ranged from avoidance to claims of inability. Ultimately, Vallance took widespread refusal in the army and a dearth of parish returns as ample evidence of the fact that the oath was "short lived" and generally at odds with popular opinion. His assessment fits with a wider tendency among scholars of the period to view the Vow and Covenant as the middle of three oaths of allegiance – as "the Protestation's successor," or the forerunner to the Solemn League and Covenant.[51] While not incorrect chronologically, such explanations downplay the significance of the Vow and Covenant and the reactionary Sacred Oath as markers of ideological escalation and, as importantly, mobilization.

More recently, scholars have alluded to the oath's immediate implications and wider significance. Andrew Hopper, for instance, has suggested that parliament's aggressive pursuit of the oath "led some of its supporters into reconsidering their positions or even changing sides."[52] Braddick, meanwhile, has claimed that the purpose of the Vow and Covenant played an important role "to stabilize allegiances."[53] Julia Merritt proposed that the enforcement of the oath led to an "intrusive inquisition" in nearby Westminster.[54] The Vow and Covenant, for John Walter, amounted to a "radical text and explicit commitment to oppose the king's forces," and a text that, significantly, "removed" some of the "limitations imposed by the final text of the Protestation."[55] By this measure, the oath stands as a serious marker in the distinctions between opposing forces that were coalescing behind the titles of "royalist" and "parliamentarian," and indeed as a central component of the political polarization that characterized the summer. Although London's parish records provide only six surviving lists of Vow and Covenant returns – a point which, as Vallance readily admits, makes "corroborating the comments of the Venetian ambassador difficult" – these provide an important means for assessing how Londoners interacted with the oath. Rather than limit an assessment of the overall reception of the Covenant, the areas of returns highlight some of London's most active and radical centers of mobilization – areas in which there is, again, a clear intersection between an active and militant civic leadership, pro-war preaching, and popular political engagement.

Militants had long sought to implement some of the terms laid out in the new Vow and Covenant; earlier petitions such as the one promoted by Watkins and Shute in December 1642 bore a striking resemblance to the oath, as did Bowles' *Plaine English* from January 1643, and the *Remonstrans Redivivus* petition from March of the same year. Seen within the context of these earlier radical proposals, and especially in light of the summer "low tide" in the war effort, the Vow and Covenant transforms. It ceases to appear simply as the short-lived middle example of national covenanting tradition; instead, it stands on its own. Rather than function as a modified version of the Protestation, which "removed the limitations imposed by the final text of the" earlier oath, or as a litmus test for the later Solemn League and Covenant, the Vow and Covenant served as a means to measure the extent to which Londoners might embrace the radical program mobilizing en masse, for what would be the general rising.

The oath's reception can be gleaned from the surviving records of a handful of London parishes. The vestry minutes from St. Mary Magdalen Milk Street, for example, contain a printed and pasted down copy of the Vow and Covenant followed by 120 signatures. The first of these is marked by the parish's godly rector and chaplain to Pennington, "Tho[mas] Case Lecturer," and is followed by "Anne his wife."[56] In St. Margaret Lothbury, the petition was copied out by hand "fair written" as parliament's orders stipulated, and 251 signatures of the men and women of the parish are recorded. The first signature is that of Leonard Cooke, the "Godly, Learned, and Orthodox Divine" who was appointed to the parsonage of the parish according to a sequestration order from February.[57] The first three pages include the signatures of men only, while the last two pages consist of the names of nearly 100 women and a few additional men.[58] The "Names of such of the Parishioners" from St. "Clements East Chepe as tooke the Covenant According to an Ordiance & Command of both Houses" remains in the back of their churchwardens' accounts. The single folio contains 120 signatures, including those of Walter Taylor, their rector, Edmond Brome, minister, and their two churchwardens. If 120 signatures is a relatively small number, it is in fact more than the 105 signatures from 8 October that accompany the Solemn League and Covenant.[59] At St. Martin Orgar, the entire Vow and Covenant was copied out along with the names of 175 male subscribers.[60] Orders in the vestry book at St. Stephen Coleman Street state clearly that the "oath and covenant" were to be taken "in the Afternoone" following a "Sermon in all the Parishes Churches and Chappells" throughout London. Orders were clear, moreover, that the "oath and Covenant shalbee tendred to every man within the parishes within the Bill of Mortality." Those who were unable to take the Vow and Covenant were expected to swear to it "the next Fast day." Following the orders is an impressive list of signatures beginning with John Goodwin and totaling 780 names, and just under half of which – some 372 – belonged to women. St. Stephen provides the single largest example of subscriptions to the Vow and Covenant. Other parishes list yet more names. St. Benet Fink, for instance, recorded the names of 131 male parishioners who agreed to the oath.[61] Yet it was a parishioner from St. Stephens, one John Wells, who added his name with the caveat that he was "savinge my alegants to my kinge and the only just Suepreme majesty and the laste prottistacion."[62] Parishioners, like their counterparts in the army, took seriously both their commitment to the oath and the binding nature of the agreement. In total, six City vestries recorded the names of at least 1,577 Londoners who took the Vow and Covenant. John Wells offered the sole example of refusal based on allegiance. While this number cannot necessarily be used as a means to extrapolate and estimate the number of Londoners who agreed to the Vow and Covenant, the survival of 1,577 signatures does suggest that the oath gained at least some traction in the City.

Further insights can be gleaned from London's six surviving lists. The number of signatures put down in the parishes, for instance, can be compared with the numbers of signatures collected for the later Solemn League and Covenant, which was a "divisive" affair in its own right.[63] As we have seen, lists of signatures from St. Clement Eastcheap reveal that fifteen fewer parishioners signed the Solemn League and Covenant than did the earlier Vow and Covenant. Similarly, some seventy-six fewer parishioners from St. Margaret Lothbury signed the Solemn League and Covenant than signed the Vow and Covenant.[64] Various reasons might explain the disparity in signatures. One obvious possibility is that the Vow and Covenant's subscribers believed again that subscribing to a second oath would leave them breakers of their first. A smattering of additional evidence might save us from perpetual speculation about the controversial nature of both oaths. Nathaniel Symonds, for one, seems to have taken far more issue with the Solemn League and Covenant than he did with the prior Vow and Covenant. On 22 February 1644, he agreed to give a "hearty" apology in his native St. Clement Eastcheap for speaking "rashly and wickedly against the parliament" and their new covenant. At the same time Walter Taylor, St. Clement's rector, signed a written statement to confirm that Symonds had in fact "taken the league and covenant." Whereas Symonds' signature was written clearly on the return for the Vow and Covenant, it was harshly crossed out on the later return for the Solemn League and Covenant.[65] Symonds, like others, may have found the idea of a pact for mutual defense with parliament less troubling than the establishment of a national presbytery.

Clearly, contemporaries saw the Vow and Covenant as something more than a fleeting or passing issue; at the time of the Vow and Covenant's signing there was no guarantee that parliament would enter into a fighting agreement – let alone a national covenant – with the Scots.[66] And while it may still be difficult to "corroborate the Venetian Ambassador's claims" regarding the extent of popular resistance to the Vow and Covenant, there is reason to consider what the practical terms of the oath meant for Londoners. Indeed, doing so reveals that the Vow and Covenant helped to reframe – and indeed intensify – the ideological parameters of the war effort sought by London's militants.

Beyond the modest insights that stand to be gained from a close look at individual oath-takers from six parishes, there is compelling evidence to suggest that a number of parishes did in fact intentionally remove – and perhaps even destroy – their lists of subscriptions. One rather straightforward explanation for the removal of lists could be the parliament's order to return names within the brief twenty-day window. Records from St. Mary Colechurch reveal a pasted down copy of the Vow and Covenant, but the opposite page – presumably one of signatures – was torn out.[67] Again, this raises a number of questions. Was the list removed for return to parliament, as the Vow and Covenant's instructions stipulated, or was it intentionally taken out at a later date, perhape even upon the arrival of the Solemn League and Covenant? No matter the case, the removal of lists implies that there were more signatures; more than 1,577 Londoners swore to uphold the terms of the Vow and Covenant.[68] Julia Merritt, moreover, points to circumstantial evidence that lists were made in the Westminster parishes of St. Clement Danes, where "two paper books used for the Covenant" were recorded, and St. Mary le Strand, where a book was purchased to record the names of parishioners "who were to take a new oath and covenant."[69] Our initial six parishes thus made way for nine in which names were likely recorded and returned according to parliament's order.

Parishes that retained signatures – or at least traces of the oath, as was the case in St. Mary Colechurch, St. Clement Danes, and St. Mary le Strand – provide yet more evidence of the intersection between preaching and parochial mobilization. We need look no further than St. Mary Magdalene Milk Street, St. Stephen Coleman Street, and St. Mary Colechurch to find substantial links between a godly ministry and engagement with parliament's new oath. Thomas Case and John Goodwin played instrumental respective roles "stirring up" support for the war effort with their sermons, just as they did when it came time to promote the Vow and Covenant. Although one of London's smallest parishes, St. Mary Magdalene Milk Street was home to a receptive audience that included an active "civic leadership" and common councilors. St. Stephen Coleman Street needs little introduction at this point;

the large City parish was home to upwards of 400 families and had close ties to activists and radicals.[70] The place where John Goodwin's congregation met, and where Richard Overton's secret printing press operated, was, incidentally, also home to 780 signers.[71] Mayor Pennington's home, the very place where the five members were said to have hidden from the king in January 1642, was also within the boundaries of Coleman Street.[72] Although it ultimately touted less robust radical credentials, St. Mary Colechurch was home to a number of leading military men, including Thomas Jackson, John Towse, and, most notably at this point, Randall Mainwaring.[73]

But what of the remaining parishes of St. Margaret Lothbury, St. Martin Orgar, and St. Clement Eastcheap? Although each varied in size and social composition, it may come as little surprise that each was also home to political activists who supported parliament. The smaller parish of St. Margaret Lothbury harbored known opponents to the Crown, including the later regicide Miles Corbet. Sixty-five of St. Margaret's parishioners loaned £389 to parliament's cause on 27 November 1642.[74] Parishioners from St. Martin Orgar, a large but poor parish on the north side of the river in Bridge Within Ward, regularly heard sermons from the independent minister Thomas Brooks in 1643, and their receptiveness to wartime rhetoric might be guessed at since they had already played an enthusiastic part in the removal of their previous rector, the Laudian Brian Walton.[75] St. Clement Eastcheap, according to Liu, was home to "a number of well-to-do tradesmen and relatively well-known civic leaders" and was "undoubtedly Puritan in the earlier years of the revolutionary era."[76] Indeed, twenty-nine of St. Clement's parishioners loaned £301 to parliament on 26 November 1642, and many of the same parishioners had actively petitioned parliament in February 1642 in order to replace Ben Stone, their incumbent minister, with Walter Taylor.[77] London parishes that retained evidence of their participation in the Vow and Covenant were, then, on the whole, also home to important agitators and wartime activists, including Pennington and Mainwaring.[78] It might therefore come as little surprise that areas that recorded robust financial support for parliament's effort overlap with areas that retain evidence of Vow and Covenant returns. Indeed, St. Mary Magdalen Milk Street was at the base of Cripplegate Ward, on the edge of Cheapside and near to the bustle of Bread Street Ward. St. Stephen Coleman Street stood alone in its activism just east of Guildhall, a stone's throw from St. Margaret Lothbury, a church straddled between the wards of Coleman Street and Broad Street. All three of the above parishes had engaged in the program for iconoclasm. In terms of continuity and mobilization, we are left with a picture of a handful of centrally located parishes that supported the war effort at its beginning and remained committed through the low tide of summer 1643.[79]

City Cash Accounts note a single payment for printing "200 Copies of the Oath" that were "to be taken by the Captaines and Shoulders of this

Citty."⁸⁰ Soldiers might naturally be expected to "distinguish the good and well-affected party from the bad," but Waller's plot added new reason to assume that the vast majority of Londoners should be expected to do the same.⁸¹ In June 1643, Londoners once again faced the dilemma of choosing sides in the conflict between the king and parliament. This time, they were presented with stark terms: they could swear to the Vow and Covenant, or they could be labeled as refusers and subjects of "His Majesties command." Well aware of the tension caused by these options, royalist printers made a concerted effort to promote the Sacred Oath. New tracts such as *The Anti-Covenant* were printed with the hope that they might dispel fears that "a popish army" was being "raised" by the king "for the subversion of the true Protestant Religion." There was also *A Letter to A Noble Lord at London from a Friend at Oxford*, which made clear that the "*Sacred Vow and Covenant*" along with "the discovery of the great Plot" were little more than deceptive attempts to replace the "possibility of hope or Peace" with "blood and desolation."⁸² Plainly, the struggle for the hearts and minds of Londoners raged on. *Merculius Aulicus* waited nearly a month before claiming "that the designe and purpose of the new Oath and Covenant" did finally "begin to shew itself." Soon thereafter, on 22 July, the newsbook suggested that parliament's Vow and Covenant was part of a plan set in motion by "grand contrivers" who were still working out new ways to access "the goods and monies of all those that take it."⁸³ Here *Aulicus* missed a crucial point. For Pennington and likeminded activists, the Vow and Covenant was not only a pathway to the sinews of war; rather it was also a means to check on the preparedness of Londoners to rise up en masse.

The general rising

While the oath was being tendered in London, militants moved forward with their program for a general rising.⁸⁴ Indeed, their plans were already well under way. In late May, the "L[or]d maior and Cittizens" arrived in Westminster to present *An Humble Proposal of the Safety of Parliament and Citie*. Their proposal was only the latest in a series of radical petitions and tracts that sought to unleash London's full military potential, but it was also by far the boldest example to date. Not only did Pennington deliver the proposal to Westminster, but it was, as Thomason's annotations indicate, timed to "oppose the Accomodation that the Lords would have made about may 25." In the place of peace, *An Humble Proposal* offered ten steps that would fully mobilize London, a City that could "yet afford" to raise "100000 men." Most of the proposal's suggestions were breathtakingly radical in scope. First, London was to "secure Horse," "victuall the

Citie" and "clear [out] the Prisons." Next, it was expected that all members of the Commons and Lords would "go forth personally into the Field, for foure or sixe dayes time" so that they might "encourage" or even "lead" residents who wished "to discover their affections." Londoners were then expected to establish a *Campus Martius*, a "Field of Mars" modeled on the one that Romans had dedicated to their god of war. London's *Campus Martius* would house sixteen or eighteen "tents or boarded houses" that could "be raised in *Finsberry* Field, or else-where." Twelve tents were to be allocated for "the listing of Souldiers" and "the other six to receive Moneys and Subscriptions." Each of the tents would be organized to accommodate "five or six trades" so that tradesmen and apprentices might "encourage each other more cheerfully" to enlist. Meanwhile, "shops in London and the Suburbs" were to be "kept shut" so that "men may have nothing to hinder them from appearing." Ministers would be called upon again to bring attention to the entire proposal, to rally Londoners, and "move them affectionaly with the deep consideration" of the "Protestation," which "Parliament breaches." Achieving these ends, claimed the petitioners, would "put" London "in a gallant posture" and ensure an eventual victory; failure to do so would prove "ominous and dreadful." If any Londoner doubted the consequences of inaction they needed merely "remember the curse, Jer. 48.10 *Cursed be he that doth the work of the Lord negligently, and cursed be he that withholds the Sword from blood.*"[85] These were the terms of the general rising.

The timing of *An Humble Proposal* was important; not only was it made on the heels of reports that parliament had suffered a crushing defeat and the loss of Cornwall at the Battle of Stratton on 16 May, but it came as the specter of peace was rising again in the Lords. The proposal, offered up as a viable alternative to peace "in this time of present danger," was initially met with silence.[86] Yet parliament soon found itself in a more receptive mood. News of Waller's plot broke just a week after the proposal; two weeks later, the Vow and Covenant was being read and subscribed to throughout the City; by the end of the month, on 30 June, parliament would suffer yet another shocking defeat at Adwalton Moor. Conflicting reports of a "great Victorie" won by royalists were countered by suggestions that Fairfax was "giving barrel to the Popish Army" in the north.[87]

On 7 July, just two days after Tompkins and Chaloner were publicly executed in London, a new version of the proposal for a general rising was made available in print as *Instructions and Propositions*. The updated collection of proposals, which professed to be "a Worke worthy" for "consideration" by "all true and honest-hearted Christians," couched May's *An Humble Proposal* in less onerous terms. The new *Instructions and Propositions* nevertheless called for a number of similar measures, including, most notably, "the raising of an Army of ten thousand Vountier Souldiers." In light of the threats of June, the proposed army would be tasked foremost with the protection of London, and be "additionall to the Army raised by both houses of Parliament, under the command of *Robert* Earle of *Essex*." Six instructions were included so that the order might be put "into the hands of honest men."[88]

On the following day, Common Council agreed to petition both houses to approve of their desire to add seven new members to the committee meeting at Salters' Hall. Of twenty-one names considered, a group of "seven freemen of this City" were finally agreed upon, including Edward Cooke, Sergeant Major Turner, Lieutenant Colonel Tichborne, Tempest Milner, William Andrews, Captaine Thomas Player, and Sergeant Major Harsnett. A further request from the council sought to supplement the presence of military men with "the right honorable Isaack Pennington," leading common councilors, and livery company representatives, including John Kenderick, Alderman Richard Turner the "senior merchantailor," William Hobson the "haberd[asher]," Theophilius Riley the "draper," and Richard Bateman the "skinner." For the first time, the committee's composition would take into account the interests of leading livery companies. Pennington's request to join the committee came with the caveat that although he "was Lord Maior for the time being," he also expected to "take and contynue of the said Committee after his Maioralty shalbe ended" in October 1643.[89] The Lord Mayor and his allies expected that the general rising, once established, would remain in place for the foreseeable future, and indeed that they would retain control over an army that put London's interests first. More than the addition of thirteen leading militants to the Militia Committee, the petition proposed that "an ordiance may be granted" to see to it "that all the forces raised and to be raised aswell within the said Citie and Liberties" and "within the parishes and places adiacent mencioned in the weekly bill of mortality" would be placed "under the sole Command of the Committee for the Militia of this Citie." Not only did Londoners expect to gain control of the Militia Committee and place Pennington at its head, but they also apparently intended to extend the Committee's reach into Westminster, Middlesex, and Surrey.[90]

London's militants were given more reason to move ahead on 10 July, when the Commons read a letter in which the Lord General openly recommended the pursuit of a peace settlement with the king. Essex raised a number of serious issues, including the "settling of Religion" and "the Lawes and Liberties of the Subject," but he also conjured up troubling suggestions of a "just Trial" for "those chiefe Delinquents that have brought all this mischief to both Kingdomes," a clear condemnation of the king's evil counselors, but one that seemed to imply guilt on both sides.[91] The

Lord General's letter sent yet another series of shockwaves throughout the City, and not least among proponents of the new Militia Committee. The question of peace had not only been renewed by the Lord General, but it had been done with the possibility of singling out and punishing some "chiefe" individuals who could be blamed for the war. This all sounded problematically sympathetic with the king's tendency to blame and pursue a select few opponents.

If at first a matter of concern for proponents of the general rising, it was soon clear that Essex's equivocation might in fact spur mobilizing efforts. Indeed, much less a boon for the prospect of peace, Essex's letter served to align and reinvigorate the interests of the war party in parliament and the City – it would, in short, add yet another reason to move ahead with concerted and uniform plans to raise an army that would be effective and independent of the Lord General. Ironically, then, it was parliament's leading military commander, perhaps more than anyone else, who moved radicals in London and Westminster to coordinate their efforts over the summer. Common Council meanwhile held an emergency meeting to discuss the presence of "ill affected" people who were gathering "in great multitudes" around London. They concluded new plans for "the speedy raysing of mony to be employed for the speedy raysing of many for the defence and safety of the Citie." Anyone who loaned more than £50 would receive "the bond of the Major."[92]

Counted among parliament's men in favor of a "subsidiary Army" were several individuals whom D'Ewes repeatedly identified in his journals as "fiery spirits." These included the younger Vane, Marten, Strode, and a rotating cast of sympathizers such as Martin Bond and even, on occasions, Pym.[93] On the rare occasions when he took up his seat in the Commons, Mayor Pennington joined their ranks. "*Isaac* and his faction," as we have seen, included Venn, Mainwaring, Fowke, Browne, Harvey, and Tichborne – and leading petitioners and ministers such as Watkins, Shute, Burroughs, and Peter.[94] This coterie and their network of orbiting allies, which Lindley estimated to include "100 activists," and which had long promoted robust efforts against the king, also professed radical ideas in writing and conversation.[95] Marten, who soon became chair on the Committee for the General Rising, was an outspoken and unequivocal promoter of the war and of republicanism. He had already drafted *The Rights of the People of England*, in which he argued that supreme authority rested with "inhabitants gathered into a body In the masse."[96] Burroughs espoused equally radical views, claiming infamously in 1638 that "supreme power is in the supreme magistrate," which was the "people's power." The collective authority of magistrates and other temporal rulers, he went on, could be understood by referencing cases of elective power such as Poland and Venice where "they did originally choose their kings and prescribe them conditions and limited their power by laws."[97] The "radical" credentials of leading proponents of the general rising are, thus, beyond question.

Essex's letter became a lightning rod in the push to gain support for a general rising. Most historians agree that the earl's suggestion of peace marked a political turning point in parliament's war effort. Lindley believed that the letter generated "some criticism of his generalship in radical quarters," while Brenner concluded that it ultimately incentivized radicals to initiate their "offensive." The letter, claimed Hexter, "spread through London" and made it so that "all the voices that had been sporadically raised against him" could finally join "in one magnificent chorus." For Pearl the letter marked a logical turning point, a time when "radicals" who had for months been "campaigning against the inefficiency and over-cautiousness of Essex and his army," could seize the initiative.[98] As David Como has suggested more recently, it was Essex, with "his wounded honour," that required "an antedote."[99] The obvious solution lay in the creation of an army free from Essex's dithering command and self-importance, and now, clearly, his willingness to entertain the king's tactics of singling out enemies.

Indeed, segments of the City had come to view Essex with a mix of disenchantment and open hostility. His leadership had been associated with "the dilatory proceedings of the parliamentary army" and his perceived incompetence in the field had since returned to the forefront as a popular topic of gossip.[100] "If I am not mistaken in Physognomie," claimed one anonymous Londoner in a note from 1 July 1643, "he loves to have noe harme." Rather than pursue a fight, the author went on, the earl seemed more inclined "to be quiet if he might"; rather than seek the king, "he layes [in] sleepe [and has] good diett."[101] Sloth and gluttony were recent additions to the list of popular charges against the earl, ones that grafted easily upon his lasting reputation as "the great Cuckold" whose "prick" could never be "as long as thy pipe."[102] Behind such open, and at times crude attacks were deeper – and indeed by the measures legitimate – points of concern about Essex's commitment to parliament's cause. Criticism of Essex had grown steadily in the City since the shocking news of Brentford the previous November, and amplified further in light of a lengthy winter of inactivity and the losses of the spring and early summer.[103] By this measure, Essex's letter was just the latest upsetting piece of news. But in this case it elevated what already seemed a crisis by sparking renewed criticism of parliament's military leadership. Disconcerted, many Londoners came to openly express their hostility toward the earl. Wallington, for one, took the suggestion of a settlement as yet another example of punishment from a God eager to "unbutton" the faithful "from our vaine hopes."[104] The Lord General had, with a single letter and apparent about-face, confirmed the fears of many; questions of targeted arrests and peace settlement thus returned to the forefront in both parliamentary and demotic debates.

Upon hearing Essex's letter read in the Commons on Monday 10 July, "Mr Strode, Sr Peter Wentworth and some other violent spirits" were stunned and could be "observed to pluck ther hatts over ther eyes."[105] Such immediate reactions were to be expected from "fiery" parliamentarians, but they cannot be taken to represent the entirety of the House. Pym proposed to end a discussion over peace the following day, claiming that "wee could not safely intertaine the motion because wee had seen that all our offers of peace had been reiected by his Majesty and our safety been also indangered by them." Sir Philip Stapleton "spake against" peace and the younger Vane complained that Essex had "done well to stirre us upp," but that the matter of "propositions of peace" had already been attempted and failed "to take effect." Rather than weigh in on such matters, Vane went on, suggesting that the earl should be content to "doe his dutie" as Lord General. Debate over the matter continued through Thursday when Essex sent a second "scoffing" letter in which he suggested that Vane should come out personally to advise him about the best way to attend to "the great affairs of the kingdome." Although the younger Vane was not in the house, his father was said to look "very blancke" upon hearing the letter read. Debate over the matter, which revealed "some for and some against the treaty of peace," persisted.[106] Essex's proposal had had an altogether polarizing effect.

Pennington and his allies secured a major victory the following week. On 18 July "intelligence received from the House of Commons" reached Common Council and warned that "the Kings forces were come neere unto this City" and further that "people ill affected" to parliament's cause had risen "in Armes in severall palces in Kent and Surrey." The "imminent danger" of an uprising provided a third opportunity to call for a volunteer army.[107] That night, orders were drawn up and issued as a single sheet calling upon "all sorts of well-affected Persons" to gather at the Merchant Taylors' Hall on Wednesday 19 July between "4 of the clock in the morning till 8. in the Evening" so that all present could "heare, and subscribe a Petition to the Parliament (to which Thousands have already subscribed) for raising the whole *People* of the *Land* as one *Man*, against those Popish-blood-thirsty Forces raised, to Enslave, and Destroy *Us*, and our *Posterity*."[108] A second round of orders were printed the next day so that "those who did not appear on Tuesday last" might go to Grocers' Hall "between the houres of eight in the morning, and eight at night." Ending the order was the simple exhortation that participants might "*shew this to your Friends*," and that "*If it be stuck up, let none presume to take it downe.*"[109] The full extent of the program for collecting signatures was made clear on the following day, 20 July, when petitions with upwards of 20,000 names were presented to the Commons. Subscribers made clear that they had "of long time been silent observers" and that they now sought "some more powerfull meanes (then as yet hath beene applyed to raise the whole people both in the City of *London*, and all other parts of the Kingdome)."[110] It seemed as if a program might finally be making some headway.

The 20,000 signatures were presented to the lower chamber by John Hat, Sir Giles Overbury, John Norbury, and Fulke Greville, a relative of the late Lord Brooke. The process, as D'Ewes recalled, was both "irregular" and "contrary to the Proceedings and Privilige of Parliament."[111] The petitioners not only called for the establishment of a committee with the reaching ability to "chuse a new Generall for the Army" and "compel men that were unwilling," but they had requested that "they themselves" who put their "names in their petition," would be appointed to lead the committee. In a highly irregular manner, petitioners were instructing "the howse not only whom they should chuse" but also "what trust they should repose in them and what power they should give them."[112] The suggested "worthy members" were to be led by none other than "My Lord Mayor." Following were the names of several familiar war party members, including "Mr. *Morley*, Mr. *Blackiston*, Mr. *Bainton*, Mr. *Ashurst*, Mr. *Strode*, Mr. *Bond*, Mr. *Gourdon*, Mr. *Marten*, Mr. *Hoile*, Mr. *Rigbie*, Sir *Henry Heyman*, and Sir *William Masham*."[113] In a remarkable turn of affairs, Mayor Pennington had navigated into a position in which he would preside over a committee that was tasked with the consideration of his own petition. Moreover, it was to be a committee with the power to finally oversee the creation of London's new volunteer army. The petitioners' success and the subsequent establishment of the committee stood out to Brenner as "the culminating effort" in radical designs "to create an autonomous army since the previous autumn." Of the thirteen appointed committeemen, ten "would end up as political independents" and "eight would be nominated to the High Court of Justice."[114]

Despite the "irregular" nature of the petition's presentation, both houses agreed to take the proposals into consideration. It was, D'Ewes concluded, "the present desperate condition" of parliament's war effort that ultimately led parliament to agree and establish a new Committee for the General Rising. The new body was granted space to meet at Merchant Taylors' Hall on Threadneedle Street in Billingsgate.[115] The Committee immediately set about implementing the very terms proclaimed in the petition for its establishment: "to lift and dispose as many of the Petitioners as are willing, and all others of like affection to the Cause in a warlike manner, into Companies and Regiments," and further to "appoint a Commander in chiefe" and order "subscriptions for Mony, Ammunition, Armes, Horses, and any other necessary Provision[s]." All of these powers, the petition noted, were needed in light of the "most hellish plot contrived, and countenanced by the Kings own Hand," and "according to the true intent of the late Covenant."[116] Petitioners acknowledged that the recent developments were in fact connected: the new Committee's extensive reach was granted as a result of the threat of Waller's plot and made in accordance with the "intent" of the Vow and Covenant. Essex's letter added a third disconcerting dimension to the equation.

These already complex matters are complicated further by the fact that the original petitions were lost, or perhaps even destroyed. Fragmentary notes must therefore be relied upon as a means to estimate how Londoners participated over the short two-day period when signatures were collected. Salvetti, for instance, claimed that the petition had "la sottoscrizione di circa quindici mila persone, la maggior parte di gente ordinaria."[117] Upwards of 15,000 signatures were collected between Merchant Taylors' Hall and Grocers' Hall, and most had come from "di gente ordinaria" – from "ordinary people." Others suggested that the signatures were put down by "thousands" who were "throughly sensible" and eager to proceed in light "of the miserable condition of the Common-wealth."[118] "I with many others," recalled William Walwyn, "petitioned Parliament for the general raising and arming of the well affected."[119] Efforts were not, in the end, undertaken solely by a coterie of militants. Rather, the general rising depended on the mobilization of a wide cross-section of Londoners. It appeared, by all outward signs, to be a true *levée en masse* – the result a groundswell of efforts by radical civic leaders and their fellow "ordinary," "well-minded," and politically informed Londoners.

Militants remained energized in the wake of the petition. "Make use of this opportunity to preserve your selves," claimed *A Memento to the Londoners* on 25 July, "or expect suddenly to be destroyed." "Nothing," the broadside went on, "can preserve you but a general rising." Prevailing concerns suggested that a great deal was in fact at stake. The king's approach was impending; a second Turnham Green loomed on the horizon, and Londoners should "rise up" unless they wanted their "Religion, Lawes, Liberties, your Lives, Wives, Children, Estates, [and] all" to be "lost."[120] Four days later, on 29 July, Common Hall met and reiterated the "humble desire" for "a present gennerall Riseing": it was to be an effort "wherein every on[e] may give assistance in person or Purse, by an Equall Levie, To be made by Fit persons appointed for that End." Any who "shall refuse may be Secured & theire Estates seized on for the use of the Kingdome." It had become painfully clear to Common Hall's attendants that "there is no way left in humayne Reason to preserve this our Cittie and perishing Kingdome from the power & Rage of those Cruell Tyrants & bloodthirsty Papists now in Armes against us."[121]

Royalists were dismayed by reports of London's planned rising, and indeed of the accusations made by its leading proponents. Samuel Butler lamented that "many Thousands" had recently produced a petition that revealed an "obstinate aversion from Peace." With this, Londoners had cast numerous unfair aspersions on the king, including the claims that he "*hath raised an Army of Papists, Out-lawes, and Traitors, for the Robbing, Burning, Murthering, and destroying of His Religious, Honest, and well meaning People.*" The same "pernicious men" who concocted the rumors, Butler concluded, were the ones who had proposed "the raysing of a new Army" and nominated "*Pennington* the pretended Lord Major, *Strode*, one of the five Members, *Harry Martin*, Plundermaster Generall, and *Dennis Bond*, Burgess of Dorchester." Each of these "desperate Traitors" had devised to create "the late Covenant" as means to force honest Londoners "to joyne with them in this Rebellion."[122]

On the same day that *A Memento to Londoners* was printed, and five days after the petition for a general rising was delivered to parliament, "the truly valiant" Sir William Waller rode into the capital on a train of 100 horses. He "was with much joy received by the whole City" who fired off ordnance "from the workes as hee made his entrance" and gathered in "multitudes" to process behind him as he made his way to his City residence. From his home, he went on to be "bravely feasted" by the Lord Mayor.[123] On that same day, the 30 March *Petition and Remonstrance to Common Council and to Parliament* was reprinted as *Remonstrans Redivivus*. The "recycled remonstrance" reiterated popular concerns over "the usuall misconstruing and perverting" of law and the suggestion "*that kings can doe no wrong.*" Reasserted also was the commitment to *salus populi suprema lex esto* and the view "that the safety of the people is the Supreme Law."[124] Two days later, the newly formed Committee for the General Rising decided that Waller should serve as general of London's new volunteer army.[125] Parliament approved their selection on the same day, promising Waller a new commission. Waller next traveled from Westminster to Merchant Taylors' Hall where members of the Committee for the General Rising, including the Lord Mayor, aldermen, and metropolitan inhabitants had gathered to enlist and to subscribe "money, horse, and arms, in a very free manner." Waller then gave a brief rousing speech that echoed Skippon's words at Turnham Green the previous year, and in which he swore that enlistees' willingness "to hazard their lives in this cause" meant that "he [too] would go along, and spend his blood with them."[126] He was cheered on by crowds who looked upon "William the Conqueror" as the answer to their hopes. London's mood, for the time being, remained electric. Writing to his wife in late July, the royalist Thomas Knyvett concluded that "this towne is all madd for raising a newe Army for Sir William Waller who, they saye, the city will have [as] ther generall."[127] If overwhelming at the time, sanguine spirits soon cooled.

Rupert's capture of Bristol on 26 July renewed a sense of alarm in the capital. The "great loss" of the strategic port left Gloucester as parliament's last strategic stronghold in the west; its fall, most agreed, might spell disaster for parliament, as it would leave nearly all of the west in royalist hands. Little could then be done to stop royalist armies from marching east toward London.[128] In light of these developments, the House decided that the Lord General – and not Waller – should march west with a brigade of London's trained bands. Both generals awaited their new armies, but it was for the time being decided that all forces should remain under the sole authority of the Lord General. In one swift action, parliament had frustrated high hopes for the general rising; rather than focus on his new position, Waller – like Skippon the previous autumn – was to remain subordinate to the Lord General. On 1 August Waller traveled to the City's artillery yard with the expectation that he might meet and "[en]list those multitudes of men which had long expected him." Upon arrival, he found that the vast numbers of recruits were in fact "so thinne and small" that he soon left "ashamed of the disappointment."[129] The very next day, the Council of War decided that Waller's time in London might be better used for "the speedy raising and arming" of 6,500 horse that would be used specifically for the relief of Gloucester.[130]

Although their efforts were clearly hindered, radicals did not give up hope in their new army and its general. Henry Marten complained to the Commons about these developments on 5 August, suggesting that the slow progress raising a new army owed primarily to want of a commission from Essex. The Commons put forth considerable effort to persuade the Lord General of the need for Waller's commission. Letters had reached Essex, and the House even agreed to a special commission that would meet and hear the Lord General's complaints. This was finally secured, but when it arrived in London on 7 August it was revealed to be largely untenable; this conferred upon Waller the right to command London's militia – a title that had already been granted to Major-General Philip Skippon the previous year. The ambiguity of Waller's new "joint appointment" prompted the Commons to seek yet another new commission. Their request, which was far more specific, called for "a Commission to Sir William Waller to levy Ten Regiments of Foot, and Ten Regiments of Horse; and to be Serjeant Major General, and Commander in chief of those Forces." To this was added a further note that Waller should have "such further Power as is usually given in Commission of the like Nature."[131] Parliament made clear that they would no longer tolerate prevarication. Finally secured, Waller's new commission would ultimately do little to help prospects for a volunteer army. Indeed, by 8 August, *Aulicus* could claim that the Committee for the General Rising had not yet managed to enlist "above 600" men.[132] More favorable toward parliament's cause, *Mercurius Civicus* reported that "the truly valliant" Waller was searching high and low for his volunteer army. At the "Butchers Hall neere New-gate-market," he encountered "divers able and lusty Butchers" who "voluntarily listed themselves."[133] If not exactly what Waller had been promised, these "lusty" new enlistees offered a step in the right direction. Two months later, Waller found himself at the head of an army cobbled together out of existing London regiments and a handful of newly impressed men; only a fraction had joined up as part of the proposed general rising. Essex, meanwhile, would soon march out of the City at the head of an army 15,000 strong. Three weeks later, the Committee for the General Rising was ordered to transfer its collections to the committee sitting at Grocers' Hall. The general rising, to borrow Pearl's phrase, seemed "as good as dead."[134]

A close consideration of surrounding political developments reveals that the same currents that led to the call for a general rising also presaged its collapse. Waller's recruits were not forthcoming as had been hoped from the outset; but this owed more to the pressing need to relieve Gloucester than it did to a discernible lack of support for the rising. By this light, radical efforts to control an army may have failed to materialize, but London had once again stepped up to provide the manpower needed to maintain parliament's war effort. The program for the general rising might therefore look less disastrous. The ultimate "failure" of the program has, since Hexter's assessment in *King Pym*, been explained in terms of confusion and political infighting that led to a "squabble" between parliament's Militia Committee and the newly created Committee for the General Rising. Pearl suggested that its failure stemmed "from a lack of recruits and lack of compulsive powers." Lindley, meanwhile, has echoed Pearl's claim, stating simply that "recruits were not forthcoming." More recently, Brenner concluded that efforts to raise a new army ended for "reasons that remain unclear," but that the most likely explanation still came down to tactical disputes that left radicals "quarreling among themselves." It was, Ian Gentles claimed succintly, "a flop."[135] Each of these explanations is, admittedly, cautiously correct; the rising never materialized a volunteer army of 20,000. Yet each of these interpretations limit their purview to cover the immediate circumstances surrounding the general rising's collapse and the failure to create a new army. This in a sense fails to fully recognize the program's wider political significance and legacy for parliament's war effort. "The fact that London did not rise," as Sarah Barber observed, "is surely not the point."[136] The program, in other words, was more significant than its immediate outcome. Indeed, the general rising was merely the latest in a series of efforts that had sought to mobilize Londoners en masse since the outbreak of the war – or earlier yet if efforts to relieve the Irish Rebellion are taken into account. If failed, the general rising was also the most successful attempt at mobilization to date, and it was the one that saw Londoners gain the greatest influence over national politics. In his portrayal of parliamentarian radicalism,

David Como has taken this line of inquiry a step further to suggest that "the General Rising arranged the template" that would create "the New Model Army."[137] Surely this was among the most important and lasting legacies of the program; but more, on balance, remains to be said.

Indeed, the significance of the rising comes into clearer focus when it is set within the context of metropolitan affairs between the months of May and August. Seen in this light – in what might, for lack of a better phrase, be termed a "medium range view" – the program becomes both increasingly nuanced and multivalent. It might thus remain the "template" for the events of eighteen months later described by Como, but it looks far less like the "flop" described by Gentles. In what might just as soon be called a "long range view," the rising looks more like a central mobilizing moment in efforts that spanned from efforts to relieve Ireland in early 1642 on to the creation of the New Model Army between late 1644 and 1645. The rising, on the one hand, sheds considerable light on the degree to which parliament's war effort had come to place a disproportionate burden on the City, and, in turn, how Londoners, despite their reservations, remained willing to shoulder such a burden. On the other hand, it redefines the scope of the rising itself, showing that the movement was not simply an *ad hoc* military program for enlisting troops; it was, as we have seen with respect to the implementation of the Vow and Covenant, and as we will see with regards to the production of demotic print and crowd action in early August, part of a wider scheme to mobilize the metropolis, to deliberately agitate and engage ordinary people, through protest, in parliamentary politics.

Two days prior to the presentation of petition for the general rising, the Commons had already agreed to pass an ordinance "for the raising of 6500 horse" within London, Westminster, and the adjacent counties. These were to be raised by the Militia Committee and used by the earl of Manchester's new "flying army."[138] Politicians seem to have been fully aware and little concerned over the extent to which competing efforts to raise armies would impact efforts to establish a general rising. News of the loss of Bristol on 26 July only exacerbated matters, adding yet more urgency to the need to locate men who would be willing to march into the west. Essex appeared before the Lords on Friday 28 July to complain about "remedies" for issues in his own forces that included arrears, the loss of recruits to "other Employment," the "Scandals laid upon his Excellency," and a request for "an inquest into the causes of the loss of the West."[139] Upon consideration, and in light of Bristol, the House agreed that Essex "should be recruited with 4000 foote," but they voted against an inquiry into Waller's leadership.[140] *The Parliament Scout* thus had good reason to warn that "it might prove good to the Enemy, and none to the Citie" if "both parties" failed to "joyne in one" as they set about recruiting. "The Committee by them named" for a General Rising had to work with "others that had subscribed at Grossers-Hall" – namely the Militia Committee – so that, "hand in hand," they could both create "the best worke that hath yet beene set on foote."[141] Coordinating recruitment was one issue; a shortage of recruits was another matter altogether. Both issues, it would seem, proved detrimental to the immediate goals of the rising.

Contemporaries warned about a shortage of willing men from the outset. Among the many "divers Citizens" who flocked to show support at Merchant Taylors' Hall in late July, were some who also had misgivings about how others might "escape from being demanded to subscribe according to ability." "Without compulsive power," some warned, the great project "would be retarded, and nothing done."[142] They were ultimately correct to express such concerns. Given the need to relieve Gloucester, compulsory power for raising an army was used to support Essex, and not Waller. Thus, the same "ordinary" Londoners who put their names to the 20 July petition did not enlist in the general rising. Far from being the army of 100,000 hinted at in *An Humble Proposal*, or indeed one of the 20,000 who signed *The humble Petition*, only a handful actually enlisted to serve. *Aulicus* could finally mock in mid-August "that of 5000 men which would have no peace, no fewer than fifteen sturdy fellowes (in words at length and not in figures)" actually "listed their names upon the *Roll* to pursue the *Warre*."[143] D'Ewes offered a more judicious assessment of the abysmal turnout, claiming that "there were not yet in near upon a weeks space about 300" who were prepared to march alongside Waller.[144]

Essex, despite his overtures to peace, retained support from vital segments of parliament. On 18 August, the Lord General's troops were ordered to repair to their colors "upon pain of Death," and on the same day parliament issued an order to deliver £200 of coat and conduct money to impress 2,000 soldiers for his army.[145] By the time of his marching out of the City on 26 August, Essex was at the head of a brigade of trained bands and auxiliaries made up of between 6,000 and 8,000 men along with some 1,500 horse.[146] Waller, meanwhile, was still in London seeking out generals.

Accounting for the slow progress of the general rising in late July, Agostini wrote that *"the violence shown in administering the oath"* – the Vow and Covenant – had in fact done *"great harm to the parliamentarians"* and their war effort. Londoners, Agostini reckoned, remained devoted to the cause; but it seemed unlikely that their willingess to take up pens would ever be matched by an enthusiasm for drawing swords. They had already weathered the summer's military losses, news of Waller's plot, the aggressive pursuit of the Vow and Covenant, and what seemed daily threats of an attack by royalists. In line with these developments, Londoners participated in a massive petitioning campaign between 18 and 20 July that briefly stunned parliament and made way for a committee that broke with precedent by proposing its own membership and authority over metropolitan mobilization. Two weeks later, Agostini returned to the issue of the general rising, claiming that it "proceeds slowly, not for lack of money, as the citizens vie with each other in their zeal to do their utmost, but of men, of whom there are few left who are ready to take service."[147] Most of London's willing recruits had already enlisted in service with the auxiliaries.[148] Another indication of trouble came the following month, when on 25 May the Committee for the Advance of Money ordered that "moneys still in arrears unpaid may be gotten in & imployed for the arming of the auxiliary Soldiers now raised or to be raised by the care & industry of the committee sitting at Salters hall in Breadstreet London" and further that "the same may be allowed upon the accoumpts of the Committee at Weavers hall."[149] Indeed, programs for raising London troops had been up and running for the better part of a year; many of the willing were already trailing pikes and hauling muskets on the march west toward Gloucester. Nevertheless, even Pym could not help but marvel at the persistence of "the comon people of the City" who in early August still "seem to cry latly & savortest to unite in a body & shut up all their shopps."[150] Their haste to "unite" did not, after all, equate to an eagerness to fight. Rather, as we shall see, it made space for a popular agitation that would fundamentally alter the course of the civil war.

The Lord Mayor and the multitude

Years later, when reflecting on the significance of the general rising, William Walwyn revealed that he had no misconceptions about the program's importance. Although it "took not its proper effect, and came not to perfection," it nevertheless successfully "mated the common enemy, and set all wheels at work at home." More important than the rising's immediate realization, Walwyn concluded, was the fact that it proved to be "the spring of more powerfull motions and good successes."[151] Walwyn only hints at the nature of the "successes" that were to come; one clearly came in the shape of the relief force that marched from London for Gloucester. Another came days before, in the first week of August, when Pennington and his fellow militants once again called upon Londoners to join in a "general rising" – in this case, however, the proposed "rising" was not a matter of delivering propositions, putting hands to a petition, or creating a new volunteer army. It was, instead, a call to protest and action. On 7 August 1643, thousands of Londoners heeded the call to rise up and descended on Westminster's Old Palace Yard in protest against peace and in favor of war. Far more than the petition of 20 July, the "general rising" of early August proved the crowning achievement of radical metropolitan mobilization in 1643 – a time when the

Lord Mayor and London's "multitude" came together to subvert the will of parliament.

Charles was well aware of the political advantage afforded by his summer victories. Richard Cust has argued convincingly that the king and his advisers took full advantage of their opportunity by issuing "a carefully judged declaration" that sought three main objectives: the celebration of military victories "in providential terms," a reaffirmation of the king's "commitment to the Protestation," and renewed commitment to the royalist cause. The king's declaration, which was issued on 30 July, and was almost certainly written by Clarendon, also took a decidedly conciliatory tone; rather than tout the victories at Adwalton Moor, Roundway Down, and Bristol, it proposed a return to peace. This was, as Cust suggests, almost certainly a calculated move – a shrewdly timed effort to cleave the parliamentarian war effort in two by separating proponents of peace from their belligerent opponents.[152] Charles and his advisers were acutely aware of the divisions that plagued London and Westminster; much like the attempt on the seven Londoners, or indeed the decision to issue the Sacred Oath of June, they hoped that their new declaration might inspire loyalists in the capital and beyond.

Indeed, developments in Westminster suggested that his tactics might succeed. On 2 August, the Lords appointed a committee to consider new terms of peace. Bedford and Holland led the charge. Two days later, the Lords requested that the Commons might join them the following day at eleven o'clock in the Painted Chamber as a Committee of Both Houses and in order to discuss "certaine propositions to be sent to his Ma[jes]tie."[153] The meeting was postponed to allow the members of the lower chamber time to consider some specifics of the proposals. When Manchester delivered the Lord's propositions on to the Commons the next morning, they revealed a preamble outlining reasons for a new peace settlement. These claimed that their willingness came "by reason of a Protestation which they had seen lately in Print," and "in which" the king had apparently "declared that he would maintaine the Protestant Religion without and connivance at Popery." The subsequent proposals included a number of concessions, but they also required the disbanding of armies, "that the Church-government might be reformed," that a pardon would be issued to all men, and that all delinquents "questioned in Parliament before January 1642 might be proceeded against."[154] Their terms bore a striking resemblance to the recently aborted Oxford Treaty.

On Saturday, the Commons began a lengthy debate over whether or not the propositions could be considered in earnest. After three hours, Pym rose to speak against proceeding, claiming that the propositions were unfit since "wee had sent for the Scotts to assist us." A vote was cast, revealing that ninety-four members supported proceeding and sixty-five were opposed. D'Ewes and "many others" were thus overjoyed with thoughts that "the worke of peace" would proceed. Yet "violent spirits" who had long opposed peace engaged in "their cunning practices to overthrow what had been done." Members of the war party next proposed that the propositions could not be considered in full due to the parliament's vulnerability to an open attack. After several members had departed for the day, confident that debate would resume on Monday, a second vote was demanded. This revealed seventy who opposed a discussion of the propositions against sixty-eight who wished to continue. "And so we lost it by two voices," lamented D'Ewes.[155] Undeterred, proponents of peace pressed the matter until nine o'clock in the evening, until it was finally agreed to that discussion should resume on Monday.

Desperate to prevent the peace proposals from moving forward, Pennington and his allies turned to the City. That night, after the house adjourned, they set their plans in motion. Two main strategies were employed: first would be an official response from Common Council. Second would be a deployment of hundreds of printed tickets that called upon the masses to descend upon Westminster.

Wallington heard rumors that councilors "did sit up all night in framing a petition for the parliament" to prevent the surrendering of forts and the delivery of the City's magazine to the king.[156] Such rumors proved well founded. On Sunday, 6 August Common Council was called for an emergency meeting so that they could "read the draught of a petition" that would be submitted to the Commons by "the Lord Maior Aldermen and Commons of the Citty of London." In this they wished to make clear their express opposition to "such propositions and offers" that "have bin lately sent from the house of peers" to the Commons. They claimed to be "much dejected" by the proposals, which "would be utterly destructive to our Religion, Lawes, and Liberties." Their hastily drafted petition was ready for presentation the following morning "by as many Aldermen and Commons as can intend to go."[157] Foremost among their concerns was the loss of the Tower of London, the lieutenancy of which had just become vacant.[158]

Meanwhile, "divers violent and ill disposed persons" met together on "Saturdy night" to "contrive a Libellous and scandalous writing," which they planned to scatter "up and downe in the City of London." Their writing was picked up and "indiscreetly read in some pulpitts" on the following day.[159] The "scandalous" writing took shape as printed tickets that contained a simple set of instructions and an unmistakable warning: "*All such as desire there may be a general raising of the people against those* Irish *Rebels, and blood thirsty Papists now in Armes (fully purposing to destroy us, our Religion, Lawes and Liberties) are desired to meet at* Westminster *Hall, to morrow morning by nine of the clock.*" The same Londoners who hoped for a general rising were once again called upon to respond to the cause by descending upon Westminster. Added to the ticket was the threatening claim that 20,000 Irish rebels had "come over" to take the City.[160] More than simply propose a second rising, the "seditious" authors agreed that "if the Propositions of peace went forward," they would "by violence seize upon leading promoters of the propositions for peace from both Houses." Eight members were targeted, including Northumberland and Holland, along with Denzil Holles, John Evelyn, William Pierrepoint, Sir William Lewis, Harbottle Grimstone, and John Maynard. D'Ewes had no doubts as to who the ringleader behind these designs was. "Isaak Pennington," he wrote in his journal, "was iustly suspected to be a raiser and contriver of all this plot and tumult." It was the "Arch-hypocrite" Lord Mayor who devised the plans, just as he had "sent about in show and pretence to forwarne all men from coming to Westminster."[161] If D'Ewes is to be believed – and indeed there is, on balance, little reason not to believe him – Pennington was behind both the petition and the libelous tickets, plans which were proceeding according to plan.

On the morning of Monday 7 August, the full scope of radical efforts was made apparent. Converging on Westminster's Old Palace Yard that day "was a great concourse of people out of the city" who "filld all passeges," along with City aldermen and councilors who had come to present their petition.[162] Arriving by boats and carriages at the same time were members of the Commons and Lords prepared to resume their discussion from two nights earlier. Some in the crowd accosted "the Lords as they passed into the house," insisting with shouts that they should "remember" their "great promises at Guild-Hall at the entrance into this Warr," and that they had once promised to "live and die with us." Others simultaneously "cried no Peace."[163] D'Ewes believed that the "seditious multitude" who had arrived "according to the Libells dispersed yesterday" were there to "overawe the members of the house of Commons" and prevent them from giving "consent to the Propositions for peace." After finding some "occasion to passe along through part of the old Pallace yard," D'Ewes was shocked to see "it almost filled up." The same "multitudes" set to provoking "Bedford, Holland and Clare" with "base and scandalous language" in the hopes that they might retaliate and thus be "murdered and destroied." Fearing for their lives, the earls apparently fled, making "haste towards *Kingston*," and on to the king's court at Oxford.[164] Londoners had successfully disrupted the Lords, but there was still the matter of debate in the Commons. The scene, Thomas Knyvett opined, "would have made any honest peac'able spirit hart have bledd."[165]

Around this time, Alderman Thomas Atkins, a close ally of Pennington and future Lord Mayor, was accepted into the House to present Common Council's petition. Accompanying the petition was a new draft ordinance that sought to provide a legal framework for pursuing the terms of the general rising. Most notably, this called for the closing of shops and the compulsory enlistment of 30,000 Londoners and the procurement of 10,000 horses. The House offered "hearty thanks" and guaranteed that the petition would be taken up "in a manner as shall be fitting." Significantly, they also agreed to move forward with the request to draft propositions for an ordinance "for the Safety of the City, and the Peace of the Kingdom."[166] It thus appeared that Pennington and his allies had jumped the final hurdle in their race to create a volunteer army; an ordinance would soon provide them with compulsory power to enlist Londoners for their long-anticipated rising.

Meanwhile, the Commons set to debating how to handle the crowd at their door, the likes of which, D'Ewes later concluded, was much less a "dangerous tumult" than an "unlawfull conspiracy." Pennington declared that he had done "his endeavor to suppresse" the crowd. Yet few did "believe it" since he had also come "down to vote against the Propositions for peace, having not been there before for some monethes past." Debate ensued after Pennington finally agreed that he would go to greater efforts to prevent future tumultuous gatherings. After less than two days of strategic maneuvering that included a rapid print campaign to agitate London's "multitude" and a hastily drafted petition, the Lord Mayor took his seat in the Commons to cast his vote against the peace propositions. The votes were counted to reveal a narrow margin of seventy-nine for and eighty-eight against proceeding. "That night," Knyvett reported sadly to his wife, "it was carried by the Maior vote against these propositions."[167] The path to "peace and tranquility," D'Ewes mourned, was thus avoided by just a handful of voices.[168]

On the following day, 8 August, a new group of protesters descended upon Westminster. This time the gathering was composed almost entirely of women who demanded a far different outcome from their counterparts of the previous day. The new crowd, which wore white ribbons in their hats and purportedly included some "Irish" women and others who "came out of Southwark Westminster and other places without the cittie," had apparently taken their cue from their counterparts, but this time they marched up "to the very doore of the house of Commons to cry out 'Peace, Peace'." Like Monday's "tumultuous gathering," which had targeted eight leading proponents of peace, Tuesday's protesters threatened to "plucke out certaine members of either house" whom they identified as "enemyes to peace." According to Whitaker, the crowd became more agitated as the day wore on so that by the afternoon they started shouting out for "Lord Say and Mr Pym." Arrests were finally made and the remaining women dispersed, walking "back to Southwarke" and "parts adjoyning."[169]

Unsatisfied, two to three thousand women returned to Westminster the following morning with a petition for some "speedy course" toward "settlement." Next, an even "greater tumult" ensued, with the crowd becoming so packed in that messages could "not passe from one House to the other." Matters deteriorated rapidly when the "many civilly disposed women" ascended the stairs to the Commons and began banging on the doors and shouting out "for the blood of" members who were "averse to peace." Some in the crowd took to heckling passersby. Orders were issued to reinforce the regular palace guards with City trained bands and two troops of horse. Taunts gave way to violence when some of the crowd began to "fling stones and brickbats."[170] Thus provoked, some of "the troopers" responded with "bullets in their own defence." Others drew their swords and "cut them on the face and hands." One woman apparently "lost her nose."[171] The day ended with three protesters dead. Two of these were men of "meane Condition." The other was the daughter of a "spectacle maker" in Westminster "who was Slayne casually by a Pistoll shot off" by the trooper Humphrey Taylor.[172] Another account claimed that one of the victims was "a Balladsinger with one arm."[173] Understandably, the "casual" slaying of Londoners threatened to do considerable harm to parliament's reputation and the cause at hand. Matters were only made worse when it became known that Taylor served under Waller – ergo, the people's army had turned on the very people it was expected to protect. This may have raised questions about Waller's purpose. Clearly it also did little to champion mobilization.

Reports of the affair varied considerably. Most weighed in on the origins and quality of the protesters as a means to either question their legitimacy or, alternatively, enhance sympathy. Of the 5,000 who came to Westminster, most, claimed the Venetian ambassador, were "lower inhabitants," with some "women" who were "with their children in their arms." After being "fomented by soldiers," the "rascals" were attacked, leaving ten dead and "more than 100 injured."[174] Newsbooks offered their own sensationalized views of the day's violence. *Certaine Informations* asserted that the protesters were fewer in number than had been reported elsewhere, and that they were in fact "two or three hundred Oyster wives" who should be counted as "dirty and tattered sluts."[175] *The Kingdome's Weekly Intelligencer* suggested that the "women were for the most part, Whores, Bawdes, Oyster-women, Kitchen-stuff women, Beggar women, and the very scum of the Suburbs, besides some abundance of Irish women."[176] If perhaps more credible, *Mercurius Civicus* proved only slightly less hostile, claiming that there were "some two or three thousand" who had gathered, but that "most of them were of the inferior sort" and had come to Westminster from "about the City of London and the Suburbs thereof." One of the ringleaders could be singled out "amonst the rest" by her "being a most deformed Medusa or

Hecuba with an old rusty blade by her side."[177] Less eager to villainize the crowd, *Aulicus* harped on the loss of life and limb, reporting that "three [were] killed directly," and that "thirteene or fourteene" were left injured.[178] Walter Yonge ended the day convinced that most of the rabble were not in fact women, but were men dressed in women's clothing.[179] Peace protesters were keenly aware of political developments and they likely came from a range of stations. Most were probably common and middling sorts. They were, as Lindley has suggested, probably "respectable married women."[180] In some cases they were almost certainly the wives or widows of husbands who had departed for war, and in others they were simply inhabitants who hoped for a resolution. No matter their assumed "quality," the assault on the protesters shocked the nation and left Londoners to contemplate the hazards of popular protest, or indeed the extent to which the war had left them divided and vulnerable.

Remarkably, in the span of just four days, Londoners had mobilized en masse both for and against peace. Protests, on the one hand, marked the culmination of ideological cleavages that began in autumn 1642 and had widened significantly over the course of 1643. On the other hand, they spoke of a lasting and momentarily heightened hope for peace. Collectively, the agitation and protest witnessed in late July and early August reveal the extent to which mobilizing efforts and crowd action could influence national politics. On Monday, 7 August, a group of protesters had disrupted parliamentary proceedings and subsequently terminated peace propositions that stood to end civil war.

What differed, in essence, between the competing peace and war movements, was the fact that the push for war had the backing of important civic leaders – not least the Lord Mayor – who adeptly engaged with multilevel, and at times seemingly coordinated, tactics of agitation and mobilization. Thus, on Saturday night, while some were drawing up a petition for an emergency meeting of Common Council, others were busy printing tickets for distribution throughout the metropolis. The subsequent crowd mobilization, which successfully terminated parliament's peace propositions and nearly granted the Committee for the General Rising compulsory powers for enlisting Londoners, marked something of a radical meridian, a high point in a program for mobilization that had been developing even before the outbreak of war the previous year. Rather than create an army, calls for a general rising had, in the end, agitated a crowd. But at the crucial political juncture of early autumn 1643, this action was enough to keep parliament's cause alive. The driving off of leading peers – vestiges of high level loyalism in London – at the hands of a riotous crowd, proved militants' crowning achievement. For the time being, it marked the end of nearly two years of maneuvering by peers who were at times implicitly, and at others outspokenly, in favor of a peace settlement; it signaled, in other words, the supersession of militant interests over peaceable ones, *both* in parliament and the City.[181] Although high hopes for a new volunteer army proved short-lived, peace had been averted and a City brigade was preparing to march to Gloucester.

In the midst of July's turmoil, yet another significant development took place. The quiet retirement and replacement of John Conyers as Lieutenant of the Tower merited little comment by contemporaries. But the occasion would be of lasting significance for London's relationship to the civil war. On 20 July, it was agreed in the Commons that the London Militia Committee should "recommend to the House a fit Person to supply the Place of the Lieutenant of the *Tower*." On the following day, Pennington's name was proposed for the office.[182] The "usurper" thus found a third appointment beyond his status as Member of Parliament and Lord Mayor of London – in this case as the Lieutenant of the armory and stronghold of the City, the magazine prize that had been at the heart of the struggle since before the outbreak of war. Pennington celebrated his new appointment on Sunday 20 August with a sermon preached in the Tower Church by Samuel Kem, a godly army chaplain who had previously given a "violent republican sermon" to members of London's Military Garden at their annual meeting at St. Mary Overie in 1640, and had since taken to preaching in uniform. This time, Kem wore a buff coat and scarf (presumable in parliamentary orange), and marked the occasion with the claim that those who died for parliament's cause were "blessed" in the eyes of God.[183] Laud, who was at the time imprisoned in the Tower, was purportedly made to suffer through the sermon by parliament's self-fashioned military preacher.[184] If Pennington's mayoral term was approaching its end date, he nevertheless carved out a position of lasting importance for the City and the cause.

As Walwyn later proclaimed, the rising's ultimate lack of "perfection" ultimately mattered little; what did in fact matter was the extent to which agitators for the general rising had inspired popular protest, and specifically the impact that their efforts had on renewed attempts to establish a peace settlement. If largely unwilling to enlist, Londoners had nevertheless revealed their collective alacrity for petitioning and protest. Together, in the early days of August, they had delivered their desires from the streets of the metropolis to the very chambers of Westminster; their actions dictated the course of metropolitan politics and, by extension, the civil war.

Notes

1 BL Harley MS 165, fol. 124r; BL Add MS 40883, fol. 188v. See in particular *A Miraculous Victory* (London, 1643).
2 BL Add MS 40883, fos. 128v–129r.

3 Brenner, *Merchants and Revolution*, p. 457; John Adamson, "The Employment of Robert Scawen," in Ian Gentles, John Morrill, and Blair Worden (eds), *Soldiers, Writers and Statesmen of the English Revolution* (Cambridge, 1998), p. 42; Ian Gentles, *The English Revolution and the Wars in the Three Kingdoms, 1638–1652* (Harlow, 2007), p. 165.
4 *Mercurius Aulicus*, July 9 1643 E.62[3], p. 36.
5 *A Declaration and Motive of the Persons Trusted* (London, 1643); BL Add MS 31116, fol. 58r. This particular passage relates to 23 June 1643.
6 HMC 14th Report, *Portland* MSS, vol. 3, p. 113.
7 William Ingler, *Certaine Informations*, 31 May (London, 1643), p. 158. E.105[2].
8 *Mercurius Aulicus* (London, 1643), pp. 300–301. E.55[14].
9 See Hexter, *Reign of King Pym*, 122–147; Pearl, *London*, pp. 269–273; Lindley, *Popular Politics*, pp. 314–319; Brenner, *Merchants and Revolution*, pp. 448–459. Recently, David Como has made this connection more explicitly, noting that the terms of the general rising were "prominently used to mobilize the city to oppose the Lords' latest, most threatening attempt to resurrect peace negotiations," but space remains for emphasizing the extent to which the protests in Westminster were not simply inspired by the general rising, but were a successful outcome of the wider effort to mobilize Londoners to participate in a total war effort. See Como, *Radical Parliamentarians*, p. 175.
10 BL, Harley MS 165, fol. 145r.
11 John Pym, *A Discovery of the great Plot for the utter Ruine of the City of London* (London, 1643), sig. A2r.
12 Thomason's copy of *A Discovery* was marked "June 9th 1643."
13 *A True Discoverie of the Late Intended Plot To ruine the Citie of London and the Parliament as it was informed by Mr. Pym, young Sir Henry Vane, Mr. Solicitor, and Mr. Glyn* (London, 1643), sigs. A3r–A4r. Thomason marked his copy "June 13."
14 Ward, Lock and Co., *Ward and Lock's Pictorial Guide to the Environs of London* (London, 1878), p. 29. For the order to seize and transport Crispe's goods "to London for the use of the Parliament," see TNA, SP 19/1/134.
15 Geoffrey Smith, *Royalist Agents, Conspirators and Spies: Their Role in the British Civil Wars, 1640–1660* (Farnham, 2011), pp. 53–54.
16 Braddick, *God's Fury*, p. 291.
17 Hexter, *Reign of King Pym*, pp. 9–10.
18 Pearl, *London*, p. 265.
19 Vicars, *God on the Mount*, p. 248.
20 Hexter, *Reign of King Pym*, p. 32. For a useful discussion of previous attempts to usher in oaths of association, see Edward Vallance, *Revolutionary England and the National Covenant* (Woodbridge, 2005), pp. 53–55.
21 BL, Add MS 37343, fol. 263v.
22 *CSPV* vol. 26, p. 277.
23 BL, Add MS 27962 K(i), fos. 109r–v. Salvetti referred to "the military commission provided to a member of the Lower House."

24 *Mercurius Aulicus*, Monday, 1 June 1643, p. 291.
25 Conrad Russell, "The First Army Plot of 1641," *TRHS*, 38 (1988), p. 85.
26 *Mercurius Aulicus*, Wednesday, 7 June 1643, pp. 301, 355.
27 *A Declaration of the Loyalty of the Citizens of London to the King and Parliament Wherein Their Fidelity and true Affection to the Publicke good is clearly manifested, by their Voluntary Contributions, Personall Actions, and Strong Fortifications, for the safety of the King, Parliament and Kingdome* (London, 1643), sig. A2r.
28 BL, Add MS 31116, fol. 55r.
29 BL, Add MS 31116, fol. 55r.
30 The normal monthly fast-day sermons were to be preached by Herbert Palmer, Thomas Hill, and Thomas Carter. See *CJ* vol. 3, p. 110.
31 BL, Add MS 31116, fol. 55r. According to the *Commons Journal*, 152 members took the "New Oath and covenant" on the afternoon of the 6th, while sixteen requested more time to consider specific aspects of the document.
32 These included Lord Howard of Escrick, Lord Lovelace, Lord Wharton, Viscount Conway, Viscount Say and Seale, the earls of Portland, Bollingbrooke, Clare, Holland, Denbigh, Salisbury, Pembroke, Montgomery, Bedford, Rutland, Northumberland, and Manchester. See *LJ* vol. 6, p. 87.
33 HL, Hastings Correspondence Box 17/9692.
34 *A Discoverie of the Great Plot* (London, 1643): ESTC R22271; ESTC R230621; ESTC R235655 and *A True Discoverie of the Late Intended Plot To ruine the Citie of London and the Parliament as it was informed by Mr. Pym, young Sir Henry Vane, Mr. Solicitor, and Mr. Glyn* (London, 1643): ESTC R6095.
35 *A True Discoverie*.
36 *A Copie of the Commission sent from his Majestie to The Conspirators of the Citie of London* (London, 1643).
37 BL, Add MS 31116, fol. 57r.
38 *A Brief Narrative of The late Treacherous and Horrid Designe [...] Together with a true Copie of the Commission under the great Seal, sent from Oxford, to severall persons in the Citie of London* (London, 1643). These were printed for Edward Husbands, and are to be sold at his shop in the Middle Temple. June 15. A second edition was printed on 12 July, ESTC R23812. See BL Harley MS 165 fol. 112r, Wednesday 14 June 1643. The *Parliament Scout* provided a relation of "the late plot." See John Dillingham, *The Parliament Scout* (London, 1643), p. 4.
39 *A Brief Narrative of The late Treacherous and Horrid Designe*. This passage is taken from the orders on the title page: "Ordered by the Commons in Parliament, That this Narration and Commission be read in all Churches and Chappels, in the Cities of London and Westminster, and the Suburbs thereof, on the day abovesaid."
40 Stephen Marshall, *The Song of Moses the Servant of God* (London, 1643), p. 39.
41 Obadiah Sedgewick, *Haman's Vanity* (London, 1643), p. 31.
42 Charles Herle, *Davids Song of Three Parts* (London, 1643), p. 22; Edmund Calamy, *The Noble-Mans Patterne* (London, 1643), p. 45.

43 BL, Add MS 40883, fos. 105v–106r, 108v. As David Booy has pointed out, Wallington's troubled morning and reflection had to do with another "royalist plot to regain governmental power under cover of petitioning for peace." See *The Notebooks of Nehemiah Wallington, 1618–1654: A Selection* (Aldershot, 2007), p. 193 n. 267. It seems entirely possible that both plots had become convoluted in Wallington's mind.
44 *CSPV* vol. 26, p. 277.
45 *A Sacred Oath or Covenant* (Oxford, 1643).
46 Ibid., pp. 3–4. This list includes 191 names.
47 *CJ* vol. 3, pp. 147–148.
48 *A Sacred Oath or Covenant*; *A Sacred Vow and Covenant* (London, 1643), pp. 5–6.
49 Edward Vallance, *Revolutionary England and the National Covenant: State Oaths, Protestantism and the Political Nation* (Woodbridge, 2005), p. 57.
50 *CSPV* vol. 27, pp. 291–307.
51 Vallance, *Revolutionary England and the National Covenant*, pp. 57, 115–119; Edward Vallance, "Religious Justifications for the English Civil War," *HLQ*, 65 (2003), pp. 402–403.
52 Hopper, *Turncoats and Renegadoes*, p. 6.
53 Braddick, "History, Liberty, Reformation and the Cause," p. 128.
54 Merritt, *Westminster*, p. 146.
55 Walter, *Covenanting Citizens*, p. 260. This may also begin to tell the story of the Protestation's "long afterlife, whose full history," as Walter suggests, "has yet to be recovered," p. 244.
56 LMA, MS P69/MRY9/B/001/MS02597/001, fos. 66–67.
57 *A&O*, pp. 82–83.
58 LMA, MS P69/MGT1/B/001/MS04352/001, fos. 156r–157v. It should be noted that fol. 157 is in fact a duplicate in the pencil notation. This should be 158v.
59 LMA, MS P69/CLE/B/007/MS00977/001, unfol., but the list is pasted in the back of the book.
60 LMA, MS P69/MTN2/B/001/MS00959/001, fos. 381v–382; See Vallance, *Revolutionary England*, p. 116.
61 LMA, MS P69/BEN1/B/005/MS01303/001, unfol. No other information accompanies the list, but the location of the chronology of the list in relation to other accounts suggests that it is in fact from the Vow and Covenant.
62 LMA, MS P69/STE1/B/001/MS04458/001/002, undated return pasted at the end of the book; see also Vallance, *Revolutionary England*, p. 118.
63 Vallance, *Revolutionary England*, p. 57.
64 LMA, MS P69/MGT1/B/001/MS04352/001, fos. 156r–160r. [174 as opposed to 251].
65 LMA, MS P69/CLE/B/007/MS00977/001, unfol.
66 Vallance, *Revolutionary England*, p. 59.
67 LMA, MS P69/MRY8/B/001/MS00064, fos. 34v–35r. Signatures were also removed for the 1641 Protestation and the Solemn League and Covenant. I could not find evidence of these lists in the Parliamentary Archives.

68 Vallance notes that "there is much evidence that after 1660 the records of the more politically sensitive oaths of the civil war period were destroyed, either in belated acts of vengeance or in an attempt to cover up any collaboration with the Parliamentarian regimes," in *Revolutionary England*, p. 108.
69 See Merritt, *Westminster*, p. 146. Merritt notes that "the context makes it clear that this was not the National Covenant." See also City of Westminster Archives Centre, vol. 22, fol. 399v.
70 See Liu, *Puritan London*, p. 39.
71 See Christopher Hill, *Economic Problems of the Church from Archbishop Whitgift to the Long Parliament* (Oxford, 1956), p. 255; Adrian Johns, "Coleman Street," *HLQ*, 71 (2008), pp. 33–54.
72 John Rushworth, *Historical Collections*, vol. 4 (London, 1708), p. 239.
73 Thomas Horton, Colechurch's rector, served as Professor of Divinity at London's Gresham College.
74 LMA, MS P69/MGT1/B/001/MS04352/001, fol. 149v.
75 See *The Articles and Charges Prov'd in Parliament Against Dr Walton* (London, 1641). Walton was finally sequestered in June 1643, just prior to the administering of the Vow and Covenant.
76 Liu, *Puritan London*, pp. 27, 139.
77 LMA, MS P69/CLE/B/001/MS00978/001, fos. 7–8, 11.
78 Julia Merritt likens vestries to "mini-commonwealths" in "Contested Legitimacy and the Ambiguous Rise of the Vestries in Early Modern London," *HJ*, 54 (2011), p. 28.
79 Milk Street's parishioners remained active supporters of the cause. On 21 June 1644, "the parishioners" of Milk Street agreed to send £60 that was intended "for the raising of Forces" on to "Treasurers for Money and Plate att the Guildhall." See LMA MS P69/MRY9/B/001/MS02597/001, fol. 79.
80 LMA, MS COL/CHD/CT/01/004, fol. 223v.
81 *A Sacred Vow and Covenant* (London, 1643).
82 *The Anti-Covenant, Or a sad Complaint Concerning The new Oath or Covenant* (Oxford, 1643), p. 10; *A Letter to a Noble Lord at London from A Friend at Oxford* (Oxford, 1643), p. 1.
83 *Mercurius Aulicus*, 22 July, p. 390, E.63[2].
84 Brenner has correctly suggested that the general rising should be seen as part of a wider systematic effort by radicals to establish an independent fighting force in London that extended from autumn 1642 until September 1643. *Merchants and Revolution*, pp. 452–459.
85 *An Humble Proposal Of Safety to the Parliament and Citie* (London, 1643). See the title page for Thomason's note about the presentation.
86 Ibid., title page.
87 *Mercurius Aulicus* E.60[18], pp. 349–350; *The Kingdomes Weekly Intelligencer* E.59[22], pp. 197–198.
88 *Instructions and Propositions Drawne up and agreed on by divers well affected persons in the City of London ... for the raising of an Army of ten thousand men of godly conversation* (London, 1643), title page, pp. 1, 6.

89 LMA, MS COL/CC/01/01/041, fol. 67r; for the petition, see PA, MS HA/PO/JO/10/1/153, fol. 83v.
90 LMA, MS COL/CC/01/01/041, fol. 17v.
91 *The Earle of Essex His Letter To Master Speaker* (Oxford, 1643), p. 3.
92 See LMA, MS COL/CHD/MN/02/015, Miscellaneous Papers, 1643–1690, "Extracts and notes regarding the security of the City and the raising of money at the time of the Civil War, 1643."
93 Sears McGee offers a perceptive discussion of these men in *An Industrious Mind*, pp. 393–400.
94 *Mercurius Aulicus*, Sunday, 16 July (1643), p. 370.
95 Lindley, *Popular Politics*, p. 308.
96 BL, Add MS 7532, fol. 5r.
97 Essex Record Office, T/B, 211/1, #39. See also Brenner, *Merchants and Revolution*, p. 440.
98 Hexter, *Reign of King Pym*, p. 118; Pearl, *London*, p. 269; Lindley, *Popular Politics*, p. 305. Most parliamentary journals account for this episode and the subsequent debate in the Commons.
99 Como, *Radical Parliamentarians*, pp. 169–171.
100 Pearl, *London*, p. 267.
101 Museum of London, MS 46.78/673, "An unsigned note relating to Lord Essex," 1 July 1643.
102 HL, Huntington MS 16522, "Poems and Ballads," p. 140. See Donagan, *War in England*, p. 252.
103 For an earlier criticism of Essex's eating, drinking, and wasting of time, see BL, Harley 164, fol. 318r.
104 BL, Add MS 40883, fol. 128v.
105 BL, Harley MS 165, fol. 122v. See also Jason Peacey, "Disorderly Debates: Noise and Gesture in the 17th-Century House of Commons," *PH* 32 (2013).
106 BL, Harley MS 165, fol. 123v–124r, 125v.
107 Ibid., 127v.
108 *All sorts of well-affected Persons* (London, 1643).
109 *All that wish well to the safety of this Kingdome* (London, 1643, E.61[10]); see Peacey, *Print and Public Politics*, pp. 353–354.
110 *To the Right Honourable the Knights, Citizens, and Burgesses in PARLIAMENT ASSEMBLED* (London, 1643); LMA, MS COL/CC/01/01/041, fols. 162v–163v; PA, HL/PO/JO/10/1/153, fol. 83; *CJ* vol. 3, pp. 175–176.
111 Ibid., p. 176. D'Ewes notes "Sir Foulke Griffith" in BL, Harley MS 165, fol. 128r. See Pearl, *London*, p. 270; Lindley, *Popular Politics*, p. 315.
112 BL, Harley MS 165, fol. 128r.
113 *The humble Petition of thousands of well affected Inhabitants* (London, 1643) C26:3[86]; C5:1[81].
114 Brenner, *Merchants and Revolution*, p. 457.
115 BL, Harley MS 165, fol. 128v.
116 *The humble Petition of thousands of well affected Inhabitants* (London, 1643).
117 BL, Add MS 27962 K(i), fol. 130r/136r.

118 *A Declaration of the Proceedings of the Honourable Committee* (London, 1643), p. 3.
119 William Walwyn, *A Whisper in the Ear* (London, 1646), p. 4.
120 *A Memento to the Londoners: To put them in minde how neere their destruction is, and what means is left to prevent it* (London, 1643). These terms were almost identical to those made by Philip Skippon at Turnham Green on 13 November 1642. See Chapter 2.
121 Bodleian Library, MS Nalson 13, fol. 389r/p. 183.
122 Butler, *A Letter*, pp. 31–32.
123 *Mercurius Civicus*, 20–28 July, p. 1; *Mercurius Aulicus*, 31 July, p. 411; *A Perfect Diurnall*, 24–31 July sig. E2r.
124 *Remonstrans Redivivus*, p. 3. Pennington may have been involved in the production of both the *Petition and Remonstrance* and *Remonstrans Redivivus*. See David Laing (ed.), *The Letters and Journals of Robert Baillie* vol. I (Edinburgh, 1851), pp. 274–275. Pennington had played a key role in the petition from 11 December 1640. See Pearl, *London*, pp. 210–216. See also Anthony Fletcher, "Power, Myths and Realities," *HJ*, 36 (1993), pp. 211–216.
125 Henry Marten confirmed the appointment in a speech at Guildhall the next day. *Three Speeches Delivered at a Common Hall* (London, 1643), pp. 17–18.
126 *A Perfect Diurnall*, 24–31 July, sig. E3r; *A declaration of the Proceedings of the Honourable Committee of the House of Commons at Merchant-Taylors Hall* (London, 1643); see also John Adair, *Roundhead General: The Campaigns of Sir William Waller* (Gloucestershire, 1997), pp. 104–107.
127 Bertram Schofield (ed.), *The Knyvett Letters (1620–1644)* (London, 1949), p. 121.
128 BL, Egerton MS 2643, fol. 13.
129 *Mercurius Aulicus*, p. 428. E.65[26].
130 *CJ* vol. 3, p. 192.
131 Ibid., p. 198.
132 *Mercurius Aulicus*, p. 428. E.65[26].
133 *Mercurius Civicus*, p. 87. E.65[4].
134 Pearl, *London*, p. 273. Waller returned his commission to the Speaker of the House on 9 October.
135 Hexter, *Reign of King Pym*, p. 127; Brenner, *Merchants and Revolution*, pp. 458–459; Pearl, *London*, p. 272; Lindley, *Popular Politics*, p. 319; Ian Gentles, "'This Confused, Divided and Wretched City': The Struggle for London in 1642–43," *Canadian Journal of History*, 38 (2003), p. 476.
136 Barber, *A Revolutionary Rogue*, p. 8.
137 Como, *Radical Parliamentarians*, p. 176.
138 BL, Harley MS 165, fol. 127v.
139 *CJ* vol. 3, pp. 187–189. Pym relayed these points to the Commons the following day.
140 BL, Harley MS 165, fol. 132v.
141 *The Parliament Scout*, pp. 39–40. E.61[26].
142 *A Declaration of the Proceedings of the Honourable Committee* (London, 1643), pp. 5–6.

143 *Mercurius Aulicus*, pp. 434–435. E.65[26].
144 BL, Harley MS 165, fos. 135r–v; Hexter, *Reign of King Pym*, p. 126.
145 *LJ* vol. 6, p. 186.
146 See John Day, *Gloucester and Newbury 1643: The Turning Point of the Civil War* (Barnsley, 2007), p. 86.
147 *CSPV* vol. 27, pp. 305–306; the legal dimensions of the Vow and Covenant remained a central topic of debate throughout the autumn. See Samuel Clarke, *Englands Covenant Proved Lawfull & Necessary also at this time, both by Scripture and Reason. Together With sundry Answers to the usuall Objections made against it* (London, 1643); *Observations upon the Instructions for the taking the Vow and Covenant* (Oxford, 1643); *A Vindication of the Late Vow and Covenant* (London, 1643). For approval of the proposal by the Commons, see BL, Add MS 31116, fol. 66.
148 See Chapter 4, pp. 153–154.
149 See TNA, SP 19/1/155.
150 BL, Egerton MS 2643, fol. 13.
151 Walwyn, *A Whisper in the Ear*, p. 4.
152 Richard Cust, *Charles I: A Political Life* (Harlow, 2005), pp. 378–379.
153 BL, Harley MS 165, fol. 135v.
154 Ibid., fol. 138r.
155 Ibid., fos. 141r, 142r–v.
156 BL, Add MS 40883, fol. 138r.
157 LMA, MS COL/CC/01/01/041, fos. 69v–70r.
158 On 29 July, the same day that the committee proposed William Waller's place as commander of the new army, they also suggested "that the care & custodie of the Tower of London should be committed to the Lord Mayor & sheriffs." See BL, Harley MS 165, fol. 131v. See p. 215.
159 BL, Harley MS 165, fol. 145v. Peacey notes the significance of the event in *Print and Public Politics*, p. 354.
160 *Mercurius Aulicus*, pp. 431–432. E.65[26]; BL, Harley MS 165, fol. 145v.
161 BL, Harley MS 165, fol. 145v.
162 *Knyvett Letters*, p. 126.
163 *The Kingdome's Weekly Intelligencer*, p. 228. E[65].11.
164 BL, Harley MS 165, fos. 146r–147r; *Mercurius Aulicus*, p. 432. E.65[26].
165 *Knyvett*, p. 126.
166 *CJ* vol. 3, p. 197; Lindley, *Popular Politics*, p. 318.
167 *Knyvett*, p. 126.
168 BL, Harley MS 165, fos. 147r–148v.
169 BL, Harley MS 165, fol. 149v; BL, Add MS 18778, fol. 13v; BL, Add MS 31116, fol. 69r.
170 Bodleian Library, MS Clarendon 22, fos. 117r–v; *Mercurius Civicus*, pp. 87–88. E.65[4].
171 *The Kingdome's Weekly Intelligencer*, p. 229. E.65[11].
172 BL, Add MS 31116, fol. 69r.
173 *The Kingdome's Weekly Intelligencer*, p. 229. E.65[11].
174 *CSPV* vol. 27, p. 8.

175 *Certaine Informations*, p. 231. E.65[8]. See Patricia Crawford, "'The poorest she': Women and Citizenship in Early Modern England," in Michael Mendle (ed.), *The Putney Debates of 1647* (Cambridge, 2001), pp. 209–210. See also Ann Hughes on female agency and political awareness in "Gender and Politics in Leveller Literature," in Susan Amussen and Mark Kishlansky (eds), *Political Culture and Cultural Politics in England: Essays presented to David Underdown* (Manchester, 1995), pp. 179–222.
176 *The Kingdome's Weekly Intelligencer*, p. 229. E.65[11].
177 *Mercurius Civicus*, p. 87. E.65[4].
178 *Mercurius Aulicus*, p. 434. E.65[26].
179 BL, Add Ms 18778, fos. 13–15.
180 Lindley, *Popular Politics*, p. 352. See also TNA, SP 24/1/39, 45.
181 For an early example of popular opposition to the conservative voting of the peers, see *To the Honourable the House of Commons Assembled in Parliament: The humble Petition of many thousand poore people, in and about the Citie of London* (London, 1642). See Michael Mendle, *Dangerous Positions: Mixed Government, The Estates of the Realm, and the Making of the Answer to the XIX Propositions* (Tuscaloosa, 1985), pp. 167–168. For the most recent discussion of this move, see Como, *Radical Parliamentarians*, pp. 115–116.
182 *CJ* vol. 4, pp. 176–177.
183 Gordon Goodwin, "Kem or Keme, Samuel (1604–1670)," in Sidney Lee (ed.), *Dictionary of National Biography*, vol. 10 (London, 1908), pp. 1250–1251; see John Rouse Bloxam, *A Register of the Residents, Fellows, Demies ... of Saint Mary Magdalen College* (London, 1876), p. 112. Kem's sermon from 1640 was *The New Ford of true honour made impregnable* (London, 1640). Barbara Donagan notes a separate occasion in Bristol where Kem was "said to have preached in a buff coat and scarlet coat and scarlet cloak with pistols on the cushions beside him." See Barbara Donagan, "Kem, Samuel (1604–1670)," *ODNB* (Oxford, 2008).
184 Thomas Longueville, *A Life of Archbishop Laud* (London, 1894), p. 419.

5

A "rebellious city"?

Bristol's fall on 26 July left doubts about parliament's ability to control the wider Severn Valley.[1] When news reached the capital that Gloucester's governor, Colonel Edward Massey, had no intention of surrendering to encroaching royalists, Londoners could pause for a collective – if also momentary – period of calm.[2] Should Gloucester fall to the king, there would be little to stop royalists from turning their attention back toward London and the east. Eager to avoid this fate, parliament turned to the City.

London's response was unequivocal. The very day after peace protesters had been slain in Westminster, an ordinance passed for the collection and delivery of £10,000 raised by a tax of the twentieth part on London, Westminster, and "adjacent areas." The funds were to be employed for William Waller's new army. Essex, who up to this point had been busy deliberating over how he might avoid granting a commission to Waller, wrote to the Commons on 9 August, claiming that he "was ready and willing to hazard himselfe in person for the raysing of the siege" in Gloucester so long as arrears could be paid and he might also be granted a "competent number" of new soldiers.[3] Two days later, on 11 August, Common Council agreed to pass on requests to livery companies for a new £50,000 loan, a sum that would help fund Essex's march west. Orders bearing Pennington's name were printed, accompanied by familiar warnings about the "greate and imminent danger to this Citty," "the neere approaching of the kings forces," and the "greate and weighty cause" at hand.[4] Liveries had only to respond, but the matter of their ability to do so remained in question.

Parliament's request for yet another loan also marked the beginning of a new phase in the civil war, a period of escalating financial strain, of fracturing political associations, and of a fundamental rearticulation of the way in which Londoners would engage with mobilization. Doubtless, much of this shift owed to extant and deepening divisions between parliamentarians. "War" and "peace" factions had of course long been at odds; pressurized over the developments of July and August, and not least the matter of relieving Gloucester, the tenuous bonds that held parliament's coalition together began to crack.

Compounding issues over how parliament should continue to wage war – or indeed, which military commander might be best positioned to lead a relief effort for Gloucester – were persistent and deepening concerns over religion, both in terms of structure and faith. Scholars such as Ann Hughes and Elliot Vernon have delineated well how religious concerns cleaved Londoners apart, leading to the creation of factions, counter-factions, and new loosely formed coalitions.[5] Hughes in particular has shown the power of print in these developments, and how Thomas Edwards, a man who "apprehended his world as divided into good and evil parties" in 1644, would eventually produce *Gangraena*, the heresiography that led to yet more "fracturing of the parliamentarian cause."[6] Edwards and his polemics in a way exemplified many of the complex processes that were in play, and London was often at the center of these matters. To once again borrow Como's succinct phrasing, the London of 1644 resembled a "churning environment of sectarian religious experimentation" that was readily "threatening to tear itself apart."[7] But even prior to this, in late 1643, questions over the war, and indeed over the Solemn League and Covenant, were forcing into the open questions that might previously have been avoided.

Driving matters of political and religious polarization were several practical concerns. Not least were changes to parliament's leadership in late 1643.[8] Parliament's war coalition lost an important leader when Henry Marten was expelled from the House. Not long after Londoners had diverted the course of peace by marching on Westminster, Marten openly expressed personal views in parliament that were too extreme to go unchecked; when asked to reflect on the views of John Saltmarsh, a preacher whose personal papers contained scribblings about how to "destroy" the king and his heirs, Marten apparently professed that he could find no reason why "any one family should be put in the balance with the destruction of the whole Kingdom." Urged to clarify his meaning, Marten proclaimed that the "one family" under consideration was none other than that of the king "and his Children." The House responded decisively: Marten was sent to the Tower for a fortnight and banned from parliament for three years.[9] Sarah Barber, Marten's biographer, has suggested that the Commons lost more than a radical and known incendiary with the ejection; lost also was an industrious committee member who deserved credit for having "successfully kept the fractious Londoners on board" with parliament's war.[10] Although this assessment might grant Marten somewhat more credit than he deserves, it must be acknowledged that his removal in August altered the makeup of parliament's "war party" coalition.[11] It came, moreover, at the height of developments surrounding the general rising and the push to relieve Gloucester.

More troubling to the wider parliamentarian coalition and cause was John Pym's death on 8 December. Reports of Pym's demise were accompanied by royalist rumors of a "foule carkasse" that was riddled with worms.[12] The symbolism, if apocryphal, said as much about royalist perceptions of parliament's leadership as it did about the statesman's centrality to the parliamentary cause. Pym's rapid decline was striking given his central role in the politics of the previous two years, as momentous a matter for parliament as it was for his opponents. Members of both houses recognized the loss with an elaborate funeral in which the Assembly of Divines escorted Pym's body from Essex House to Westminster Abbey to hear Stephen Marshall give a lengthy commemorative sermon.[13] The occasion, claimed Gentles, afforded an important opportunity to seek unity and "bolster" what many perceived to be "sagging morale" among "parliament's supporters."[14] Doubtless the "heraldric" ceremony had some effect on the Londoners who watched as Pym's elaborate funeral procession passed by. A leading spokesman of the cause had been silenced.[15] Yet Pym's departure also cleared the way for new parliamentary leaders who were eager to have their say over what directions parliament's war might take. The loss of Pym, Pearl states, cleared space for a parliamentary "middle group" that would come to orbit around Oliver St. John.[16]

Others have put somewhat less stock in the significance of Pym's passing. Pym was far less central for Kishlansky, who sought to remedy scholars' "continued taxonomic confusion" and "uncertainty" by suggesting that the period operated according to a politics of consensus.[17] For Adamson, Pym's departure marked the loss of a single leader who was part of a large and cohesive artistocratic junto. Party interests were clear from the outset, claimed Adamson; precisely how party structures permutated over time, however, and what Pym's loss meant to this equation, must still be shown.[18]

Scholars have had decidedly less to say about the ways in which London's changing leadership impacted the civil war. Save for passing comment by Pearl, who noted that John Wollaston's "moderation as Lord Mayor in 1643–44 was in marked contrast to the conduct of his predecessor, Pennington," we know surprisingly little about what the dramatic change to the mayoralty did to alter London's relationship to the war. In fact, we know very little about many of the leading Londoners who remained as gatekeepers between parliament's interests and the City's vast resources over the course of late 1643 and 1644.[19] Indeed, the conclusion of Pennington's mayoral term in October 1643 was arguably of far greater significance to metropolitan mobilization than were changes to parliament's coalition that came as a result of Marten's ejection and Pym's death. A Staffordshire native and goldsmith, Wollaston embarked upon a mayoralty that was characterized by less active participation. When it came to several previously important aspects of metropolitan mobilization, including matters of dealing with "malignancy," shepherding petitions, or acting as a mediator between parliamentary requests and corporate, parochial, and trade company interests, a less robust picture emerges.

From the outset of war, parliament had relied heavily on the City militia, both as a collective defensive force and for its regiments, which were readily deployed for combat. From 1644 onwards, however, this relationship changed precipitously. Parliament's attention turned increasingly to large and reliable extrametropolitan armies. The most obvious of these were the Scots, whose alliance with parliament was formed in November, shortly before Pym's death and following England's adoption of the Solemn League and Covenant in September 1643. In January 1644, an impressive Covenanter army, some 20,000 strong, marched south under the command of Alexander Leslie, earl of Leven. In light of Scottish intervention, and in light of the growing importance of the Eastern Association, demands for London's militia diminished. This is not to say that the City stopped deploying armies; London brigades continued to march out from the metropolis, but it is to say that pressure on Londoners to find new soldiers had lessened.

From autumn 1643 onwards, London's relationship to the civil war on the whole changed. Less a provider of emergency armies and stopgap loans, the City saw its role redefined to be that of the assumed "parliamentarian stronghold." Maimed, sick, and wounded soldiers continued to cross into the metropolis in search of pensions and care. With new political leaders in the ascendant, and while questions loomed large about how the war against the king might best persist, Londoners embarked upon a new and uncertain phase of wartime mobilization.

Financing a relief force

Given their professed financial dire straits, the speed and extent to which London's livery companies fulfilled parliament's request for £50,000 for Gloucester was nothing short of remarkable. Outstanding loans – not least for the £100,000 from the previous year – had yet to be paid back; several companies had already recorded the sale of plate and other goods to help cover forced loans to parliament. More than simply a matter of recovering past debts, diminished trade, increased taxes, and disrupted sales had pushed some companies to the brink of insolvency. As with previous collections, the greatest assessments and burdens fell upon the City's prestigious twelve "great" companies.

Although they had grown deeply indebted to their own members, the Grocers acquiesced to Pennington's letter and the request for £4,500, nearly one-tenth of the entire £50,000 loan.[20] Haberdashers were assessed just slightly less at £3,850, which they apparently paid speedily.[21] Likewise, £3,000 was requested from the Fishmongers, who summoned their members to a meeting in which they "unanimously consented" to pay their part.[22] Mercers, who had already sold plate in excess of £699 to cover outstanding debts, were assessed £3,250. They nevertheless consented to raise the loan by 25 August.[23] Goldsmiths likewise agreed, returning their written "assent unto the raysinge of the sum[m]e of money by this Company according to the Contents of the lord maiors letter." The formalities of their letter belied the state of their finances; returning £3,500 forced the company to sell "all or soe much" of the plate "as they have in a readiness." Silver spoons were saved in the nick of time when Wollaston, who was "lately elected Lord Major for the yeare ensewinge," expressed his view that "itt is not thought fitt to sell or melt downe any of the said plate" since he planned to "borrow" it for his use while serving as Lord Mayor.[24]

Other companies were more open about the strains caused by the loan. Responding to a request for £3,750, Drapers claimed that their "wardens shall take the best care they can" to obtain the sum.[25] Given the "greate pressing and urgent occasions" of their need "for money aswell for the payment of their debts," Clothworkers ordered "all the Stock of plate which this Company hath shall be forthwith sold at the best rate." They apparently raised the total of £2,750 by September, but the effort sunk the company another £1,000 into debt.[26] If encumbered by their debts, most companies nevertheless managed to raise the sums requested by parliament. Where stores of plate did not suffice to cover loans, companies borrowed directly from their own liverymen and freemen. Salters concluded that raising their £2,400 required that they seek members "to lend & pay w[it]hout taking the same upp att interest upon the Companies Seale." Like other trading companies, they succumbed to the sale of plate, ordering that "there shalbee 200^l worth of the Companies Plate or more sold att the discreon of the M[aster]r & wardens for the necessary occasions of this Company."[27] Skinners were in a similar position when they agreed to likewise to pay their "loane of 2100," which they hoped to "rayse" by selling off "parte of the Comanyes plate."[28]

Where stores of plate ran short and members could not help cover costs, companies had to look elsewhere to raise cash. On 7 September, for instance, a vestry held by the parish of St. Lawrence Jewry recorded that both the Salters and the Grocers were in desperate need of cash. With their reserves of plate depleted and credit exhausted, the companies apparently turned to parishioners. Together the companies borrowed "tewe hundred poundes upon Consideration they will give there Companyes seall" and under the condition "that it maybe be payd in within six wekes after nottis given unto them when it shall growe dew."[29] In an unexpected turn of events, London's most prestigious guilds asked parishioners to help raise money to supply what looked to be another forced loan for parliament. Merchant Taylors, Vintners and Ironmongers soon found themselves in similar positions to the Salters and Grocers. Merchant Taylors, who had experienced "the ascendancy of eminent royalist citizens in the court" over the course of 1643, nevertheless acquiesced and agreed to pay their assessment of £5,000. According to Nigel Victor Sleigh-Johnson, the company's decision to pay can be traced to their "assembly," which on the whole "proved more enthusiastic than the Company governors." Yet collecting £5,000 proved more difficult than company members had anticipated; like others, they were forced to sell plate and depend on loans from their own liverymen and freemen. Rather than deliver the large lump sum, the company paid in installments, the first of which was made in January 1644. A full fifth of their loan remained outstanding in May of the same year; aside from the selling of plate at a company dinner, no further mention of the loan appears in their records.[30]

Vintners, who had shown reluctance in the case of previous loans, petitioned the Committee for the Advance of Money with a "humble" list of seven reasons why they might be relieved from raising their assessment of £2,500. Their reasoning seemed beyond reproach: they had "long since" been owed £624 of interest on previous loans and they had already "delivered armes out of their store to divers Captaines for the Parliaments service." Commitment was not, then, the issue. What was, the company went on, was the fact that they were "idebted at interest for £7000" worth of rent.[31] Pleading aside, the company gave "absolute consents" that they should have £500 worth of plate "pawned" so that they could forward a fifth of what had been requested.[32] Their token gesture failed to mollify the committeemen; with £2,000 in arrears, the Committee for the Advance of Money threatened a sequestration order that would allow for the seizure of their lands and goods. Vintners responded with a petition warning that sequestrations would have unintended but terrible consequences. Sequestration might cause the company to collapse, and a collapse, they cautioned, might leave no one to execute wills or care for the poor. Who, they pressed, would be left to care for "the stocks of orphans and other trustees?" Left unpaid, they cautioned, outstanding debts would bring "disgrace" upon both the company *and* parliament.[33] The petition sufficed for the time being; committeemen for the time being passed their concerns on to the consideration of the Commons. More persuasive than their petition, perhaps, was the fact that the company had agreed to "humbly take notice of the ordinance" passed on 11 September that secured the "payment of £5 per ton excise on all wynes wee hereafter buy and the halfe excise for all wynes on our handes." Bankruptcy – if not for the sake of orphans, but rather for parliament's ability to administer its new excise – was best avoided. Parliament "seemed to rest satisfied" with the promise that the company would continue "to their utmost abilities" to collect the remainder of their loan.[34] The matter thus rested until June of the following year when the Vintners were reminded again to pay the £2,000 still owed toward the maintenance of "the garrison of Gloucester."[35]

Vintners were not the only ones to face legal pressure in light of insolvency and indebtedness. £1,700 requested from Ironmongers was revealed to be excessively burdensome. Company members debated how to manage the matter, deciding finally to send a response to Pennington's initial letter to say they could not afford to pay since they "formerly lent to divers Lords and to the Parliament for reliefe." Previous loans, they went on, had rendered their members "disabled and impovereshed." Their next move was to invite Pennington and the Court of Aldermen to review their account books directly so that they might see for themselves the "disability to performe the said Loane." Fidelity to the cause, they professed, could be seen in the £500 they spent to impress men for Ireland, and indeed in the £3,400 that they had already raised "for [the] reliefe of Ireland." Like their contemporaries, the Ironmongers saw Ireland's relief and parliament's war as one and the same. Company debts at the time of Pennington's request amounted to £6,994.[36] Their "answare" ultimately proved "not satisfying" and a new request was issued for £1,700, "or soe much thereof as could bee provided." The matter carried on until the Committee for the Advance of Money finally summoned members to appear on 19 September. Once again, they claimed that their previous loans, including an outstanding sum of £5,100 loaned to parliament, had not received "satisfaction," and that they could not possibly be expected to find an additional £1,700. Partially contented, the Committee next demanded that they pay at least £300 within a two-week period ending on 7 October. The matter of their outstanding loan carried on through February 1644, when the company received a new threat: if they failed to deliver £1,300 to the Guildhall they would be forced, "or els," to produce a list of "the names of the Livery of the Company" and the amounts that they had loaned. The threat was temporarily avoided due to the calling of a Common Hall, which provided a legitimate reason for dodging the summons. But this was by no means the end of the matter. Subsequent meetings in April, October, November, and December 1644 failed to resolve the issue of "default of payment."[37] Ironmongers found themselves in the same unenviable position at the end of 1645. The "ancient" company thus teetered on the brink of insolvency for two years, with their daily operations disrupted.

If extreme examples, cases pertaining to the Merchant Taylors, Vintners, and Ironmongers offer important examples of the cumulative burden that wartime loans had placed on London's livery companies. While the majority of the City's twelve "great" companies managed to raise and pay their part of the £50,000 loan, they often did so largely under duress. Outstanding debts and the economic strains of wartime taxation left liverymen and freemen to sometimes consider their situations in rather stark terms: lend or face summons. Failure to pay would in all cases result in exertion of additional pressure by the Committee for the Advance of Money. Dire cases, as we have seen, risked sequestration. In the end, London's twelve leading companies were asked to raise £38,300 – more than three-fourths of the £50,000 loan to send a relief force to Gloucester. Collecting the remaining £11,300 remained important. As was the case with previous loans, "lesser" trade guilds made payments that reveal the wider dimensions of wartime finance, and suggest, at times in idiosyncratic terms, the extent to which segments of the City were supportive or discouraging of parliament's effort. In the case of the loan to mobilize for the relief of Gloucester, the main impediment to collection was not simply a matter of faith and fidelity towards parliament's cause, but it was now a matter of widespread impecunity and potential bankruptcy.

Although their records are far less detailed than those of the leading twelve, evidence suggests that London's other liveries dealt with pressures that were largely the same.[38] It is telling that the issue of payment was taken up on 29 September when parliament ordered that "special care" be taken "to negotiate with the City" for collecting £20,000 of the £50,000 loan.[39] Like their preeminent counterparts, many of London's smaller liveries promptly did what they could to deliver cash to the Guildhall. Several companies paid outright. Cordwainers, for instance, delivered their £400 without delay.[40] Likewise, the Turners, a company that boasted a long record of support for the cause, and which had even paid £1 13s 4d to dine with Mayor Pennington on two occasions, quickly sent along their £85. This sum, they noted, was simply their "allotted" payment made "towards the 50000l."[41]

Other trading companies meanwhile offered a range of responses to Pennington's request. Some were clearly concerned that the loan might strain their day-to-day operations; others, meanwhile, expressed frustration over their valuations and assessments. In most cases the burden was passed on to a handful of wealthy liverymen who were willing and able to lend. Five brewers pledged £165 toward their £690 assessment, for example. Although generous, their payments covered less than a third of the total, leaving £525 outstanding. On 22 August, senior members of the company met and agreed to sell plate "to the utmost value thereof." This allowed them to raise an additional £298 9s 8d, which appears to have been an adequate sum for settling the matter.[42] Saddlers, meanwhile, simply recorded that they were "altogether unwillinge" to pay their £600 assessment "in regard of the greate sums they owe[d in interest] already." Their tone changed remarkaby when the assessment was reduced to the "sum of five hundred pounds," which they believed to be a more accurate assessment since it was based on "old proportion of one hundred quarters of wheate" in their stores. The full £500 was forwarded to the Guildhall on 22 August, with £300 coming from a single wealthy member, John Burt, £100 from John Bardwell, and the final £100 from the company treasury.[43] Tallow Chandlers agreed to pay their £650 outright, but they soon found that they were only able to collect £500. £300 of this came from Andrew Walker, a freeperson of the company who expected that he would be repaid his principal with £12 interest by 21 February 1644. Yet again, the Committee for the Advance of Money stepped in to demand that they fulfill their obligation to raise the remaning £150 that was outstanding. The company responded to requests in February by claiming that they could "by noe meanes raise any further or other summe of money towards the payment of the said 650l." They were finally ordered to forward the names of company members so that the Committee could deal with matters directly. As of July 1644, Walker had only been paid back half of his principal, but this came with £15 in interest.[44] Similar issues arose when the painters and stainers sought to defer the issue of their £75 loan at a meeting on 18 August due to "the smallness of appearance" on their members. But the issue came back to haunt them when the Committee for the Advance of Money pursued the payment, which led to a petition about "the takeing of £60 imposed on the Company" in February.[45] Presumably this led to action since company minutes make no further mention of the matter.

Parliament seemed altogether willing to overlook smaller shortcomings in the payment of loan assessments, or in some cases allow companies extra time to raise their loans. Blacksmiths scraped together £50 of their £80 loan by 29 September; no further record was made of their outstanding £30 debt.[46] Proceeding with caution, inholders paid £150 of their £300 assessment immediately and decided to keep the other £150 "in the Companies cheast until farther order bee taken."[47] Stalling, as they had learned from experience, could be to their benefit. Tillers and Bricklayers "speedilie" raised their £125 by selling company plate. They apparently did not raise the full amount, however, as it took until 7 February for them to take the last £25 "out of the house stock."[48] £125 requested from plumbers led to the raising of £100 "where it cann bee had." Although £25 short, the matter seemed thus settled.[49]

Entrepreneurial interest can be detected behind some lending. Robert Campion paid outright the entire £250 assessed to the Cordwainers. Campion's terms for lending were simple enough: he stipulated that his money was to be repaid in full and with interest no later than 23 February of the following year.[50] Campion's willingness to front the money may have owed less to his fidelity to parliament's cause and to the relief of

Gloucester than it did his hope for a return of 8 percent. Fellow company members seemed all too happy to have some additional time to raise the cash. Campion, like many other lenders, was a successful merchant and investor. Some of his £250 may have come from a £1,000 investment that he recently withdrew from the East India Company. The promise of a return by February may ultimately have seemed a propitious wartime investment.[51]

£50,000 was of course a substantial sum, and the matter of outstanding debts and unpaid loans weighed on lenders. But the loan was in the end one of several financial expedients that parliament had come to depend upon. Merchant Adventurers, for instance, had singlehandedly loaned some £90,000 to parliament over the course of 1641–2. In early October 1643, they were called upon again to raise £30,000 for parliament's navy, which they apparently did without issue. Cash was not unobtainable, but lenders had grown increasingly cautious in light of unpaid debts and widespread uncertainty. More important than the amount of the £50,000 loan, moreover, was the cumulative impact that rasing the money had on the day-to-day operations of companies. The range of corporate responses to the August loan suggest the impact that more than a year of lending had on the metropolis, and more specifically it exposes webs of metropolitan finance that spanned from the corporations themselves to parochial communities that sometimes depended on company charity (and perhaps vice versa in terms of the loan to the Salters and Grocers). Here, then, were a series of burdened communities caught between the ideological parameters of a war (couched in all the normalized language of necessity and defense) and the practicalities of lending.

Trepidation on the part of livery companies might therefore seem well founded; indeed, repayment of the loan from August 1643 did not begin until May 1645, and when it did finally commence only a handful of companies received a third of their initial investment along with interest on that third. Already, in April 1644, companies were being asked by Mayor Wollaston and Common Council "to forbeare their monies lent towards the 50000l" on account of a desire to "mainteyne a considerable number of horse" and to preserve momentum in the wake of "the great victory given by" Waller and Sir William Balfour at Cheriton.[52] What, it had to be asked, would prevent parliament from seeking yet more loans? Although most liveries maintained day-to-day operations, many were left strained, and in some exceptional cases diminished. Numerous companies, as we have seen, were reduced to selling plate, objects that were of intrinsic, and in some cases historical, value. If feigned for political reasons, or whether due to real financial strain, some trade companies ultimately failed to meet the challenge of raising the £50,000. Indeed, a handful of corporations remained embattled over the loan well into the middle of the decade; others, like the Cordwainers, were still reeling over the impact of lending to parliament into the early 1650s.[53] Ordered by the Lord Mayor and backed by the Committee for the Advance of Money, the majority of the £50,000 loan nevertheless quickly reached parliamentary coffers, providing lifeblood for the expedition to relieve Gloucester. Although there was little to suggest it at the time, Pennington's request for £50,000 would mark the end of direct lending toward parliament's war by London's liveries. Depleted and strained to the breaking point, companies could no longer shoulder the burden of being parliament's financial stopgap.

Gloucester, Newbury, and Alton

Confident that his combined forces might still take Gloucester, Charles was said to have claimed that "Waller is extinct, and Essex cannot come."[54] The king's assessment, and indeed his presumptions about the ease with which Gloucester could be wrested from parliamentarian control, proved misplaced. As one parliamentarian captain later proclaimed, the city "manfully withstood" the siege and successfully repelled "the fury of the Cavaliers."[55] While livery companies scrambled to pay their new loan, parliament was busy determining how to best save their besieged city in the west. On 18 August, parliament ordered troops to repair to their colors and prepare for departure. Those who failed would be rounded up and "proceeded against according to the Law of War." Next, as we have seen, parliament authorized the impressment of 2,000 new soldiers from London, Westminster, Southwark, and areas within the Bills of Mortality.[56] Whitaker remarked that the newly raised men would serve to supplement four active regiments of "the City Forces."[57]

Little is known about the quality and quantity of the impressed. The rumor mill that was *Aulicus* suggested that the men were mostly "popish Walloones" who were "lately quartered at Putney"; others were apparently being scrounged from the dregs of Greenwich and upriver at Kingston.[58] Efforts under way for Waller and Manchester seem to have pushed the search well beyond the City. On 21 August, the Militia Committee issued orders for citizens to "shut up their shops" and "continue them so shut untill *Glocester* be relieved." In the meantime, trained band and auxiliary forces were ordered to muster so that they could be selected for service "by lot."[59] Six regiments marched out of the capital in total, including the Red and Blue regiments, the Red, Blue, and Orange auxiliaries, and the personal regiment of Sergeant-Major-General Randall Mainwaring. Essex's combined London Brigade, made up of veteran militiamen and some newly impressed men, was said to total some 15,000, most of whom came directly from London and its surrounding environs.

Looking after their own, Londoners took special care to ensure that the departing soliders were adequately supplied and refreshed. Churchwardens from St. Bartholomew-by-the-Exchange paid 2s 6d to "Mr Fox for [a] Cart to Carry the bread and chees to the artillery" so that his mustering men could be fed.[60] The inhabitants of St. Mary Abchurch, St. Mary Aldermanbury, St. Mary Woolchurch, St. Michael Cornhill, St. Botolph Aldersgate, St. Botolph Billingsgate, and St. Lawrence Jewry took similar actions.[61] The parishioners at St. Bride's were among the most active supporters when it came time to victual soldiers. They collected bread and cheese from "about the parish," and paid for baskets to cart food all the way to Windsor. Rather than wait idly, remaining regiments set to improving the City's defenses. Rowland Wilson and the Orange regiment, for instance, engaged in "trench work" on the Lines of Communication. Thankful for their efforts, St. Bride's churchwardens paid £1 16s for "two hogsheads of beere" that were "carried into the fields when Captayne Wilson and his Company went to diggin." An additional 8s was collected the following month to pay "for bread wyne and Cheese" that was given to soldiers working to maintain City fortifications.[62] Should Gloucester fall, Londoners wanted to be certain that their defenses were prepared.

On 26 August, Essex departed the capital at the head of his impressive new army. That same day, Common Council agreed that Londoners should pay fifty subsidies, a highly divisive measure that amounted to a forced loan in all but name.[63] Indeed, the prospect of raising the fifty subsidies led to a report on 9 September that "divers freemen" of London had "of late absented and withdrawn themselves and their families" out of the City and "into the Country" so that they might "avoid payment of the monies imposed upon them by ordinance of Parliament and Acts of Common Council." London's belligerents, meanwhile, remained eager to see Waller at the head of his own army; espying that fears over an attack on the City might still be used to legitimize the raising of a new force, Common Council approved of a measure whereby the Militia Committee "shall use their best indeavours" to raise "aswell auxiliaries" who would be "under the comand of Sir William Waller on this present Expedicion for the safety of this City."[64] Waller – having finally gained his commission – spent the next month busily seeking new recruits in London while Essex marched "with his warlike bands of Souldiers" toward Gloucester.[65]

If decidedly less impressive than Essex's London brigade, Waller nevertheless managed to cobble together an army. Slow progress once again made impressment necessary. On 4 September, Agostini reported that the matter of raising men was entirely in the hands of "the city of London," which had "usurped practically absolute power" and thereby "formed a council for the militia composed of citizens with the supreme authority to do what is considered necessary for self defence." Refusal to enlist could be met by "court martial" or "even with death." Agostini lamented that the course of actions had led to "an oath worse than the first" and which was imposed on Londoners "one by one." The actual "pressing" of men, he reported, was done "with so much inhumanity that many of the objectors have been injured and five killed."[66] On 7 September, lots were drawn, placing the Green auxiliaries and the Yellow regiment under Waller's command.[67]

Five days later, on 12 September, the Commons issued orders for impressing yet another 5,000 soldiers. 2,000 of these were to be found within the Lines of Communication and parishes within the Bills of Mortality. The remaining 3,000 were to come from the surrounding counties of Essex, Kent, Middlesex, Surrey, Hertfordshire, and Sussex. The deplorable conditions of the recent "press" demanded that new measures be taken. Extra incentive to enlist was granted in the shape of an "Ordinance for Indemnity" for watermen, which amounted to a guarantee "that the Time of such Apprentices" spent under Waller's command would count toward their indentured apprenticeships.[68] The next day, the House appointed a Committee of Accounts for Waller's Army, which was headed by John Trenchard, MP for Dorset. The Ordinance for Indemnity proved to be of little or no avail. For one, Essex had delayed Waller's commission for far too long, despite, as *Aulicus* could taunt, "the readinesse of the *three Houses* (the House of *three Lords*, the *Lower House*, and the *Common-Counsell*) to recruit his Forces."[69] Even the parliamentary newsbook *Mercirus Britanicus* commented on Essex's delay, claiming "*Waller* hath got a Commission, but with such restrictions as will do him little good."[70] The second issue stemmed from Trenchard's Committee of Accounts, which, as John Adair has suggested, "tended to pick and choose among warrants which they received from Waller, favouring captains of their own political persuasion."[71] This observation was corroborated yet again by Agostini, who wrote on 18 September that Waller had "more officers than soldiers" and faced extreme "difficulty" when "obtaining volunteers and the unsatisfactory service to be expected from pressed men."[72] Protracted as the process was, Waller had finally found his army. Their condition remained to be seen. The royalist William Levett observed the forces mustering in Finsbury Field on 26 September, and estimated that there were 13,000 men-at-arms, an impressive figure given that five City regiments were already fielded with Essex.[73]

Reports soon reached the capital of parliament's great military success at Gloucester and Newbury, along with mention of the admirable performance of London's soldiers. According to one account of Newbury, the City brigade "were often charged by the horse and foot" under Rupert's command, but they "stood to it with undaunted resolution."[74] Later in the day they held crucial ground to protect parliament's baggage train. Sergeant Henry Foster, who fought that day in the Red regiment, offered an alternative and particularly detailed account of the march from London that was printed on 2 October. Foster acknowledged that the nearly 5,000 Londoners who marched out from the metropolis were unaccustomed to the conditions of war, and in particular the nights when they had to "lay all in the open field upon plowd-land, without straw, having neither bread nor water." But cold evenings passed and hunger could be satiated. It was, Foster claimed, a shared sense of God's favor that "enabled our Souldiers to undergoe it cheerfully." Their true test came at Newbury. London's Red and Blue regiments experienced some of the most "dreadful" moments of the battle; both withstood repeat charges by royalist horse and cannon fire so that "mens bowels and brains flew in our faces." But God once again "gave unto them" the "courage and valour" needed to fight on, and so, by the end of the day, it could be reported that Londoners were "fighting like Lions in every place." Londoners lost several noteworthy men in the fight, including Captain Richard Hunt from St. Mary Woolchurch, Captain George Mosse from St. Mary Aldermanbury, Captain John Juxon of the City Horse, and William Tucker, Lieutenant Colonel of the Red regiment.[75] Few, in the end, could deny that the City's soliders had fought admirably. Clarendon, for instance, later recalled that members of the trained bands and auxiliary regiments "were in truth the preservation of that Army that day."[76]

The days that followed saw only minor skirmishing, and so Essex's forces soon headed back toward London. They reached the Lines of Communication on Thursday 28 September, where they were greeted by thousands of cheering onlookers. The Lord Mayor, City sheriffs, aldermen, and common councilors rode out on horseback to profess "their great affection unto them" and follow them on to Temple Bar where they were "entertained" with great fanfare.[77] The returning troops basked in praise, with "most of them (imitating the ancient Romans)" by marching "through the City with greene boughs in their hats in signall of victory, and also with all their Colours and Ensignes, which (to their perpetuall honour) they brought away triumphantly."[78] Churchwardens from St. Bride's, which sat adjacent to Fleet Bridge, paid 2s each so that ringers could keep bells pealing throughout the day's celebrations, while Holy Trinity the Less in north Queenhithe paid 1s 6d for ringers to do the same.[79] With the return of the brigade, Londoners could breathe another collective, if short-lived, sigh of relief; Gloucester, and thereby the west, seemed saved.

If reason for celebration, victory at Newbury also signaled the end to lingering hopes for a general rising. The outcome of the battle did much to revive the reputation of the Lord General, who returned to the matter of Waller's commission after his triumphant return to the City. On 3 October, the earl informed the Lords of his opinion that Waller should remain under his command. Four days later, Essex pressed the matter further by threatening to "resign and go beyond the seas" if Waller retained his original commission.[80] His pettish claims had their desired effect. A dedicant to the cause above all else, Waller proclaimed himself "ready to receive and obey his Excellency's Commission," and thus he agreed to the termination of his prior fraught, short-lived, and ultimately ineffective one.[81] Waller's compliance amounted to little more than papering over cracks. Essex's threat did even less to foster the good will of London's militants. Rather, it served to reaffirm lingering hopes that parliament might one day establish an army free from his sole command. If seemingly settled for the time being, Essex's move assured that the concerns that elevated Waller in the eyes of militants would persist into the following year.

But moods soon darkened for other reasons. Rebuffed at Newbury, royalist forces managed to rally and take Reading on 3 October, refreshing fears over a royalist advance. Six days later, Common Council passed an act stipulating that the nightly watch should consist of no fewer than 1,097 individuals – all of whom would be provided by City wards. Later that month, during Pennington's penultimate Common Council session, it was agreed that inspections should be conducted in order to assess the City's total stores of grain and that means should be devised for establishing new secured granaries, a precaution that might help maintain the capital in case of a siege.[82] At the same time, the Militia Committee urged Common Council to ready seven regiments of the trained bands and auxiliaries so that they could "march according to the discipline of warr with the forces under command of his Excellency to regayne the Towne of Redding."[83] On Tuesday, 17 October, the Militia Committee followed up the City orders with a declaration "that was published in severall places about *London*" and required all soldiers to "randevuos" the following morning in St. James's Fields. Soldiers were expected to arrive "completely armed, and fit for service by seven of the Clock." Tardiness of an hour would result in a fine of 5s; two hours would be 10s. Showing up after noon would result in the closure of shops and potential "expulsion out of the lines of Communication." London's vestries were expected to prepare tables that would stand "fixed within the respective Churches wherein shall be inscribed the Names of all such Soldiers." Each of these would, the Committee professed, stand as a "testimony of their good affections and a perpetuall memorial to the honour of them and their Posterity."[84]

Honour was without doubt an important motivator for some, but clearly other measures were needed when it came time for citizens to close up their shops and leave their families for war. Bulstrode Whitelocke, for one, marveled at the commitment shown by veterans and new enlistees. He wondered at London's "gallant" regiments and the "strange affection" they bore toward the fighting cause. How, he asked, could men be convinced to trade "a soft bed, close courtains and a warm chamber" for "the hard and cold earth?" What could possibly drive them "to leave the choicest and most delicate fare of meates and wines for a little course bread, and durty water, with a foule pipe of tobacco?" Who, he asked, would dare depart from "pleasing discourse and conversation of friends, wives and children" and instead endure "the dreadfull whistling of bullets, and the shriekes and cryes of dying bodyes dropping dead att ones feet?" Joining the fight, Whitelocke concluded, must have more to do with commitment to "religion and to the rights and liberties of the countrey" than it did to the fines threatened by either the Militia Committee or Common Council.[85] Like many of his contemporaries, Whitelocke had come to associate Londoners' martial valor with a distinct politico-religious idealism, a romantic if perhaps unreasonably broad notion of the extent to which the City's inhabitants were committed to parliament's cause, and one that bore some similarity to assumptions made months earlier about the success that could come from a general rising. Whitelocke's assessment likely mattered far more to observers than it did to participants, and especially those of the latter group who were pressed to join and threatened with expulsion for failing to muster.

Indeed, England's autumn weather had a way of dispelling optimism. On Monday, 16 October, seven regiments of the London trained bands marched out of the capital under Waller's command. Lieutenant Elias Archer of the Yellow regiment recorded their progress as they headed westward. On 5 November, Londoners came up against a "very cold night" and were forced to quarter "in the fields neere a Village." The conditions proved "tedious to many of our men which never were accustomed to such lodging."[86] Spirits sunk further upon engagement with the enemy at Basing House in Old Basing, Hampshire. The Westminster Liberty regiment suffered badly on the third day of the siege; their first line fired outside of range of the enemy and prompted their later ranks to open fire upon "their own front," a mistake which broke their entire formation so that they "slew and wounded many of their own."[87] The siege ended in utter failure, driving morale lower yet. Waller's attempt to rally spirits led to opposing chants of " 'Home, Home,' " and left him with little option but to "threaten to pistol any of them that should use that base language." Writing to Speaker Lenthall on 16 November, Waller explained that his inexperienced and disobedient soldiers had forced him to halt progress at Farnham. Soon thereafter a full "mutiny broke out" with the London brigade refusing to "march one foot further."[88]

On 12 December, Waller rallied his downbeat and homesick men for one last effort. Most were under the impression that they would be "discharged" and allowed to "march homewards on the morrow." But Waller had other plans. According to Archer, Waller rode to "the head of every Regiment" where he "gave us many thanks, for our service past, and told us that according to his promise and our expectation we were to be discharged" the following day. Waller went on, however, raising the important point that reputation was at stake, and that departing early would strip away "much honour in respect of the bad success we had in our chiefest service." Convinced by Waller's speech, Londoners apparently gave their "full consent to stay" and proceed.

Their opportunity arrived the following day at Alton where the City's Red, Green, and Yellow regiments played a decisive part in the defeat and capture of nearly 1,000 royalists under the command of the earl of Crawford.[89] Sir Ralph Hopton's southern forces were served a crushing blow. Keeping his promise, Waller next granted the soldiers their discharge, allowing them to march back to London in time for Christmas.

If recalcitrant and at times mutinous, the London soliders who marched into the west during the autumn of 1643 nevertheless provided an invaluable service to parliament's war effort. In a year that was characterized at first by far more royalist successes than defeats, Londoners had financed, joined, and deployed brigades that helped to secure crucially important victories against the king. Some 10,000 Londoners marched with Essex to relieve Gloucester on 26 August; less than a month later, on 20 September, a City brigade played a pivotal role at Newbury. Yet again in early October, Londoners marched out under the command of William Waller. And although they grew more wearisome and homesick by the day, they also stood their ground to earn a decisive victory on 13 December at Alton. The path had thus been cleared for the entry of the Covenanter army, a development that owed in no small part to efforts by City soliders.

New political leaderships, the Committee of Both Kingdoms, and Basil Brooke's plot

Flagging enthusiasm and the troublingly persistent threat of royalist attacks helped to cement the view that a Scottish army might save parliament's war. Following their string of defeats in the spring, parliament had already sent commissioners in July to "persuade" the Scots "to join with us in the common Cause." Their undertaking eventually paid off with the first official reading of the Solemn League and Covenant on 26 August – incidentally, the same day that Essex departed to Gloucester and the same day that Common Council approved the payment of an additional fifty subsidies for parliament's army.[90] A copy of the Covenant was next sent to the Assembly of Divines in Westminster who set about considering the "lawfulness of taking it."[91] With the Assembly's approval, the oath was administered in both Houses in September, was given to Londoners in October, and was next ordered to be taken throughout the nation in January 1644.[92] Pym had long sought an alliance with the Scots, but the fashioning of the covenant was, as Hexter has rightly acknowledged, "the work of young Sir Henry Vane and the Scot, Archibald Johnston of Warriston."[93] Vane and Johnston's roles in drafting the architecture of the Covenant, as we shall see, helped to lay the foundation for their leadership in parliament's Committee of Both Kingdoms, the successor to the Committee of Safety. More importantly, the adoption of the Solemn League and Covenant and the arrival of Scottish soldiers altered the dynamics of the civil war, and by extension the politics of mobilization in the capital. Although London was to remain an integral component of parliament's strategy, City forces would soon take a back seat to serve in a supportive role, sending out brigades when needed. With parliament's military hopes newly cast upon the Scots, Londoners were asked to bolster the effort in other ways: expectations were that they would continue to supply the sinews of war and that they would maintain the Lines of Communication, but added to these were increased responsibilities with regards to the care and maintenance of sick and wounded soldiers.

Financing parliament's new allies was the first order of the day. Prior to marching south, the Scottish forces required funds to cover outstanding arrears for their previous service in Ireland. As we have seen, the response to the most recent loan of £50,000 left the prospect of requesting more money from livery companies out of the question. This meant that other innovative programs for raising money needed to be pursued. An early effort came by way of *An Order for the speedy raising of Money for the Advancing of the Scotch Army*, which was printed on 7 October 1643 and distributed throughout London in light of "the desperate designes and Plots of Papists, Prelates, and other ill-affected persons." Again the order was for "the Ministers of every Parish," along with "Churchwardens of every Parish to cause an Assembly of the Parishioners to morrow [*sic*] after Sermon in the afternoone" to subscribe what "summes of money" they could. Again the letter bore the name of Lord Mayor Pennington.[94] More robust programs started on 28 September when parliament established its Committee for Compounding with Delinquents, which met at Goldsmiths' Hall. The Committee's first task was to meet with the Lord Mayor and Common Council "to appoint a Committee to meete with a committee of this house for the raysinge of money for the Scots." On 12 October, the Committee was granted "power to present the names of such Persons as they shall thinke fitt and able to send Moneys for the service within the Cittyes of Lond[on] and Westminster and parishes within the Bills of Mortallity for the borrowing of such summes of Money of them as shallbe thought fitt to be assessed upon them by Ordinances of both houses." That same day, £40,000 was assigned as a first payment "to the Scotts out of the Sequestracion Moneys."[95] Two days later, on 16 October, parliament passed an ordinance for a loan of £200,000 to be guaranteed according to sequestered estates and the sale of "delinquents' coals."[96] According to Coates, the loan, which was overseen by the newly formed Committee for Scottish Affairs at Goldsmiths' Hall, would amount to "the largest voluntary subscription" made to parliament "after the propositions."[97] The first printed ordinance from 27 October called for "a free and voluntary loane" of £66,666 13s 4d, which would be one-third of the total proposed for "the speedy bringing of our Brethren of Scotland into this Realme."[98] Londoners responded positively to the ordinance, paying approximately 85 percent of their proposed £80,000 sum.[99] Be it for eagerness to alleviate their own burdens of war, or due to newfound confidence in the loan's security, raising the £200,000 amounted to a rare unqualified success. Collectors from St. Bartholomew-by-the-Exchange, where John Lightfoote served as lecturer, delivered in just under £268 36s 8d, with several parishioners promising to lend an additional £74. Just seven parishioners refused to lend toward "our brethren of Scotland towards payment of ther Army raised for our defence," while six others could not due to their being "out of towne," including "Dr Zouche" who was "att Oxford."[100] Although parish accounts remain conspicuously silent on the matter, Robert Ballie noted on 17 November that "some" £30,000 had already been collected "from twenty-eight parishes of London."[101] Throughout the war, Richard Waring and Michael Herring, treasurers for the Committee of Scottish Affairs, sat at a subcommittee for provisioning at Turners' Hall, where they used the money to fulfill contracts that ranged from securing victuals such as peas and oatmeal to ordering clothing and muskets.[102]

Aside from its success, the new loan underscored the extent to which London's mobilizing efforts had changed. On the one hand, the anticipation of a foreign professional fighting force stood to relieve pressure on the City. On the other, it led to the rapid ratification of an agreement with the Scots, who on 29 November officially agreed to a treaty to send their armies south. Marching on English soil under the command of Alexander Leslie, earl of Leven, would be some "18000 foote 3000 horse and between 4 and 500 Dragoneer[s]" along with an impressive "120 great guns, and other train of Ammunition, very full and large."[103] It was no coincidence that the

29 November treaty called for exactly "18,000 foote," a force comparable in size to London's trained bands and auxiliaries. The Scottish army thus provided parliament with the first viable alternate to an army cobbled out of volunteers and militias. It was, moreover, an army made up of many seasoned veterans; many had served in the Bishops' Wars or further afield on the Continent during the Thirty Years' War; doubtless their expertise would be a welcomed addition to parliament's effort.[104] Some Londoners must have wondered if the arrival of the professionals meant that they might be able to trade in their muskets for brooms and go back to shopkeeping.

From this point forward, concerted efforts were made to maintain close communications between the new Lord Mayor, Common Council, and parliament's new Committee of Both Kingdoms. The political leanings of the Committee, which was established by ordinance on 16 February, and was tasked with managing the joint parliamentarian and Scottish war effort, can be gleaned in part by its membership. Several members of the new Committee came over from the previous Committee of Safety, including Essex, Northumberland, and Saye and Sele. New peers included Manchester, Wharton, and Robartes, a veteran of Edgehill and Newbury. Appointees from the Commons included William Armyne, Samuel Browne, John Crewe, Oliver Cromwell, Oliver St. John, Robert Wallop, and both Henry Vanes. Each of these men, save perhaps for the more moderate leaning Crewe, should be counted as a vigorous opponent of the king. The younger of the two Vanes brought with him a particular vehemence and eagerness to manage parliament's fight. Other holdovers from the Committee of Safety included William Waller, William Pierrepoint, and the militants John Glynne and Sir Philip Stapleton. Scottish members included the earl of Loudon, Viscount Maitland, Jonston of Wariston, and Robert Barclay. In his attempt to characterize the Committee, Wallace Notestein concluded that proceedings offer "foot-notes on the involved and subterranean policy of Sir Henry Vane and his friends." Although there is, on balance, little to suggest that Vane managed the affairs of the Committee of Both Kingdoms to the same extent that Pym had supposedly managed those of the Committee of Safety, it became increasingly clear in early 1644 that the new Committee would allow Vane to pursue his distinct political interests.[105]

Vane's energetic leadership proved consequential for London's mobilization; for one, it soon became clear that Vane did in fact have every intention of inheriting Pym's mantle of leadership. In her political biography on the subject, Violet Rowe has suggested that Vane had remained content "cooperating with Pym and St John, and to a much lesser extent and only on occasions for specific purposes, with Marten and Glyn." But the balancing act changed precipitously in late 1643 and early 1644; Pym's death and Marten's ejection from the House left ample room for Vane to establish a new role for himself as the leader of parliament's war party. Prior to realizing this goal, Vane and his allies needed to wrestle with a second emerging political coalition that had formed around Denzil Holles, a peace proponent and friend to Essex in the Commons. For Rowe, Vane's ultimate success is revealed, in part at least, by the fact that "the king himself" took to "referring to Vane as the leader of a party in the House." For David Scott, who identified Vane's group as "the Say-St John group," it became clear that, with the backing of their new Scottish allies, parliament's war proponents soon found themselves "in the driving seat at Westminster."[106] City leaders, as it turns out, often found their interests closely aligned with the dominant Vane group, an association that was to have serious implications for mobilizing efforts in London.

The extent to which disunity plagued the parliamentarian coalition over the winter of 1643–4 is perhaps best illustrated by the aftermath of Basil Brooke's plot, an effort to divide parliament and the City. Historians have claimed that the plot afforded an important but ultimately underutilized opportunity for parliamentarians. It was, as Andrew Hopper notes, at best "a supposed plot." Geoffrey Smith, meanwhile, found it to be little more than "an insignificant and obscure conspiracy."[107] If close to the mark, their assessments deserve some slight qualification, even if only for the sake of London's part in the matter. Indeed, there is evidence to suggest that Brooke's plot, like Waller's plot before it, left contemporaries gripped. Signifcantly, the entire affair was quickly seized upon and readily manipulated as a means to align the interests of Lord Mayor Wollaston and Common Council with Vane, St. John, and their allies. The entire affair unfolded over a relatively brief period beginning in late December 1643 and ending in January 1644, but it was from its first "discovery" widely sensationalized. Brooke, a Catholic, had managed to facilitate communications between the king and queen and several leading Londoners. Some of these connections, as Lindley has suggested, enabled communication between what would otherwise be "unlikely associates."[108] They included Theophilus Riley, the former radical activist and the City's scout-master general, Thomas Violet, a goldsmith who had previously failed to pay taxes and was jailed under then-Wollaston's authority as City sheriff in June 1643, and Colonel Read, who one critic considered a "grand Jesuitied Papist," who had, despite his religious convictions, played an important role intervening on behalf of Protestants in Ireland. The conspirators apparently met in King's Bench jail and took up a correspondence under code names such as Riley's "Man in the Moone." Outside of prison, their meetings continued "at the three Craines," a tavern near to the river "in Vintree." Evidence of their plotting was made clear by the timely "discovery" of two letters. One came by way of Lord Digby to Brooke and made reference to a second letter, which was apparently addressed from the king to Mayor Wollaston. The main aim of the conspirators, who used Benyon's petition from 24 February 1642 as a model for their plan, was to divide parliament and the City by persuading the Lord Mayor and common councilors to issue peace proposals, to oppose the alliance with the Scots, and to recognize the legitimacy of the parliament in Oxford over the one sitting in Westminster. At the very least, the conspirators hoped to foment divisions that would help to "impede the proceedings of Parliament" and prevent "the Scots coming into this kingdome."[109] Once discovered, Brooke, Riley, and Violet were committed to the Tower. Brooke remained there until May 1646, when he was transferred back to King's Bench, while Violet, for his part, remained until 1652.[110]

Once revealed, the plot served to have the opposite of its intended effect. A Common Hall was scheduled to meet on 8 January and members of a special delegation were appointed to deliver invitations of attendance from the Guildhall to parliament. That same day, parliament sent members of a special committee that could "communicate the Matter of the late Design." The committee included Henry Vane, Gilbert Gerard, Arthur Haselrig, and then Alderman Pennington.[111] Two days after the meeting, and in light of "theis tymes of yminent danger," Common Council placed keys for "all the severall gates" of the City "into the custodie of the Sherifs of London."[112]

A second meeting came ten days later, on 18 January, during a day of public thanksgiving. London councilors nominated John Fowke to deliver invitations to parliament, the Lord General, and the Scottish Commissioners. The day's events began with a sermon given at Christ Church Newgate Street by Stephen Marshall, who set the tone for the gathering when he asked attendants to "feast" their *"soules with the fat things of Gods house"* before they "feast" their *"bodies."* Marshall proceeded to discuss Chronicles 12:38–40, and the view that God's guidance was the reason why "so many treacherous desines, secret treasons, and open violences" had been avoided. He next asked his audience to take note of the quality of their fellow attendees, whom he introduced directly. Essex and Warwick were also in attendance, and by their sides sat an "abundance of noble and resolute Commanders" who had "faces like unto Lions." With them was the entire *"Representative body of the City"* and the *"Militia"* who had earned "the honour of" preserving London, which stood resolutely as "the greatest meanes of the salvation of the whole kingdome." Next were the Scottish Commissioners, who by Marshall's estimation represented "the wisdom and affection of their whole Church and Nation." All had apparently come together in an expressed "unity of hearts, and concurrence of spirit."[113]

Thomas Juxon, a captain in the City's Green regiment who was present, recalled the day's events in his journal, noting attendance that included "the Houses of Parliament, the Scots commissioners and assembly," along "with his excellency and many commanders." After Marshall's sermon, the group processed on to Merchant Taylors' Hall, while "the trained bands, on each side, made them a guard." Mayor Wollaston proceeded on foot and was followed closely by the sheriffs and aldermen who rode on horseback. Flanking the City leaders and parliamentary officials were soldiers and throngs of onlookers.[114] The afternoon feasting – which purportedly cost £4,000 and came only days after Common Council had revived the controversial plans for a weekly meal tax – provided an opportunity for the City to express their "great happiness" for the "contynuall vigilance" shown by the parliament toward "the Safety and Preservacion not only of the Kingdome in generall but of this City in particular."[115] Dinner was followed by a singing of a psalm before leftovers were cleared from tables and carried off to feed refugees from Bristol and others in "several prisons." Like previous plots, Basil Brooke's had been conveniently discovered and thus conveniently backfired. Juxon recalled that the "design which was intended for division" had thus provided an "occasion for a brotherly meeting" and a chance to "counter-mine" divisions.[116] Good as this may have seemed, it was more papering over cracks.

The thanksgiving, for one, seemed to serve war party interests best; beyond sermons and feasting, the occasion led to renewed commitments for a mutual defense between parliament and Common Council, a pact that helped to align City interests with those of the Committee of Both Kingdoms. Soon thereafter the Commons sent "their hearty and cheerefull thanks" to the court for "their great expressions of Love in their Late enterteynment at marchant tailors hall."[117] Besides the generation of a ceremonious affirmation of friendship and unity of purpose, the uncovering of the plot revealed the persistence of a royalist – and indeed, in this case, "papist" – fifth column within London. Although leadership in parliament and the City had changed, the threat to the metropolis remained the same; hostile elements still lurked up and down the City. In light of this, Wollaston's commitment to the fighting cause seemed beyond reproach; the new Lord Mayor, who had supported previous radical plans such as the weekly meal, who himself served as colonel to the City Yellow regiment, and who acted as president of Bethlem and Bridewell, was to remain sympathetic to war party interests.[118] As telling, perhaps, was the fact that John Fowke and Alderman Pennington, now veterans of the cause, each played a part facilitating the arrangements.

Another clarifying political development came in the wake of the plot's revelation. On 26 January, Common Council met to discuss "a humble peticion of the Lord Maior Aldermen and Comons of the Citie of London in Comon Councell assembled." Their petition left few to doubt which side of parliamentary politics the new City government landed on. In this, they openly called for the removal "of all such Comanders and Officers in the Armie under the command of his Excellency the Earle of Essex which are conceived unfit." Such commanders and officers, the London petitioners believed, were the root cause of the "divisions betwixt the parliament and Citie." Reforming the Lord General's army, they hoped, would heal the "spirit of divison which hath walked in the darke betwixt the parliament and the Citie" and which "hath ben alike active betwixt his Excelencie his Army and Citie." The petition, which was delivered to parliament three days later, was presented by the same Londoners who had delivered the invitation to dine at Merchant Taylors' Hall. In this, they hoped to see proof that officers in Essex's army were "well affected to the cause" and further that "there may be such a new establishment such as a Councell of warr" tasked with bringing about "disciplyne in the said Army." Thus, London's militants hoped they might finally bring the Lord General to heel.[119] The revocation of Waller's commission meant that they would need to seek other means to implement their interests. What better opportunity than the Lord General's own army, a force which had already absorbed considerable numbers of Londoners on the eve of the march to relieve Gloucester.

If a regular means to lodge complaints, the petition also signaled an important escalation and entrenchment of the rivalry between belligerent segments of London and parliament and the peace-seeking earl of Essex and his supporters. By March 1644, parliament had successfully established a committee to investigate the composition of Essex's army. By November, the same committee would be responsible for reporting on divisions and accusations that had arisen between Cromwell and the earl of Manchester – forerunners of the later Self-Denying Ordinance.

Within the scope of rapidly diverging politics, Basil Brooke's plot and the subsequent 18 January thanksgiving celebrations helped to establish a limited – but nontheless important – unity of interests. The City petition of just over a week later made certain that the fractious political divisions of the previous year would, if shifted in their application, remain largely intact; in place of Mayor Pennington's close association with the Committee of Safety, there had arisen a new alliance between Mayor Wollaston and Vane and St. John's emergent Committee of Both Kingdoms. The persistence of divisions made one thing certain: the earl of Essex would continue to see his sole leadership over parliament's armies challenged. Avoiding another debacle like the one that surrounded Waller's commission marked an important step in streamlining military efficiency, if also setting parliament's armies on the path toward the Self-Denying Ordinance. Importantly, Londoners had once again insisted that they should have a say over military affairs. It was, as they made clear, reasonable that they should have some control over a war effort that had until recently endured "divers miscarriages" and all the while depended on their "treasure." As Brenner has suggested, Londoners may have given "their blessing to the Scottish alliance," but they did so only once they had gained assurances that they would also retain a degree of control over the conduct of war.[120] The new Lord Mayor and his allies apparently had every intention of seeing that their Common Council would continue on as a "third house of parliament."

The costs of war

Perhaps more than anything else, the petition against the Lord General revealed that Londoners were acutely aware of the disproportionately large burden that parliament's war effort had placed on their "already exhausted" treasuries. Doubtless, Londoners had good reason to express their concerns; they did in fact pay more on average than their suburban counterparts. Livery company loans, as we have seen, were largely exhausted in the wake of the autumn request for £50,000. Monopolies provided another means to extract cash. It was, William Palmer has suggested, a desire "to avoid imposing further tax burdens" that led parliament to take up the highly controversial project of granting monopolies to trading companies in late 1643 and early 1644. This appears to be part of the motivation behind a loan of £40,000 given by the Merchant Adventurers between October 1643 and January 1644. Other sums raised included £6,000 from the East India Company and another £8,000 from the Levant Company.[121]

The main issue in 1644, however, was the addition of yet more excised commodities. On 9 January, parliament "imposed new excises on flesh and salt," followed in July by "additional excise duties on imported hemp, flax, tow, pitch, tar, resin, and tallow" along with "cotton wools."[122] Although a full third of the money raised by the excise was to be used to repay those who had already contributed goods and services toward the war effort, such as food, carts, and supplies, the burden nevertheless fell hard upon London's liveries, merchants, and tradesmen. This was especially true for those who dealt in meat. As Coffman explains, London's butchers "were not allowed to slaughter animals without the excise ticket" and "all cattle were to have the excise paid upon being brought into the city." Failure to pay the tax could result not just in fines, but also in a charge of malignancy.[123] Additions to the excise program in late 1643 and early 1644 thus marked an important point of expansion for parliament's developing tax program, and by extension an important, if perhaps necessarily "indifferent," moment in the development of the state's bureaucratic coverage. The addition of malignancy charges afforded additional leverage over transgressors.[124]

Contemporaries at no point lost sight of the burdensome and increasingly thorough nature of parliamentary taxation, part of what some were beginning to liken to tyranny. With once underground verse out in the open, royalists were all too happy to remind Londoners of the cause of their suffering.[125] One could easily hear taunting songs or read lurid verse, like the popular claim that

> a horse got Pym
> and Pim begot a Roundhead.
> This Roundhead got a Cittizen
> that great tax-bearing Mule.[126]

Mock petitions might just as soon belittle Londoners for scraping up the "scummings of the Citty" and their seemingly endless ability to "turne their Franticke wealth, and squeeze their purse proud spunge till the publique faith cannot passe for a private pott of ale."[127] Doubtless, such jests could sting. Some livery companies, as we have seen, were still under immense pressure to pay outstanding loans in 1644. Fishmongers, for instance, who had "unanimously consented" to pay their portion of the £50,000 August loan, were still "very much prest" by the "Lord Maior and the Courte of Aldermn to pay in" their remaining balance of £2,100 in February.[128] Royalists were not entirely off target with their claims that prolonged war and diminshed trade revealed many who had

> growne poore,
> as any Common whore,
> That hath been long a fadeing
> ther's no body will buy
> you may leave to sweare and lye,
> as you were wont to do in your trading.[129]

Other long-standing programs continued to take a toll. Customs fees in the port of London generated vast sums of money for parliament at the expense of merchants and traders, while weekly collections for Ireland persisted well into 1644. Ben Coates has estimated that "a total of £1,414,726 was received by Parliament's customs' commissioners from 2 July 1642 to June 1650," a figure which made "customs the largest source of taxation from London in the 1640s."[130] The controversial "meale weekly," which was first introduced by the Salters' Hall subcommittee in May 1643, was revived and presented again by the subcommittee to Common Council in January 1644. Debated over the course of January and February, the proposal was finally submitted to parliament by Wollaston as an ordinance for "one meale in the week towards the charge of Arming and forming into Regiments the Auxiliary forces now in raysing within the Lynes of Communication."[131] The previous year's plan had simply been repackaged to fit the new recruitment expectations of Common Council and the Salters' Hall subcommittee. Their hopes were finalized in the shape of an ordinance that called for the collection of a weekly meal intended to "ease and relieve" the exhausted trained bands.[132] As if these large-scale matters of parliamentary finance did not already place a great burden on the people of the City, there were other important matters that needed to be addressed by politicians and citizens. None of these, as we shall see, proved more serious than the need to care for the sick and wounded.

When visiting the Savoy hospital with his wife on a cold day in December 1643, Nehemiah Wallington noted the "very sad specticls of misery of our Souldiers" which caused him to "pety and to pray for them as also my heart was much stered up to praise God for the presarving of me and mine."[133] Having walked the short distance from his home in Eastcheap, Wallington found himself face-to-face with suffering that left him acutely aware of the horrors of war. Other Londoners had come to view similar sights in their own parishes; since the outbreak of fighting, maimed, sick, and injured soldiers had steadily streamed into the metropolis; their arrival challenged popular views of war and caused some to pause and reconsider their reasons for supporting the effort in the first place. Caring for the maimed became more burdensome as the war progressed, and especially after the conflicts of autumn 1643. Families lost fathers and sons with each new battle, and in many instances those who returned home bore injuries that left them incapable of resuming their trades, providing for their families, and in some cases caring for themselves. In light of these terrible circumstances, families turned to the Court of Aldermen for military pensions. Long waits meant that most had to rely on parochial charity.

Crowded hospitals and limbless beggars had become quotidian matters in early 1644. Historians have explored the conditions endured by London's sick and maimed, showing that death on the battlefield was just part of a larger picture of suffering.[134] Recent work by Eric Gruber von Arni has revealed glaring differences in the way that parliamentarians and royalists cared for their sick and maimed soldiers. According to his findings, the two sides managed diametrically opposed systems; parliament maintained a "full centralized responsibility for those killed or incapacitated in service," whereas the royalists lacked central oversight and therefore managed care through a number of "regimental commanders."[135] One result of these discrepancies is that London, as the capital and home of parliament's effort, saw the arrival of a disproportionate number of injured soldiers who were seeking care. Not only were parliament's sick and wounded concentrated in and around the City, which "remained the only Parliamentary base sufficiently secure and equipped to provide stable and permanent hospital facilities," but London almost certainly attracted wounded royalists in search of respite.[136]

Parliament recognized the importance of caring for the maimed from the outset of the war; early attempts were made to assure that those who lost life or limb in parliament's service would receive pensions. A parliamentary ordinance from 24 October 1642, designed "for better Encouragement in the Service," declared that an "allowance" would be provided "for such of them as shall be maimed, and thereby disabled by their Labour to provide for themselves, their Wives, their Children, as formerly they did." Initially, funds for "allowances and Rewards" came from collections overseen by the Committee for Maimed Soldiers in parishes in London, Southwark, and Westminster, but these areas were eventually expanded to all of the areas within the Bills of Mortality in 1643.

Early care for the sick and wounded was overseen by the parliamentarians Robert Jenner and Cornelius Holland, whose receipts totaled, according to Gruber von Arni's account, "just over £1,690" between the dates of 14 November 1642 and 31 May 1643.[137] The first comprehensive effort to establish a fund for the maimed did not occur until October 1643, when Richard Hutchinson, William Greenhill, John Pocock, and John Randall were given the unenviable jobs of overseeing the disbursement of £3,980 to sick and maimed soldiers. As Geoffrey Hudson has shown, the "fund, which was supposed to operate for six months" and which was to be distributed in sums of 4s or less per week, ended up operating for seventeen years. Supply for the fund was later replaced by revenue generated by the excise.[138] Further assistance came that same month in the form of a parliamentary ordinance that called for increased collections for the sick and injured: it "levied upon the City of London and Westminster the some of 1200." Most parishes appear to have paid their proportions of the levy accordingly. Officials from St. Mary Aldermanbury – one of the few parishes that kept a record of their payments – "agreed that eaighteen pounds" would be "gathered for maimed Soulders" over the course of the year. After the levy, they increased their sum to £20, which was again to be "payd in acording as the Ordinance doth require."[139] Scheduled payments for the maimed had therefore increased by 10 percent between March and October 1643. Gruber von Arni points out that parliament issued new orders on 1 November 1643 "to raise £4,475 to cover the costs of maintaining financial provision for the wounded over the next six months." This money was to be collected in London and several other counties that were under parliamentary control.[140]

The "allowances and Rewards" that were distributed by parliament's Committee for Maimed Soldiers seldom provided enough to cover more than basic necessities. Some of the sick and injured were fortunate enough to receive stipends from bequests left to London's corporations. Philip Strelley, a goldsmith who died in September 1603, left one such bequest. Strelley's will stipulated that £10 be distributed to the sick and maimed on an annual basis for a full ninety-nine years. Naturally, some of the money that Strelley left behind benefited soldiers who returned to London during the wars of the 1640s. The charity, for instance, provided for thirty-eight soldiers 5s each in 1642, while just six men were fortunate enough to receive 6s 8d each in 1643.[141] The amounts that were given varied by year and according to internal circumstances in the company. On good years forty soldiers were granted funds out of Strelley's charity. As can be expected, members of the Goldsmiths were often given preference; "6 maymed souldiers members of this Company" were given 9s each on 22 December 1643. Distribution of the remaining "parte" of the £10 had to wait until the company received "the rest of the rents" before it could "bee ditstributed to maymed Souldiers." The company may have borrowed from Strelley's fund in order to cover some of their outstanding debts, so that the money was simply not available to distribute all at once.[142]

Most injured apprentices and tradesmen returned to find less propitious circumstances. Indeed, few companies could afford to distribute charity on the level of the Goldsmiths, and perhaps with good reason when the pressures of lending are taken into account. Soldiers who could not obtain pensions were often left at the mercy of parochial charity. According to the annual accounts kept by Clement Underhill, the City collected their usual assessment of £175 1s 4d in 1643, along with £162 4d for pensions, sums which could hardly be stretched to cover the needs of the City's rapidly accumulating sick and wounded.[143] This resulted in an apparent shortage of pensions; most of the maimed were therefore left to wait for the "next available" pension, a process that usually required a space to open due to death. There existed, then, a considerable backlog of maimed men who waited to receive pay from the state. A list of fifty-six new pensioners from 1643 reveals that twenty-nine were given to soldiers who had entered service in 1635, and that only four new pensions were made available for men who began service in 1641. There were, then, no new pensions available for men who had actually served since the outbreak of war in 1642. Less than £165 was divided up between the fifty-six injured soldiers who were fortunate enough to hold pensions at the time, suggesting that individual pensioners received payments that ranged between £2 and £4.[144]

Numerous petitions to the Court of Aldermen reveal the extent of the injuries and hardships suffered by the maimed. Robert Gulson, a haberdasher and resident of "Broaken wharfe," was promised a "souldiers pention" in November 1642 after he was "lately maimed in the Battell att Newbery." Promises, however, did little to help those who lost the ability to care for themselves. Richard Anderton may have found some comfort in January 1644 when he received notification that he was next in line for a "souldiers pention which shall happen to fall voyd." This clearly could not come sooner, since he "lost the use of both his hands in the Battaile att Edgehill" fourteen months earlier. After being "shott in his Arme & shoulder att the fight att Newbery," Henry Dawes, "a very poore man" from the City Blue regiment, found "compassion" from the court, which agreed in February that he should receive "the next Souldiers pencion." New petitions for pensions arrived daily, exposing some of the devastating circumstances that returned home with London's soldiers. Petitioners included Rowland Swinarton, who "lost the use of his left hand" at Alton, and Richard Lacon, who "lost the use of his right hand in the parliament service." A steady stream of petitions overwhelmed the courts. In July one Valentine Hamilton of the Blue trained bands petitioned for relief since he "had his backbone broken" at Newbury and since then found himself "utterly disabled to doe any thing." Hamilton's petition seems to have been the last straw for the court, which immediately decided that several men should be appointed to investigate "under whose Command such souldiers went forth in the publique service and from what place and where they received their hurte and maymed."[145]

Parishioners had of course maintained annual charitable payments for the sick and wounded since long before the outbreak of the war. Yet the system of collections that extended back to the thirteenth year of Elizabeth I's reign did little to prepare London for the scope of what was needed after a year and a half of "intestine" war. Payments to the maimed and injured were determined by the size of the parish and the most common annual assessment was £1 14s 8d, but rates varied so that some parishes paid as little as £1 6s per annum. Some paid the larger annual sum of £2 3s 4d. Parishes did, however, also make regular charitable donations on an *ad hoc* basis, a fact that leaves the full scope of parochial charity a matter of debate. Records only occasionally account for the payments made to individual maimed and sick soldiers, and where payments can be found they are often lumped together with generalized payments to the poor and needy. For example, the parishioners of St. Swithin London Stone paid out £6 1s 6d from Easter 1642 until Easter 1643 to help care for needy "lame Souldiers and other poore people."[146] St. Bartholomew-by-the-Exchange made record of payment of two shillings and six pence over the course of 1643 to 1644 "to sundry maim[e]d souldiers and other distres sad people in the perishes behalf."[147] Similar records abound in churchwardens' accounts. Some churchwardens made specific note of the occasions when they gave to the maimed. The churchwardens at St. Mary Somerset on Upper Thames Street, for instance, recorded three payments; eight pence was "given to three Souldiers" between May 1642 and April 1643, while six pence "given to a poore sicke and lame Soldier" and an additional eight pence given to another "poore sicke and lame Soldier" sometime between 1643 and 1644.[148] Most remained nameless, like the "poore man in Kentstreet that was hurt in the warres" and received 1s from St. Mary Newington, Southwark.[149]

Adding to the problem was the fact that refugees never stopped coming out of Ireland. "Poore and disressed" refugees had flooded into London for months preceding the outbreak of war, and their presence, as readers might recall, often added unwelcome strain on parochial resources. Although they could scarcely be blamed for their "want and misery," their arrival drained coffers and ultimately depleted resources prior to the arrival of England's own sick and needy soldiers.[150] The first sizable wave of maimed soldiers returned to London shortly after Edgehill in late October 1642, and from that point onwards numbers steadily increased.

Money raised in the parishes was sent on to treasurers for the maimed, who in turn distributed funds to hospitals where sick and injured soldiers received care. Many were at first admitted to hospitals of St. Bartholomew, St. Thomas Southwark, or the Savoy, where Wallington solemnly walked in December 1643. Some less fortunate soldiers ended up alongside criminals in the depths of Bridewell. After recovering, most were discharged and left to fend for themselves. As if the difficulties of securing pensions, navigating parochial charity, and begging were not bad enough, there is also evidence that the sick and wounded had to contend with local governors who were prone to granting preferential treatment. The problems became so widespread that a group of maimed soldiers banded together in March 1644 to address the problem to Common Council. Their petition listed some of the many issues faced by "wounded and maimed" soldiers who had been "in theis Warre in the Parliament service." Their main issue was with the management of Sutton Hospital of the London Charterhouse in Smithfield, which they claimed was being run by governors who were not only negligent, but "in Armes against the parliament." These "royalist" governors had apparently tampered with the pensions system so that all new "places void" were in fact given to men "in noe necessity." The petitioners hoped that Common Council might rectify the issue by petitioning the Commons to remove all soldiers who had previously been "preelected" to pensions so that those more needy "may be placed in their roomes."[151] The petition was eventually sent on, and on 16 April the Commons ordered the creation of a Committee for Sutton Hospital which met that afternoon in the Star Chamber to look into the allegations and make sure that no "reversioners be admitted" and that those who were previously admitted should have their positions voided.[152] Sutton Hospital offers a rare glimpse into an active and adapting system of wartime care, of how petitioners were able to quickly move their concerns from the street to parliament.[153]

Apart from the new "state-run" hospitals, parish records make note of numerous scenarios in which local inhabitants cared for the maimed. The service, usually taken up by widows, provided some jobless Londoners with a modest living. This seems to have been the case with Maudlin Gowler of St. Botolph Without Bishopsgate, who received one shilling per month in May and June 1643 for "keepeinge two sicke souldiors."[154] 3s 6d was "given to the sicke Souldier that lay at Lewes his house" in the parish of St. Ethelburga Bishopsgate in 1644.[155] Two soldiers, one Thomas Lee and another known simply as "Steeuven," were cared for over the course of sixteen weeks in St. Stephen Walbrook at a total cost of £3 4s.[156] Other parishes, meanwhile, took the matter of pensions into their own hands. Officials at St. Martin Ludgate decided in 1643 that one "George Emery a Maymed Soldier shold have allowed him a pentcion of Two shillins a weeke."[157] Caring for the sick and wounded was doubtless costly and time-consuming, but the overflow from hospitals left little choice. Churchwardens from St. Giles in the Fields, Westminster, provide an unparalleled account of the "monies disbursed to sick and Maymed Souldiers Commanded by Ordinance of Parliament" over the calendar year from April 1643 until April 1644.[158] Parishioners "payed in" a total of £21 to care for sick and maimed soldiers, which included money distributed to both maimed soldiers and war widows. More than 181 monthly payments were made throughout the parish. Money was not simply distributed, but instead could be used in some cases to purchase goods. One John Harris, for example, required the parish "to buy him shooes," while his fellow maimed pensioners, Peter Frotheringham and Robert Parker, sought and received multiple monthly cash payments.[159]

The loss of limb affected families as well. In October, the *Parliament Scout* complained that, besides being "unfit" for military service, the "absence" of "house keepers" left London families to "stand at home." Worse yet, an untimely "death" was "usually the beggaring of wife and children."[160] Indeed, absence, deaths, and severe injuries could be enough to ruin families. War widows "were given preference as nurses" in metropolitan hospitals, which was fortunate, as it not only provided care for the wounded, but also generated income for the living.[161] Others were forced to join the queue and seek charity alongside the injured. St. Giles in the Fields paid 1s to "Mary Manning a Souldiers wife" in September 1643, and 1s 6d "to a poore woman in bloomsbery that lost her husband at Turnbridge" in October 1643. Churchwardens regularly categorized payments to war widows in lists for the "sick and Maymed."[162] Countless similar examples can be found in the parochial records, revealing the extent to which wartime deaths and injuries interrupted – or worse yet, fractured – families. St. Olave

Old Jewry, for instance, provided charity for numerous war widows. 1s went to a "widowe" who suffered for "her husband beinge slayne" in 1643, while in 1644 another 5s was given to five other women, including one "whose husband lost his legge in the Army," another who lost "her husband beinge slayne," and another "poore woman" who "lost her sonne in the Army."[163] Churchwardens at St. George the Martyr in Southwark gave 17s "att severall times to Goodwife Wilson & her children" after "her husband" died of a wound.[164] These brief records stand as a valuable reminder that the miseries of war were regularly compounded. Orders for "maintayning of maymed soldiers widdowes and fatherles children" remained a common occurrence in churchwardens' accounts throughout wartime London, and indeed well after the war ended.[165]

Fast days provided one solution to the depletion of coffers. Aside from promoting the welfare of those who fought on behalf of parliament, monthly fasts were increasingly used as occasions for promoting and collecting on behalf of the sick and wounded. Parliament regularly issued orders for collections, such as the one from 22 March that ordered money to be paid "upon the next Fast Day, to be employed for the Relief of the poor maimed Soldiers and Soldiers Widows."[166] Fast days provided ideal opportunities for collections, not only because attendance was compulsory, but because parishioners might be particularly compelled to give after hearing ministers condemn negligence and extol the virtue of charity.

Officials from St. Saviour Southwark kept a nearly complete collection of printed orders and receipts of payments made for the maimed on fast days. Their records reveal a regimented system of fast-day collections that began in March 1644 and continued on until January 1645. Small printed receipts reveal names, dates, and amounts collected. When printed receipts were not made available, parish officials recorded the amounts of their collections by hand. All collections "for and towards the reliefe of sick and maimed Souldiers" were then to be passed on to any of the four treasurers who sat at Tallow Chandlers' Hall.[167] William Greenhill, one of the treasurers for the maimed, signed receipts following fast in March when £4 15s was collected, and again after the November fast day when parishioners gave £3 18s.[168] Thomas Underhill signed for £4 collected on January 1644, while Richard Hutchinson signed for £3 that was raised in February 1645.[169] Orders were not made solely for the collection of money, but also for "necessity of Linen and Woollen Cloathes" which were needed to help dress wounds and keep men warm so that they could "cure of their wounds and sickness."[170]

Printed orders, moreover, reveal precisely what was expected of the preaching ministry on fast days. "All ministers" who preached in London's "severall parishes and Chappels" were expected to "earnestly perswade the people freely to contribute to this so pious charitable, and honourable a work," with the goal of helping men to recover from their injuries and "be ready againe (when God shall enable them) to venture their lives for the defence of all our Lives, Liberties, and Religion."[171] The degree to which ministers throughout the City followed these orders can only be guessed at, but the regular fast-day sermons given in Westminster at St. Margaret may have set the tone for the City. Although they never explicitly called for financial contributions for the maimed, fast-day sermons such as Joseph Caryl's from 23 April made clear that action was desperately needed, and that all auditors should help to "raise your hearts yet to more activitie of endeavours."[172] Most hearers, likewise, would conclude with Thomas Hill's suggestion, made during an August fast-day sermon, that they should "act" their "Prayers" and "worke and do good according" to their "Petitions" to God.[173] In calling for godly conduct and actions, ministers suggested – even if only implicitly – the importance of contributing toward, and caring for, the maimed.

Both parliamentary and metropolitan officials worked diligently to establish care for the needy, but consistently overburdened facilities and a steady increase in the number of wounded regularly forced care into the hands of parishioners. On 22 May 1645, more than a year after petitioners had requested that changes be made at Sutton Hospital, two hundred soldiers from the Savoy Hospital petitioned the Commons on "the Behalf of Fifteen hundred Soldiers, and the Widows of Soldiers" who benefited from weekly distribution of money at Christ Church and Parsons Green. Their petition spurred parliament to increase their weekly payment from £200 to £250 with money collected out of the excise. Parliament ordered that collections made at the next three fast-days (except for those held in St. Martin in the Fields and St. Margaret Westminster) would "be employed for the relief of maimed Soldiers." An additional £1,000 was to be collected from the estates of delinquents in order to pay for the arrears owed to surgeons and apothecaries who had already rendered services.[174] If remarkable in scope, the solutions put forward by parliament could only offset what had become a systemic issue; by October 1644, Common Council was receiving reports about overcrowding at Bridewell, a facility that had fallen into a state of "detryment" due to the burden of "Soldiers" who had arrived "from time to tyme."[175] The issue of caring for the sick and maimed required constant assessment, reevaluation, and adaptation; seeking new means to account for the needs of London's wounded began well before the outbreak of the civil war and persisted well past its end.

War-weariness and the maintenance of the cause

On 2 July 1644, nearly half a year since the success at Alton, William Waller wrote to the Committee of Both Kingdoms to complain that he was "extremely plagued with the mutinies of the Cittie Brigade, who are growne to that height of disorder, that I have no helpe to retayne them." They had, he went on, returned "to their old song of home, home." Little, it would seem, had changed. Exasperated, Waller could not help but continue his complaint: "an Army compounded of these men" would never be entirely reliable, since they "never goe through with their service." Rather than prolong their action, he went on, parliament should seek "an Army meerly your owne" and "that you may command." Until such a time arrived, it would remain "impossible to doe any thing of importance."[176] The creation of an army of their "owne," of course, had to wait; in the meantime, Waller had revealed his growing frustration with the young apprentices who filled London City's Yellow and White regiments.

Experienced commanders such as Captain Robert Harley could not help but notice the condition of new soldiers as they marveled at the world outside of London; some, he claimed, could scarcely tell "what manner of things cows were."[177] If green by most accounts, the young soldiers were nevertheless often eager to participate. Opportunity knocked in late March 1644 at Cheriton, Hampshire, when Waller's combined parliamentarian forces managed to win an important victory over Lord Hopton's royalists. The London brigade proved instrumental to parliament's success; Sir Arthur Haselrig's now veteran Lobsters received most of the credit for the day since they apparently held the left flank of the field. Yet portions of the City White regiment also fought hard and managed to advance and occupy ground on the right flank. London's press characteristically made the most of the occasion. Captain John Jones wrote a letter on the day of the battle that later made its way into print: "our London Regiments, but above any, our Major General [Richard] Brown[e], hath bin a prime means for our present welfare."[178] Another account printed in the capital suggested that Browne was indeed "a special instrument" since he had personally led 100 men in a charge to "throw the Enemies body and put them to a rout."[179] News of the success prompted Londoners to ring church bells and celebrate with thanksgivings. In a sermon preached to the Lord Mayor and aldermen at St. Paul's, Cornelius Burgess and Henry Wilkinson offered praise to the Almighty "for the victory obteyned by gods mercy against the forces under the Comand of the Lord Hopton."[180] Reports of Haselrig's sturdy Lobsters and Browne's decisive command afforded Londoners with yet another example of their "brave boys" upholding the cause.

Indeed, Hopton's defeat gave both politicians and citizens new hope and reason to see that their "tears were wiped away."[181] As with similar occasions in the past, celebrations were soon tempered. The festive mood in the capital was a far cry from the battlefield, where Londoners had mixed feelings about the state of war, and where thoughts often roamed back to home. Good news almost inevitably came with some bad. First came reports that the Tower Hamlet auxiliaries had performed "very honourably and stoutly" at Cheriton on 29 June, and held "back the enemy" at Cropredy Bridge.[182] But their actions were not enough to win the day. According to Peter Gaunt, the "disorganized and fragmented encounter" left some "700 dead or captured" and worse yet delivered yet another blow to morale.[183] Cropredy gave Londoners reason enough to return to "their old song of 'home, home'."[184] Rather than march on, many simply deserted to find their way back to the City. After Major-General Browne arrived in Northampton to reinforce Waller with fresh troops, including some new men raised in London, 400 soldiers from the Southwark White auxiliaries decided to march back to London and carry with them their dead commanders, Colonel James Houblon and Captain Francis Grove. Waller was left distraught, complaining to parliament that "2,000 Londoners" had simply picked up, and set out "withough wanting for further orders." Browne's reinforcements were of unquestionable importance, but Waller could not help feeling "very much weekened" as he watched his London brigade disintegrate.[185]

Few if any Londoners were to be found at the decisive battle of Marston Moor on 2 July. Instead, the day was won by the combined ranks of the Eastern Association and the Covenanters. It was at this point clear that the war effort could and indeed would continue without the help of London's forces. This is not to say that they were completely finished fighting – indeed, "London boyes" who served under Browne's command would win praise as "most heroicke spirits and trusty Tojeans" for taking Greenland House in Oxfordshire on 9 July – but the London militia had, in their absence from the field of battle a week earlier, largely defined their own obsoletion.[186]

Apart from the entry of the Scots, efforts had been under way to seek other major forms of support for parliament's war effort. The Eastern Association, which formed in December 1642 out of the militias from the parliamentarian counties of Cambridgeshire, Essex, Hertfordshire, Norfolk, and Suffolk, and later incorporated Lincolnshire and Huntingdonshire, was coming to occupy a prominent role. The associated counties spent much of their early existence dealing with royalists in the north, but they gradually assumed a larger part in parliament's war effort. In August 1643 their commander, Lord Grey, was replaced by the earl of Manchester. From that time forward, the Association proved indispensable to parliament's war effort, functioning, according to Clive Holmes, as "the largest and most effective Parliamentary army then in service."[187] The Association's forces were at the center of the siege of York in May 1644, but their single greatest achievement came on 2 July, when they helped to secure a decisive victory for parliament.

Marston Moor was significant for a number of reasons. It was, for one, parliament's first major defeat of royalist forces. Second, it marked the end of royalist control over the north, a change that allowed parliament to reconsolidate military attention to the south and west. The success, moreover, proved to be both tactical and symbolic, since it was the result of cooperation between parliamentarian forces of the Eastern Association and some 16,000 Scottish Covenanters who made up "the bulk" of the army under the command of the earl of Leven.[188] The conspicuous absence of a City brigade at so decisive a battle speaks volumes about both the shifting state of parliament's war effort and the waning significance of London's militia. Indeed, Londoners had repeatedly helped to secure parliament's limited successes in late 1643 and early 1644, but the same could not be said in the aftermath of the battle of Marston Moor; from July forward it was clear that the future of parliament's war would depend on the skill of resolute commanders such as Cromwell, Fairfax, and Leven, and not Londoners who remained preoccupied with their tune of "home." Questions turned instead to a consideration of how to best supply parliament's army, and how to manage the Lord General and the Eastern Association alongside the Scots.

On 6 July, official letters reached London and confirmed that the combined Covenanter and Association armies had defeated Rupert and the marquess of Newcastle.[189] Just six days later, a remarkable meeting of diplomats took place in Westminster. Walter Strickland, who had served as parliament's Ambassador-General to the Netherlands since 1642, helped to arrange the reception of a small group of Dutch ambassadors by both Houses. The Netherlands had taken a neutral stance with regards to the war, but the importance of their diplomatic assembly, and the opportunity that it presented for furthering parliament's military interests, was lost on few. The Dutch ambassadors were first "solemnly received in the Lords house," and from there they were "carried into the inner Court of Wardes chamber" which had been "prepared for them as a withdrawing roome." Next, they were escorted to their main reception, which took place in the "Commons, where chayres were sett for them," and where they came upon a spectacular scene. As the doors of the House opened "the Speaker and all the members stood up in their places uncovered," with their hats in their hands, so that they could salute the ambassadors "as they passed by." In the center of the room strewed about and "in their view," rested the "48 colours taken from the Kings forces in the Battle of Marston Moore." The ambassadors delivered a brief speech in which they offered "the affection of their Masters to these Kingdomes and their desire to mediate an accord between the King and his Parliament."[190]

The placement of so many hard-won banners – doubtless stained from battle – was meant to send an important message.[191] Parliament had won a decisive, and, indeed demonstrable, victory over the king. The elaborate reception was of course meant to impress the Dutch visitors and suggest a sea-change in the civil war. More specifically, the invitation to observe proceedings in parliament was part of a wider political effort – a strategic display of strength – that was intended to forge new bonds between parliament and the Low Countries. The flagging enthusiasm of Londoners and the near insolvency of livery companies left parliament increasingly aware of the need to court alternative avenues of support. The Continent, despite being preoccupied with its own wars, offered opportunities; in particular, the Low Countries, as Peter Edwards has shown in his exhaustive study of the origins of the arms and armor used during the civil wars, provided a vast majority of what could be purchased in terms of contracted arms and armor. The Dutch supplied "Royalists and Parliamentarians alike" with "the bulk of their imports." Both sides drew upon their respective links with the region; Henrietta Maria attempted to curry favor for the royalist cause through a marriage alliance, and she did in fact manage to procure implements of war that were sent on to arm royalists early in the conflict. Parliamentarians, meanwhile, relied upon their shared links with Dutch merchants who were sympathetic to their religion, in some cases at least.[192] Apart from London, which loaned stopgap supplies and over time generated numerous contracts for supplying implements of war over the course of 1642 and 1643, the United Provinces were the second largest suppliers of wartime supplies, save for gunpowder.[193] Parliament thus had very good reason to display their military prowess in the chamber. Although national production of supplies had increased steadily over the course of 1644, parliament was still perennially short of arms, armor, and munitions. A table littered with royalist banners stood as a bold suggestion of what might be expected from future engagements – an appeal, in short, to Dutch sensibilities about their proclaimed neutrality.[194]

Indeed, leading parliamentarians had been courting outside support for the war effort for some time. In November 1643, William Boswell, parliament's diplomat to the States General since 1632, noted the coming of the "Notorious Bloe coale" Hugh Peter. Peter's "precipitate" arrival agitated Boswell, who made special note of the fact that the infamous minister had "allreadie begunne to open his packe at Amsterdam in two sermons."[195] Peter had of course been a leading proponent of the war effort and he had to date preached a number of rousing and incendiary sermons both in London and "into the field."[196] His arrival in Amsterdam provides yet another clue to the shifting dynamic of the parliamentarian – and by extension metropolitan – mobilization. Orders for Peter's mission had in fact come directly from the Committee of Safety on 27 September 1643, and in response to an early "Ordinance of Both Houses" for sending "over Mr Samuel Hoover into Holland with instructions to make triall amongst the well affected Persons of the United Provinces for the borrowing of divers sumes of Monye for sypplye of the great pressing nexessityes of this Kingdome." Peter's mission came with detailed instructions, too, including the order that he should "be carefull to give the People in those parts notice of the Covenant and strict union betwixt the two Kingdomes of England and Scotland for defence of the Religion and Libertyes in both" and further to see that "the true Lovers of Religion may bee more effectually provoked to give us their ayde" and become acquainted "with the justice of out Cause in the present unhappy differences and Civil warr" and the "micheivous principles and deignes of the Papists which doe equally threated all other States professing the Protestant Reformed Religion."[197] Rather than continue to trumpet the cause in London's parishes, or serve as a chaplain in the field, Peter's talents would be better utilized in the Netherlands where he might employ his oratorical gifts to remind audiences about the international Protestant cause and about England's moment of need.[198] The recently formed alliance with Scotland presented a new bargaining chip in these efforts. After Amsterdam, Peter was to take his message on the road and travel on to meet with sympathetic audiences in several cities including "Rotterdam, Bergen-op-Zoom, Goes, Flushing, and Middelburg."[199]

Similarly, sometime in late 1643 or early 1644, a set of "additional instructions" were sent to Richard Jenks and William Barker, parliament's ambassadors to Sweden and Denmark. These included the expectation that the men might attempt to "rectifie" the "misconceipts" on the part of the king of Denmark, Christian IV, and take special pains to gain approbation – and perhaps even support – for parliament's effort. Both men were ordered to be careful not to offend the sensibilities of their fellow Protestants who were "of the Lutheran Religion" and might have "some obiections" to parliament's recent "proceedings against Prelacie or Episcopacy." Acutely aware of these confessional sensitivities and the difficult task at hand, both Jenks and Barker were expected to relate "how much their Bishops doe differ from those we doe here reject," and further how parliament's hand was forced by numerous "dangerous & bloodie plots made against Our lives, Religion, & Libertie" by members of "the Prelatical and Papisticall partie." Jenks and Barker carried copies of "our last Covenant taken by both kingdoms of England & Scotland (translated in Latin, French & german)," which they were expected to display as tokens of parliament's earnest desire "to stand, as brethren, together for so just & great a cause in mutual defence."²⁰⁰ If less clandestine than Peter's mission to the Low Countries, their purpose was analogous – parliament was seeking help from allies who might be sympathetic and who might recognize that the spotlight of the Protestant cause now shined most brightly on England.

Londoners, as one royalist observer noted, were well aware of their own burdens and the disproportionate "hopes" that had been placed on "their blessed brethren the Scotts."²⁰¹ Besides the earl of Leven's armies, the most obvious places to look were the tried and tested Protestant states that were beginning to emerge from their own protracted struggles against international Catholicism. England, as parliament's agents were instructed to profess, had become embroiled in a war shaped by "those mischievous principles and designes of the Papists which doe equally threaten all other States professing the Protestant Reformed Religion."²⁰² Yet not all Londoners were pleased by the prospect of dependence upon foreign powers. John Green, for instance, was averse to the idea and in 1643 he did "beseech God that I might never see this our unhappy Warre made a Warre merely for religion, and that neither side might make use of foreign auxiliaries." His hopes were dashed by the outset of 1644; it was clear by the start of the year that "the King hath already brought over the protestant forces" out of Ireland and that "the parliament" was "in dayly expectation of the Scots."²⁰³ Green's qualms over the use of foreign soldiers may have subsided in the wake of Marston Moor, but his concern was doubtless shared by many in the City.

Keeping the Scottish armies in the field required £30,000 a month, an issue that required parliament to maintain a robust program of taxation on the City. Indeed, there was no guarantee that the procurement of more international support would alleviate the financial burdens placed on Londoners. Rather, it might increase. Taxes had come to provide a consistent and readily available source of wartime income. The excise had become so successful that parliament began to use the tax in place of the "public faith" as backing for loans. This led to a request for £20,000 in April 1644 "to send forth and mainteyne a considerable number of horse and foot." The loan was unsuccessful; a mere £6,000 had been collected by the beginning of the following month, forcing the "lord maior to intreat" lenders and collectors to secure the remaining sum from money collected to repay livery company loans. From this point forward, however, the excise, no matter how unpopular, became the primary means for backing London loans.²⁰⁴ Short of Pennington's bullying requests and ordinances, war party leaders sought any possible means to raise needed funds. On 23 July, three weeks after Marston Moor, the subcommittee at Salter's Hall issued new orders for weekly meal collections, threatening doubled fines, the sale of chattels, and arrests.²⁰⁵ Distressing as these matters were, Londoners increasingly found themselves preoccupied by other incipient political and religious divisions – divisions which, in the wake of England's adoption of the Solemn League and Covenant, were slowly coalescing around presbyterians and independents, diffuse and problematic labels which contemporaries were often quicker to apply than define, and which have subsequently attracted considerable scholarly attention that need not be rehearsed here.[206] Amidst these developments, parliament's war effort required both management and maintenance. If painfully obvious by this point, the press and the pulpit remained some of the best methods to win over the hearts, minds, and pocketbooks of war-weary Londoners, including those who were attempting to navigate London's emerging political alignments.

Emerging divisions

As we have seen, the dynamics of promoting parliament's cause to Londoners changed rapidly over the course of 1644. London's interpretation of parliament's effort had become focused on communications between Mayor Wollaston and the Vane and St. John group that dominated the new Committee of Both Kingdoms. Pressing questions about the conduct of war and how best to settle religion were, in light of these political developments, inescapable. If the management of the war were the first order of the day, religion remained a close second. The prior matter left parliamentarians and Londoners further divided, with some hopeful that Essex might remain Lord General while others were eager to see him dismissed. The primary debate on the table with regards to religion had far less to do with the dismantling of episcopacy and vestiges of Laudianism, as it had in previous years, than it did with the extent to which the Westminster Assembly would determine the shape of the English church and the scope of religious toleration.[207] Parliament's primary objective – by necessity, to win the war – remained ostensibly the same as it had over the previous year, but the ways in which they hoped to achieve their goal, and indeed their expectations for what might follow in case of a success, had changed dramatically. The royalist upset at Marston Moor, which, as we have seen, owed in no small part to the efforts of the Scots, further goaded contemporaries, driving deeper the questions over the shape of a religious settlement between political groups that wished to see a limited toleration stifled or promoted.

Save for the pioneering work of Ann Hughes and Elliot Vernon, whose respective research has assisted tremendously in how we might better understand the changing dynamics and nuances of presbyterianism in the capital, and indeed the adversarial politics that followed these changes, studies of London proper have been inadequate with regards to the ways in which metropolitan inhabitants navigated these turbulent times.[208] Lindley's treatment of the subject commenced rather abruptly with a consideration of "Presbyterians and Independents" that seemed to take its cues from S. R. Gardiner's chapter of the same title from more than a century earlier.[209] Lindley focused primarily on "the Presbyterian campaign" to establish "a strict Presbyterian church" in 1645 and on the "reluctant acceptance" of a "conservative political settlement and the suppression of religious diversity" in 1646. Only passing mention is made of the wide coalition of "radical activists from 1641–2" who were critical to these later campaigns. The crucial years of 1643 and 1644 seem to play little part in shaping the dynamics that would follow.[210] Brenner has afforded us a somewhat fuller account, observing that "the peace-party and moderate factions" that eventually made up "the core of political presbyterianism" were in fact the same groups that had at first "opposed Parliament's alliance with the Scots" due to the fact that it would intensify "military conflict" and "political instability."[211] Brenner thus identified an important aspect of the political developments of the period by linking earlier "coalitions" from 1643 and 1644 with their later "political presbyterian" and "independent" factions. These links, however tenuous or seemingly minor, help to bridge the gap between the ideological escalation of 1643 and the period of open presbyterian and independent divisions that came to the fore in 1645.

The significance of these divisions was on full public display by the end of January 1644. And once again, a plot was to blame for their exposure. The plot, which was revealed on 26 January and followed closely on the heels of Brooke's plot, was apparently concocted while the royalist Captain Thomas Ogle was imprisoned in London at Winchester House in late 1643, and depended upon Ogle's belief that congregationalists would be willing to take up arms on the king's behalf in both London and Aylesbury since their "jelosy of the Pressbytery remains greater then their displesur against the Einglish prelat." Part of the plot saw Ogle contacting the London independents John Goodwin and Philip Nye, both of whom had recently been involved with their fellow "dissenting brethren" in the production of the *An Apologeticall Narration*, a theological pamphlet that has traditionally been seen as a promotion of congregationalism, but which important recent scholarship has framed as an "attempt to keep the godly united."[212] Contemporaries believed that both Goodwin and Nye might be willing to stir "the cyttysons" of London to take up arms for the king.[213] Unbeknown to Ogle, his entire correspondence was being recorded as part of a trap. When Lord Wharton revealed the plot to the Lords, he made clear that both Goodwin and Nye were free from complicity, and that they had in fact served as double agents.

Although the plot ultimately served to discredit both Ogle and the king, it had an unforeseen secondary consequence: it revealed a crucial point of contention that would precipitate divisions and exacerbate tensions between presbyterians and independents both inside and outside of the capital. Indeed, the historian Robert Paul argues that Wharton's exposure of the plot was particularly important, not because it served to further deplete Charles I's reliability – which, of course, it did – but rather because it came at the "opportune" time to sway popular opinion about the reliability of London's existing congregations.[214] Rather than give their support to a plot against parliament and the City, Goodwin and Nye had seemingly reaffirmed their loyalty to parliament's rule and cause.

Regardless of their intentions, the concurrent printing of *An Apologeticall Narration* exacerbated divisions between the two politico-religious camps; indeed, Como has argued that the tract's publication "rendered public a series of discussions that had hitherto been carried out largely outside the realm of print" and resulted in "rancorous debate, conducted in pamphlet, pulpit, and private conversation."[215] If true about *An Apologeticall Narration*, these terms were equally true of the failed plot; even if Goodwin and Nye had established their loyalty to the cause by refusing Ogle's invitations, they had also unwittingly betrayed the extent of religio-poltiical divisions within the metropolis, and further revealed that London's congregationalists were perfectly capable of forging powerful political alliances beyond the reach of both parliament and the Westminster Assembly. Juxon believed as much, noting that Ogle had "conceived some hopes of gaining the Independent party to the king," and with the express understanding that "the synod was like to discontent them."[216] By this light, both the publication of *An Apologeticall Narration* and Ogle's plot were as revealing of divisions as they were of commitment to parliament's cause.

There were, on measure, other more explicit pronunciations of the growing divisions between the inchoate presbyterian and independent coalitions. Londoners grew increasingly wary of the many printed works that extolled their successes, and royalists could easily mock claims for a militia

> Th'ave gott many a glorious victory,
> As there Preachers and Pamphletts loudly crye,
> But most men beginne to know truth from a lye.[217]

After the better part of two years of war, and after encountering mountains of printed propaganda, inhabitants were left to choose for themselves. The realignment of politics in late 1643 and early 1644 – and in particular the adoption of the Solemn League and Covenant and the entry of the Scots – made way for yet more new ideologically charged tracts. Although significant, *An Apologeticall Narration* was, in the end, just one of these tracts. Sifting through the range of printed opinions of 1644, which Como fittingly calls "a sectarian slurry," reveals the extent to which new political and theological ideas were being experimented with and hashed out.[218] If ultimately intended for a "national audience," London was also a natural testing ground for new works that proclaimed to have answers to the trials and tribulations of the time; inhabitants seem to have been well aware of the bitter and contentious divisions at hand, and surely of the extent to which they might "beginne to know truth from a lye." Within this heady environment, distinctive views coalesced, so that by the end of 1644 something approaching "partisan identifies" were in fact discernible. Indeed, much of what would come to define political "independents" and "presbyterians" had entered the public domain in the early months of the year. Like *An Apologeticall Narration*, Richard Overton's controversial *Mans Mortalitie* was available to London audiences in January.

Presbyterian responses came quickly. *An Apologeticall Narration* received a full rebuke by Thomas Edwards, whose lengthy *Antapologia* reached Thompson on 13 July.[219] In this, Edwards could already offer his audience "a true glasse to behold the faces of Presbyterie and Independencie."[220] Other attacks followed.[221] Samuel Rutherford's nearly 500-page promotion of presbyterianism, *The Due right of Presbyterieis*, was also printed and made available in London in 1644. Meanwhile, somewhat "less memorable" – and decidedly less lengthy – works had already gone to press and were circulating throughout the capital, suggesting the extent to which Londoners were already being persuaded to "choose sides." One anonymous pamphlet from 9 March set out to show how the Solemn League and Covenant was little more than a "*conspiracy*" of "unlawfullnesse," and counter to "the oaths of Allegiance and Spremacy."[222] While in London, the Scottish pamphleteer George Gillespie wrote numerous tracts and dialogues, including *A Recrimination in Defence of Presbyterianism*, an outright attack on religious toleration.[223]

Responses did not simply espouse some central tenets of religious toleration, but could even be seen to suggest ideas of the coming Leveler movement.[224] By the autumn, the range of printed material suggests a further convergence of ideas. In September, William Prynne's *Independency examined, unmasked, refuted* provided Londoners with twelve easily digestible attacks on the "Independent Platforme."[225] The following month, Thomson acquired a copy of *The Confession of Faith, Of those Churches which are commonly (though falsly) called Anabaptists*, a work "subscribed in the Names of seven Churches in *London*" and which had come together to dispel assumptions made against the congregations as a "*black brand of Hereticks.*"[226] Save for Overton's *Mans Moralitie*, which was printed in Amsterdam, the vast majority of the polemic output was printed by and for Londoners.

Sermons and lectureships afforded another important means for disseminating new divisive opinions and ideas. Although we can only guess at the content of Thomas Goodwin's lectures from his time at

St. Christopher-le-Stocks on Threadneedle Street, it can be assumed with some degree of confidence that his views concorded with his writings elsewhere. In these, which were eventually published decades later, Goodwin set out to explore "three eminently differing Opinions" regarding church governments and discover which of the three would "prove to the Truth of God." God's "Truth" he concluded, was neither presbyterian nor universal, but was that He "hath appointed and ordained the visible Saints on Earth, being diffused all the World," and that such saints were "knit together in particular bodies."[227] There were, by Tai Liu's estimate, "no less than forty-five parishes in the City of London" where independent ministers maintained "a presence." These included the important congregations such as Henry Burton's at St. Matthew Friday Street and John Goodwin's at St. Stephen Coleman Street. But they also included some less-known London players such as Nicholas Lockyer, an associate of Goodwin who was brought to the attention of authorities, and Dr. Nathaniel Homes, an associate of Burton. Lectureships were often held concurrently so that it can be readily assumed that ministers reached wide audiences. Jeremiah Burroughs had positions at St. Mildred Breadstreet, St. Michael Cornhill, and St. Giles Cripplegate, while William Bridge was active at both St. Magnus and St. Margaret New Fish Street. When back from the Low Countries, as he was in early 1644, Hugh Peter could be found giving lectures in All Hallows Lombard Street, St. Magnus, or even at the Three Cranes Tavern in Vintry.[228] This same year, a church "constituted by the Mutuall Consent and agreement" first met in Stepney. Led by William Greenhill, the founding members included Henry Burton and his wife, John Odingsell, William Parker, and John Pocock, who had all agreed to "walke in the ways of Christ held out to them in the Gospell." An additional twenty-four members joined the gathered church in 1644, and came from throughout the metropolis – from Basinghall and Coleman Streets in the west to the Artillery Grounds and on to Wapping Wall and Limehouse in the east.[229]

While it has recently been suggested that dividing religious convictions between presbyterians and independents may not have posed a significant disruption to parliament's effort at this point, and would not necessarily hinder the coming of the New Model Army, it must be admitted that the multitudinous opinions exhibited in London's sermons and lectures could do scarcely little to bolster what broader unity of purpose lay behind parliament's war effort.[230] Indeed, printed and often antagonistic espousals had become commonplace in 1644. Presbyterians, for their part, systematically sought to quash the dangers of an aborning sectarianism. Gillespie brought his presbyterian sympathies before the Commons on 27 March when he preached a sermon in which he made clear that "the Word of God" stood as "a pattern for Presbyteriall Government over many particular

Congregations."²³¹ Richard Vines, who held the rectory at St. Clement Danes, jumped at the opportunity to preach against "schisme" during the Easter sermon given before the Lord Mayor and Aldermen at Christ Church. Vines suggested that sectarianism needed to be "faced and fought against" outright so as to not "anger the Gangrene."²³² Thomas Case soon joined the fray, printing his sermons from the previous year at St. Mary Magdalen as *The Quarrell of the Covenant, with the Pacification of the Quarrell*.²³³ Those ministers who hoped to disseminate presbyterian sympathies often engaged with largely sympathetic or receptive audiences; yet the same must be said to be true of London's congregationalists.

Debate over the *Apologeticall Narration* and other lesser tracts continued throughout the year, but exchanges were overshadowed by events on 18 September when a group of "divers Ministers of the City of London" petitioned the Commons in the hope that they might hasten the establishment of a church settlement. The petitioners requested that twenty-three individuals – all of whom were presbyterians – should be ordained as "Ministers *pro tempore*."²³⁴ Their proposal came just days before the Commons began to debate terms of a peace settlement that would result in a set of twenty-seven propositions in November 1644. News of the petition spread quickly. Walter Strickland reported in October that a copy of the "petition made by certain ministers in London" and which showed "the daunger religion was in respect of divisions" was being discussed in the Low Countries and considered as "a thinge more preiudicall to our affaires then any thing whatsoever in respect of mens apprehensions."²³⁵ The terms of these proposals – and in particular those portions addressing a presbyterian settlement – further polarized politics.

Parliament's terms were delivered to the king as the Uxbridge Propositions in early 1645. If agreed to, these would effectively end the war. As in the past, Common Council wanted to be certain that any propositions that might reach the king should also take their interests into account. On 26 October, councilors petitioned parliament, forwarding six provisions designed to preserve and protect London's jurisdiction over legal and military affairs. These included the request that the City militia would remain under the command "of the Lord Maior Aldermen and Comons in Comon Councell assembled" and further "that the Militia of the parishes without London and the Liberties within the weekly bills of mortality may be under the Command of the" same. Lastly, they sought assurance that all of their laws passed since the beginning of the war would remain in place, and "that the Citizens or forces of London shall not be drawne out of the City into any partes of the kingdome without their owne consent."²³⁶ Rather than obstruct peace proposals, as had been done in the past, London's leaders wanted to make sure that a settlement would not lead to the loss of their control over the militia. Both Houses agreed to the terms of their petition and on 10 Novemebr they issued an order so that the duke of Richmond and the earl of Southampton would have safe passage to travel through London "without any Lett, Hindrance, or Molestation."[237]

Unlike Common Council, which sought simply to qualify any peace propositions, the dissenting brethren rejected the proposals outright. They left no room to misinterpret their reasoning: the propositions stipulated that the English church would be modeled on the presbytery of Scotland, and so the king himself would be forced to subscribe to the Solemn League and Covenant. The dissenting brethren spent considerable energy explaining their position over the course of November and December and their aptly titled *The Reasons of the Dissenting Brethren against the Third Proposition Concerning Prebyterial Government* was ordered to be printed in December alongside Westminster Assembly's *The Answer and Solution of the Assembly to the said Reasons*.[238] The appearance of these works together served to both better define their respective purposes and in the process alienate detractors, marking yet another important moment in which ideological coalescences bring us closer to a politico-religious landscape populated by presbyterians and independents. By weighing in on how best to move ahead with war and peace, both "parties" escalated the terms of war. But more importantly, it was at this point the dissenting brethren and *not* London's corporation that opposed outright the terms of a peace settlement with the king. London's Corporation, which had so often moved lockstep with war part interests in 1643, and in particular under the former aegis of Mayor Pennington, had now diverged dramatically from their former political viewpoint regarding war.

The supersession of London's militia, Laud's attainder, and the birth of the New Model Army

Born nearly four decades earlier in the political hotbed that was Bread Street, John Milton felt that 1644 marked something of a high water point in London's efforts. "Behold now this vast City; a City of refuge, the mansion house of liberty," he wrote in *Areopagitica*,

> the shop of warre hath not there more anvils and hammers waking, to fashion out the plates and instruments of armed Justice in defence of beleaguer'd Truth, then there be pens and heads there, sitting by their studious lamps, musing, searching, revolving new notions and idea's wherewith to present, as with their homage and their fealty the approaching Reformation.[239]

Praise was due to London's many "pens" that were active beneath "studious lamps," yet clear also was the fact that 1644 had shaped up to be far quieter than 1643 in terms of the movement of money and men. Marston Moor left few in doubt about the extent of what a combined Covenanter and Eastern Association army could achieve on the battlefield. Londoners might still boast about their lightning-fast reflexes when it came time to mobilize in self-defense, but it seemed undeniable that a new air of war-weariness had settled over the City; what few engagements Londoners participated in revealed waning enthusiasm and diminished commitments. Waller's condition improved little over the course of July. The "mutinies of the Cittie Brigade" continued to hamper efforts; likewise, Major-General Browne's City forces were in "no very good temper."[240] Desertions and mutinies continued throughout the month, leading to cashiering and even in some cases executions. On 23 July, arrest orders were issued for Major Edward Wood for shooting one of his own men with a pistol. He was released when it became clear that he had killed "a mutineer in the Southwark White Auxiliaries" who refused to fulfill his obligations "as Adjutant-General of the Foot."[241] In the wake of these reports an ordinance was issued to press 1,000 soldiers to reinforce Major-General Browne's thinning brigade.

More troubling news came out of the southwest where Essex was cornered deep in the Cornish countryside. The royalist pursuit ended in early September; encircled, having lost artillery and a previous vantage at the nearby Castle Dore, and in fear of an imminent defeat, Essex abandoned his command to Major-General Skippon. Rather than lose the field or suffer being captured, the earl boarded a fishing boat and made toward Plymouth, leaving his men to an unknown fate. Exhausted and vastly outnumbered, Skippon had no choice but to surrender. Some 6,000 soldiers – many of whom were Londoners – were taken as prisoners and escorted toward Southampton. While on the road, some were plundered and abused by royalists and Cornishmen alike, stripped naked and exposed to the "wet and stormy" conditions; the humiliating treatment killed some, while others were left for dead.[242] The once widely celebrated Lord General who had repeatedly utilized London brigades, found himself on the defensive again, shamed and derided for failing his men and the cause. As one libelous ticket that was purportedly "written by some Independent against L[or]d Gen[eral] Essex" and was "scattered about the Streets in the night" would proclaim, the earl had revealed himself to be "an open enemie" to the fighting cause. All that he set out to "doe," he did in fact "undoe."[243] Essex's decision to flee Lostwithiel damaged his reputation beyond repair; but as importantly, wider questions about military competence and the conduct of leaders had been returned to the fore.

Back in the capital, news of the defeat led to new rounds of finger-pointing and panicked fits of mobilization. Parliament's immediate answer was to designate 12 September as a day of public humiliation and fasting. In light of the "late diasaster sustain'd in the West," John Goodwin preached two sermons at St. Stephen Coleman Street, marking the occasion with a consideration of the "distinguishing character" of "*Presbyterie*" and the recent "restraint" of "*Independencie*." Goodwin's sermon amounted to a clear attack on presbyterianism, made acceptable by the fact that military defeat was a most obvious example of divine reprisal, a providential sign that the ascent of presbyterianism must come to an end. According to John Coffey, Goodwin's sermon was part of an attempt "to strip the civil magistrate of authority in religion," and thereby "undermine the authority of synods in general and the Westminster Assembly in particular."[244] Thomas Juxon, who could hardly be noted for impartiality, saw the matter in similar terms; Juxon recording in his journal that "Goodwin, minister of Coleman Street" had recently "preached that the parliament had no power to command any way of government in the Church."[245] If Essex's shameful retreat was a tragedy for the wider parliamentarian effort, it also apparently afforded a moment to take stock of the state of politics and religion.

On 13 September, the House requested that Wollaston and Common Council might take into account "what strength" they could "supply" as part of an effort to "repell the Enimy which is marching towards us from the west." Royalist fortunes looked to be in the ascent after Lostwithiel, and the capital yet again found itself in a defensive posture. One week later, Common Council made note of the joint decision between the City Militia Committee and the Committee of Both Kingdoms for "the raising and sending out" of a combined brigade made up of the "Trayned bands of Wesminster, one of the trained bands of Southwarke, and the Auxiliaries of the Hamletts." Joining their effort were the "Redd and Blew Regiments."[246] Some delay regarding their funding followed, with one proposition that the money needed to pay them might come from a fine of £10,000 imposed on Edmund Waller for his part in the plot of the previous year. Ultimately, the City was made responsible for raising £20,000 to fund the new City brigade.[247] On 15 October, a force that Juxon estimated to be 4,500 strong, marched out of London under the command of Sir James Harrington, colonel of the Westminster militia.[248] Days later, on 26 October, the brigade camped opposite royalist forces at the field of Newbury, Berkshire.

The subsequent battle, which could hardly be counted as a victory for either side, led to a series of yet more accusations and new rounds of finger-pointing. Most contemporaries concluded that the engagement should have been easily won given parliament's numerical advantages on the field. However, rather than take the opportunity to pursue the king, orders were given to desist. As a picture of the day's proceedings came into focus, authors began casting blame. Eager not to "alledge," *Perfect Passages* suggested that the day was lost primarily for "the want of a presence of a Generall."[249] *The Parliament Scout* clarified that Haselrig, Waller, Skippon, Balfour, and Cromwell "were for fighting" and hoped to see the day's "success" determined by "the King of Heaven." Thus, absolved, blame for the day seemed to rest with Manchester and Crawford.[250] Soon after "the lord general's officers" could be heard crowing in London that they would have seen a great victory that day had Essex been able and willing to lead parliament's army. The failed pursuit of the king's armies, which Juxon ultimately blamed on "the Lord Manchester and Crawford and Balfour," led him to conclude bleakly that the year's advantages had "thus ... been shamefully lost."[251]

If it provided an easy opportunity for parliamentarian commanders to cast blame, Newbury had also afforded only a limited role for the London brigade. The highlight of their participation came with the storming of Speen, a small village west of Newbury, and their subsequent recovery of ordnance that had been taken by royalists at Lostwithiel. Little more could be said of their actions.[252] Thereafter, the brigade was divided up to help replenish dwindling garrisons and help with the siege at Basing House. Some of the regiments returned to London on 14 December while others went on to reinforce Abingdon, another small but strategically important town to the south of the king's headquarters at Oxford. Those Londoners who remained encamped for the winter suffered inhospitable conditions. Major General Browne, who was appointed governor, sent a series of desperate letters to the Committee of Both Kingdoms in which he revealed appalling conditions and complained of daily desertions. But he was not entirely unsympathetic to the plight of his fellow Londoners: "their duty is hard, their Quarters very strait" and their "victual very scant." Orders soon came for the consolidation of the remnants of three London auxiliary regiments, to which Browne tersely replied, "I shall obey." Later that month, Browne confessed that he thought consolidation would merely prolong their inevitable "Dissolucion."[253] Abingdon thus stood as fitting testament to the war-weariness of Londoners, of service and exhaustion in the face of an ever-changing cause. As Marston Moor had revealed months earlier, and as the stalemate at Newbury had recently underscored, new strategies would be needed if parliament hoped to gain a lasting advantage in the war.

Reports of mass desertions and failed military command did little to sober opinions in London, where all eyes had turned to the dilatory proceedings against William Laud. Fault, claimed many, rested squarely upon the Lords, who had come to see the popular attack on the archbishop as an implicit criticism and attempt to undermine their political authority. Eager to preserve their status and to prevent the Commons from acknowledging growing cries for a means to bypass their chamber, the Lords sat in stasis, refusing to proceed against the former archbishop.[254] Matters thus remained until Londoners assembled a mass petition in which they demanded that "justice be done upon Delinquents," and "especially the Archbishop of *Canterbury* and Bishop *Wren*."[255] Paranoid and exhausted, Laud suspected that the petition, which was delivered on 28 October by Thomas Ayres and purportedly contained 10,000 signatures, was the work of William Prynne.[256] When considering if the petition should be refused, William Strode acted as teller in the Commons for a vote of "noe." City interests had again found access via the Lower Chamber, adding a sense of gravity to the proceedings. It seemed to Laud and others that the interests of the "rude multitude" were once again pitted against the peerage.

On the same day that Ayres brought the petition into the House, Alderman Pennington presented a set of six "City Propositions" that had been agreed upon in Common Council. These represented the distillation of twenty-eight earlier propositions that were determined to be too numerous for consideration.[257] The remaining six propositions sought to both affirm and extend the rights of the Corporation. Of the six, three points in particular are worth visiting in greater detail. First was the matter of London's militia. Not only was the "Militia of the Citie of London" to remain under the control of the "Lord Maior, Aldermen and Commons in Common Counsell assembled," but the "Militia of the Parishes without London and the Liberties without the weekly Bills of Mortality" were expected to "be under the commnad" of the same. Second, was the stipulation that "the Citizens or Forces of London shall not be drawne out of the Citie into any other parte of the Kingdome without their owne Consent." Pennington, for his part, found the assurance that Lieutenant of the Tower – the office overseeing London's armory and the fortress – would continue to be "in the Government of the Citie of London."[258] The appointment that had come to Pennington by way of a Militia Committee recommendation to parliament fifteen months earlier, would therefore remain with the Corporation. As one contemporary observed in song: "Isaacke would always bee Lord Mayor and soe / May always bee as hee is now."[259] The Corporation, meanwhile, had gained the assurance that they would control all of the forces raised within the Lines of Communication, a matter of increased importance given the surfaced rivalries between commanders.

The prevailing mood in the City and the Commons was echoed on 30 October when the presbyterian Edmund Staunton preached *Phineas's Zeal in Execution of Judgement*, a fast-day sermon to the Lords in which he pled that they might "executeth" their own "judgement" against Laud as a "way to pacifie Gods wrath." This was a bold address, and in his subsequent epistle, Staunton claimed that his "argument" had been made on the grounds of "*the Citie Petiiton for execution of Judgement*" and the Lord's own "*Golden Ordinance, for giving no quarter to Irish, or Papists borne in Ireland, taken in Armes against the Parliament.*"[260] On the following day, the Commons terminated their impeachment proceedings and moved instead to create an attainder ordinance, a notable break with precedent, which

Clarendon later claimed to be tantamount to a "murderous act."[261] The ordinance was eventually sent up for review on 22 November. Six days later, precedent was challenged yet again when the Commons nominated Strode to deliver a message imploring the upper chamber to proceed. Tensions were made worse by Strode's decision to add to the message that the slow pace of proceedings amounted to a denial of "justice by multitudes."[262] Essex, for one, apparently voiced his disapproval, asking "is this the liberty which we claim to vinticade by shedding our blood?" He concluded that the war to "deliver" the nation from "the yoke of he king" had led instead to subjection to the will of "the common people."[263] The Lords continued to drag their feet in December, expressing annoyance with the popular "disorders" that had moved parliament to produce the attainder ordinance and the subsequent imposition upon their rights.[264] Tempers were cooled temporarily by the brief trial and execution of the Hothams. In Agostini's view, the Lords simply could not find "anything treasonable against the Archbishop," and therefore the Commons turned to "the people of London to sign a petition in favour of his death."[265] All the while, London's press made certain to keep the matter exposed to the light of day. *Britanicus* presented the view that the Lords were "resolved with all speed to hasten their determinations"; *Civicus*, meanwhile, speculated that the delay in proceedings against the "grad delinquent" owed to a statutory technicality; *Perfect Passages* was content to proclaim that "the Lords do daily make further progress"; *The Parliament Scout*, likewise, could claim on 8 December that "one day more will fit them for judgement."[266] Canterbury's doom seemed all but certain.

Pressed on all sides – by the Commons, Londoners, and perhaps even the Scots – the Lords finally acquiesced, agreeing on 4 January 1645 to a bill of attainder.[267] William Laud was to suffer a traitor's death of hanging, drawing, and quartering. Pleas that he might be pardoned, or at the very least, be beheaded, were made to no avail. While the Lords agreed that Laud might have the benefit of an attendance by clergymen of his choosing, and that he should be executed by beheading, the Commons refused – a rebuke that likely owed less to their concern for Laud's suffering than it did to their frustration with the Lords' refusal to consider the newly proposed Self-Denying Ordinance and suggestion that efforts might be made so that "the Army" could "be new molded."[268] It was not until three days later – the day before his death – that the Commons finally agreed to a beheading.

On 10 January 1645, Isaac Pennington and some other "publique Officers" arrived at Laud's chamber to conduct him to a scaffold erected at Tower Hill.[269] After nearly a year and a half as Lieutenant of the Tower, the one-time "pretended Lord Major" found himself leading the nation's one-time "Arch-Incendiary" to his death – doubtless a welcomed culmination to his efforts to purge London's pulpits back in 1642–3. From out of the Tower, Pennington and Laud walked together and into the view of the City sheriffs and throngs of onlookers who had gathered to "see him executed."[270] While he passed, the crowds shouted "opprobrious language" and applauded his ascent on the scaffold like a "vulgar herd."[271] From beneath the stage Laud could see Londoners who had gathered to catch his blood with handkerchiefs. For all of the spectacle, Juxon recalled Laud "dying in a most calm and composed manner." The sun "burst forth as soon as the blow was given."[272] Peter Heylyn, Laud's leading apologist, claimed that the "many who came with greedy eyes to see him suffer" left "with weeping eyes when they saw him dead." Laud's execution was, for Heylyn at least, a culminating moment. It marked a low point for "that City, whose Pride and Faction raised the Fire, and whose Purse added fewel to it, for enflaming the Kingdom."[273] Regardless of the legacy of Laud's death, the political maneuvering that led to his execution had made "the feebleness of the Upper House ... ever more apparent."[274] The Lords had succumbed to pressure on all sides, and not least from preaching to popular petitioning in the City, and in so doing they gave ground in their long-standing conflict with the Commons.

Parliament still, of course, had to determine what to do with their rival commanders. They needed to find a lasting solution to the squabbles, open resentments, and increasingly acrimonious debates over how to manage the war. On 9 December, Zouch Tate reported official committee findings to the Commons, revealing that recent troubling accusations and the string of military blunders lay not with any one man, but rather with the "pride and Covetuousness" of many. Oliver Cromwell addressed the Commons next, proclaiming "that if the army be not put another method, and the war more vigorously prosecuted, the people can bear the war no longer, and will enforce you to a dishonourable peace."[275] After some discussion, Tate proceeded to introduce a proposal for "self-denying" offices in parliament's army, a matter that led to more than an hour of "grave and long debate."[276] As the Londoner John Greene recorded, the "great vote past" in the Commons, where it was resolved "that noe member of either house should have any office in the Army."[277] That same day, Londoners found copies of the libelous ticket attack on Essex and Manchester that had been "scattered about the streets" the previous night. Three days later, after the Commons voted in favor of the bill, a petition from "divers Londoners" reached the House, "commending" their decision.[278] London's newsbooks took a similar view; *The London Post* called the vote "the greatest business" undertaken "since the Parliament began"; *The Kingdomes Weekly Intelligencer*, which at first questioned the nature of the vote "to take away the scandall that lyes upon some parliament men," later approved of it, concluding that the solution was necessary since maintaining the "war as the Parliament hath hitherto managed it, is certainly to undo us." *The Scottish Dove* saw the vote as great vindication of the Commons, who had thus "manifested their Impartiality, and really vindicated themselves from the aspersion of covetousnesse or self-seeking."[279]

As was the case with Laud's attainder, peers took a decidedly different view of the proposed bill. From 21 December the upper house, which had for the previous two years proven its willingness to engage in peace negotiations, was left to determine the fate of legislation that stood to trample precedent and exclude members from service. Rather than "enfeeble us," as one observer reported, they hoped to "keep the sword in their own power."[280] Another contemporary noted that the "extraordinarie" ordinance would deprive "the Peeres of that honor wch in all ages have beene given unto them" and serve as an insult to "their due honor."[281] Thus, the contentious bill sat untouched, with the Lords refusing to even consider amendments. In the wake of their refusal, the Commons "proceeded about the new Model of the Army," determining "that it should be 21000 horse and foot" and have Lord Fairfax as its leader.[282] It was not until the start of April that the peers, under light of renewed military threats and the breakdown of treaty negotiations with the king, agreed to the bill.[283]

Prior to the passing of the Self-Denying Ordinance, parliament needed to decide how it might go about funding a new army and how it might find officers that both houses could agree upon. Common Council offered an obvious answer to the prior issue, and perhaps a somewhat less obvious answer to the latter one. In March, parliament arranged for a committee to visit Common Council and relay information about "the progress in the proceedings" at Uxbridge and their resolution "to put their forces into the best posture they can for the vigorous prosecucion of the warr."[284] By the end of the month, Common Council had agreed to a loan of £80,000 – money that would serve as the foundation of the New Model Army.

Many of the loan's subscribers, notes Coates, came from "conservative political backgrounds," including six who had signed Benyon's petition from February 1642 supporting the loyalist mayor Richard Gurney and even Sir John Cordell, Pennington's opponent for the mayoralty in 1642 and a frequent refuser of parliament's loans.[285] The presence of such men should not, however, be taken as confirmation of the heterogeneous political outlook of the loan's backers; clearly much water had passed under the bridge since the outbreak of war, and of the seventy-eight subscribers to the loan, many, as it turns out, had been leading activists and eager promoters of a robust effort against the king. Indeed, when attempting to assess the character of the backers of the loan, which was secured by "Sir Henry Vane etc.," Juxon, whose own political and religious convictions remain difficult to tag down, concluded that the loan was "procured of the puritans" in

London. Juxon's suggestive, if not necessarily pejorative, reference to the makeup of its supporters is telling.[286] In the absence of his own clarifying remarks, Juxon's sense may be gleaned by a closer consideration of the loan's subscribers.

Nearly half of all the subscriptions for the £80,000 loan were for £1,000, while other amounts ranged from as little as £50 to £5,250. The repayment of the loan came in portions and was completed on 13 January 1646, with a total of £3,610 2s 4d paid in interest. Eight citizens together loaned a staggering £36,150, nearly half of the entire loan.[287] Aldermen Thomas Adams, Thomas Andrewes, John Warner, and John Wollaston each loaned £5,250, while Francis Allein, Abraham Chamberlain, John Dethick, and George Wytham gave £3,787 10s. Of these subscribers, the top four had all been treasurers for parliament since 1642. Warner was a known promoter of the cause, having served as colonel in the trained bands, he also pushed the drapers toward the £100,000 loan in 1642. Several other lenders held sympathies for independency. Chamberlain and Dethick, who were both parishioners in St. Andrew Undershaft, Aldgate had given generously to parliament's cause since 1642.[288] Dethick was a member of the radical Weavers' Hall subcommittee and later an independent.[289] Francis Allein went on to join Robert Scawen's Army Committee of "anti-Essexians," where he acted, according to Adamson, as "the most active" of the London treasurers. His commitment to independency, suggests Adamson, was beyond question.[290] Smaller sums came from several leading City activists and militants. Contributors included Samuel Warner (John Warner's brother), who was an engaged reformer in his home parish of St. Stephen Walbrook, and went on to become a leading independent, gave £1,000. The same came from Alderman John Fowke, one of the seven accused Londoners in early 1643 who had since become a close ally of Vane and St. John in 1644. Robert Tichborne, Stephen Estwicke, Richard Shute, and John Kendrick also loaned £1,000 each. Tichborne, Shute, and Kendrick went on to be leading political independents as well. Shute, as we have seen, was an architect and promoter of radical City petitions in 1642 and 1643. Estwicke had been a Lunsford petitioner and early supplier of war provisions. Tichborne, meanwhile, could be seen as something of a template for City radicalism; he served as a captain of London auxiliaries, was one of seven accused citizens, became member of the Salters' Hall subcommittee on Bread Street, and went on to sign the king's death warrant. A cornerstone of the support for the loan came from wealthy merchants and activists, many of whom were, as Juxon suggested, "the puritans."

The £80,000 played a crucial role getting the New Model Army off the ground. In Gentles' view, the loan request amounted to a "subtle ruse" made by war party members who wished to put pressure on recalcitrant peers and were eager to prevent them from forwarding objections to lists of officers that were compiled by Fairfax.[291] Plans moved ahead, and the Commons voted almost immediately to use £7,000 of the loan to pay for new army volunteers. Responsibility for raising the new forces fell to the London Militia Committee, the Committee of Both Kingdoms, and Thomas Fairfax. Major-General Skippon, who had marched his "brave boys" to Turnham Green in 1642, and who had more recently suffered alongside some of the same men in the Lostwithiel campaign, saw to it that the remnants of Essex's army would find their way into parliament's new army. Some 6,600 horse troopers and 7,226 foot were cannibalized from the respective armies of Essex, Manchester, and Waller, which left 7,174 soldiers to be raised. Of these, 2,500 (more than a third of the total) were to come from London; Essex, Kent, Norfolk, and Suffolk were each expected to raise 1,000 men.

Orders for impressing men stipulated "any man, or the son of any man, rated at £5 in goods or £3 in lands could not be pressed." This left the majority of the recruits to come from apprentices and the poor. "Conscripts," notes Gentles, "came in slowly, and nowhere more slowly than the city." This was, he went on, part of a "strange" disappointment regarding otherwise high hopes for recruitment. A familiarity with the previous three years of metropolitan mobilization might render the disappointment somewhat more intelligible. Londoners had fought on numerous occasions since the outbreak of war in 1642; brigades repeatedly marched into the west where they stormed enemy lines, participated in protracted sieges, and held their ground in some of the most challenging battles to date. Often, their decisions were made under the express threat of an attack on the capital by the king and his supporters. In nearly each instance, Londoners had been urged to act in order to defend their lives, livelihoods, families, and religion. Unlike the droves of young recruits who had gathered in Finsbury Fields in 1642, or indeed the considerable numbers who turned out to join the auxiliaries in 1643, Londoners were, by and large, disinterested in the prospect of enlisting in a new professional parliamentary army. What few volunteers turned out came mostly from "poor and suburban parishes."[292] In a report to the Commons on 7 October, Robert Scawen revealed that the City had raised just fifty-seven of their proposed 1,469 men.[293] Nearly three years of civil war had bred a palpable aversion to the prospect of serving.

If unwilling to take up swords, Londoners had fewer aversions to opening their pocketbooks. Contracts reveal the extent to which the City's inhabitants might benefit from the new undertaking. 9,200 swords were arranged for by the Cutlers; 8,000 shoes from the shoemakers, along with numerous other goods in large quantities.[294] Within days of receiving London's loan, the new Army Committee took to fulfilling contracts. On 7 April, saddlers received £540 for 600 saddles. One fourth of the contract for shoes was filled by Jenkin Ellice and Francis Marrett, who were paid £225 for 2,000 pairs at a cost of 2s 3d per pair. 3,000 had already been contracted from Francis Mariott, John Hones, and Robert Botley for £337 10s. Horses were at the top of the list. On 1 April, £1,500 was paid "in part" of a contract for 1,200 horses. Eight days later, £2,500 was paid for 1,200 horses. That same day, an additional £400 was paid for 200 horses "for dragoons." Outfitting the new army required numerous contracts for clothes and weapons. Christopher Nicholas, for instance, received £425, payment "in full" for supplying 3,000 "Lockeram Shirts att two Shillings ten pence a peece." Edward Harris and Arthur Dew took £400 as "part of their Contract for one Thowsand Coates and Breeches." Benjamin Hawkins had £580 6s 8d, payment "in full" for 2,500 swords and belts at 4s 8d per pair. That same day, Robert Geffrey received £233 6s 8d for 1,000 swords and belts. Supplies, no matter how small, were accounted for. £6 11s was disbursed to General Hammond to pay for "two colors," "two partizans" and "four halberts." 2,000 "Cotton Stockens," meanwhile, were procured at a cost of 12s per dozen for a total of £100.[295] With £80,000 in hand, and an efficient committee managing contracts, the full potential of metropolitan mobilization was finally being revealed.

In some instances, committee contracts were awarded to like-minded City militants. As Gentles first observed, this manifested most clearly with "a consortium of cloth merchants."[296] Most of these men had long been at the forefront of radical City politics. On 6 March 1646 a contract for coats, breeches, and shirts worth £2,339 1s 3d was awarded to Stephen Estwicke and "his Partners," Thomas Player and Tempest Milner. Having loaned £1,000 for the New Model the previous March, Estwicke was beginning to reap financial rewards for his efforts.[297] Other London radicals benefited as well. Owen Rowe was paid £500 to supply 1,000 "backs breasts and potts," and another £100 for "one Thousand Long Pikes." The merchant and activist Francis Webb received £85 for 200 "Dutch Pike" and the same number of "Dutch swords and Belts."[298] It would of course be easy to simply assume that the extensive contracting made by the Army Committee would eventually come to benefit leading activists, many of whom were themselves also merchants.[299] The payment of thousands of pounds to men like Estwicke, Milner, Player, Rowe, and Webb might likewise simply seem a coincidence. Yet chance becomes less plausible when their later political endeavors are taken into account. Each, save for Webb, emerged as a leading political independent in the coming "Counter-Revolution."[300] Their ability to finance, manage, and outfit the New Model Army was the culmination of nearly three years of radical trial and error, of seeking to agitate and implement new initiatives to mobilize the metropolis. The extent to which their early radicalism presaged later events would, for the time being, remain unclear. That culmination would have to wait until August 1647, when the army that they had helped to create in 1645 – the army that would soon defeat the king at Naseby – marched on London.

Conclusion: a "Monument of Mercies"

From the vantage point of 1646, Londoners might take a moment to reflect on their passage through the past four years of turmoil. The "victory" at Naseby on 14 June 1645, Juxon concluded, proved that "God" stood ready to "vindicate His honour" and remind all that he "looks not as man, but by the despised subdues the mighty."[301] Many of Juxon's fellow Londoners surmised that their preservation owed to providential favor. How else could they have escaped from so many narrowly averted crises? Printed in late 1646 as a single broadsheet, *Englands Monument of Mercies in her Miraculous Preservation* urged readers to acknowledge their great fortune and show "thankfulnesse unto God." In accounting for England's preservation, the anonymous author of the broadsheet counted a staggering eighty-six "plots, Conspiracies, Contrivances and attempts of forraigne and home-bred treacherous Enemies," which ranged from the Army Plot of 1641 to "the peace with Irish Rebels" in 1645. Amidst the years that saw an almost exponential increase in plots were a number of other events that have long aided our understanding of the civil war, including familiar episodes such as "the breaking forth of Rebellion in Ireland" in November 1641 and the "demanding of the five Members by the King" in January 1642. But *Englands Monument* showcased several other matters, matters which, if less readily acknowledged in modern scholarship, offer salient clues about what most concerned contemporaries.

It was, after all, no mere coincidence that most of England's "mercies" unfolded in the metropolis. First was the "design against the City of London" from January 1643 that resulted in the calling of "a speciall Common-hall" in which the king's messenger "*Herne* read his message" that demanded the arrest of the seven leading citizens who were accused of treason by the king – the king's ill-fated attempt on the seven Londoners. Next was the terrible plot of May 1643, when Waller and members from "the Court and the City" pursued a plan "to surprise the City and to let in the Kings Army" so that they could seize leading belligerents including Saye, Wharton, Pym, Strode, and "the L[ord] Mayor." Following these pivotal moments was the time in August when "rewd women about London" put their hands to a "petition for a peace" and "came in an abusive way to the House of Parliament." The year 1644 saw its own fair share of mercies, but among the most troubling was the time when "Sir *Bazill Brooke*" teamed up with "*Vilet* a Gold-smith and *Riley*" to foment "another divillish design to divide the Parliament and Cite." Later was the "wicked plot endeavoured by the instigation of the E. of *Bristoll*, and Serjeand-Major *Ogell*, to betray the Citie of London, by causing a division between the Presbyterians and Independents."[302]

Here, then, were some of the many "mercies" for which peccant Londoners should rightfully give thanks to God. Recounted thus, explicitly and with purpose, the "mercies" were intended not simply to chide, but were instead to stir thanks in a sympathetic and informed readership, a part of the populace that likely remembered well enough – or perhaps even lived through – several of the eighty-six "designs" and "plots" outlined on the single sheet. Much more than an opportunity to reminisce, moreover, *Englands Monument* helped to fashion a remarkable narrative of war, and by extension, a popuar account of London's resilience. Central to the sheet, and printed in detail, were the portraits of nine leading individuals who were behind some of the more troubling developments of the past half decade. Included were Thomas Wentworth, earl of Strafford, Laud, and Rupert. But so too were the traitors Catherine Howard, Lady d'Aubigny, and Basil Brooke. Thus, the faces of plotters in the City could be joined by the ranks of leading royalist enemies. "Published according to Order" of parliament and sold in "shops in great Woodstreet, and in the great Old-Baily" – locations near to the Guildhall and St. Paul's Cathedral, respectively – acquiring copies of the broadside was likely easy enough. Of two known surviving copies, both of which belonged to Thomason, only one copy remains intact; a second copy has been carefully edited, with the images of the perpetrators cut away.[303]

Like his fellow Londoners, Thomason had come a long way past the events of late 1642, past the shocking news of Brentford and Edgehill, and past Turnham Green where Skippon proclaimed London's cause "for God, and for the defence of yourselves, your wives and children." Londoners had since worked collectively to build trenches and fortify their City and its suburbs behind the Lines of Communication; they had since weathered the abysmal parliamentarian losses of the spring and summer of early 1643, and they had since repeatedly sent brigades made up of the trained bands and auxiliaries to aid parliament's forces in the counties. From the relief of Gloucester to the shattering defeat at Lostwithiel, Londoners remained steadfast in their commitment to, above all else, themselves.

Indeed, self-defense was a defining aspect of London's wartime mobilization. Pennington and his fellow activists, despite all of their efforts, saw their projects repeatedly shelved in light of Londoners' collective desire to maintain, foremost, their lives and livelihoods. This was a double-edged sword; like the infamous clubmen of the countryside, Londoners might be seen to champion an aggressive war effort one moment, and abandon their commitments the next. William Waller experienced this fickleness first-hand in late 1643 when soldiers from the capital turned to their songs of "Home, Home," only to fight courageously the following day. Efforts to mobilize Londoners could be equally fraught and frustrating. Outside of the official production of ordinances and precepts, activists turned to printed tracts, sermons, petitions, and increasingly to innovative means of communication, including tickets. Unlike petition campaigns, including the infamous 1 December 1642 petition and the later *Remonstrans Redivivus*, tickets afforded a cheap, speedy, and potentially surreptitious means of disseminating news and meeting political objectives. Single sheets could be printed and cut into numerous small tickets, ready for rapid distribution. Richard Browne thus posted tickets throughout London in hopes that he might quickly recruit troops in January 1643. And again, during the turbulent days of early August 1643, Pennington and his allies turned to printed tickets to relay the terms of the general rising and move Londoners to descend on Westminster – a tactic, which, as we have seen, triggered a popular protest that ultimately derailed peace negotiations. In the wake of Lostwithiel and in light of increasingly acrimonious divisions between parliament's leaders, tickets were once again deployed. It was a "libelous ticket" that helped to influence parliamentary debate and further cleave divisions between inchoate political parties in London and Westminster. Tickets, as a largely new and innovative means of mobilization, had come to function as part of what Jason Peacey identified as a "sophisticated and multi-purpose deployment" of print – as tools of action, which helped, in their demotic capacities to shape and harden public opinions, and in practical terms could also help trigger popular mobilization, participation, and protest.[304]

Within this climate, coercion became an increasingly important tactic. Access to the bureaucratic processes and legal frameworks of the mayoralty and Common Council took on new meanings as the war progressed; these instruments of civic rule, put to good use for parliament, reminded onlooking royalists of a veritable "third house." With the full power of the office at his disposal, and with the support of various parliamentary committees, such as the Committee for the Advance of Money and Harley's Committee, Pennington worked tirelessly to channel London's wealth and resources toward parliament's coffers. As suggested above, the Lord Mayor and his allies increasingly relied upon precept orders and official ordinances to move the sinews of war. Amidst efforts to establish an autonomous army such as the one proposed in the autumn of 1642 – and eventually in terms of the general rising of 1643 – Pennington and his allies acted as conduits between parliament's wartime operators and London's vast resources. These efforts manifested in the shape of orders made to livery companies for the delivery of money, arms and armor to the Salters' Hall subcommittee, a radical body that met at the heart of London's Bread Street Ward and was busy overseeing the program for raising auxiliary forces. Even after he stepped down from the mayoralty, Pennington retained important links to the City's war effort in a number of capacities, acting as an alderman, a City MP, Lieutenant of the Tower, and even as a member of the Committee for Compounding Delinquents.[305] Pennington thus made certain that he would remain an essential communicant between London and parliament. But so too did his fellow activists, and not least his fellow accused. Fowke, for instance, remained an active go-between for the City and parliament in 1644, serving on the Militia Committee and lending for the New Model Army. Along with Pennington, John Venn, Edmund Harvey, and Robert Tichborne ended up regicides.

By raising armor and weapons and delivering cash at crucial junctures, livery companies provided lifeblood to parliament's early effort. As we have seen, the first of these loans, some £100,000 initially – perhaps even ostensibly – collected to help fund relief for Protestants in Ireland, was soon appropriated in order to help launch a war against the king. Later, loans of money and arms were made expressly for London and parliament and in the name of Mayor Pennington. This was the case with the £50,000 loan from August 1643 that financed a relief force for Gloucester. The pressure of lending left many companies with their coffers depleted, their plate pawned, and their armories empty. Thus the ancient and sturdy foundations of the City's guild and trade association steadily decayed. Coates rightly points out that demands for money amounted to "a major blow to the finances of the livery companies"; the pressure of raising loans not only "diminished the role they played in London society," but also "contributed to their declining importance in the second half of the seventeenth century, "part of a process that saw ancient guilds eclipsed by overseas ones like the Merchant Adventurers."[306] A warring parliament, like a warring king, could scarcely satisfy its financial appetite. Rather than reveal a case in which livery companies "had exchanged an insatiable royal borrower for a slightly less insatiable Parliamentary one," it looked to be the other way around.[307] While the decline of London's liveries doubtless accelerated due to the runaway cost of war, and indeed due to Pennington's relentless demands, there can in the end be little doubt that their collective sacrifice helped catalyze parliament's success. From this process we may also glean a sense of the coming systematization of taxation, and of developing methods of coercion over individual and corporate wealth that would in time become crucial components of the state.

Apart from livery companies, parochial communities served as the other great wellspring of parliament's financial and military mobilization. Parishioners helped to supply an almost endless influx of cash during the early war. They provided essential ground-level support for parliament's efforts, from repeatedly lending, like they did with the oversubscribed £30,000 loan from November 1642, to the provision of chains to block streets, shovels to build trenches, and cheese and beer to refresh soldiers drilling in London's artillery grounds. Parishioners, moreover, were the targets of myriad novel financial expedients, some of which led, in due course, to established programs of parliamentarian wartime finance. Thus, parishioners often found themselves presented with *ad hoc* proposals for collecting loans and revenue. Subcommittee efforts, such as those of the Weavers' Hall and Salters' Hall, and controversial plans such as the weekly meal, all depended, at their core, on civic, and thus parochial, engagement. Together, these disparate financial expedients – along with other programs and *ad hoc* efforts like Hugh Peter's mission to the Netherlands, which produced some £30,000 – kept parliament's effort moving forward. As the war progressed, expedient measures gave way to fully realized programs for generating revenue, forerunners, and in some cases eventually components of, early state formation.[308] With each success, a cautious confidence replaced widespread uncertainty. Proposals for a £60,000 loan in early 1643, which was backed by the new monthly assessment, generated a mere £23,000, for instance, while loans backed by sequestration funds to pay for the Scots were an overwhelming success. The £80,000 loan from late 1644, which was also backed by the monthly assessment, was collected in full and proved crucial for securing the City contracts that got the New Model Army off the ground in 1645. The first three years of the City's war witnessed the birth of numerous wartime measures that would in some cases fail, but in others would become fixed components of parliamentarian finance – aspects of mobilization that were increasingly associated with "parliamentary tyranny."[309] In terms of their lifespans, none of these measures would be more important than the excise, a tax that came to dominate parliamentarian finance and find a lasting place in the state apparatus.[310] Londoners often found themselves at the forefront of such developments, from inception to implementation.

Parishes underwent dramatic changes over the early years of war. "Delinquent" ministers were sequestered in favor of "godly" replacements, lead crosses were hacked off steeples, and stained-glass windows were made clear. From their local pews, parishioners could listen as some of the nation's most capable preachers conjured a distant past to explain the present. It was of course St. Stephen's Coleman Street where Londoners first heard John Goodwin, "the Great Red Dragon," warn of Meroz in 1641, and it was Christ Church Newgate Street where Joseph Caryl preached his furious *Davids Prayer for Solomon* in 1643. It was, likewise, from the confines of the Tower Chapel that Samuel Kem relayed divine "blessings" to those who died for parliament's cause.[311] We might do well at this point to once again acknowledge that sectarian stars were not alone in parliament's constellation – they were not the only ones to bellow tales of ruin as the likely alternative to parliamentarian success. Indeed, presbyterian leaders had genuine stakes in the war since the very beginning. Men like Stephen Marshall, Edmund Calamy, and Thomas Case were among the first preachers to step into metropolitan pulpits and promote the cause with vigor. Many, as we have seen, found early success in the crowded spaces at the heart of the metropolis, in the parishes that fell within Bread Street Ward and nearby wards of Queenhithe and Farringdon Within, or indeed slightly east in the wards of Dowgate, Candlewick, and Billingsgate.

London's crowded streets all the while swelled due to the arrival of refugees and maimed soldiers who inspired sympathy, required care, and served as daily reminders of the physical and spiritual costs of war. The maimed soldier who wrote *Idolaters Ruine, and Englands Triumph* urged his fellow soldiers in early 1645 to continue to "shew their love and affection to the cause of Christ; and fear not to venture their lives, limbes or estates." Failure to do so, he cautioned, could bring about a fate as terrible as Meroz, which "was not cursed for any evill that he did," but rather "was cursed" because it "did no good." Just as the author (or authors) of *Englands Monument* hoped to give thanks to God for delivery from "manifold Plots, Conspiracies, Contrivances and attempts," the writer of *Idolaters Ruine* wished to see the war maintained until the same God cast "confusion" upon "all such cursed Rebels."[312] If parliament's war effort gradually became less dependent upon the efforts of Londoners, the outcome of the conflict still depended on divine approbation.

Records of parochial lending paint a picture of a metropolis that was never simply parliamentarian, but was instead persistently divided, and at times by discernible ward and parish boundaries. From the first efforts to relieve Ireland, through to the Ward Assessments for Non-Contributors, and on to the numerous mobilizing efforts of 1643, including the Vow and Covenant returns, distinct areas of support and recalcitrance come into view. Efforts to raise money for parliament were most successful in the center of London around St. Paul's Cathedral, and again just north of the Thames and east of London Bridge. If irregular in composition and size, the parishes that saw the greatest financial, military, and social mobilization also often enjoyed a healthy intersection between preaching and parochial activism. Taken together, this suggests that parochial communities, as resilient centers of religious and social life, were crucial to parliament's success. We might thus appreciate an extension of Ian Archer's observation regarding Elizabethan parishes, and note that during the civil wars they still provided "an important unity of identity," and that their unique identities persisted during times "of considerable stress."[313] Doubtless, in light of the upheavals of the early 1640s, their resilience was tested to the breaking point. Underscored here, again then, is the extent to which parochial mobilization depended upon an active ministry. Preachers had, from the earliest exhortations for Ireland, to the repeated efforts to collect money for the maimed, worked diligently to "stir up" their auditors. This helps to explain why from the outset of his mayoralty, Pennington, along with leading aldermen and councilors, actively sought out new venues for Paul's Cross sermons, and why, again, efforts like the City's Camden House Committee were implemented. Contemporaries understood – even if often only sometimes implicitly – that control over London's pulpits could be translated into a command over money and men. Mobilizing efforts were thus carried out at first by a broad coalition that included committed militants alongside networks of likeminded godly supporters; it was not until later, when the pressures and demands of war shifted, as wartime alliances both fractured and coalesced, that the parameters of radicalism shifted too.

Another obvious, if largely unintentional, outcome of mobilizing efforts was the rapid politicization of Londoners. Appeals to action, by means of concerted efforts to propagandize and, increasingly, coerce, led to a novel climate of popular participation – a milieu in which political elites repeatedly, and often out of necessity, interacted with "ordinary people." This interaction helped to broaden the space of participatory politics, leaving Londoners – in civil government, in trade associations and companies, and throughout their local parochial communities – with an unprecedented say over the dialogue of national politics, and, on some occasions, the conduct of war itself. Among the most important episodes considered here are the times when metropolitans assembled en masse in response to popular agitations – times such as the night of 6 January 1642 when thousands armed themselves in response to rumors of a "cavalier" army; or again in November of the same year when Skippon and the militia sprung into action to defy the king at Turnham Green; or yet again on 7 August 1643, when scores of Londoners heeded printed tickets calling for a "general rising" and descended on Westminster, intimidating peers and helping to terminate parliament's consideration of peace propositions. Thousands placed their names on monster petitions against bishops in December 1641, just as they did again with the petitions headed by Richard Shute in November and December 1642, and again in October 1644 with the petition for Laud's execution. It was during these moments of popular political agitation and participation that the intentions of London's wartime activists (of Pearl's "upper sorts") dovetailed with what we might still call the "politics of the streets." Throughout the period spanning from late 1641 to early 1645 we thus encounter progressive, and at times outspokenly revolutionary, ideologies and interests inspiring popular protests and demonstrations – reifications of inchoate and disparate concerns that helped to define parliamentarianism, both in terms of its "radical" ideological parameters and its innovative financial expedients. With all of this in motion, we might also rightly understand that civil war London was crucial to the progress of the early modern state; it was a place where the warring state found some of its first opportunities to extract the sinews of war. We might also finally put to rest lingering notions that the City persisted "without a popular uprising."[314] To assume that the capital's revolution happened solely in its Corporation, or indeed to suggest that the City's agitated crowds somehow lacked political initiative, is to strip agency from where it is most due; it is to wrest from the hands of Londoners their collective ability to engage with the politics of their day, a politics that was as much about supporting parliament's war against a misguided monarch as it was about the streets where that struggle was being defined.

Notes

1 *Mercurius Aulicus* (Oxford, 1643, E.65[26]), pp. 433–434.
2 Braddick, *God's Fury*, p. 301.
3 BL, Harley MS 165, fol. 149r.
4 Drapers' Company Library, Court Minutes and Records, 1640–1667, fol. 31r; see also LMA, MS COL/CC/01/01/041, fol. 70r.
5 See Hughes, *Gangraena*; Elliot Vernon, "The Sion College Conclave and London Presbyterianism during the English Revolution" (unpub. Ph.D. thesis, University of Cambridge, 1999).
6 Hughes, *Gangraena*, pp. 50–51, 440.
7 Como, *Radical Parliamentarians*, p. 209.
8 Jack Hexter offers the classic example with *Reign of King Pym*. See also David Como, who is the most recent to follow this trajectory, and has provided an excellent account in *Radical Parliamentarians*, pp. 176–178.
9 BL, Add MS 31116, fos. 70v–71r. See Brenner, *Merchants and Revolution*, p. 457; Como, *Radical Parliamentarians*, p. 177.
10 Sarah Barber, *A Revolutionary Rogue: Henry Marten and the English Republic* (Stroud, 2000), pp. 8–10.
11 Hexter of course saw his ejection as a move by Pym who was eager "to silence the attacks of the war party on the monarchy." *Reign of King Pym*, p. 60.
12 *Mercurius Aulicus* (Oxford, 1643, E.79[1]), p. 703.
13 *The Churches Lamentation* (London, 1644).
14 Ian Gentles, "Political Funerals during the English Revolution," in S. Porter (ed.), *London and the Civil War* (London, 1996), pp. 209–210.
15 Harding, *The Dead and Living in Paris and London*, p. 257.
16 See Valerie Pearl, "Oliver St. John and the Middle Group in the Long Parliament: August 1643–May 1644," *EHR*, 81 (1966), pp. 490–519. See also Lotte Glow, "Political Affiliations in the House of Commons after Pym's

Death," *Historical Research*, 38 (1965), pp. 48–70; William G. Palmer, "Oliver St. John and the Middle Group in the Long Parliament, 1643–1645: A Reappraisal," *Albion*, 14 (1982), pp. 20–26. For more recent and important reconsiderations of the "middle group" matter, see David Scott, *Politics and War in the Three Stuart Kingdoms* (Basingstoke, 2003); Jason Peacey, "Perceptions of Parliament: Faction and 'The Public,' " in John Adamson (ed.), *The English Civil War: Conflict and Contexts, 1640–49* (Basingstoke, 2009), pp. 82–105; Scott, "Politics in the Long Parliament," pp. 32–55.

17 Mark Kishlansky, "The Emergence of Adversary Politics in the Long Parliament," *Journal of Modern History*, 49 (1977), pp. 617–640; Mark Kishlansky, *The Rise of the New Model Army* (Cambridge, 1979).
18 Adamson, *Noble Revolt*. For Adamson's earlier claims, see in particular J. S. A. Adamson, "The Baronial Context of the English Civil War," *TRHS*, 40 (1990), pp. 93–120.
19 Pearl, *London*, p. 330.
20 GL, MS 11588/4, fol. 83.
21 GL, MS 15842/1, fol. 318r.
22 GL, MS 5570/3, fos. 688, 692.
23 Mercers' Company Libraray, Acts of Court, 1641–1645, fos. 84v–r, 79r.
24 Goldsmiths' Company Library, Court Minute Book W, fos. 84r–v, 85v, 91r.
25 Drapers' Company Library, Court Minutes and Records, 1640–1667, fol. 32v.
26 Clothworkers' Company Library, Orders of Courts, 1639–1649, fos. 83r, 94v.
27 Salters' Company Library, Court Minute Book, 1627–1684, p. 246.
28 GL, MS 30708/3, fol. 205v.
29 LMA, MS P69/LAW1/B/001/MS02590/001, fol. 340.
30 Sleigh-Johnson, "The Merchant Taylors Company of London 1580–1645," pp. 222, 224–226.
31 GL, MS 15201/1, fol. 125.
32 Ibid., fol. 127.
33 Ibid., fol. 129.
34 Ibid., fos. 130, 136.
35 Ibid., fol. 151.
36 GL, MS 16967/4, fol. 398.
37 Ibid., fos. 400–432.
38 Ben Coates explores this matter briefly in *Impact*, pp. 70–71.
39 *CJ* vol. 3, 29 September 1643, pp. 258–259.
40 GL, MS 7352/1, fol. 262.
41 GL, MS 3297/1, unfol.
42 GL, MS 5445/17, unfol.
43 GL, MS 5385, fol. 242r–v.
44 GL, MS 6153/1, fos. 220r–223v, 226r, 230r.
45 GL, MS 5667/1, fos. 179, 186.
46 GL, MS 2881/5, pp. 138, 141. No further mention of the remaining £20 is made in the account.
47 GL, MS 6649/1, fol. 12r.
48 GL, MS 3043/2, 1620–63, fos. 153r–154v.

49 GL, MS 2208/1, 1621–47, unfol.
50 GL, MS 5204/003, unfol.
51 For a note on this matter, see Coates, *Impact*, pp. 79–80, 184.
52 LMA, MS COL/CC/01/01/041, fol. 94v–95r.
53 Coates, *Impact*, pp. 71–72.
54 W. A. Day (ed.), *The Pythouse Papers: Correspondence Concerning the Civil War, the Popish Plot, and a Contested Election in 1680* (London, 1879), p. xliii.
55 John Williams, *London love to her neighborus in generall* (London, 1643), p. 10.
56 *CJ* vol. 3, 18 August 1643, pp. 209–211. An additional 2,000 were ordered to be impressed "out of the Counties of Kent, Surrey, Sussex, and Hampshire."
57 BL, Add MS 31116, fol. 72r.
58 *Mercurius Aulicus*, Monday, 28 August 1643, p. 474.
59 *Whereas the Committee for the Militia* (London, 1643).
60 LMA, MS P69/BAT1/B/006/MS04383/001, 1598–1698, fol. 432r.
61 LMA, MS P69/MRY1/B/006/MS03891/001, unfol.; LMA, MS P69/MRY2/B/005/MS03556/002, unfol.; LMA MS P69/MRY14/B/006/MS01013/001, fol. 143r; LMA, MS P69/BOT4/B/008/MS04524/002, fol. 79r; LMA, MS P69/BOT3/B/007/MS00942/001, fol. 165v; LMA, MS P69/LAW1/B/008/MS02593/002, fol. 67.
62 LMA, MS P69/BRI/B/016/MS06552/001, fos. 123r, 124v, 125r, 126v.
63 Coates estimates that the fifty subsidies generated £80,589. *Impact*, p. 51.
64 LMA, MS COL/CC/01/01/041, fol. 73v.
65 Williams, *London love*, p. 11.
66 *CSPV*, p. 13.
67 See the Draft Ordinance from 6 September 1643 in PA, HL/PO/JO/10/1/156, fol. 20r-v.
68 *CJ* vol. 3, 12 September 1643, p. 238.
69 *Mercurius Aulicus*, 27 August 1643, p. 472.
70 *Mercurius Britanicus*, 5 September 1643, p. 17. E.67[8].
71 Adair, *Roundhead General*, p. 120.
72 *CSPV*, p. 18.
73 National Army Museum, MS 6807-53, William Levett, "The Enseigns of the Regiments in the rebellious Citty of London both of Trayned Bands and Auxiliaries"; see Richard Symonds's copy of Levett in BL, Add MS 986, "The Ensignes of the Regiments in the Citty of London: Both of Trayned Bands and Auxiliaries," fos. 1r–72v. Both Levett's original and Symonds's copy are included in Harold Arthur Dillon, "On a MS. List of Officers of the London Trained Bands in 1643," in *Archaeologia* 52 (London, 1890), pp. 130–144. See also Nagel, "The Militia of London, 1641–1649," p. 131.
74 *A True Relation of the late Expedition of His Excellency* (London, 1643), pp. 1, 13.
75 See Nagel, "The Militia of London, 1641–1649," pp. 127–128.
76 Ibid., p. 128; Clarendon, *History*, vol. II, p. 268.
77 *The True Informer*, 30 September 1643, p. 11; Henry Foster, *A True and Exact Relation* (London, 1643), sigs. A4r, B3r–v, B4v.

78 *The True Informer*, 30 September 1643, p. 11.
79 The ringers at St. Bride were paid two shillings "when the Trayned bands came home from Gloucester." See LMA, Ms P69/BRI/B/016/MS06552/001, fol. 124v; LMA, Ms P69/TR13/B/004/MS04835/001, unfol.
80 Adair, *Roundhead*, p. 121.
81 *CJ* vol. 3, 7 October 1643, pp. 265–268.
82 LMA, MS COL/CC/01/01/041, fos. 78r–79r; see also *Mercurius Civicus*, 12–19 October 1643, p. 166.
83 LMA, MS COL/CC/01/01/041, fol. 78v.
84 *Mercurius Civicus*, 12–19 October 1643, pp. 166–167.
85 BL, Add MS 37343, fol. 280r.
86 Elias Archer, *A True Relation* (London, 1643), p. 3.
87 Ibid., p. 6.
88 *Historical Manuscript Commission. Thirteenth Report, Appendix, Part 1 MSS of the Duke of Portland*, vol. 1 (London, 1891), pp. 154–155.
89 Archer, *A True Relation*, pp. 10–13. Archer puts the total number of prisoners at 1,100.
90 *A&O*, pp. 197–202.
91 *CJ* vol. 3, pp. 219–220. See also, Vallance, who also quotes this in *Revolutionary England*, p. 59.
92 See, for instance, LMA, MS P69/BAT1/B/001/MS04384/001, fol. 12, which includes forty-two signatures including the lecturer, John Lightfoote. See above for a brief discussion of the relationship between the Solemn League and Covenant and the earlier Vow and Covenant.
93 Hexter, *Reign of King Pym*, p. 151.
94 *An Order for the speedy raising of Money for the Advancing of the Scotch Army* (London, 1643).
95 TNA, SP 28/1 fols. 1–4.
96 *A&O*, pp. 311–15.
97 Coates, *Impact*, pp. 57–58.
98 See TNA, SP 16/498/70r; *An Ordinance of the Commons Assembled in Parliament* (London, 1643), sig. A2r; TNA, SP 16/498/73; *An Ordinance of the Lords and Commons Assembled in Parliament, Declaring the causes wherefore ... the ruines of both Kingdomes* (London, 1642), p. 2.
99 Coates, *Impact*, p. 58.
100 LMA, MS P69/BAT1/B/001/MS04384/001, fos. 13–14. Coates cites the total from St. Bartholomew as £276, *Impact*, pp. 57–58.
101 David Laing (ed.), *The Letters and Journals of Robert Ballie, 1637-1662*, vol. 2 (Edinburgh, 1841), p. 104.
102 TNA, SP 46/106 fos. 21, 23, 38, 79.
103 *A Full Relation of the Scots martch from Barwicke to Newcastle* (London, 1644), A2v.
104 See in particular Matthew Glazier, "Scots in the French and Dutch Armies during the Thirty Years' War," in Steve Murdoch (ed.), *Scotland and the Thirty Years War: 1618–1648* (Leiden, 2001), pp. 117–142.

105 Wallace Notestein, "The Establishment of the Committee of Both Kingdoms," *AHR*, 17 (1912), p. 477.
106 Violet Rowe, *Sir Henry Vane the Younger: A Study in Political and Administrative History* (London, 1970), pp. 32–33; David Scott, *Politics and War in the Three Stuart Kingdoms, 1657–49* (Basingstoke, 2003), pp. 70–71.
107 Hopper, *Turncoats and Renegadoes*, p. 51; Smith, *Royalist Agents, Conspirators and Spies*, p. 54 n. 58; see also Lindley, *Popular Politics*, pp. 353–355.
108 Lindley, *Popular Politics*, p. 354.
109 *A Perfect Diurnall*, 1–8 January 1644, sig. A4r; *The Kingdomes Weekly Intelligencer*, 2–9 January 1644, sig. P2r. For the implication of Watkins, see Lindley, *Popular Politics*, p. 354. For a valuable account of the entire episode, see Bertha M. Gardiner (ed.), "A Secret Negociation with Charles I, 1643–1644," in *Camden Miscellany*, 8 (Westminster, 1883).
110 For the best account of the plot, see Amos Tubb, *Thomas Violet, a Sly and Dangerous Fellow: Silver and Spying in Civil War London* (Lanham, 2017), pp. 43–50. Tubb argues that Riley, who could previously be counted as a City belligerent and promoter of parliament's cause, was turned by the prospect of the Scots' entry into the war and the adoption of the Solemn League and Covenant.
111 *CJ* vol. 3, p. 360. For the best contemporary account of the plot, see *A Cunning plot to Divide and Destroy the Parliament and the City of London* (London, 1643). E.29[3].
112 LMA, MS COL/CC/01/01/041, fol. 82v.
113 Stephen Marshall, *A Sacred Panegyrick* (London, 1644), sigs. B1r–v, p. 24.
114 *The Journal of Thomas Juxon, 1644–1647*, ed. Keith Lindley and David Scott (London, 1999), p. 40.
115 LMA, MS COL/CC/01/01/041, fol. 84v. See fol. 83v for the discussion of a weekly meal. Lindley cites *The Letters and Journals of Robert Ballie*, vol. 2, pp. 134–135 for the figure £4,000. See Lindley, *Popular Politics*, p. 355.
116 *Juxon*, p. 40.
117 LMA, MS COL/CC/01/01/041, fol. 86r.
118 LMA, MS COL/CC/01/01/041, fol. 86v for his promotion of the controversial weekly meal.
119 See *CJ* vol. 3, p. 380; LMA, MS COL/CC/01/01/041, fos. 88r–v.
120 LMA, MS COL/CC/01/01/041, fol. 88v; Brenner, *Merchants and Revolution*, p. 466.
121 William Palmer, *The Political Career of Oliver St. John, 1637–1649* (Delaware, 1992), p. 91.
122 Coffman, *Excise Taxation*, p. 38. See p. 102 for a table that compares the excise paid by London and the counties; *A&O* vol. I, pp. 394–395.
123 Coffman, *Excise Taxation*, p. 39.
124 For his important distinction between "purposeful" and "indifferent" aspects of state formation, see Braddick, *State Formation*, p. 1.
125 See Thomas Cogswell, "Underground Verse and the Transformation of Early Stuart Political Culture," *HLQ*, 60:3 (1997), pp. 303–326.

126 HL, MS 16522, "A Collection of Poems & Ballads in ridicule of the Parliamty Party during the Quarrel with Ch. I." Thomas Weaver's song was "set to the tune of ye Pedigree," p. 7.
127 HL, MS Ellesmere 7802.
128 GL, MS 5570/3, fol. 714.
129 HL, MS 16522, p. 62.
130 Coates, *Impact*, p. 39.
131 *A Declaration and Motive of the Persons Trusted* (London, 1643); LMA, MS COL/CC/01/01/041, fos. 86v, 88v–90v.
132 *A&O*, pp. 405–409.
133 BL, Add MS 40883, fol. 188v.
134 Carlton, *Going to the Wars*, p. 214.
135 Gruber von Arni, *Justice to the Maimed*, pp. 21, 34.
136 Ibid., p. 49.
137 Ibid., pp. 65, 68.
138 *A&O* vol. I, pp. 36–37; Geoffrey L. Hudson, "The Relief of English Disabled Ex-Sailors, c. 1590–1680," in Cheryl A. Fury (ed), *The Social History of English Seamen, 1485–1649* (Woodbridge, 2012), pp. 236–237.
139 LMA, MS P69/MRY2/B/001/MS03570/002, unfol.
140 Gruber von Arni, *Justice to the Maimed*, p. 50.
141 Goldsmiths' Company Library, MS 223, "Strelley's Charity Book, 1603–1790."
142 Ibid.; Goldsmiths' Company Library, Goldsmiths' Court Minute Book W, 1642–1645, fol. 108v.
143 LMA, MS COL/CA/01/01/061, fol. 61r. The total assessments for the maimed collected between 1635 and 1643 was £1435 15s, while the total collected for pensions for the same period was £1337 4d.
144 LMA, MS COL/CA/01/01/061, fos. 62v–63r.
145 LMA, MS COL/CA/01/01/061, fos. 15r, 34r, 59r, 65v, 70v–71r, 174r–v.
146 LMA, MS P69/SWI/B/004/MS00559/001, fol. 44r.
147 LMA, MS P69/BAT1/B/006/MS04383/001, fol. 430r.
148 LMA, MS P69/MRY12/B/002/MS05714/001, fos. 133v, 139r, 143v.
149 John Harvard Library, St. Mary Newington Churchwardens' Accounts, 1632–1734, unfol.
150 LMA, MS P69/LAW1/B/008/MS02593/002, fol. 29; LMA, MS P69/ALH8/B/013/MS00823/001, unfol.
151 LMA, MS COL/CC/01/01/041, fol. 91v. For information on Sutton Hospital, see Gruber von Arni, *Justice to the Maimed*, p. 145.
152 *CJ*, vol. 3, p. 460.
153 See in particular the Civil War Petitions project, www.civilwarpetitions.ac.uk.
154 LMA, MS P69/BOT4/B/008/MS04524/002, fos. 78v, 79r.
155 LMA, MS P69/ETH/B/006/MS04241/001, p. 384.
156 LMA, MS P69/STE2/B/008/MS00593/004, unfol.
157 LMA, MS P69/MTN2/B/001/MS00959/001, fol. 137v.
158 Camden Local Studies and Archives Center, MS VOL P/GF/M/4, unfol.
159 Ibid.

160 *The Parliament Scout* (London, 1644, E.12[12]), p. 543.
161 Hudson, "The Relief of English Disabled Ex-Sailors," pp. 236–237.
162 Ibid.
163 LMA, MS P69/OLA2/B/004/MS04409/002, unfol.
164 John Harvard Library, Churchwardens' Accounts of St. George the Martyr, 1621–170, fol. 170r.
165 LMA, MS P69/JNZ/B/014/MS00590/001, fol. 190v.
166 *CJ* vol. 3, p. 435.
167 LMA, P92/SAV/1944, Printed Proclamation from 31 March 1644.
168 LMA, P92/SAV/1940; LMA, P92/SAV/1942.
169 LMA, P92/SAV/1949.
170 LMA, P92/SAV/1945, Parliamentary Proclamation for Collecting Wool and Clothes from 13 June 1644.
171 LMA, P92/SAV/1944, Printed Proclamation from 31 March 1644.
172 Joseph Caryl, *The Saints Thankfull Acclamation* (London, 1644), p. 48.
173 Thomas Hill, *The Season for Englands Self-reflection* (London, 1644), p. 12.
174 *CJ* vol. 4, p. 153.
175 LMA, MS COL/CC/01/01/041, fol. 146r.
176 TNA, SP 21/16, fos. 87v–88r.
177 Quoted in Adair, *Roundhead General*, p. 159.
178 *A Letter from Captain Jones* (London, 1644), lacks pagination and signatures.
179 *A Fuller Relation* (London, 1644), lacks pagination and signatures; for the royalist mockery of Browne, see Keith Lindley, "Sir Richard Browne, first baronet (*c.* 1602–1669)," *ODNB* (2004).
180 LMA, MS COL/CA/01/01/061, fol. 106v.
181 *Juxon*, p. 49.
182 Thomas Ellis, *An Exact and Full Relation of the Last Fight* (London, 1644), p. 5.
183 Peter Gaunt, *The English Civil War: A Military History* (London, 2014), pp. 182–183.
184 Cited in Nagel, "The Militia of London, 1641–1649," p. 197.
185 Ibid.
186 *Mercurius Civicus*, 11–17 July (London, 1644). Opinions were initially divided over where London regiments might serve. By September and early October, it was determined that five regiments should go to Sir James Harrington. See *Juxon*, p. 59.
187 Clive Holmes, *The Eastern Association in the English Civil War* (Cambridge, 1974), p. 1.
188 Braddick, *God's Fury*, p. 330.
189 BL, Harley MS 483, fos. 92r–94r. My thanks are due to Sears McGee for providing me with a transcript of this journal.
190 BL, Add MS 37343, fos. 308v–309r.
191 For a valuable discussion of these banners and their meanings see Ian Gentles, "The Iconography of Revolution," in Ian Gentles, John Morrill, and Blair Worden (eds), *Soldiers, Writers and Statesmen of the English Revolution* (Cambridge, 1998), pp. 91–113. For more examples of banners, see Alan

R. Young, *The English Emblem Tradition vol. 3: Emblematic Flag Devices of the English Civil Wars, 1642–1660* (Toronto, 1995).

192 Edwards, *Dealing in Death*, pp. 196–197.
193 Ibid., see in particular Table 8, which is compiled from TNA, SP 28/261–4.
194 Ibid., pp. 149–150, 211.
195 TNA, SP 84/157 fol 221r. My thanks to Jason Peacey for bringing this letter to my attention.
196 Hugh Peter, *The Case of Mr. Hugh Peters* (London, 1660), p. 3.
197 Bodleian Library, Clarendon MS 22, fol. 128r–v. Walter Strickland served as Peter's contact in the Netherlands. The order from September was signed by Say and Seale, Sir Gilbert Gerard, John Pym, and Anthony Nicoll.
198 See Adams, "The Protestant Cause." For the cause in the 1620s, see Thomas Cogswell, *The Blessed Revolution: English Politics and the Coming of War, 1621–1624* (Cambridge, 1989).
199 Keith Sprunger, *Dutch Puritanism: A History of English and Scottish Churches of the Netherlands in the Sixteenth and Seventeenth Centuries* (Leiden, 1982), p. 384.
200 BL, Add MS 72436, fol. 36r. My thanks are due to Sam Fullerton for bringing these instructions to my attention.
201 HL, MS HA Correspondence Box 17 #9695.
202 Bodleian Library, MS Clarendon 22, fol. 128r.
203 "The Diary of John Greene (1635–59)," ed. E. M. Symonds, *EHR*, 43 (1928), p. 528.
204 LMA, MS COL/CC/01/01/041, fos. 91v, 94v; Coates, *Impact*, pp. 60–64.
205 *At the Sub-committee at Salters Hall in Breadstreet* (London, 1644). For the increased reliance on the weekly meal, see LMA, MS COL/CC/01/01/041, fos. 92r, 93ar–v. On 8 April, the Common Council agreed to use "credit of the weekly meale" to contract 3,000 muskets and 1,000 pikes to arm City auxiliary forces.
206 This issue draws from a lengthy and at times contentious historiography. See, for instance, J. H. Hexter, "The Problem of the Presbyterian Independents," *AHR*, 44 (1938), pp. 29–49; David Underdown, "The Independents Reconsidered," *JBS*, 3 (1964), pp. 57–84; Valerie Pearl, "'The Royal Independents' in the English Civil War," *TRHS*, 18 (1968), pp. 69–86. As a number of scholars have pointed out, the process of political "polarization" that came to define presbyterian and independent "parties" was rarely clear-cut, but rather shifted on a regular basis over the course of the 1640s. Both "indepdents" and "presbyterians" are perhaps best understood as "heterogeneous groups," as Austin Woolrych suggested, or perhaps in terms of a "broad coalition," as Whitney Jones observed. See Austin Woolrych, *Soldiers and Statesmen: The General Council of the Army and its Debates, 1647–1648* (Oxford, 1987), pp. 5–8; Whitney Jones, *Thomas Rainborowe (c. 1619–1648): Civil War Seaman, Siegemaster and Radical* (Woodbridge, 2005), p. 45. For the most recent assessment of these categories, both in terms of their values and shortcomings, see Como, *Radical Parliamentarians*, pp. 239–242, 266–283.

207 See Sears McGee, "Francis Rous and the 'scabby or itchy children': The Problem of Toleration in 1645," *HLQ*, 67 (2004), pp. 401–422; Hunter Powell, *The Crisis of British Protestantism: Church Power in the Puritan Revolution, 1638–44* (Manchester, 2015), pp. 91–212.

208 Again, see Hughes, *Gangraena*, *passim*; Vernon, "The Sion College Conclave and London Presbyterianism duing the English Revolution," chapter 2.

209 Gardiner, *History*, vol. I, pp. 299–323.

210 Lindley, *Popular Politics*, pp. 356–403.

211 Brenner, *Merchants and Revolution*, p. 464.

212 Thomas Goodwin, Philip Nye, Sidrach Simpson, Jeremiah Burroughes, and William Bridge, *An Apologeticall Narration, Humbly Submitted to the Honourable Houses of Parliament* (London, 1643/1644); see Powell, *The Crisis of British Protestantism*, pp. 91–212; see also Ethan Shagan, "Rethinking Moderation in the English Revolution: The Case of *An Apologeticall Narration*," in Stephen Taylor and Grant Tapsell (eds), *The Nature of the English Revolution Revisited* (Woodbridge, 2013), pp. 27–51.

213 This account draws heavily from John Coffey, *John Goodwin and the Puritan Revolution: Religion and Intellectual Change in Seventeenth-Century England* (Woodbridge, 2006), pp. 107–108; see also Laing, *Letters and Journals*, vol. 2, p. 111; Gardiner, "A Secret Negociation with Charles the First, 1643–44," pp. i–xviii.

214 Robert S. Paul, *The Assembly of the Lord: Politics and Religion in the Westminster Assembly and the "Grand Debate"* (Edinburgh, 1985), p. 235.

215 Como, "Print, Censorship, and Ideological Escalation in the English Civil War," p. 826; Murray Tolmie suggests that *An Apologeticall Narration* was toned down on purpose as a way to maintain parliamentary support for independents. *The Triumph of the Saints: The Separate Churches of London, 1616–1649* (Cambridge, 1977), pp. 94–99.

216 *Juxon*, p. 40.

217 HL, HM MS 16522, p. 11.

218 Como, *Radical Parliamentarians*, pp. 205–211.

219 It is worth noting, as Ann Hughes does in *Gangraena*, that Edwards claimed "no 'unkindness' between him and the authors of the *Apologeticall Narration*." Hughes, *Gangraena*, pp. 32–33; Thomas Edwards, *Antapologia: Or, a Full Answer to the Apologeticall Narration* (London, 1644), preface, sig. A4r.

220 Edwards, *Antapologia*, sig. A1r.

221 See Adam Steuart [*sic*], a Scottish covenanter and energetic polemicist who was living at the time in London and wrote a number of attacks on the *Narration* beginning with *Some Observations and Annotation upon the Apologeticall Narration*. For examples of the subsequent polemical exchanges, see *Reformation of Church-Government in Scotland, Cleered from some Mistakes and Prejudices* (London, 1644); Thomas Goodwin, *A Coole Conference Between the Scottish Commissioners Cleared Reformation, and the Holland Ministers Apologeticall Narration* (London, 1644); Adam Steuart, *An Answer to a Libell* (London, 1644), dated "Apr 16"; *C. C. the Covenanter Vindicated from Perjurie* (London, 1644), by a "Friend to the Coole Conference"; Thomas

Goodwin, *A Short Answer to A. S. Alias Adam Stewards Second part of his overgrown Duply to the two Brethren* (London, 1644). Thomason dated this "London. Feb 3d"; see also *A Reply of Two Brethren to A.S.* (London, 1644), which Thomason dated "July 11th [1644]." These exchanges diverged into a number of texts, including, notably, an attempt at reconciliation with *A Letter from a Person of Honour Reconciling The Dissenting Brethren (commonly called Independents) and the Presbyterians* (London, 1644), Thomason dated this work "November 30th."

222 *The Iniquity of The Late Solemne League* (London, 1644), pp. 1, 8.
223 George Gillespie, *A Recrimination in Defence of Presbyterianism* (London, 1644); see also Gillespie, *A Late Dialogue Betwixt a Civilian and a Divine* (London, 1644).
224 See, for instance, *A Vindication of the Treatise of Monarchy* (London, 1644); *The Arch Cheate, or the Cheate of Cheats* (London, 1644).
225 William Prynne, *Independency Examined, Unmasked, Refuted* (London, 1644), p. 2.
226 *The Confession of Faith, Of those Churches which are commonly (though falsly) called Anabaptists* (London, 1644), sig. A2r. See Como, *Radical Parliamentarians*, p. 209; B. R. White, "The Doctrine of the Church in the Particular Baptist Confession of 1644," *The Journal of Theological Studies*, 19 (1968), pp. 570–590.
227 Thomas Goodwin, *Of the Constitution, Right, Order, and Government of the Churches* (London, 1696), pp. 1, 3.
228 See Liu, *Puritan London*, pp. 106–107, 120 n. 22; these placements are verifiable through Thomas Edwards's *Antapologia* (London, 1644); Thomas Edwards, *Gangraena* (London, 1646).
229 Tower Hamlets Local History Library and Archives, W/SMH/A/1/1, "Church Book," fol. 1r.
230 See Como, *Radical Parliamentarians*, especially pp. 215–229, 367–371.
231 George Gillespie, *A Sermon Preached* (London, 1644), p. 41.
232 Richard Vines, *The Impostures of Seducing Teachers* (London, 1644), p. 37. Interestingly, Essex was a parishioner at St. Clement Danes and Vines gave his funeral sermon.
233 Thomas Case, *The Quarrell of the Covenant, with the Pacification of the Quarrell, Delivered in Three Sermons* (London, 1644).
234 *CJ* vol. 3, p. 630; BL, Thomason MS 669, fol. 10.
235 BL, Trumbull MS 72435, fol. 35r.
236 LMA, MS COL/CC/01/01/041, fos. 115r–v. The six provisions appear to be a finalized version of the twenty-eight that they initially considered at the beginning of the month. See fos. 108r–110v.
237 *CJ* vol. 3, p. 720.
238 See *The Reasons of the Dissenting Brethren against the Third Proposition Concerning Prebyterial Government* (London, 1645), title page.
239 Milton, *Areopagitica*, p. 31.
240 TNA, SP 21/16, fol. 88r.

241 Adair, *Roundhead General*, p. 196. This account is from Kent Record Office Brabourne Mss., "Military Papers, 1644."
242 Donagan, *War in England*, pp. 202–203.
243 *Alas pore Parliament* (London, 1644).
244 John Goodwin, *Theomachia: Or the Grand Imprudence of men running the hazard of Fighting Against God* (London, 1644), p. 40; John Coffey, *John Goodwin*, pp. 113–115; see also Como, *Radical Parliamentarians*, pp. 276–277.
245 *Juxon*, p. 61. Juxon also notes that Goodwin was subsequently "convened before a committee of parliament, who examined the business (Mr Prynne being most fierce and bitter against him, as formerly against Colonel Fiennes) and, in fine, was by the parliament suspended." Goodwin's sequestration did not happen until the following year. See n. 136 and BL, Add Ms 15669, fos 66, 68v, 74.
246 LMA, MS COL/CC/01/01/041, fol. 106v; *CJ* vol. 3, p. 624.
247 LMA, MS COL/CC/01/01/041, fos. 107r–v.
248 *Juxon*, p. 59.
249 *Perfect Passages* (1644), p. 32, E.17[1].
250 *Parliament Scout* (1644), p. 586. E.17[4].
251 *Juxon*, pp. 63–65.
252 Adair, *Roundhead General*, p. 213.
253 TNA, SP 21/17 fol. 175v, 183r; records from the "Office of the Excise in Broadstreet" reveal that Browne received £1,000 on 16 January and another £1,000 on 18 March. See SP 28/144, part 1, fol. 76r.
254 It is not beyond reason to assume that some peers had come to understand that Laud could be used as a bargaining chip in their increasingly acrimonious dealings with the Lower House, and indeed that his life would be an important component of any potential peace talks with the king.
255 *CJ* vol. 3, p. 680.
256 Leonie James, *"This Great Firebrand": William Laud and Scotland, 1617–1645* (Woodbridge, 2017), p. 167; for Ayres, see J. B. Boddie, "Edward Bennett of London and Virginia," *The William and Mary Quarterly*, 13:2 (1933), p. 117.
257 See LMA, MS COL/CC/01/01/041, fos. 108r–110r.
258 PA, HP/PO/JO/10/1/176, fol. 156.
259 See HL, MS HM 16522, p. 85.
260 Edmund Staunton, *Phineas's Zeal in Execution of Judgement* (London, 1645), Epistle, pp. 10, 30.
261 Quoted by James, *"This Great Firebrand"*, p. 167.
262 BL, Add MS 31116, fol. 177r.
263 *CSPV* vol. 27, pp. 156–167; see also S. R. Gardiner, who quoted Agostini: "Is this the liberty which we promised to maintain with our blood?" *History*, vol. 2, p. 102.
264 BL, Add Ms 31116, fol. 177r.
265 *CSPV* vol. 27, pp. 156–167.
266 *Mercurius Britanicus* (London, 1644, E.21[8]), p. 476; *Mercurius Civicus* (London, 1644, E.22[12]), p. 765; *Perfect Passages* (London, 1644, E.21[13]), p. 59; *The Parliament Scout* (London, 1644, E.21[15]), p. 616.

267 For the matter of the Scots, see James, "*This Great Firebrand*", pp. 169–170.
268 *The Parliament Scout* (London, 1644, E.21[15]), p. 616.
269 Peter Heylyn, *A Briefe Relation* (Oxford, 1644, E.269[20]), p. 15.
270 Tatton Park, MS 68.20, p. 11; see Booy, *The Notebooks*, p. 219.
271 Heylyn, *A Briefe Relation*, p. 15.
272 *Juxon*, p. 72; *The Kingdomes Weekly Intelligencer* made a similar note about the clouds E.24[18], p. 706.
273 *Cyprianus Anglicus: Or, the History of the Life and Death of ... William* (London, 1668), pp. 536–537, 539.
274 *CSPV* vol. 27, pp. 168–175.
275 BL, Add Ms 3116, fol. 188. See Ian Gentles, *The New Model Army in England, Ireland, and Scotland* (Oxford, 1992), pp. 6–7; Como, *Radical Parliamentarians*, p. 291.
276 *The Scottish Dove* (1644), p. 477, E.21[36]; D'Ewes claimed that the debate extended a full hour and a half after his arrival between noon and one o'clock. See BL Harlein Ms 483, p. 127.
277 "The Diary of John Greene," p. 601.
278 BL, Add MS 37343, fol. 347v.
279 *The London Post* (1644), p. 8. E.21[11*]; *The Kingdomes Weekly Intelligencer* (1644), E.21[11], p. 677, and E.21[25], p. 683; *The Scottish Dove* (1644), p. 477 E.21[36].
280 *Juxon*, p 72.
281 HL, Ellesmere Papers MS 7778, "a written protest against the Self-Denying Ordinaince in 1645."
282 BL, Add MS 37343, fol. 354v.
283 See Gentles, *New Model Army*, pp. 6–16.
284 LMA, MS COL/CC/01/01/041, fol. 125r.
285 Coates, *Impact*, p. 62; Pearl, *London*, p. 298.
286 *Juxon*, pp. 7, 76. Como sees at this stage an accordance between Juxon's interests and those of proponents of Independency, one which pre-dates his later siding with the New Model in 1647 (see *Radical Parliamentarians*, pp. 374–376, 383).
287 TNA, SP 28/350/5, part 2. Coates accounted for £36,250. See *Impact*, p. 61.
288 For Chamberlain and Dethick, see Liu, *Puritan London*, p. 84.
289 Lindley, *Popular Politics*, p. 229.
290 See John Adamson, "Of Armies and Architecture: The Employments of Robert Scawen," in Ian Gentles, John Morrill, and Blair Worden (eds), *Soldiers, Writers, and Statesmen of the English Revolution* (Cambridge, 1998), pp. 37, 51–52.
291 Gentles, *New Model Army*, p. 19.
292 Gentles, *New Model Army*, pp. 31–32, 35. The ordinance for impressing troops was first read on 25 February 1645. See *CJ* vol. 4, p. 62.
293 *CJ* vol. 4, p. 299.
294 For specific details about contracts, see Museum of London, MS 46.78/709, "Contracts for the supplying of the Army of Sir Thomas Fairfax in the year 1645."

295 TNA, SP 28/29 fos. 164, 188, 192, 194, 195, 199, 200, 204, 207, 208, 209, 210.
296 See Gentles, *New Model Army*, p. 42.
297 TNA SP 28/36, fos. 188–189.
298 TNA SP 28/352, part 1. fos. 14r–15r, 17r–19r, 32v, 122r–123r. For Webb, see Lindley, *Popular Politics*, p. 207.
299 See John Adamson, "The Triumph of Oligarchy: The Management of the War and the Committee of Both Kingdoms, 1644–1645," in Chris Kyle and Jason Peacey (eds), *Parliament at Work: Parliamentary Committees, Political Power and Public Access in Early Modern England* (Woodbridge, 2002), pp. 101–127.
300 *Juxon*, pp. 10, 156, 160. Lindley, *Popular Politics*, p. 381; see Valerie Pearl, "London's Counter-Revolution," in G. E. Aylmer (ed.), *The Interregnum: The Quest for Settlement, 1646–1660* (London, 1972), pp. 44–56.
301 *Juxon*, p. 80.
302 *Englands Monument of Mercies in her Miraculous Preservation* (London, 1646).
303 See *Englands Monument* 669.f.10[85] and supplement 816.m.1[75].
304 Peacey, *Print and Public Politics*, p. 354.
305 For Pennington's appointment to the Committee for Compounding Delinquents in November 1643, see TNA, SP 28/1 fol. 4.
306 Coates, *Impact*, p. 72.
307 Sheilagh Ogilvie, *The European Guilds: An Economic Analysis* (Princeton, 2019), p. 59.
308 Again, see Braddick, *State Formation*, especially on the fiscal-military state, pp. 177–286.
309 Ann Hughes, "Parliamentary Tyranny? Indemnity Proceedings and the Impact of the Civil War: A Case Study from Warwickshire," *Midland History*, 11 (1986), pp. 49–78.
310 For the legacy of excise, see Coffman, *Excise Taxation*.
311 See John Goodwin, *Irelands Advocate* (London, 1641), title page; Joseph Caryl, *Davids Prayer for Solomon* (London, 1643). For the description of Goodwin as a dragon, see Thomas Edwards, *The Second Part of Gangraena* (London, 1646), p. 31.
312 *Idolaters Ruine and Englands Triumph; or the Meditations of a Maimed Souldier* (London, 1645), pp. 35–36. Thomason dated this work to 17 January 1645.
313 Archer, *The Pursuit of Stability*, p. 92.
314 Pearl, "Change and Stability in Seventeenth-Century London," p. 5.

Archival materials

Bodleian Library, Oxford

Add Ms. D/114	Oxford Siege Book
Ash Ms. 826	War Accounts
Carte Ms. 80	
Clarendon Ms. 22–23	March 1643 – January 1644
English History Ms. C 53	Diary, 1642–1644
Nalson Ms. 13	
Rawlinson Ms. B 48	London in Arms Displayed
Tanner Ms. 62–63, 66	

British Library

Additional MS 968	London Regiments by Symonds
Additional MS 5494	Accounts and Papers Relating to Sequestered Estates, 1642–1648
Additional MS 7532	The Rights of the People of England
Additional MS 10114	Papers of John Harington
Additional MS 18777–18779	Diary of Walter Yonge
Additional MS 18781–18782	Reports of sermons in London, 1642–4
Additional MS 22619	Collection of original papers
Additional MS 27962	Salvetti correspondence
Additional MS 31116	Diary of Lawrence Whitacre
Additional MS 34253	Correspondence relating to the civil war
Additional MS 34315	Committee of Safety receipts

Additional MS 37343	Whitelocke's Annals vol. iii
Additional MS 40630	Cassiobury Papers
Additional MS 40883	Diary of Nehemiah Wallington
Additional MS 71534	Henry Marten Papers
Additional MS 72435	Trumbull Papers [Walter Strickland's correspondence]
Additional MSS 39940–39942	Notes on sermons
BL Egerton MS 1048	London Petitions from December 1642
BL Egerton MS 2643, 2654, 2647	Barrington Papers
BL Harleian MS 162–166	Diary of Sir Simonds D'Ewes
BL Harley MS 479	Diary of John More
BL Sloane MS 654	Letter correspondence
BL Sloane MS 922	Letter book of Nehemiah Wallington
BL Sloane MS 1465	Petitions and letters
BL Sloane MS 1457	A Memoriall of Gods Judgment
BL Sloane MS 1467	Petitions and Speeches in Parliament
BL Stowe MS 142	miscellaneous historical letters

Camden Local Studies and Archives Centre

VOL P/GF/M/1	St. Giles in the Fields, Vestry Minutes, 1618–1719
VOL P/GF/M/4	St. Giles in the Fields, Churchwardens' Accounts, 1640–1694

Clothworkers' Company, London

Orders of Courts, 1639–1649

Drapers' Company, London

Court Minutes and Records, 1640–1667

Essex Record Office

T/B, 211

Goldsmiths' Company, London

Book 02-W   Company Minutes, 1642–1645
MS 223   Strelley's Charity Book, 1603–1790

Huntington Library, San Marino

Ellesmere MSS   Papers of John Egerton, earl of Bridgewater
Hastings MSS
Huntington MSS
Stowe MSS

John Harvard Library, Southwark

St. George the Martyr Churchwardens' Accounts, 1621–170
St. Mary Newington Churchwarden' Accounts, 1632–1734

Lambeth Palace Library, Southwark

MS 679
MS 703
MS 930
MS 932

Leathersellers' Company, London

Court Minutes, 1608–

London Guildhall Library

MS 182/2	Court Minute Book of the Paviors' Company
MS 913	Court Minute Book of the Society of Tacklehouse and Ticket Porters
MS 1207/3–4	Court Minute Books Armourers' and Braisers' Company
MS 2208/1	Court Minute Book of the Plumbers' Company
MS 2881/6–7	Court Minute Books of the Blacksmiths' Company
MS 2883/1	Wardens' Account Book of the Blacksmiths' Company
MS 3043/1	Court Minute Book of the Tylers' and Bricklayers' Company
MS 3293/1–2	Court Minute Books of the Turners' Company
MS 3297/1	Wardens' Account Book of the Turners' Company
MS 4329/4–5	Court Minute Books of the Carpenters' Company
MS 4655/5–6	Court Minute Books of the Weavers' Company
MS 5177/4	Court Minute Book of the Bakers' Company
MS 5204/3	Court Minute Book of the Brown-Bakers' Company
MS 5220/2	Court Minute Book of the Gunmakers' Company
MS 5257/5–6	Court Minute Books of the Barber-Surgeons' Company
MS 5385	Court Minute Book of the Saddlers' Company
MS 5445/3–7	Court Minute Books of the Brewers' Company
MS 5570/3	Court Minute Book of the Fishmongers' Company
MS 5603/1	Court Minute Book of the Coopers' Company
MS 5606/1	Wardens' Account Book of the Coopers' Company
MS 5667	Court Minute Book of the Painter-Stainers' Company
MS 6112/1	Court Minute Book of the Curriers' Company
MS 6122/2	Court Minute Book of the Plaisterers' Company
MS 6152/2	Wardens' Account Book of the Tallow Chandlers' Company
MS 6153/1–2	Court Minute Books of the Tallow Chandlers' Company
MS 6649/1	Court Minute Book of the Inholders' Company

Archival materials

MS 7090/4–5   Court Minute Books of the Pewterers' Company
MS 7151/1   Court Minute Book of the Cutlers' Company
MS 7158/1   Wardens' Account Book of the Cutlers' Company
MS 7353/14–15   Court Minute Books of the Cordwainers' Company
MS 8041/1   Wardens' Account Book of the Joiners' and Ceilers' Company
MS 9485/1   Court Minute Book of the Wax Chandlers' Company
MS 11588/4   Court Minute Book of the Grocers' Company
MS 14346/2   Wardens' Account Book of the Curriers' Company
MS 15201/1   Court Minute Book of the Vintners' Company
MS 15842/1   Court Minute Book of the Haberdashers' Company
MS 16967/4   Court Minute Book of the Ironmongers' Company
MS 30708/3   Court Minute Book of the Skinners' Company
MS 34017/5   Court Minute Book of the Merchant Taylors' Company

London Metropolitan Archives

CLC/180/MS07415/001   Dutch Church at Austin Friars, Afkondingen [Proclamation] book, 1643–1752
CLC/180/MS07399   Copy out-letter book, comprising copies of letters from the Consistory, mainly to other Dutch reformed congregations
CLC/270/MS03342   London in armes displayed
COL/AD/01/041   Court of Common Council Letter Book QQ
COL/CA/01/01/059   Court of Aldermen Repertory 55, 3 November 1640 – 13 August 1642
COL/CA/01/01/060   Court of Aldermen Repertory 56, 18 August 1642 – 24 October 1643

COL/CA/01/01/061	Court of Aldermen Repertory 57, 31 October 1643 – 28 October 1645
COL/CHD/CT/01/004	City's Cash Accounts, 1641–3
COL/CHD/CT/01/005	City's Cash Accounts, 1644–6
COL/CHD/MN/03/005	Warrant of the Militia Committee of the City of London to the Committee of Arrears, 24 April 1646
COL/CHD/MN/01/004	Maimed soldiers and sailors: Account book, 1665–79
COL/CHD/MN/01/006	Military and Naval Pensions, 1661–79
COL/CHD/MN/02/015	Miscellaneous papers, 1643–90
COL/CN/01/01/001	Common Hall, Corporation of London Minutes, November 1642 – October 1646
Ms. 824/1	All Hallows the Less, Vestry Minutes, 1644–1830
P69/ALH1/G/01/001	All Hallows Barking by the Tower, Vestry Minutes, 1629–69
P69/ALH1/H/05/001	All Hallows Barking by the Tower, Churchwardens' Accounts, 1628–66
P69/ALH4/B/001/MS04049/001	All Hallows Lombard Street, Vestry Minutes, 1618–53
P69/ALH6/B/001/MS04957/001	All Hallows Staining Mark Lane, Vestry Minutes, 1574–1655
P69/ALH6/B/008/MS04956/003/001	All Hallows Staining Mark Lane, Churchwardens' Accounts, 1645–79
P69/ALH7/B/001/MS00819/001	All Hallows the Great, Vestry Minutes, 1574–1684
P69/ALH7/B/013/MS00818/001	All Hallows the Great, Churchwardens' Accounts, 1616–1708

Archival materials

P69/ALH8/B/013/MS00823/001	All Hallows the Less, Churchwardens' Accounts, 1630–51
P69/ALB/B/001/MS01264/001	St. Alban Wood Street, Vestry Minutes, 1583–1676
P69/ALB/B/003/MS07673/002	St. Alban Wood Street, Churchwardens' Accounts, 1637–75
P69/ALP/B/001/MS01431/002	St. Alphage London Wall, Vestry Minutes, 1608–1711
P69/ALP/B/006/MS01432/004	St. Alphage London Wall, Churchwardens' Accounts, 1631–77
P69/TRI3/B/004/MS04835/001	Holy Trinity the Less, Churchwardens' Accounts, 1582–1662
P69/AND3/B/001/MS01278/001	St. Andrew Hubbard, Vestry Minutes, 1600–78
P69/AND3/B/003/MS01279/003	St. Andrew Hubbard, Churchwardens' Accounts, 1621–1712
P69/AND1/B/009/MS02088/001	St. Andrew-by-the-Wardrobe, Churchwardens' Accounts, 1570–1688
P69/ANA/B/010/MS00587/001	St. Anne and Saint Agnes, Churchwardens' Accounts, 1636–63
P69/ANL/B/004/MS01046/001	St. Antholin Budge Row, Churchwardens' Accounts, 1574–1708
P69/BAT1/B/001/MS04384/001	St. Bartholomew-by-the-Exchange, Vestry Minutes, 1567–1643
P69/BAT1/B/001/MS04384/002	St. Bartholomew-by-the-Exchange, Vestry Minutes, 1643–76
P69/BAT1/B/006/MS04383/001	St. Bartholomew-by-the-Exchange, Churchwardens' Accounts, 1598–1698

P69/BEN1/B/005/MS01303/001	St. Benet Fink, Churchwardens Accounts, 1610–99
P69/BEN2/B/001/MS04214/001 pt.2	St. Benet Gracechurch Vestry Minutes, 1607–1758
P69/BEN3/B/007/MS00878/001	St. Benet Paul's Wharf, Churchwardens' Accounts, 1605–57
P69/BEN3/B/001/MS00877/001	St. Benet Paul's Wharf Vestry Minutes, 1579–1674
P69/BOT1/B/001/MS01453/001	St. Botolph Aldersgate, Vestry Minutes, 1601–52
P69/BOT2/B/001/MS09236	St. Botolph Aldgate, Vestry Minutes, 1583?–1708
P69/BOT2/B/012/MS09235/002/002	St. Botolph Aldgate, Churchwardens' Accounts, 1586–1691
P69/BOT3/B/007/MS00942/001	St. Botolph Billingsgate, Churchwardens' Accounts, 1603–74
P69/BOT4/B/001/MS04526/001	St. Botolph-without-Bishopsgate, Vestry Minutes, 1616–90
P69/BOT4/B/008/MS04524/002	St. Botolph-without-Bishopsgate, Churchwardens' Accounts, 1632–62
P69/BRI/B/016/MS06552/001	St. Bride Fleet Street, Churchwardens' Accounts, 1639–78
P69/CRI/B/007/MS04423/001	St. Christopher le Stocks, Churchwardens' Accounts, 1575–1660
P69/CRI/B/001/MS04425/001	St. Christopher le Stocks, Vestry Minutes, 1593–1731
P69/CLE/B/007/MS00977/001	St. Clement Eastcheap, Churchwardens' Accounts, 1636–1740
P69/CLE/B/001/MS00978/001	St. Clement Eastcheap, Vestry Minutes, 1640–1759
P69/DUN2/B/011/MS02968/003	St. Dunstan-in-the-West Churchwardens' Accounts, 1628–44

Archival materials

P69/DUN2/B/001/MS03016/001	St. Dunstan-in-the-West Vestry Minutes, 1588–1663
P69/ETH/B/006/MS04241/001	St. Ethelburga Bishopsgate, Churchwardens' Accounts, 1569–1681
P69/GEO/B/001/MS00952/001	St. George Botolph Lane and St. Botolph Billingsgate Vestry Minutes, 1600–85
P69/GEO/B/005/MS00951/001	St. George Botolph Lane Churchwardens Accounts, 1590–1676
P69/GRE/B/001/MS01336/001	St. Gregory by St. Paul, Vestry Minutes, 1642–1701
P69/HEL/B/004/MS06836	St. Helen Bishopsgate Churchwardens' Accounts, 1565–1654
P69/JS2/B/001/MS04813/001	St. James Garlickhithe, Vestry Minutes, 1615–93
P69/JS2/B/005/MS04810/002	St. James Garlickhithe, Churchwardens' Accounts, 1627–99
P69/JNB/B/006/MS00577/001	St. John the Baptist Walbrook, Churchwardens' Accounts, 1595–1679
P69/JNZ/B/014/MS00590/001	St. John Zachary, Churchwardens' Accounts, 1591–1682
P69/KAT1/B/011/MS01124/001	St. Katherine Coleman Street, Churchwardens' Accounts, 1610–71
P69/KAT2/B/001/MS01196/001	St. Katherine Cree, Vestry Minutes, 1639–1718
P69/LAW1/B/001/MS02590/001	St. Lawrence Jewry, Vestry Minutes, 1556–1670
P69/LAW1/B/008/MS02593/002	St. Lawrence Jewry, Churchwardens' Accounts, 1640–98
P69/LAW2/B/010/MS03907/001	St. Laurence Pountney, Churchwardens' Accounts, 1530–1681

P69/LAW2/B/001/MS03908/001	St. Laurence Pountney, Vestry Minutes, 1614–73
P69/MAG/B/018/MS01179/001	St. Magnus the Martyr, Churchwardens' Accounts, 1638–1734
P69/MGT1/B/001/MS04352/001	St. Margaret Lothbury, Vestry Minutes, 1571/2–1677
P69/MGT3/B/001/MS01175/001	St. Margaret New Fish Street, Vestry Minutes, 1583–1675
P69/MGT3/B/014/MS01176/001	St. Margaret New Fish Street, Churchwardens' Accounts, 1576–1678
P69/MGT4/B/001/MS04571/001	St. Margaret Pattens, Vestry Minutes and Memoranda Book, 1640–83
P69/MGT4/B/004/MS04570/002	St. Margaret Pattens, Churchwardens' Accounts, 1558–1653
P69/MTN1/B/001/MS01311/001/001	St. Martin Ludgate, Vestry Minutes, 1576–1715
P69/MTN2/B/001/MS00959/001	St. Martin Orgar, Vestry Minutes, 1469–1707
P69/MTN3/B/005/MS11394/001	St. Martin Outwich, Churchwardens' Accounts, 1632–1743
P69/MRY1/B/006/MS03891/001	St. Mary Abchurch, Churchwardens' Accounts, 1629–92
P69/MRY2/B/001/MS03570/002	St. Mary Aldermanbury, Vestry Minutes, 1610–1763
P69/MRY2/B/005/MS03556/002	St. Mary Aldermanbury, Churchwardens' Accounts, 1631–77
P69/MRY3/B/010/MS06574	St. Mary Aldermary, Churchwardens' Accounts, 1597–1665
P69/MRY4/B/001/MS01240/001	St. Mary-at-the-Hill, Vestry Minutes, 1609–1752
P69/MRY8/B/001/MS00064	St. Mary Colechurch, Vestry Minutes, 1612–1701

P69/MRY8/B/005/MS00066	St. Mary Colechurch, Churchwardens' Accounts, 1612–1700
P69/MRY9/B/001/MS02597/001	St. Mary Magdalen Milk Street, Vestry Minutes, 1619–68
P69/MRY9/B/007/MS02596/002	St. Mary Magdalen Milk Street, Churchwardens' Accounts, 1606/7–1666/7
P69/MRY12/B/002/MS05714/001	St. Mary Somerset, Churchwardens' Accounts, 1614–1701
P69/MRY13/B/001/MS01542/002	St. Mary Staining, Churchwardens' Accounts, 1644–1836
P69/MRY14/B/006/MS01013/001	St. Mary Woolchurch Haw, Churchwardens' Accounts, 1560–1672
P69/MTW/B/005/MS01016/001	St. Matthew Friday Street, Churchwardens' Accounts, 1547–1678
P69/MIC1/B/008/MS02601/001/001	St. Michael Bassishaw, Churchwardens' Accounts, 1617/18–1715/16
P69/MIC2/B/006/MS04071/002	St. Michael Cornhill, Churchwardens' Accounts, 1608–1702
P69/MIC2/B/001/MS04072/001	St. Michael Cornhill, Vestry Minutes, 1563–1697
P69/MIC3/B/009/MS01188/001	St. Michael Crooked Lane, Churchwardens' Accounts, 1617–93
P69/MIC4/B/005/MS02895/002	St. Michael le Querne, Churchwardens' Accounts, 1605–1717
P69/MIC6/B/005/MS04825/001	St. Michael Queenhithe, Churchwardens' Accounts, 1625–1706
P69/MIC7/B/003/MS00524	St. Michael Wood Street, Churchwardens' Accounts, 1619–1871

P69/MIL2/B/001/MS00062/001	St. Mildred Poultry, Vestry Minutes, 1641–1713
P69/NIC1/B/001/MS04060/001	St. Nicholas Acons, Vestry Minutes, 1619–1738
P69/OLA2/B/004/MS04409/001	St. Olave Old Jewry, Churchwardens' Accounts, 1586–1643
P69/OLA2/B/004/MS04409/002	St. Olave Old Jewry, Churchwardens' Accounts, 1643–1705
P69/OLA2/B/001/MS04415/001	St. Olave Old Jewry, Vestry Minutes, 1574–1680
P69/OLA3/B/002/MS01257/001	St. Olave Silver Street, Churchwardens' Accounts, 1630–82
P69/PAN/B/014/MS05018/001	St. Pancras Soper Lane, Churchwardens' Accounts, 1616–1740
P69/PAN/B/001/MS05019/001	St. Pancras Soper Lane, Vestry Minutes, 1626–99
P69/PET1/B/001/MS04165/001	St. Peter Cornhill, Vestry Minutes, 1574–1717
P69/PET4/B/006/MS00645/002	St. Peter Westcheap Churchwardens' Accounts, 1601–1702
P69/STE1/B/030/MS04456	St. Stephen Coleman Street, Vellum Book
P69/STE1/B/012/MS04457/002	St. Stephen Coleman Street, Churchwardens' Accounts, 1586–1640
P69/STE1/B/001/MS04458/001/001	St. Stephen Coleman Street, Vestry Minutes, 1622–1693
P69/STE1/B/001/MS04458/001/002	St. Stephen Coleman Street, Vestry Minutes, 1694–1726
P69/STE2/B/008/MS00593/004	St. Stephen Walbrook, Churchwardens' Accounts, 1637–1748
P69/SWI/B/004/MS00559/001	St. Swithin London Stone, Churchwardens' Accounts, 1602–1725

P69/TMS1/B/008A/MS00662/001   St. Thomas the Apostle, Churchwardens' Accounts, 1612–1729

P82/AND/B/001/MS04251/001   St. Andrew Holborn Circus, Vestry Minutes, 1642–1714

P92/SAV/1898–1926, 1928, 1935–1951   Receipts for Maimed Souldiers, St. Saviour, Southwark

Mercers' Company, London

Acts of Court, 1641 to 1645

Museum of London

MS 46.78/709   Contracts for the supplying of the Army of Sir Thomas Fairfax in the year 1645

MS 46.78/673   An unsigned note relating to Lord Essex

The National Archives, Kew

E 179	Records of the Exchequer
SP 16	State Papers Domestic, Charles I
SP 19	Committee for the Advance on Money
SP 20	Sequestration Committee
SP 21	Committee of Both Kingdoms
SP 22	Committee for Plundered Ministers
SP 23	Committee for Compounding with Delinquents
SP 28	Commonwealth Exchequer Papers
SP 46	Supplementary State Papers Domestic
SP 84	State Papers Holland

National Army Museum, London

MSS 6807–53   William Levett, "The Enseigns of the Regiments in the rebellious Citty of London both of Trayned Bands and Auxiliaries," 26 September 1643

Parliamentary Archives, Westminster

MAIN PAPERS HL/PO/JO/10/1/115, 117–121, 124–139, 141–148, 150–158, 161–163, 165, 167–171, 176

BRY/10, BRY/45, BRY/57, BRY/96	Parliamentary Records
MAN/21	Warrant of the Committee of Lords and Commons
WIL/2	Papers of the Earls of Manchester

Salters' Company, London

Minute Book, 1627–84

Tower Hamlets Local History Library and Archives

W/SMH/A/1/1	Church Book

Westminster Archives Centre

E23	St. Margaret's Westminster, Churchwardens' Accounts, 1640–1
E24	St. Margaret's Westminster, Churchwardens' Accounts, 1642–3
E25	St. Margaret's Westminster, Churchwardens' Accounts, 1644–5
E2413	St. Margaret's Westminster, Vestry Minutes, 1591–1662
F2002	St. Martin-in-the-Fields, Vestry Minute Book, 1624–52
E2269	St. Clement Danes, Churchwardens' Accounts, 1627–50

William Andrews Clark Memorial Library, Los Angeles

Clark MS 1951.011	Notes from Sermons given by Richard Culverwell in St. Margaret Moyses

Index

Adams, Thomas 70
Additional Sea Adventure to Ireland 36
Adwalton Moor, battle of 180, 196, 209
Agostini, Gerolamo 136, 147, 184, 188–190, 207–208, 213, 235–236, 275, 298
Alden, Robert 101
alehouses 32, 152
All Hallows Bread Street 100
All Hallows the Great 15, 36, 101, 143, 306
All Hallows Honey Lane 102
All Hallows the Less 37, 101, 143, 306–307
All Hallows Lombard Street 95, 268, 306
Alton, battle of 258
Amsterdam 16, 25, 261, 267
Andrews, Thomas 36, 62, 65–66
anti-episcopacy 34–35
anti-popery 31, 33
An Apologeticall Narration 265–267, 269, 296
Archbishop of Canterbury 15
Archer, Edward 152
Archer, Elias 239
Areopagitica see Milton, John
Armyne, William 243
Arrowsmith, John 137
Arthur, Thomas 70
Artillery Company of London 29
Artillery Garden 19, 65
Arundel House 15

Ashe, Simeon 79
Ashurst, Richard 94
Atkins, Thomas 9, 95, 211
attempt on the seven Londoners 120, 136, 153, 165, 167, 186, 209, 281
auxiliaries 153
auxiliaries project 156
Avery, Samuel 94
Axtell, Daniell 45
Ayres, Thomas 274

Balfour, Sir William 233, 272–273
Ballie, Robert 242, 291, 292
Banks, Sir John 46
Bankside 15, 74, 146
Barber Surgeons' Company 75
Barclay, Robert 243
Basing House 239, 273
Bassishaw Ward 99, 101
Bateman, Richard 66, 119, 168, 171, 197
bell ringing 18
Bellamy, John 88
Benyon's petition 245
Besley, William 95
Bethlem Hospital 246
Billingsgate Ward 99
Bills of Mortality 191, 242, 274
Blackmore, William 152
Blacksmiths' Company 232, 304
Blakiston, John 126, 141
Bond, Martin 198
Book of Common Prayer 49

Boothby, Walter 88, 95
Boswell, William 261
Bowles, Edward 125–126, 170, 191
Bread Street Ward 88, 98–101, 117, 156, 194, 270, 286
Brentford, battle of 84–85, 89, 91
Brereton, Sir William 44, 115
Brewers' Company 134, 304
Bridewell Prison and Hospital 72, 246, 254, 257
Bridge Ward 194
Brightwell, Thomas 51, 58, 63, 95, 175
Broad Street Ward 103, 194
Brome, Edmond 191
Brooke, 2nd Baron Greville, Robert 115, 169, 180, 201
Brooke, Sir Basil 240, 244
Brooke's plot 240, 244, 247, 265, 282
Brooks, Thomas 194
Brough, William 150
Browne, Richard 62, 66, 81, 87–88, 121, 122, 129, 133, 159, 161, 258, 271, 273, 283, 294
Browne, Samuel 243
Brownebakers' Company 75
Burges, Cornelius 9, 66, 258
Burroughs, Jeremiah 45, 57, 179, 268
Burton, Henry 48, 100, 188, 268
Butler, Samuel 2, 9, 160, 202

Calamy, Edmund 8, 9, 40, 42, 46, 56, 135, 140, 187, 217, 286
Camden House 148, 152, 175, 287
Camden, Lady Elizabeth 95
campaign against crosses *see* iconoclasm
Campbell, John, 1st Earl of Loudon 243
Candlewick Ward 99
Caryl, Joseph 138–139, 173, 257, 285, 294, 300
Case, Thomas 7, 8, 44, 57, 83, 100, 113, 117, 135, 193, 269, 286, 297

Castle Baynard 88, 99
cavalier, term 1
Cavendish, William, 1st Duke of Newcastle 260
censorship 12
Chaloner, Richard 183, 196
Chamberlain, Abraham 95
Charing Cross 15, 34
Charles I, King 2, 7, 23, 27, 53, 56, 75, 86, 91, 116, 118, 168, 222, 266, 292, 313
Charles II 2
Cheap Ward 62, 99, 101, 102
Cheapside 104
Cheapside Cross 145, 147
Cheriton, battle of 233, 258
Cheshire, Thomas 149
Chestlin, Robert 24, 48, 49, 51–52, 58, 122
Cholmley, Sir Henry 82–83
Christ Church Newgate Street 93, 138–139, 245, 257, 269, 285
Christian IV, King 262
Church, Captain Thomas 74
City loan for £60,000 131
City's militia committee 94
Clarke, Sir George 95, 119
Clarke, John 152
Clarke, Matthew 151
Clegat, Captain Edward 95
Clothworkers' Company 11, 16, 33, 54, 71–72, 75–77, 111, 112, 157, 177, 228, 289, 302
Clotworthy, Sir John 141
Coates, Richard 131
Cockroft, Caleb 62, 94
Coleman Street 36, 62, 66, 88, 94
Coleman Street Ward 102–103, 194
Commission of Array 63
Committee of Accounts for Waller's Army 236
Committee for the Advance of Money 75, 92, 97–98, 104–105, 126, 156, 163, 208, 229–232, 234, 283

Committee of Association 126
Committee of Both Kingdoms 240,
    241, 243, 246–247, 258, 264,
    272–273, 279, 292, 300, 313
Committee for Compounding with
    Delinquents 241, 313
Committee for the Demolition of
    Monuments of Superstition and
    Idolatry 141–142
Committee for the General Rising *see*
    general rising
Committee for Irish Adventurers
    43, 55, 74
Committee for Irish Affairs 29
Committee for Maimed Soldiers
    156, 251
Committee for Plundered Ministers 48,
    149, 313
Committee of Safety 60, 74, 76, 85,
    128, 181, 186, 241, 243, 247,
    262, 301
Committee for Scandalous
    Ministers 48
Committee for Scottish Affairs 242
Committee for Sick and Maimed
    Soldiers 90
Committee for Sutton Hospital 254
Committee for the Vindication
    of the Parliament from the
    Aspersions thrown on them in
    the King's Answer to the London
    Petition 123
Common Council of London 4–5,
    11, 13, 17–21, 29, 35, 51, 64,
    67–68, 76, 93–94, 105–107, 109,
    119–120, 122–123, 130–133,
    135, 157, 161, 165, 167, 179,
    197–198, 200, 203, 210–211,
    214, 224, 233, 235, 238–239,
    241, 243–246, 248–250, 254,
    257, 269–270, 272, 274, 277,
    283, 295, 305
Common Hall 11, 18–19, 63, 68, 70,
    72, 119, 121, 123–124, 181–182,
    185, 202, 221, 230, 245, 306

Conyers, Sir John 215
Cooke, Edward 197
Cooke, Leonard 149
Cooper, William 151
Cordell, John 95
Cordell, Robert 95
Cordwainers' Company 73,
    231–232, 305
Cornhill Ward 88
Coulson, Captain William 101
Council of War 149, 204
Court of Aldermen 11, 18, 47, 57,
    90, 106, 140, 230, 250, 252,
    305–306
Covenanter army 227, 240
Covent Garden 1, 65
Crewe, John 243
Cripplegate Ward 88
Cripplegate Without Ward 62
Crispe, Samuel 95
Crispe, Sir Nicholas 129, 163, 183
Cromwell, Oliver 56, 243, 247, 260,
    272, 276
Cropley, Edward 73
Cropredy Bridge, battle of 259
Crosby House, London 121, 163
Cooks' Company 75, 172
Cullum, Thomas 95
Culverwell, Richard 7, 100, 314

D'Ewes, Sir Simonds 30, 53, 58, 90–91,
    106–108, 115, 125, 169, 182,
    198, 201, 207, 210–212, 220,
    299, 302
Denmark 262
Devereux, Robert, 3rd Earl of Essex 20,
    50, 63, 65, 67–68, 74, 81, 85, 87,
    89, 104, 235
Digby, Sir Kenelm 93, 244
Dowgate 101
Dowgate Ward 99, 101
Downham, John 36, 101
Downing, Calybute 9, 24, 79,
    91, 112
Drake, Sir William 90–91

Drapers' Company 11, 16, 70, 76, 111, 112, 158, 177, 228, 288, 289, 302
Dugdale, William 65, 67
Dukeson, Richard 50

East India Company 233, 248
Eastern Association 227, 259–260, 271, 294
Edgehill, battle of 61, 82–84, 86, 89–92, 113, 122, 133, 243, 253–254, 282
Edwards, Thomas 6, 225, 267, 296, 297, 300
Essex House 15, 226
Estwicke, Stephen 278, 280
Evelyn, John 38, 211
excise 24, 164–165, 178, 181, 229, 248, 251, 257, 263, 285, 292, 298, 300
excise tax 248

Fairfax, Dr. William 152
Fairfax, Thomas 279, 299, 313
Fant, Elizabeth 66
Farringdon Within Ward 99, 286
Farringdon Without Ward 62, 99
fasting and humiliation 136
Feake, Christopher 101
Fiennes, William, 1st Viscount Saye and Sele 2, 36, 63, 74, 76, 84, 92, 116, 128, 169, 243
Finsbury Fields 196, 279
Fishmongers' Company 16, 33, 70, 76–77, 157–158, 172, 249, 304
five members 1, 2, 28–31, 33, 121, 124–126, 167, 170, 194, 281
Fleet prison 121
Fleet Street 60, 89, 308
Foote, Joshua 95
Foster, Sergeant Henry 237
Founders' Company 75
Fowke, John 9, 27, 34, 91, 95, 107, 121–122, 125, 128, 165, 171, 245–246, 278
Froysell, Thomas 151

Gangraena see Edwards, Thomas
Garrett, George 70
Gearing, John 51
general rising 7, 88, 182, 191, 195–199, 202–208, 211–212, 214–216, 219, 225, 238–239, 283, 287
  committee 214
  committee formation 201
  failure 206
  petition for the 201–202
  plans for 196
George, Sir Garrett 27, 119
Gerrard, Sir Gilbert 76, 141, 161, 169, 175, 181, 245, 295
Gillespie, George 267
Girdlers' Company 75, 172
Glapthorne, Henry 122–123, 169
Glaziers' Company 73, 172
Gloucester
  £50,000 livery company loan for 234
  celebration for the relief of 237
  impressment for 235
Glynne, John 76, 90, 169, 181, 243
Goldsmiths' Company 11, 16, 71–72, 111, 134, 157–158, 172, 177, 228, 252, 289, 293
Goldsmiths' Hall 241
Goodwin, Arthur 62
Goodwin, John 83–84, 94, 102, 104, 113, 114, 116, 117, 118, 192–194, 265, 268, 271, 285, 296, 298, 300
Goodwin, Thomas 94, 140, 267
Gosse, Samuell 162–163
Gower, Thomas 153, 156
Greene, John 140, 145, 150, 173, 174, 175, 179, 263, 276, 295, 299
Greenhill, William 51, 148, 175, 251, 256, 268
Gresham College 48, 121, 219
Greville, Robert, 2nd Baron Brooke 2, 36, 80, 82–84, 92, 127, 160, 167, 282

Greville, Sir Fulke 201
Grey, William, 1st Baron of
    Warke 259
Griffith, Matthew 51, 58, 139,
    149, 173
Grimstone, Harbottle 211
Grocers' Company 16, 29, 70, 76, 110,
    158, 200, 202, 228, 305
Grocers' Hall 29, 200, 202, 205
Grove, Captain Francis 259
Guildhall 11, 15, 27, 29, 36, 43, 60,
    62, 67, 71, 77, 84, 92–93,
    101–102, 104–107, 124–125,
    130, 142, 144, 151, 172,
    181–182, 187, 194, 219, 221,
    230–232, 245, 282, 304
gunpowder plot 33, 181
Gurney, Richard 10, 19, 34, 46–47,
    61, 63, 68, 75, 102, 122,
    137, 277

Haberdashers' Company 16, 72, 76,
    92, 105, 157, 172, 227, 305
Haberdasher's Hall 97
Hacket, Richard 62
Hackett, John 51
Hall, Thomas 67
Hall, William 46–47, 57
Hampden, John 29, 74, 82, 85, 169
Harley, Robert 38, 62, 141, 175, 258
Harrington, Sir James 272
Harsnett, Samuel 197
Harvey, Edmund 62, 107, 121–122,
    129, 161, 179, 284
Haselrig, Sir Arthur 29, 38, 62,
    159–160, 245, 258, 272
Hastings, Henry, 5th Earl of
    Huntington 34, 126, 168, 186
Hat, John 201
Hawkins, William 95
Hearne, Richard 122
Henley, George 119, 152
Henrietta Maria, Queen 141, 150
Herle, Charles 44, 57, 187, 217
Herne, Henry 119, 124
Herring, Michael 242

Heylyn, Peter 167, 276
high treason 27, 121, 124, 135, 147
Hignell, William 150
Hildesley, Mark 94
Hill, Thomas 257
Hobbes, Thomas 2
Hobson, William 197
Holdsworth, Richard 51
Holland, 1st Earl of *see* Rich, Henry
Holland, Cornelius 251
Hollar, Wenceslaus 145, 146
Holles, Denzil 29, 74, 82, 84, 90, 115,
    211, 244
Holles, John, 2nd Earl of Clare 211
Holmes, Dr. Nathaniel 268
Holy Trinity the Less 143, 237, 307
Honorable Artillery Company
    19, 80, 95
Hooker, Captain Edward 51,
    153, 175
Hoover, Samuel 262
Hopton, Sir Ralph, 1st Baron 160,
    240, 258
horse conscription 161
Hotham, John 36, 180
House of Commons 15, 23, 29, 54, 87,
    91, 104–105, 109, 120, 133, 200,
    220, 221, 223, 288
Hovell, Hogan 88
Hunt, Captain Richard 237
Hutchinson, Richard 251
Hyde, Edward, 1st Earl of Clarendon
    2, 9, 18, 21, 22, 34, 45, 54,
    67, 110, 118, 153, 160, 169,
    177, 209, 222, 237, 275, 290,
    295, 301

iconoclasm
    by London soldiers 79
    as propaganda 147
    Queen's chapel 141
Inbraiders' Company 75
independency as an ideology in
    London 268
Inigo Jones 15
Innholders' Company 158

Irish Rebellion 25, 30–32, 35, 41, 54
Ironmongers' Company 16, 69, 71, 74, 175, 229, 230, 305

Jackson, Thomas 194
Jenner, Robert 251
Johnston, Archibald, Lord Wariston 241, 243
Jones, Captain John 258
Jones, Peter 119, 168
Jones, Samuel 94
Juxon, Captain John 237
Juxon, Thomas 272, 277
Juxon, William *see* bishop of London

Kem, Samuel 215, 285
Kendall, William 100, 148, 162, 175
Kendrick, Andrew 66
Kendrick, John 36, 88, 130, 172, 197, 278
Knyvett, Thomas 203, 211–212

Lambeth Palace 15, 58, 303
Langbourn Ward 88
Langham, George 62
Lansdowne, battle of 160
Laud, William, Archbishop of Canterbury 43, 56, 67, 100, 110, 148, 150, 152, 223, 273, 275, 298
Laudianism 140, 151
Lawrence, George 7
Leathersellers' Company 11, 158, 303
Lee, Richard 152
Leslie, Alexander, 1st Earl of Leven 242, 260
Levant Company 248
Levellers 84, 88, 166, 223
Lightfoot, John 242
Lilburne, John 84, 119
Lindley, Keith 3–4, 16, 22, 25, 35, 47–48, 54–55, 57–59, 64, 70, 72, 88, 100, 109–111, 114, 116–119, 142, 153, 162, 168, 174–177, 198–199, 205, 214, 216, 220–223, 244, 264–265, 292, 294, 296, 299–300
Lindsay, Ludovic, 16th Earl of Crawford 240, 273
Lines of Communication 5, 21, 120, 132–133, 138, 165, 167, 172, 182, 235–237, 241, 274, 282
    contributions 136
    parochial participation 135
    participation by livery companies 134
    planning 133
    raising money for 133
    survey and preparation 132
Lithgow, William 133, 172
livery companies 17
Lockyer, Nicholas 268
London Bridge 14, 104
London, population of 16
Long, Colonel Walter 163
Lostwithiel, battle of 271, 283
Love, Christopher 79
Low Countries 261, 263, 268–269
Lunsford petition 88, 101, 119
Lunsford, Thomas 31

Mainwaring, Captain Robert 62, 65, 161
Mainwaring, Randall 9, 34, 62–63, 91, 109, 121–122, 124–125, 132, 162–163, 194, 234 *see also* Redcoats
Maitland, John, 1st Earl of Lauderdale 243
Mall, Thomas 151
Mandeville, Viscount *see* Montagu, Edward
Marshall, Stephen 8–9, 40, 42–43, 45, 56, 79, 187, 217, 226, 245, 286, 292
Marston Moor, battle of 259–260, 271
Marten, Henry 38, 62, 65, 91, 141, 160, 169–170, 177, 183, 204, 221, 225, 288, 302
    ejection from the House 160

Massey, Colonel Edward 224
Maynard, John 90, 211
Meade, Robert 88
Meare, Captain Moses 154
Melcott, James 65
Meldrum, Sir John 82
Mercers' Company 11, 16, 71, 75, 110, 111, 112, 134, 158, 172, 173, 177, 228, 289, 313
Merchant Adventurers 233, 248
Merchant Taylors' Company 16, 19, 72, 111, 134, 158, 200–203, 229, 246–247, 289, 305
Merchant Taylors' Hall 207
Mercurius Aulicus 19, 26, 108, 118, 127, 129, 139–140, 145, 151, 153, 156, 171, 173, 174, 176, 178, 179, 181, 184–185, 195, 204, 207, 214, 216, 217, 219, 220, 221, 222, 223, 234, 236, 288, 290
Mercurius Rusticus 21, 52, 58, 59, 176
Meroz, the curse of 40, 42–46, 56, 57, 84, 102, 129, 285–286
Meyrick, Sir John 87
Middle Temple 60, 89, 189, 217
Military Garden 19, 215
Militia Committee, London 4–5, 88, 119, 122, 153, 197, 205–207, 215, 234–235, 238–239, 272, 274, 279, 284, 306
Militia Ordinance 46
Milner, Tempest 100, 197, 280
Milton, John 270
mixed constitutionalism, concept of 185
Masons' Company 75, 172
mobilization as an ideology 6
Montagu, Edward, 2nd Earl of Manchester 22, 23, 25, 26, 54, 56, 92, 113, 115, 117, 124–125, 128, 169, 170, 171, 206, 209, 217, 223, 234, 243, 247, 259, 273, 276, 279, 296, 314
Moore Fields 31, 65
Moore, James 151

Moorewood, Gilbert 36
Moorfields 102
Morton, Thomas 46–47, 51–52, 57, 59
Mosse, Captain George 237
Musicians' Company 75

Nag's Head Tavern 88
Neve, Oliver 102
New Model Army 7, 20, 157, 206, 268, 270, 277–278, 280, 284–285, 289, 299
   £80,000 loan from London 279
   London contracts for 280
Newbury, first battle of 236, 243
Newbury, second battle of 160, 273
Newgate prison 149
newsbooks 12, 180, 188, 276
Nicholas, Sir Edward 126, 161, 168, 186
Nicholson, Christopher 88
Norbury, John 201
November assessment 101–103, 149

oath taking 18
Ogle, Captain Thomas 265
Ogle's plot 266, 282
Ordinance for Indemnity 236
Osboldston, Robert 106
Overbury, Sir Giles 201
Overton, Henry 94
Overton, Richard 119, 143, 145, 174, 194, 267
   printing press 103
Oxford 50
Oxford Treaty 91, 153, 166, 209

Painter-Stainers' Company 75, 232, 304
Palace Yard, Westminster 33, 107, 182, 208, 211
Palmer, Herbert 147
pamphlets 12, 28, 80, 120, 167, 180, 187
Parker, Henry 166
parochial charity for sick and wounded soldiers 254–255

party identity 6
Pearl, Valerie 3–4, 9, 22, 24, 26, 53, 64, 108, 109, 110, 111, 116, 118, 122, 168, 169, 172, 176, 179, 183, 199, 205, 216, 220, 221, 226, 287, 288, 289, 295, 299, 300
Pembroke, 4th Earl of *see* Herbert, Philip
Pennington, Isaac 9–10, 19, 24, 27, 34, 48–52, 61–64, 67, 75–77, 81, 88–93, 97–98, 100, 103, 105, 107–108, 121–124, 127–129, 133–140, 142, 144, 147–151, 156–159, 161, 165–167, 171, 172, 179, 182, 184–185, 191, 194–195, 197–198, 200–201, 203, 208, 210–212, 215, 221, 224, 226–227, 230–231, 234, 238, 241, 245–247, 263, 274–277, 282–284, 287, 300
Pennington, Mary 10
  as alderman 27
  lieutenancy of the Tower 215
pensions for sick and wounded soldiers 253
Percy, Algernon, 10th Earl of Northumberland 211
Perne, Andrew 181
Peter, Hugh 9, 45, 57, 104, 261, 268, 285, 295
petitioning
  Shute's petition 87
petitions 108
Pierrepoint, William 211, 243
Player, Thomas 133
plots 31–32
Plumbers' Company 75, 134, 172, 304
Pocock, John 251
political providentialism 42
Portsoken Ward 98
presbyterianism as counter to independency in London 269
print as a tool for mobilization 13
printed tickets 133, 210

propaganda 14
Protestant cause 32, 84, 263
Protestation, the 8, 23, 24, 30, 42, 44, 53, 57, 100, 117, 126, 170, 175, 190–191, 196, 209, 218
Prynne, William 267, 274, 297
Pym, John 2, 19, 29, 62–63, 82, 92, 115, 124–125, 164–165, 169, 173, 181, 183–184, 209, 216, 225, 295
  speeches 125, 187

Queenhithe Ward 99, 101

radicalism, concept of 9
Randall, John 251
Rawdon, Marmaduke 72, 163
Rawlinson, John 150
Reade, Robert 33
Reames, Barny 119, 168
Redcoats 122, 124–125, 129, 163
  see also Mainwaring, Randall
regicide 94, 194
Remonstrans Redivivus 166, 179, 191, 203, 221, 283
Reynardson, Abraham 72
Rich, Henry, 1st Earl of Holland 84, 160, 209, 211
Rigby, Alexander 126, 170
Right, Edmund 102
Riley, Theophilus 63, 96, 130, 148, 175, 244
Ripple Field, battle of 159, 160
Robartes, John, later 1st Earl of Radnor 243
Robinson, Ralph 102
Roborough, Henry 188
Rogers, Nehemiah 151
Roode, Edward 150
Roundway Down, battle of 160, 180, 181, 209
Rous, Francis 141, 173, 296
Rowe, Captain Francis (brother of Owen) 96
Rowe, Owen 63, 94, 280

Royal Exchange, the 14–15
Rupert, Prince 82, 84, 203, 237, 260, 282
Rushworth, John 65
Russell, Francis, 5th Earl of Bedford 74, 209, 211
Russell, James 94

Sacheverill, Ann 66
Sacred Oath and Covenant 189
Saddlers' Company 231
Sallwey, Arthur 149
Salters' Company 11, 16, 72, 111, 112, 154–155, 157–159, 176, 197, 228–229, 249–250, 289, 295
Salters' Hall 153, 157
Salters' Hall subcommittee 153–158, 208, 249, 278, 283, 285
Saltmarsh, John 225
salus populi suprema lex esto 166, 203
Salvetti, Amerigo 121, 184, 202
Savage, Elizabeth, Countess Rivers 160
Savoy Hospital 90, 254, 257
Scawen, Robert 279
Scriveners' Company 75
Seaman, Lazarus 100
Sedgwick, Obadiah 9, 24, 79, 100
Self-Denying Ordinance 247, 275, 277
sequestration 152, 162
Sequestration Committee 162
sermons *see* preaching
Sheppard, Matthew 62
Shute, Josias 51
Shute, Richard 9, 87–89, 92, 97, 105, 126, 191, 278, 287
Simpson, John 101
Skinners' Company 16, 72, 157–158, 228, 305
Skippon, Philip 7, 19, 29, 63, 80, 85, 87, 127, 133, 161, 204, 221
Smart, Ithiel 150
Smith, James 95
Soame, Thomas 62
Solemn League and Covenant 190–193, 218, 225, 227, 241, 262, 264, 266–267, 270, 291, 292

Somerset House 15, 141, 151, 174
Southwark, borough of 5
Speen, the storming of 273
Squire, John 48, 51, 58, 151
St. Alphage 79
St. Andrew Holborn 51
St. Andrew Hubbard 96
St. Andrew Undershaft 95, 278
St. Andrew by the Wardrobe 96, 131
St. Augustine Watling Street 51, 152
St. Bartholomew by the Exchange 235, 242
St. Bartholomew the Less 46
St. Bartholomew's Hospital 254
St. Benet Fink 192
St. Benet Sherehog 96, 139, 149
St. Botolph Without Bishopsgate 55, 144, 151, 154, 255
St. Bride Fleet Street 155, 237
St. Christopher le Stocks 268
St. Clement Danes 50, 97, 193, 269, 297
St. Clement Eastcheap 51, 150, 190–191
St. Dunstan, Stepney 50
St. Ethelburga 90, 152, 255
St. Giles Cripplegate 50, 129, 155, 268
St. Giles in the Fields 5, 37, 121, 132, 142, 151, 255
St. Helen, Abingdon-on-Thames, Berkshire 150
St. James's Fields 238
St. James Garlickhithe 37
St. John, Oliver 181, 226, 243–244, 278, 288–289, 292
St. John the Baptist 101
St. John the Evangelist 100
St. John Zachary 36–37
St. Laurence Pountney 15, 101, 140, 144
St. Lawrence Jewry 37, 79, 95, 102, 132, 142, 144, 228, 235
St. Leonard Eastcheap 1, 143, 188
St. Leonard Shoreditch 48, 51, 151
St. Magnus the Martyr 142, 268

St. Margaret Lothbury 103, 149, 192, 194
St. Margaret Moses 100, 154
St. Margaret New Fish Street 151, 268
St. Margaret Pattens 144
St. Margaret, Westminster 83
St. Martin Ironmonger Lane 102
St. Martin-in-the-Fields 257
St. Martin Ludgate 43, 57, 255
St. Martin Orgar 119, 142–143, 152, 191, 194
St. Martin's Lane 15
St. Martin Thames Street 15
St. Martin Vintry 91, 149
St. Mary Abchurch 51, 132, 144, 150, 235
St. Mary Aldermanbury 79, 95, 135, 235, 237, 251
St. Mary Axe 163
  (joined to St. Andrew Undershaft) 97
St. Mary Colechurch 102, 162, 193, 194
St. Mary le Strand 193
St. Mary Magdalen Milk Street 37, 100, 117, 135, 191, 193–194
St. Mary Magdalen Old Fish Street 51, 149–150
St. Mary Mounthaw 101
St. Mary Newington 38, 55, 96, 116, 254, 293, 303
St. Mary Overie Southwark 15
St. Mary Somerset 101, 253
St. Mary Woolchurch 144, 235, 237
St. Mary Woolnoth 51
St. Mary-le-Bow 15, 95, 100
St. Matthew Friday Street 48, 93, 95–96, 100, 188, 268
St. Michael Bassishaw 101, 135, 145
St. Michael Cornhill 15, 143, 150, 235, 268
St. Michael Paternoster Royal 101
St. Michael Queenhithe 101
St. Mildred Bread Street 79, 95, 100, 268
St. Mildred Poultry 102

St. Nicholas Olave 101, 149
St. Olave Old Jewry 37, 102, 135, 142, 150–151, 175, 256
St. Olave Silver Street 97
St. Olave Southwark 142
St. Pancras Soper Lane 36, 94
St. Paul's Cathedral 15, 28, 46–47, 51, 98, 104, 140, 145, 150, 258, 282, 286
St. Paul Covent Garden 50
St. Paul's Cross 118, 137–140, 173, 287
St. Peter Cornhill 143
St. Peter le Poor 51
St. Peter Westcheap 37, 97, 143
St. Saviour Southwark 142, 256
St. Sepulchre-without-Newgate 40, 42
St. Stephen Coleman Street 36, 102, 154, 191, 193–194, 268, 272, 285
St. Stephen's Chapel 15
St. Stephen Walbrook 95, 131, 255, 278
St. Swithin London Stone 102
St. Swithin's Lane 78
St. Thomas' Hospital, Southwark 254
St. Thomas the Apostle 142, 151
Stamp, Timothy 50
Stampe, William 50
Stapleton, Philip 38, 74, 182, 200, 243
state formation 10, 12, 89, 92, 155–156, 159, 164–165, 248, 284–285, 288
Staunton, Edmund 274
Stewart, James, 1st Duke of Richmond 96, 270
Stone, Benjamin 51, 150
Stone, Thomas 95
Stratton, battle of 159, 196
Strelley, Philip 252
Strickland, Walter 260, 269, 295, 302
Strode, William 29, 84, 91–92, 116, 169, 170, 182–183, 200, 274
Stuart, Katherine, Lady d'Aubigny 183, 282

Sutton Hospital 254, 257
Swadlin, Thomas 49, 51–52, 58
Sweden 262
Sweet, Robert 88
Symonds, Nathaniel 192

Tabor, Humphrey 103, 149
Tallow Chandlers' Company 232
Tallow Chandlers' Hall 256
Tate, Zouch 276
taverns 88, 152, 244, 268
tax of eight fifteenths 133
Taylor, Humphrey 213
Taylor, Walter 150, 191–192, 194
Temple Bar 237
Thames, River 14–15, 84, 286
Thirty Years' War 59, 80, 243, 291
Thomas Player, Captain 197
Thomason, George 122, 137, 267
Thomson, William 95
Three Cranes Tavern 244, 268
Tichborne, Robert 97, 121–122, 153, 156, 179, 197, 278, 284
"To your Tents, O Israel" 28
Tompkins, Nathaniel 183, 196
Tothill Fields 64
Tower Hill 14, 275
Tower of London 31, 107, 119, 210, 222
Tower Ward 88
Towse, John 9, 36, 38, 62, 162, 194
trained bands 1, 5, 19–20, 21, 29–30, 44, 51, 62, 65, 85, 87, 94, 105, 107, 126, 139, 153–154, 163, 181–182, 204, 207, 213, 237–239, 243, 246, 250, 253, 272, 278, 282
Trenchard, John 236
Tryon, Moses 102
Tucker, William 237
tumult 34, 107, 211–213
Turner, Richard 148, 197
Turner, Thomas 164
Turners' Company 73, 134, 172, 304
Turners' Hall 242

Turnham Green 2, 7, 82, 85–89, 91–92, 129, 202–203, 221, 279, 282, 287
twelve great livery companies 73–74, 227
£50,000 loan for Gloucester 231
Tyburn 14, 45
Tylers and Bricklayers' Company 74–75, 232
Tyrrell, Thomas 60–61, 81

Udall, Ephraim 51–52, 58, 152, 176
Udall, Philippa 152
Underhill, Clement 252
Underhill, Thomas 256
Underwood, William 62
United Provinces 261–262
Uxbridge Propositions 269

Vane, Sir Henry (the younger) 91–92, 200, 241, 244, 278
Vassall, Samuel 92, 116, 140
Vaughan, Edward 88
Venn, John 9, 20, 33–34, 49, 54, 62–63, 91, 100, 121–122, 140, 162, 179, 284
Vines, Richard 269
Vintners' Company 16, 71, 74–75, 157–158, 229–230, 305
Vintry Ward 62, 88
violent spirits 210
Violet, Thomas 244
Visscher, Claes 145–146
Vow and Covenant 186, 188–196, 202, 206–207, 218–219, 222, 286, 291
  printing of 195
  reception of the 192
  returns 190, 286

Walbrook Ward 88, 99
Walker, Andrew 232
Walker, Edward 34, 54
Walker, George 100
Walker, Henry 27–28, 53

Waller, Edmund 121, 183, 272
Waller, Sir William 62, 74, 154, 168, 180–181, 203–205, 207, 213, 222, 224, 233, 235, 240, 243, 258, 271, 283
Waller's plot 183, 281
   as motivation for mobilization 185
Wallington, Nehemiah 1, 31, 84, 180, 188, 210, 218, 250, 302
Walton, Bryan 152
Walton-upon-Thames 149
Walwyn, William 88, 119, 179, 202, 208, 215, 221, 222
Ward Assessments for Non-Contributors 286
Waring, Richard 95, 242
Warner, John 36, 62, 95, 278
Warner, Samuel 38, 95, 278
Warwick, 2nd Earl of *see* Rich, Robert
Washborne, Herriot 65
Watkins, Sir David 9, 104–105, 126, 191, 287
Weavers' Company 77, 88, 114, 172, 208, 278, 304
Weavers' Hall subcommittee 92–93, 97–98, 114, 156, 159, 162, 278, 285
Webb, Francis 280
weekly assessments 130, 164
weekly meal 154–155, 246, 250, 263, 292, 295
Wells, John 97, 192
Wentworth, Sir Peter 169, 170, 200
Westminster Abbey 15
Westminster, city of 5, 11, 14–15, 21, 23, 29–30, 33–35, 37–38, 44, 50, 55, 58, 72, 78, 89, 91, 107, 115, 123–124, 126, 128, 130, 132–133, 139, 145, 147, 154, 162, 182, 187, 190, 193, 195, 197–198, 203, 206, 208–213, 216, 217, 218, 219, 224–226, 234, 239, 241–242, 244–245, 251, 255, 257, 260, 264, 266, 270, 272, 283, 287, 292, 296, 314
Wharton, Nehemiah 78–80, 162
Wharton, Philip, 4th Baron 76, 82, 84, 105, 116, 186, 217, 243, 265
Whichcote, Captain Christopher 153, 156
Whitaker, Jeremiah 137
Whitaker, Laurence 105, 160, 186
Whitaker, Thomas 212
Whitby, Oliver 149
Whitechapel 22, 132
Whitehall 27, 29
Whitelocke, Bulstrode 67, 85, 90, 114, 121, 184, 239, 302
Whitley, Thomas 19, 20
Whitmore, George 163
Wilford, Roger 78
Willett, Captain Peter 163
Williams, Richard 91
Willingham, George 162
Willoughby, William 153
Wilson, Rowland 235
Wilson, Thomas 44, 57
Windebank 33
Wiseman, Thomas 27, 29
Wollaston, John 62–63, 67, 226, 233, 245–246, 278
Wollaston, Richard 152
Worcester, siege of 159
Wrightman, Humphrey 39
Wriothesley, Thomas, 4th Earl of Southampton 270

Yonge, Walter 43, 214
York, the siege of 260

EU authorised representative for GPSR:
Easy Access System Europe, Mustamäe tee 50,
10621 Tallinn, Estonia
gpsr.requests@easproject.com